TALK – ACTION = 0

THIRTY-THREE YEARS OF D.O.A.

3,500 shows and counting

More than a million sales on fifty releases that include:
- thirteen studio albums
- thirteen singles and EPs
- one live album
- two split albums
- five split singles and EPs
- six DVDs
- two solo albums
- eight D.O.A. compilations
- more than twenty V/A (various artists) compilations
- two D.O.A. tribute albums by other artists

The tours:
close to two million miles logged by land, air, and sea (actually, it's incalculable!), and thirty countries on four different continents:
- fifteen European tours
- thirty cross-Canada tours
- twenty national tours of the US
- three tours of Australia
- two of New Zealand
- one tour of China
- one tour of Japan

Band members (the Men of Action who played two shows or more includes):
- eight bass players
- six other guitarists
- fourteen drummers plus another four who filled in for one show

Fourteen riots and countless run-ins with cops and border guards.

Vehicles (strangely enough, we've had only five vans and one school bus):
- Randy's green panel van
- The Blue Bullet
- Miss Piggy, the school bus
- Galloping Gertie
- The Iron Lung
- Reid Fleming, the white truck, purchased brand new in 1988 and still running today with 800,000 kilometres on it.

The number of motors, tires, and various parts that have blown up, I just don't like to think about.

OK, LET'S GO!

ARSENAL PULP PRESS | VANCOUVER

TALK – ACTION = 0

AN ILLUSTRATED HISTORY OF D.O.A.

Joe Keithley

I dedicate this book to my loving family, thanks for putting up with me!

A special thanks to all who played in D.O.A., all who worked for D.O.A., and especially to all the fans of D.O.A. A big thanks to everybody at Arsenal Pulp Press for believing we could make a great book!

—Joe Shithead Keithley

CONTENTS

6	Introduction
9	Chapter 1: 1977–1979
41	Chapter 2: 1980–1981
65	Chapter 3: 1982–1983
85	Chapter 4: 1984–1985
121	Chapter 5: 1986–1988
159	Chapter 6: 1989–1990
179	Chapter 7: 1991–1994
215	Chapter 8: 1995–2000
243	Chapter 9: 2001–2004
271	Chapter 10: 2005–NOW
298	D.O.A. Family Tree
300	Discography
302	Photo Credits

INTRODUCTION

When I started down this road, I had no idea where it would take me, nor did I perceive just how rough that road would turn out to be. I was a young man of eighteen, and I just wanted to play music, excite people, and change the world; I mean, how hard could it be? You just get up there and play the music that you love and dig the sheer power and thrill of it all. But like almost everything in life, tough odds, weird circumstances, and the ill-intentioned always manage to get in the way.

D.O.A. had a veritable raging river of trouble from the start. The press and the general populace perceived right away that we were troublemakers and out to fuck with anything that got in our way. The fuck-ups and problems (forget about "issues"; I hate that weak-kneed euphemism) ranged from police to border guards to rip-off promoters to stab-you-in-the-back record companies. But probably the toughest part was losing some of our comrades along the way—friends and band members like Dimwit, Ken Jensen, and Stubby Pecker, and many other pals as well.

I was first consciously inspired to be an activist when I was about sixteen years old. Events around the world, like the nuclear arms race, the war in Vietnam, and protests all across North America and Europe, stoked the fire in me. When I realized that artists were uniting and fighting together for good causes, I was drawn into activism forever. When I coupled that with the high of firing people up with our blitzkrieg form of music—that, to me, was the perfect marriage of the arts. I'll always be thrilled by riling people up while I'm on stage.

When we first heard of punk rock back in 1976, we thought it was strange and primitive. That turned out to be true, but as we got deeper and deeper into it, there was a whole lot more that wasn't visible to the naked eye or ear. What I dug about it was the freedom of expression; you could say whatever you wanted. It didn't matter if the masses thought it was crazy or unacceptable. And I loved the camaraderie, the feeling of being part of a movement, a social phenomenon that challenged the status quo.

We released the 7-inch single "Disco Sucks" in 1978, and that gave us a passport to travel the world as professional troublemakers, taking on evil-doers, slimy corporations, and scuzzy politicians, all the while having a real cool time doing it. This book illustrates, literally and figuratively, how we have done our best to fuck with the system and once in awhile make it work in our favour.

When we started, I thought the world was screwed up, but it took me a few years before I realized just how messed up it *really* was. Part of what attracted me to punk rock in the first place is that it stood up to bullshit. Bullshit like RACISM, SEXISM, GREED, and WARMONGERING. So, when people ask me why I still do what I do, the answer is easy: 'Cause the world is still full of RACISM, SEXISM, GREED, and WARMONGERING. In some ways, it's worse today than back then.
We came across the slogan TALK – ACTION = 0 on the front of an anarchist mag called *Open Road,* and we immediately knew that it fit D.O.A. like a glove. When we asked *Open Road* if we could use that phrase, they said, "Go ahead. The world and everything in it belongs to all of us." To us, that meant:

BE YOUR OWN BOSS.
THINK FOR YOURSELF.
EFFECT SOME POSITIVE CHANGE IN THIS WORLD.

And in that spirit, I thought it would be cool to share D.O.A.'s thirty-three plus years of punk, troublemaking, and fun. When I started to go through my fourteen boxes of posters, tour schedules, photos, and memorabilia, it was tough to pare it down. D.O.A. has played somewhere around 3,500 shows over the years, so there are a lot that aren't included here, given the space limitations of this book. Still, I believe that I've painted a pretty broad canvas.

While it's true that punk, like most artistic or social movements, would eventually lose some of its focus and get partially mired in self parody—much to the delight of various naysayers— that's not the whole picture. To the critics, I say: Shove it! Try getting off your butts and creating something that has a shred of meaning. Punk's positives far outweigh its negatives. When you distill what came out of punk—the-think-for-yourself, do-it-yourself ethic for helping those around you and effecting positive change—I'd say punk is still potent. So watch your step when you mess with the rebel kind. Remember this:

WE CAN AND WE WILL
CHANGE THIS WORLD
INTO A BETTER PLACE

So, my friends, I humbly say to all of you:

TALK – ACTION = 0

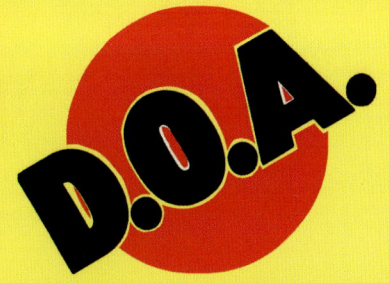

YOU ~~THINK YOU~~ WANNA MAKE A DIFFERENCE
IT SEEMS

DESTROY

Chapter 1

1977-1979

TRADITION

THE CHAOTIC START

As a teenager, I wanted to be a pro hockey player, hopefully for the Boston Bruins. Around the same time, I bought my first drum set and that was a turning point. As I went through high school, I started to become politically aware, and the '60s folk music that my older sister brought home stirred the mental pot for me as well.

In 1973, while I was in grade ten, Greenpeace was holding demonstrations against the buildup of nuclear arms between America and the Soviet Union. This encouraged us teenaged kids to skip school and demonstrate with them. In Vancouver, we marched around the US consulate downtown. This was big: I had attended my first demonstration. I no longer thought about playing for the Bruins; now I wanted to be a civil rights lawyer. I held up William Kunstler (who defended the Chicago Seven) as my role model. Oh yeah, music was still there for me too; I was busy beating the crap out of the drums in crummy high school rock bands.

Two days in September 1974 sealed my fate. The first day, I enrolled at Simon Fraser University; the next day I bought my first guitar from a pawn shop. I had to take up guitar 'cause one of my best friends, who we nicknamed Dimwit, was becoming a far better drummer than I could ever be. I was about to be kicked out of the band, so learning guitar was a matter of survival. We formed a mediocre rock band to play some club shows—our payoff was getting fired from our first gig. We collectively said, "Shit! This rock business ain't what it's cracked up to be!"

Then in '76 we heard about punk rock. Wow! What weird shit is this? It all happened pretty fast after that. We started covering Iggy Pop songs, the Ramones came to town, and singles from the Sex Pistols and the Clash started arriving at the coolest record store in town, Quintessence Records. So in June '77, we formed a band called the Skulls; we thought the name sounded "mean"! We moved to Toronto and raised shit there till February '78, when we broke up.

I arrived back in Vancouver and put an ad in the *Georgia Straight*, Vancouver's alternative newsweekly. I wanted to form a new punk rock band and take the world by storm. First I found Randy Archibald. He was an okay drummer, but not incredible, so I taught him how to play bass and nicknamed him Randy Rampage. Then I came across Chuck Biscuits, who was Dimwit's little brother, and he turned out to be one of the greatest drummers of all time. We were set.

We played a few club shows as part of the burgeoning Van City punk scene, but what really got us going was a "Battle of the Bands" contest. We didn't win, but the MC, Tom Harrison (music critic for the *Georgia Straight*), got covered with gob and stale beer when he announced we lost, which outraged the punks. Next we played an Anti-Canada Day picnic in Stanley Park; the burning of money and the Canadian Constitution and the pissing off of the police department cemented D.O.A. as Vancouver's official troublemakers.

After releasing "Disco Sucks" in June '78, we did our first road trip. We ended up at San Francisco's birthplace of punk, the Mabuhay Gardens. We did two shows, befriended the Avengers, Jello Biafra, and the Dead Kennedys as well as Negative Trend (which mutated into Flipper), and I pissed all over the crowd, which established our punk cred in SF.

With that original trio, we put out two more singles in '78 and '79 and started travelling down an unknown path. It was like punk rock pioneering; in our travels across North America, we found that bigger cities usually had their own fledgling scenes, but the small- to mid-size towns had only vaguely heard about the new threatening phenomenon of punk. So, for a lot of people, D.O.A. was their punk rock baptism. We never really had time to take in what was happening; we were just too fuckin' busy doing it.

By the end of '79, things were starting to shake for the band; we had a manager, journalist Ken Lester; we had record companies wanting to put out our records; and we had tons of offers for shows, particularly in California. We started travelling to California as often as six times a year.

We were on our way.

FIRST BANDS

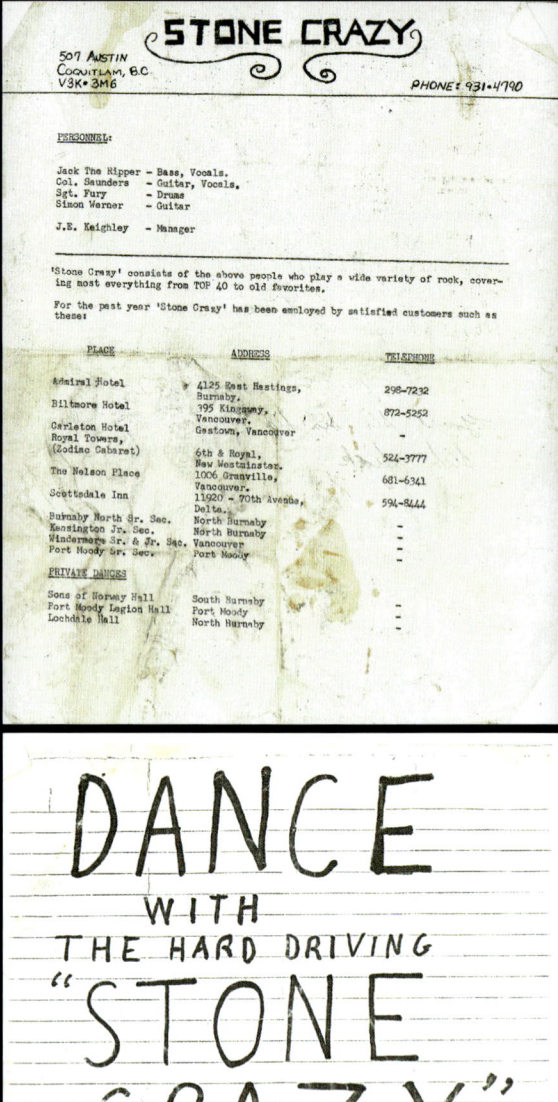

It's been a rough and rocky road. But this is how it all started for my friends and me. Our rock band Stone Crazy, which consisted of Dimwit (RIP), Wimpy, Brad Kent, and I, had our first pro gig at the Grasslands Motor Inn in Merritt, BC, where we were supposed to play Top Forty cover songs. The owner, Mussolini Joe, didn't like us, so he gave us the boot.

After the Stone Crazy firing, we started our first punk band. We needed a name; we came up with the Skulls, it had a threatening ring to it. It was Brad and me on guitar, Wimpy on bass, Dimwit on drums. This crazy Australian guy (what other kind is there?) became our lead singer.

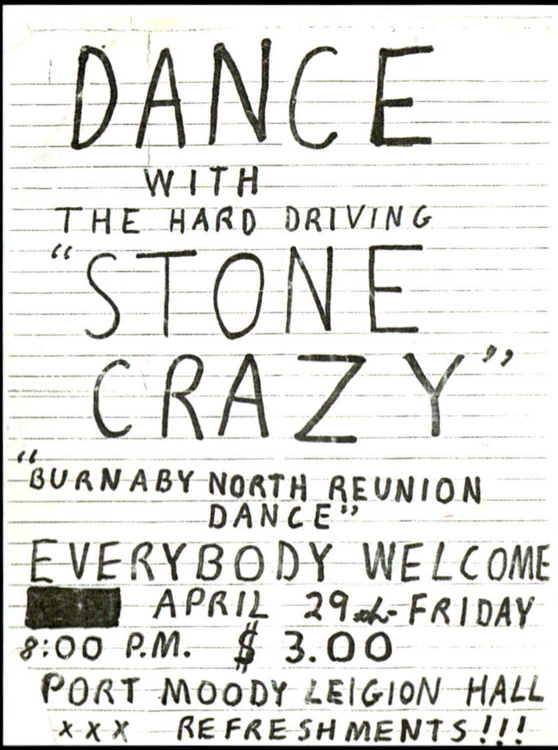

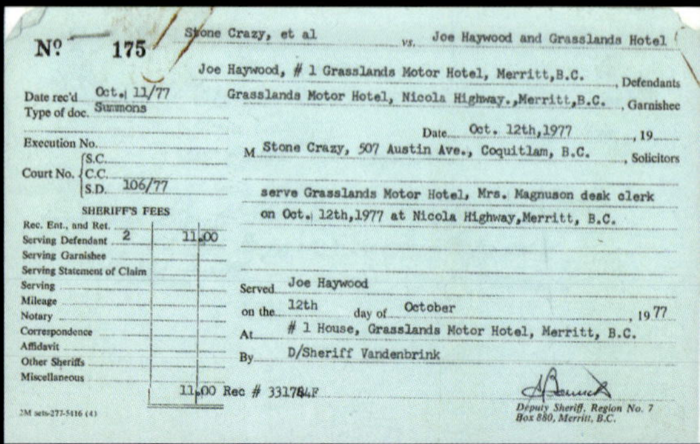

Our first show was on the beach at White Rock, BC. It was an outdoor bandshell and we snuck our way onto the bill by saying, "Yeah, yeah, sure, sure, we're just a rock band like Led Zeppelin, that kind of shit." The crowd consisted of a bunch of greaseball hippies wearing Jack Daniels T-shirts. Our set was greeted by a barrage of garbage and bottles. Our singer Lee punched a couple of those geeks in the head.

The next day I phoned up Tom Harrison and told him about the shit that had gone on. That week in the *Straight*, we were said to be Vancouver's most hated band! Wow! We were on our way. At that show we also met some of White Rock's best: Art Bergmann (Young Canadians) and John Armstrong (Modernettes).

We heard about a punk show in Vancouver at the Japanese Hall with the Lewd and the Furies. We wormed our way onto the bill at the last minute, so whenever I saw the gig posters I would write the Skulls on them with a sharpie. We opened the not-so-gala event and were met with a shitload of indifference. About halfway through I started getting egged by a guy yelling, "Man, you're so punk!" Squinting through the lights, I finally got a bead on the fucker who was doing the egging. I jumped off the stage and tackled him to the ground. Then I took the rest of his carton of eggs and smashed them into his face. I clambered back on stage and sang the rest of the set.

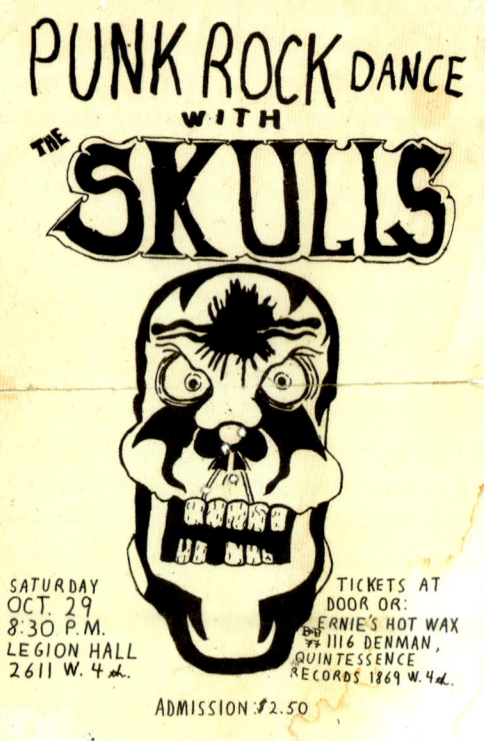

By September '77 our line-up had solidified; Dimwit on drums, myself on vocals, Wimpy, a.k.a. Labordenass, and Simon Werner (RIP) (the Pack) on guitar. At a Japanese Hall show, a huge biker from the Satan's Angels (now the Hell's Angels) came backstage to confirm that the Skulls and the Furies would play that weekend at their Labour Day run. Chris Arnett, leader of the Furies, freaked out and told the guy that he was leaving for South America the next day and couldn't do the show. The biker chased Chris around the dressing room calling him a chickenshit while throwing punches at him. Fearing for his life, Chris ran out, and the Furies never showed up. The Skulls did play the entire biker weekend; it was fucking unreal.

Now that we had established that we were a bunch of troublemakers, we quickly realized that nobody in their right mind would hire us. Damn! That was fucking smart!

So we just went D.I.Y. because when you burn your bridges, you'd better figure out how to swim. I rented the Legion Hall in one of Vancouver's suburbs, a hick town called Port Moody. Besides setting up the show, I did all the postering (hopping on and off buses) and set up the PA. The day of the show we were at the hall getting ready, and in walked two undercover Port Moody police officers. They called out, "Who's in charge of this?" I walked over and said, "That would be me." The cops said our poster was obscene. He held up the poster and said, "Look at this! Piss on You Productions! Shithead! That's sick!" I told him it was my democratic right to print whatever I wanted. The cops said they would be back later to "keep an eye on things." As the evening progressed, maybe twenty would-be punk fans/curiosity seekers showed up, as well as about twenty Satan's Angels. The bikers offered to run the door for me; well, who was I to argue? So they charged people $2 to get in and $ 3 to get out.

To actually have a show in Vancouver I had to rent the West 4th Legion Hall. We got around fifty people. There were no other punk bands in town, the Furies had broken up, and the Dishrags were stuck over in Victoria, so we started the first of what became a proud Vancouver tradition: We formed the first "fuck band." We all traded instruments: I played drums and called myself "Flab Jiggle," Dimwit played bass; Brad Kent played guitar, and Dave Noga sang. We called it Victorian Pork.

The Skulls' plan was to relocate to London to try and make it in the UK punk scene. We had all been saving up dough for the move. Then we heard about this thing called a drive through. Basically, you return a rental vehicle to its original location and just pay for the fuel. So we decided to take all of our gear and personal crap, jump in a motor home, and relocate to Toronto for awhile, before the big move to London. We left Vancouver in mid-November '77 and drove for four days straight across the icy northern wasteland to get to T.O. The drive was all right, but the toilet in the Winnebago wouldn't flush, so by the time we got there, the bowl was overflowing. Nice!

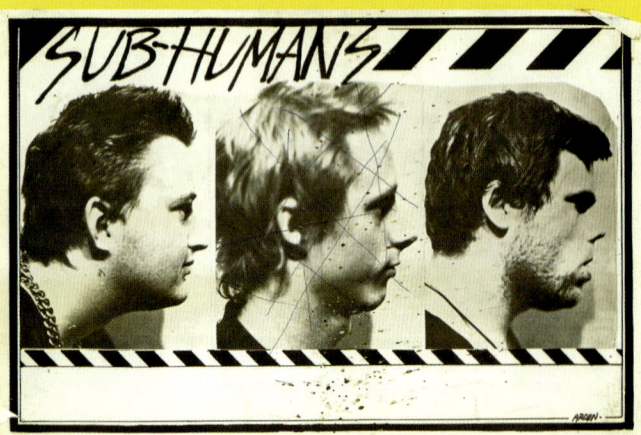

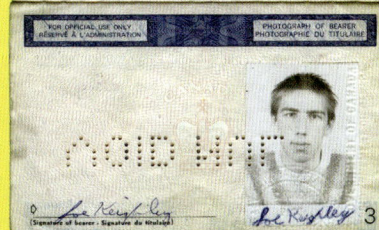

We bummed our way onto a few bills in Toronto. At first people didn't like us, but we made friends and played shows at Club David and the Shock Theatre. We played shows with the Ugly, the Viletones, and the B Girls. We were pissing away our savings for the UK move, waiting for shows that rarely came; I was bored. So to fill the time I started a fanzine called *Drones*. There was only one issue, but it was a classic, for sure. My other main occupation was spraypainting: I would tag anything I could with "the Skulls Rule!" Sometimes I would mindlessly just walk along with the spray can going, painting businesses, churches, whatever. In February '78, Wimpy and Simon Werner moved to London. Dimwit and I were supposed to follow closely behind, but we never did—we decided to move back to Vancouver, and that was the end of the Skulls. Wimpy came back in March and formed the Subhumans along with Dimwit and Brad.

When I got back to Vancouver, I recruited Randy to be the bass player. Then I discovered that Dimwit's little brother Chuck was a good drummer. We met a singer who called himself Harry Homo. He said, "You guys be the band, I'll be the singer, we'll call ourselves D.O.A., and make a million dollars." Well, that was good enough for us, and D.O.A. was born. It was February 11th, 1978, and we talked our way onto a show with the Generators at the Japanese Hall. When the Generators realized we were starting to play the same three songs over again, they pulled the plug on the power. While we had been in Toronto Victorian Pork had gotten "serious" with a new line-up. We opened for them and that was the first time D.O.A. appeared on a poster.

I've always believed that band members should be comrades, and a band should fight against the odds and try to change the world. In our case, common enemies drew Randy, Chuck, and me together. It basically boiled down to two things: the pathetic apathy of mainstream society and the slimy corruption that riddled the music business. So one night while sitting around considering our fate with a case of O'Keefe's Extra Old Stock, we came to our three basic truths:

EVERYBODY HATES US • NOBODY WILL BOOK US • WE'LL NEVER GET A RECORD DEAL

After briefly pondering those sobering realizations, I said, "Why don't we put out our own record? There's this band I used to see when I went to SFU called the Pied Pumkin String Ensemble; they did it, so why can't we?" Well, there was one big problem—we had no fuckin' dough! But like everybody else, the rock 'n' roll gods have to grind one out on a regular basis like us destitute mortals, and manna fell from heaven! Some unemployment enjoyment cheques came in. I cashed those and booked Ocean Sound in North Vancouver. We recorded and mixed the four-song *Disco Sucks* EP in nine hours. That included finishing half the lyrics in the studio. To the right is my notebook from that recording session.

WOKE UP SCREAMING

DON'T REALLY CARE WHAT THEY SAY
DON'T REALLY CARE WHAT THEY DO
JUST KNOW I'M SICK OF THEIR CRAP
[TH]E COPS THEY TOOK ME AND BEAT ME BLUE
[IT] WASN'T WHO I WAS OR WHAT I DO
[IT] WAS JUST BEING ALIVE

[TOO]K A CHANCE ON THE OTHER SIDE
[GOT] OFF THE DOWNHILL SLIDE
[STO]PPED WASTIN' MY TIME

[HA]D A DREAM, SAW A SCHEME
[SAW] A MAN, HANG ON A BEAM
[NE]XT THING WAS I WOKE UP SCREAMING
HIS EYES WERE SCREAMING
[I]T WASN'T WHO I WAS OR WHAT I DO
[IT'S] JUST BEING ALIVE
[N]OT JUST DREAMING

[TO]OK A CHANCE ON THE OTHER SIDE
[G]OT OFF THE DOWNHILL SLIDE
[ST]OPPED WASTIN' MY TIME

DISCO SUCKS
EP
1978

ROYAL POLICE

[TH]EIR BLOODY FOOLS
[WI]TH THEIR STUPID RULES
[KI]CK EM' OUT,
[B]EAT EM' ABOUT

[TH]EIR DISGUSTING
[B]UT THEIR ONLY PAWNS
[T]RAINED TO KEEP
[TH]E PUBLIC IN LINE

[N]EW STORMTROOPERS
[S]O SHUT YOUR MOUTH
[CA]USE THE MONEY BEHIND EM
[D]ON'T WANT NO RIOT

NAZI TRAINING CAMP

~~THIS PLACE IS DECADENT CRAP~~
THIS ~~PLACE IS USELESS~~ USELESS GARBAGE
~~IT'S YOUR WORLD I'M TELLIN' ABOUT~~
~~SWASTIKAS ARE IN YOUR BRAIN~~

~~I'M TALKIN~~

YOUR AT THE CATTLE TROUGH
ELECTRIC PRO UP YOUR ASS
YOU SEEM TO ENJOY IT
SWASTIKAS ARE IN YOUR BRAIN

I'M TALKIN' BOUT THE GREEDY SLUTS
I'M TALKIN' BOUT THE NIFTY PRICKS
IT'S YOUR WORLD I'M YELLIN' ABOUT
SWASTIKAS ARE IN YOUR BRAIN

Office Specialty

D.O.A.

steno note book
cahier de sténographie

book no./numéro de l'article:

to/à:

from/de:

stenographer/sténographe:

151-0734 Feint and Centre Line/Green Tint
Papier rayé avec ligne centrale/vert clair

120 pages

Punk rock was the new sensation in Vancouver and D.O.A. epitomized it, so Tom Harrison got us on the bill of the Battle of the Bands. The show was at the Body Shop, a local meat market, and the local punks came down there determined to raise shit. That they did, especially when D.O.A. were knocked out of the competition.

On July 1st, 1978 (Canada Day), D.O.A., the Subhumans, and Private School tried to play in Vancouver's magnificent Stanley Park without a permit. The bulls were having none of this. They blocked us from playing until we borrowed a permit for the park from a picnicking church group (hey, there's good people in every walk of life). The bands finally played five hours later than scheduled. Anarchists burned the Canadian Constitution and money. The concert got a lot of media coverage, so the public's perception of our less-than-savoury attitude increased exponentially around BC.

Our first road trip was to Victoria. Tim Ray and AV had asked to come over and play on the bill with them and the Dishrags. We planned to go to the Dishrags' high school (they were all sixteen) and do some flyering for the show. The Dishrags met us at the front of the school about 11 a.m., then the two bands and road crew all ran pell mell through the classrooms throwing flyers at kids. In short order we had a posse of teachers and the principal in hot pursuit. They grabbed us and kicked us out of the school. Jeez! What ingrates—we were just spreading Canadian culture. Only about fifty people showed up at the gig and, of course, we didn't get paid, but it was a lark.

Once the *Disco Sucks* EP came out, we mailed it everywhere we could think of, and about a month later it was number one on a San Francisco college radio station. That summer, I got us booked for two nights at Mabuhay Gardens, SF's home of punk. To get there, I took the train, Randy and Chuck took the Greyhound, and Brad hitchhiked. We arrived without any gear, so we borrowed some from Negative Trend, and I became fast friends with their bassist Will Shatter (RIP) (Flipper). On Friday night we warmed up for the Avengers, which was great, and the joint was packed. On Saturday night we opened for Ray Campi and the Rockabilly Rebels. The crowd was a bunch of tourists that were definitely indifferent to our brand of noise. At that time I was just singing, so to entertain the crowd I decided to try to wrap my entire body with gaffer's tape. It didn't work; the crowd stared at me with all the emotion that you might see in a shark's eye. Sensing their boredom—and having to piss like a racehorse—I unzipped and sent forth a stream that went clear across the dance floor. The yellow liquid ended up in some girl's drink about twenty feet away. Needless to say, that (wet) cemented our rep in SF. On Sunday, we didn't have a show, but the Dead Kennedys were playing at the Fab Mab. I caused such a ruckus that the bouncers threw me out. Dirk Dirksen (RIP), who ran the Mab, said I was banned for life. Jello stopped the DK's set and said they wouldn't continue unless they let "that Joey Shithead back into the club." Dirk relented and that was the start of my great friendships with Jello and Dirk.

QUADRA
3 BANDS
- **D.O.A.**
- **RABID**
- **ERNIE DICK & the POINTED STICKS**

WED   THURS
AUG. 23 – 24

NEW WAVE NEW WAVE NEW WAVE NEW WAVE
NEW WAVE NEW WAVE NEW WAVE NEW WAVE

1055 HOMER

Back home we got booked into this gay club on Homer St. called the Quadra Club (later on Club Soda, still later the Starfish Room). When we arrived for the sound check, they had a video monitor hooked up that played Deep Throat over and over again, and it was still playing when the show was over. This was Ernie Dick and the Pointed Sticks' (later just Pointed Sticks) first show.

A local college DJ, Phil Smith, booked us to play my old alma mater, Simon Fraser University. While we played, the entire ceiling of acoustic tiles got ripped out by the fans. You can see D.O.A.'s song list on the poster.

The White Noise Tour 78

Friday Oct. 6   Friday Oct. 6

D.O.A.

Dishrags   The Pointed Sticks

8.00 PM

Simon Fraser University
South Court Lounge   No Age Limit

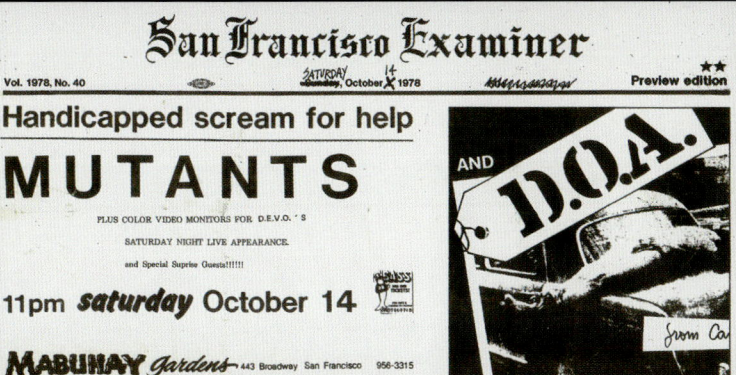 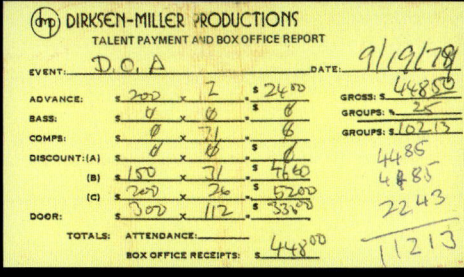

This was our second trip to San Francisco in '78. We played with the Mutants and got paid $102.13. This time we rode in style in Al Steadman's green Chevy panel van. Simon Wilde, a.k.a. Stubby Pecker (RIP) (he briefly played bass for D.O.A. in 1980) had an upside-down swastika on his jacket. By chance, Simon encountered a racist gang of whites outside the Mab and got punched out by these cretins. When we heard about the fight, our roadie, Bob Montgomery (Chuck's older brother) and I went out front to see what was going on. I was immediately confronted by the head racist, backed up by about twelve or thirteen guys. This head dick screamed at me, then ripped off his wife beater. At first I wondered if he didn't want to get it dirty while they pummelled me. He turned around and showed me a full back tattoo of an eagle clutching a swastika. It was his point of pride. We had a ten-minute argument, with the club's security standing by. Amazingly, no punches were thrown. After they left, I told Simon to never wear a stupid fucking swastika again.

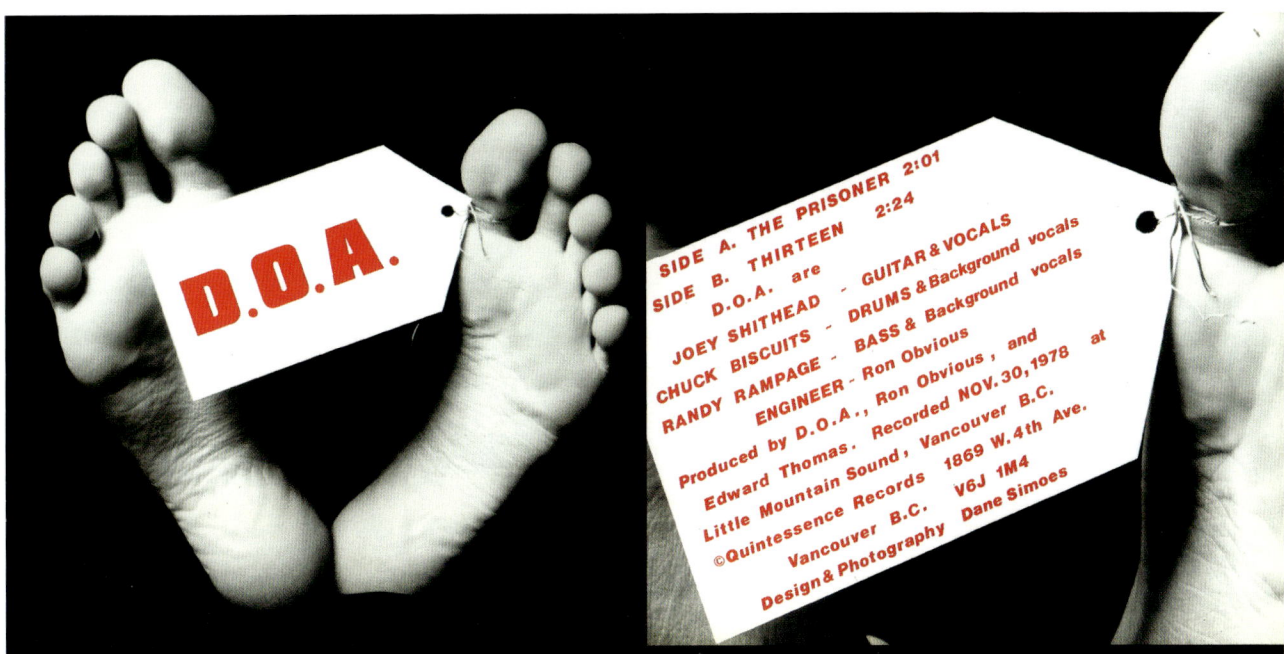

We got the Avengers up to Vancouver for a two-night stand. These were the last shows at the Japanese Hall, Vancouver's original home of punk rock. We also played in Victoria again, and the poster showed me with then-Prime Minister Joe Clark. It was the Wright brothers' (No Means No) first introduction to punk rock, and a wild one it was, as Randy, Chuck, and I took on some really moronic patrons with mike and cymbal stands.

In late '78, Quintessence Records released our *The Prisoner/Thirteen* 7-inch single, recorded at Little Mountain Sound by Ron Obvious. Bob Rock helped out on the session.

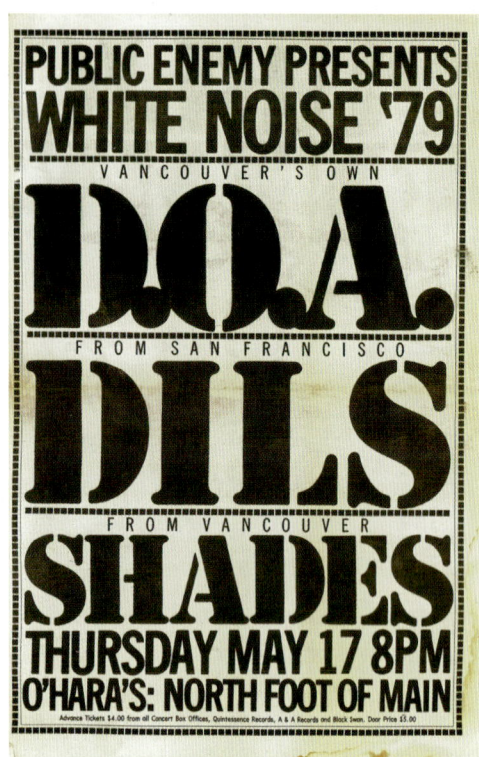

We played this new rather large club called O'Hara's with the Dils and the Shades. Sponsored by *Public Enemy* magazine, it was a good show. The next night, there was the 3D Party: D.O.A., the Dils, and the Dishrags. It was held at a squat house, one of Vancouver's oldest and most trashed, right next door to Dave Gregg's "Fort Gore" pad. So many fucking people showed up that they smashed holes in the wall that separated the hallway from the room where the bands performed. This was a better show.

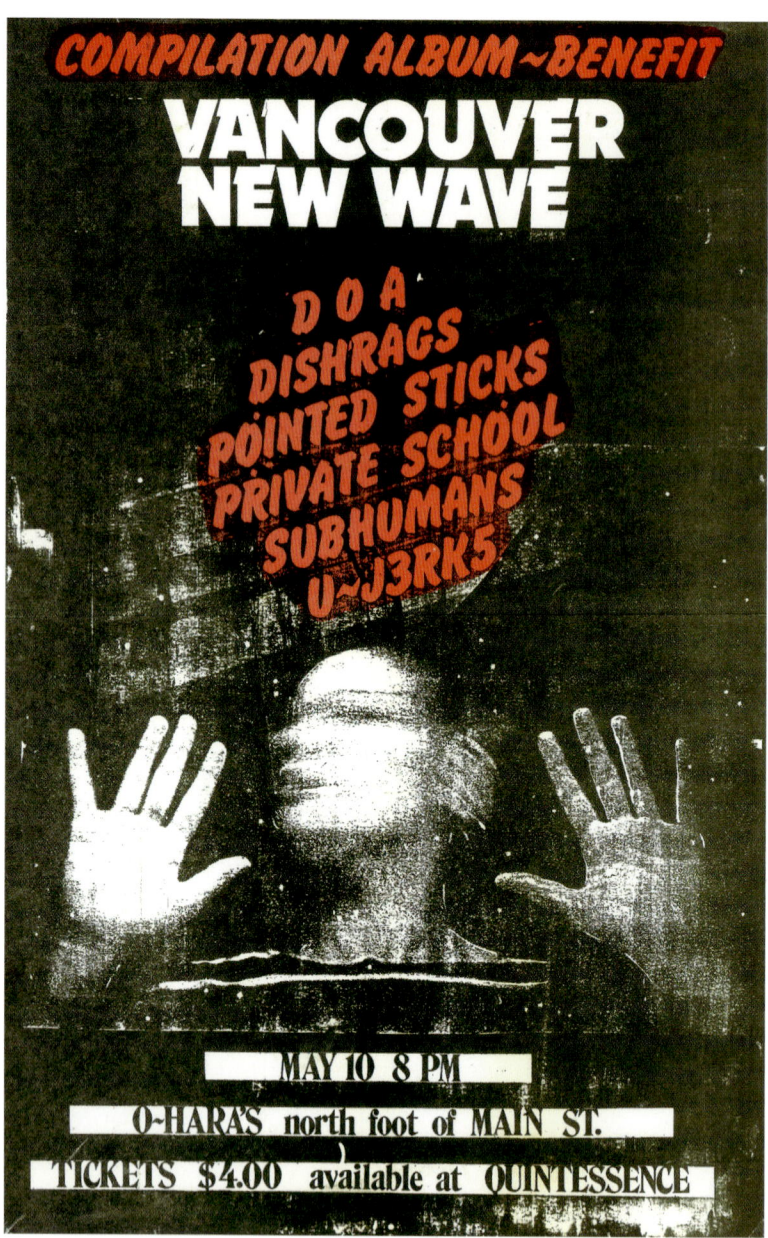

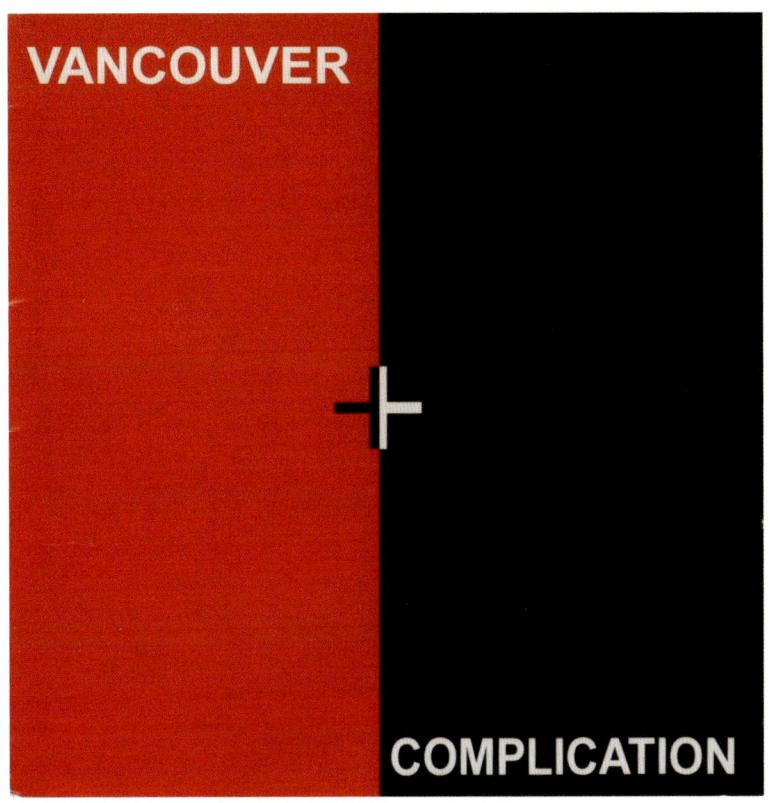

Vancouver had a really vibrant and creative punk/new wave scene. Jack Rabid of the Big Takeover called it one of the best in the world. So Phil Smith, Steve Macklam (Pointed Sticks manager), Gerry Barad (Quintessence and D.O.A. advisor), and Grant McDonaugh (Quintessence) had an idea: Let's record all the bands in the scene and put out a compilation album. Great idea, but as usual, nobody had any dough except maybe Ted Thomas (he owned Quintessence Records), but he wouldn't back it. So we found Chris Cutress (CBC recording engineer) who ran Sabre Sound, an 8-track studio in Burnaby. Chris recorded everybody for free. To pay for the initial pressing, we put together a benefit show for the compilation at O'Hara's. Despite the petty in-scene fighting, we put out a great album. It was re-issued by Sudden Death Records as a benefit for the Vancouver Food Bank in 2005.

An early version of "I Hate You."

We got invited to play a big outdoor R.A.R. (Rock Against Racism) concert in Chicago. There was a benefit show at the Smilin' Buddha to help get us there. This gave us the impetus to organize a national tour. We made our way down the west coast to San Francisco. Then we headed over to Texas, where our one show was at Raul's in Austin. We got into Austin the night before our gig and had nowhere to crash out. So along with all the band equipment, Ian Tiles (merch guy), Bob Montgomery, Randy, and Chuck all crammed into Randy's little green panel van. I said, "You guys are nuts! Look at this beautiful Texas night, I'm going to sleep under the stars in this park." That was fine till about two a.m. when a huge Texas thunder-and-rain storm opened up. Like a drowned rat, I too squished into the van.

We drove up from Austin to Chicago and arrived with just fumes of gas in the tank and no money. We got to the show at about ten a.m. They wanted us to play at eleven a.m. when nobody was there, so I talked the promoter into putting the entire concert back by two and a half hours so D.O.A. could start at one-thirty p.m. About 5,000 people showed up and we played songs like "World War Three," "The Enemy" and our anti-racist tune, "Race Riot." We won over the crowd and made a ton of friends amongst this anti-racist, anti-war collection of free thinkers. They were our kind of people.

FIRST TOUR

Then we headed straight to NYC. In Chicago, we'd met Ken Lester, a journalist for the *Georgia Straight*, and he bummed a ride to New York with us. Later that summer, Ken would become our manager till 1988. He did a great job. (Ken was one of the two people charged with inciting 1971's Gastown Riot, where Vancouver Police waded violently into a crowd on horseback. He was later acquitted.) We arrived in NYC almost flat broke. We stayed with the NY Yippies at #10 Bleecker St. (half a block from CBGB's). The night we arrived, we spent our last twenty bucks on alcohol. Yes, I know, not so wise. For the four days till our show, we hung around with the Bowery bums and threw shit at tourist buses that cruised by to look at the dispossessed. When the show finally happened, there was an electrical fire. The NYFD efficiently put out the fire, and when they asked the bar for a few free beers, the Yippies refused, so the firemen shut the show down for not having a permit. When I went to collect our $100 guarantee, they tried to weasel out on me and give me twenty bucks. I said, "FUCK THAT!" and got our $100.

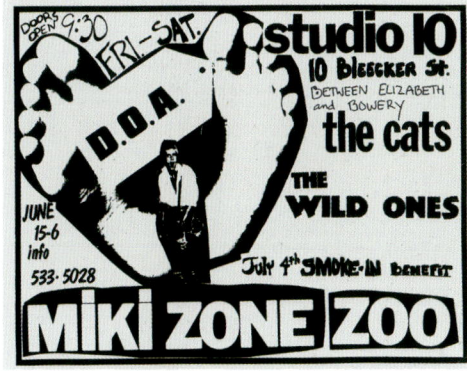

Two days later, Ken got us the support spot for one of the Dils' shows at Hurrah's Club. The Dils did a two-night stand: on the first night, we were spectators. When the Dils started playing, we ran around the inside perimeter of the club in a great circle. We were joined by Jello Biafra and a bunch of our friends who'd managed to get there from Vancouver. Now please be advised, dear readers, that this was not a punk rock club; it was a pretentious place. As we ran around the club in this great Tasmanian Devil circle, we knocked drinks out of patrons' hands and, in some cases, we knocked down the club-goers. Well, this was a real "kid's day at the beach" till one woman claimed that Randy had knocked her down and broken her wrist. The club was going to cancel our show the next night, the NYPD had arrived, and they were about to handcuff Rampage. Ken, ever the negotiator, and I talked logically to the cops. Soon there were no charges, and we played a great show the next night, opening for the Dils.

33

July 1, the second annual Anti-Canada Day Anarchist Picnic, was held again at Stanley Park, but this time at Lumberman's Arch, a place I revered as a kid and still do. My highlight was our adaptation of a Sex Pistols classic. We called it "Anarchy in BC."

The nuclear arms race between America and the Soviet Union was a nightmare, so we helped organize a Rock Against Radiation show in Vancouver. The city was totally opposed to it and tried to stop the show, but it went ahead. The next year, the mayor was leading the Stop the Arms Race parade in Vancouver. It takes people a while to catch up, sometimes.

We got invited to open for the Clash at the PNE Gardens in Vancouver. We had met the Clash and were big fans, so this was a great honour. It did not go so well, however. The Clash were a lot more uptight than when we'd met them previously; I ended up screaming at them as they were heading on stage. Mick Jones referred to D.O.A. as "that little heavy metal band." Oh well, they were still one of my fave bands.

Joey Shithead: one of twenty clones.

Ahhh! the Cambrian Hall show. D.O.A. and our fans fucked up so many venues that I was always on the hunt for a new hall that had never heard of us. I would go into the hall and rent it as "A concert for young people." That was usually cool, at least until the show was over when the hall owner saw the evidence of the hedonistic debauchery and destruction that we were becoming famous for. At this Cambrian Hall (Vancouver's Welsh Society), Ian Tiles found a bucket and kept dousing us with water as we were playing on stage. By the time we were finished, there was water everywhere, along with a plethora of broken bottles. The Welsh guy who ran the hall was looking for me. I held a guitar amp up by my head as I walked out so he couldn't lambast me, but as I walked by him I could hear him say in a thick Welsh brogue, "Where's that Joe Keithley?! Me grandmother could play better music than that!" That was our last show at the Cambrian Hall.

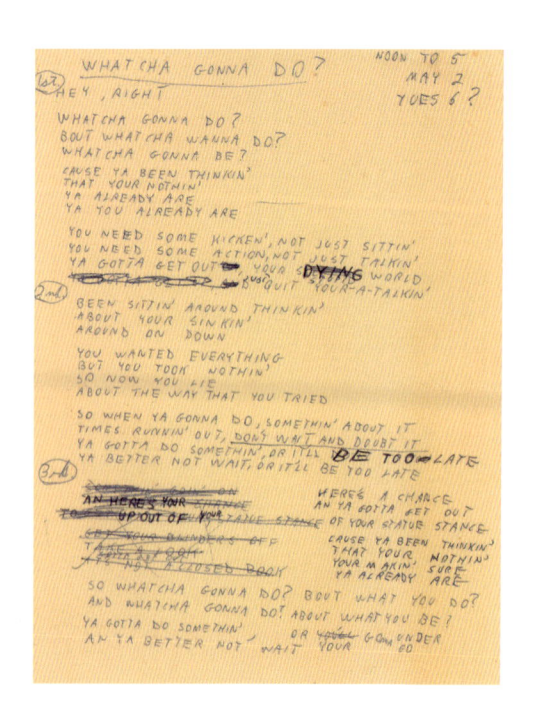

We made a second cover for this single that went overtop of the first one; Lester thought the first cover was too cutesy. Ron Obvious engineered and produced the single with the help of Bob Rock.

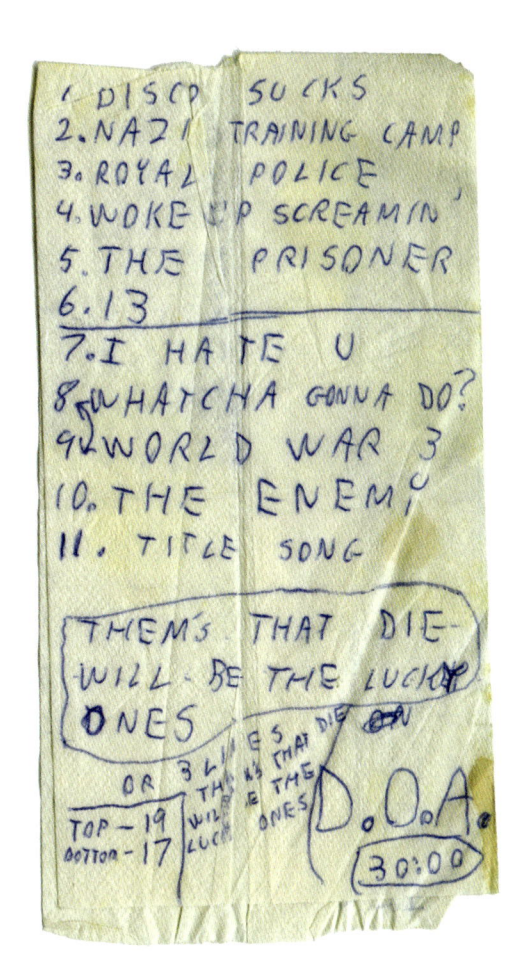

1979 was good year, but we had one last show to do on December 7 at UBC's SUB Ballroom with Female Hands. The show's organizers did one really dumb thing—they hired UBC engineering students to do security. The engineers had a rep for being out of control and pushy. When D.O.A. hit the stage, the shit hit the fan. The engineers tried to stop the punks from stagediving. The harder they tried, the harder the punks fought back, and the punks were a lot tougher than the engineers thought, so the engineers got their collective asses kicked. Part way through the set, Chuck ran out from behind his kit and urged the crowd to go nuts: "Anarchy, man! Destroy this dump!" When the crowd got out of control, Chuck ran and hid backstage, Bob Montgomery swung back and forth across the stage on the giant ballroom curtains (we later had to bail Bob out of jail), and the glass front doors of the ballroom got smashed. Backstage, Chuck quit. "D.O.A. is over," he said. A short while later after perusing the damage, I went back to the dressing room and saw three guys with Chuck's drums. I snarled, "Where the fuck do you think you're going with those?" "Hey man, Chuck just gave these to us." I charged these scumsuckers and slammed one of them into the wall. They ran down the back stairs like scared rabbits. Well, so much for having the world as our oyster; the hall was destroyed, Bob was in jail, and the band was broken up.

D.O.A. BREAKS OUT

In 1980, D.O.A. became a four-man rock band when we added Dave Gregg on second guitar. That gave us a powerful two-guitar wall of sound. We were definitely making waves across North America, so it made sense for our manager to negotiate an album deal with the newly formed Friends Records in Vancouver. That was cool; we weren't putting out just singles anymore, we would record a whole album. And we were ready for it. The songs that made up our first album, *Something Better Change,* had been performed live at least 100 times and practiced another 400 times. By the time we recorded *Hardcore 81,* we had probably played well over 200 shows and practiced all those songs at least a thousand times. As the albums came out, we took on an increasingly busy tour schedule, and we invested in a brand-new Dodge van, the Blue Bullet.

In these early years, we really found our way as a band: We would take on any subject lyrically; we got more involved in people-first politics; we would travel around North America at the drop of a porkpie hat; we became the soundtrack for a lot of political upheaval; and we popularized the phrase "hardcore."

Chapter 2

1980–1981

The original D.O.A. line-up had broken up after the riot at UBC in December '79, but I soldiered on. We had already brought in Dave Gregg as the second guitarist, so we replaced Randy with my buddy Simon Wilde, a.k.a. Stubby Pecker (RIP), and Andy Graffiti replaced Chuck on drums.

We played a few shows around town with the new line-up, which was met with mixed reviews. One night we had a show in Vancouver at a hall at 30th and Main. The PA was supplied by Jim "I" Braineater (a fabulous artist from Vancouver). The set did not go over well and there was almost continuous feedback coming from the PA, though Jim struggled to control it. The after-party was at the Hacienda (an apartment/party stop that rose up out of a parking lot next to a seedy downtown hotel on Seymour Street). The proprietors were Bill Scherk (Los Populáros) and Carol Segal (Randy's sometime girlfriend).

As fate would have it, Randy, Chuck, and I all happened to meet in the parking lot. After a brief pause, we agreed that our set that night had sucked. We decided, on the spot, to get back together and conquer the world as a four-piece; Dave Gregg would be the second guitarist, and our fearless manager, Ken Lester, would help set the course to either glory or eternal damnation.

The temporary D.O.A. line-up did the bed tracks for the whole first album, but it was never mixed or released. Part way through the recording Chuck came back. You can hear Chuck drumming all the way through, and Stubby's bass playing can be heard on four tracks, Randy's on the rest.

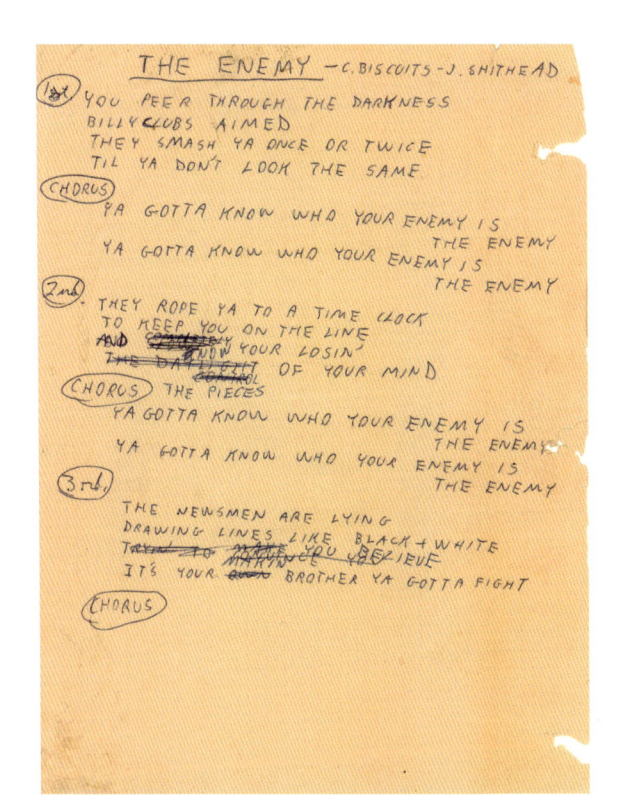

THE ENEMY — C. BISCUITS - J. SHITHEAD

(1st)
YOU PEER THROUGH THE DARKNESS
BILLY CLUBS AIMED
THEY SMASH YA ONCE OR TWICE
TIL YA DON'T LOOK THE SAME

(CHORUS)
YA GOTTA KNOW WHO YOUR ENEMY IS
               THE ENEMY
YA GOTTA KNOW WHO YOUR ENEMY IS
               THE ENEMY

(2nd)
THEY ROPE YA TO A TIME CLOCK
TO KEEP YOU ON THE LINE
AND ~~SOMEDAY~~ YOUR LOSIN'
~~THE DARKEST~~ OF YOUR MIND
~~CONTROL~~
(CHORUS) THE PIECES
YA GOTTA KNOW WHO YOUR ENEMY IS
               THE ENEMY
YA GOTTA KNOW WHO YOUR ENEMY IS
               THE ENEMY

(3rd)
THE NEWSMEN ARE LYING
DRAWING LINES LIKE BLACK + WHITE
~~TRY~~ TO ~~MAKE YOU~~ BELIEVE
IT'S YOUR ~~OWN~~ BROTHER YA GOTTA FIGHT

(CHORUS)

RUBBER ARMS
DUMB PICTURE

43

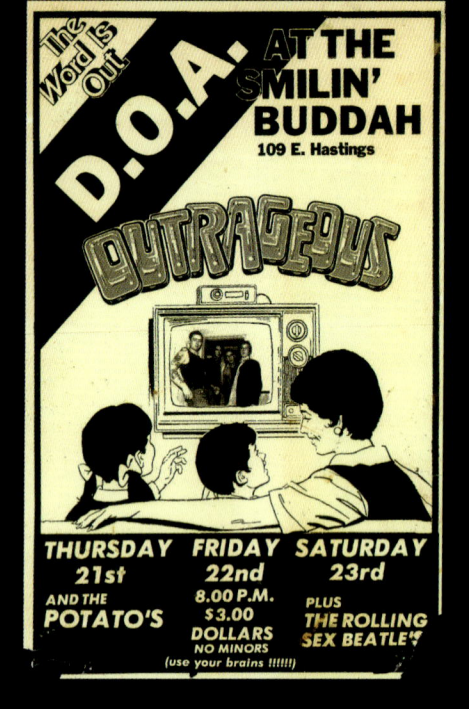

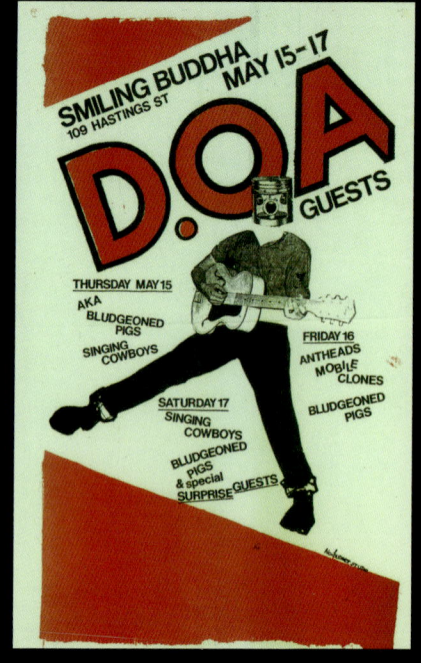

In 1979, the Smilin' Buddha Cabaret took over as Vancouver's home of punk rock—our CBGB's, our 100 Club. It was a dump, but it was our dump. I was living in a roach-infested apartment just behind the Drake Hotel on Powell Street about four blocks from the club. The owners of the Buddha, Lashman and Nancy, thought I was an upright young fellow, so they turned the club booking over to me. The same people every night tried to get on the guest list, refusing to pay the $2 admission.

WEDNESDAY
DRINK
Margaritas
FOOD
Chili & Grilled Cheese
MOVIES
Repo Man (w/ Chuck Biscuits)
The Hunger — Road Warrior
BEER
Beer

THURSDAY
DRINK
Whisky Sours
FOOD
Chili & Hot Dogs
MOVIES
Corrupt (w/ John Rotten) & Boy & His Dog
BEER
Beer

I BRAINEATER, ON DEMAND
SPACE CAKE & SPECIAL SERVICE

FRIDAY
DRINK
Cuba Libres
FOOD
Tuna Salad & Chili
MOVIES
Scarface
Serious Moonlight Tour (w/ Bowie)
BEER
Beer

"TOTALLY TRENDY, O.K. TO GO..." --Simon Le Bon sez.
SATURDAY → LOOKOUT!!

AT THE PLAZA INTERNACIONAL HOTEL & RECREATIONAL COMPLEX
JULY 25-28
1AM → 5AM
THE ONLY AFTER HOURS PARTY THAT MATTERS

"a gathering place for the backsliding artist and mediocre person"
-- VANCOUVER SCUM

D.O.A.
U-J3RK5
SUNDAY, JUNE 1, 8PM
ARCADIAN HALL (6TH & MAIN)

GUESTS & FILMS
NO BOOZE/ALL AGES WELCOME
$4 ($3 WITH SKOOL CARD)

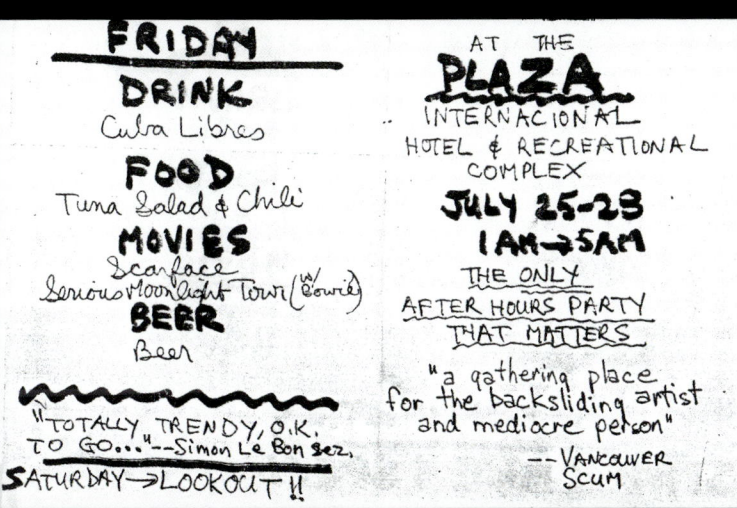

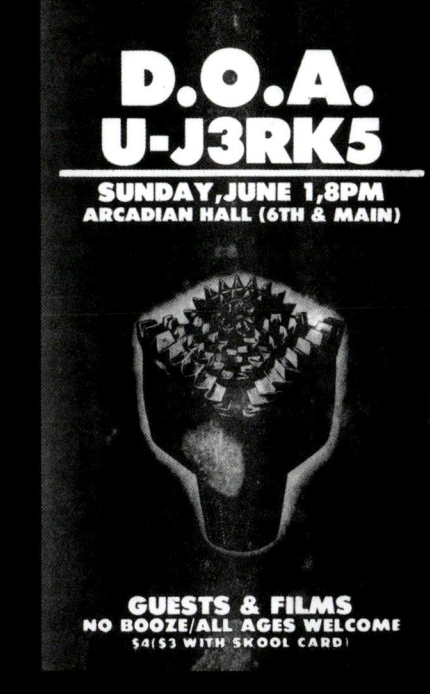

The Plaza International was our home and home to every punk rock band that came through Vancouver between 1980 and '85.

D.O.A. and the Dead Kennedys: Amazing bill, amazing show—punk rock at its peak.

PERRYSCOPE CONCERTS,
STRIVING FOR STREET CREDIBILITY,
PRESENTS

VANCOUVER'S OWN
D.O.A.
DESTROY TRADITION

FRIDAY, JULY 10, 8PM
COMMODORE BALLROOM,
870 GRANVILLE

DEAD KENNEDYS

PLUS SPECIAL GUESTS FROM OHIO
TOXIC REASONS

TICKETS $7.50 ADVANCE FROM KELLY'S TICKET WICKET, 810 GRANVILLE (669-5880),
ALL V.T.C. LOCATIONS, EATON'S, INFO CENTRES IN MAJOR MALLS, QUINTESSENCE, HOT WAX, FRIENDS, RAVE

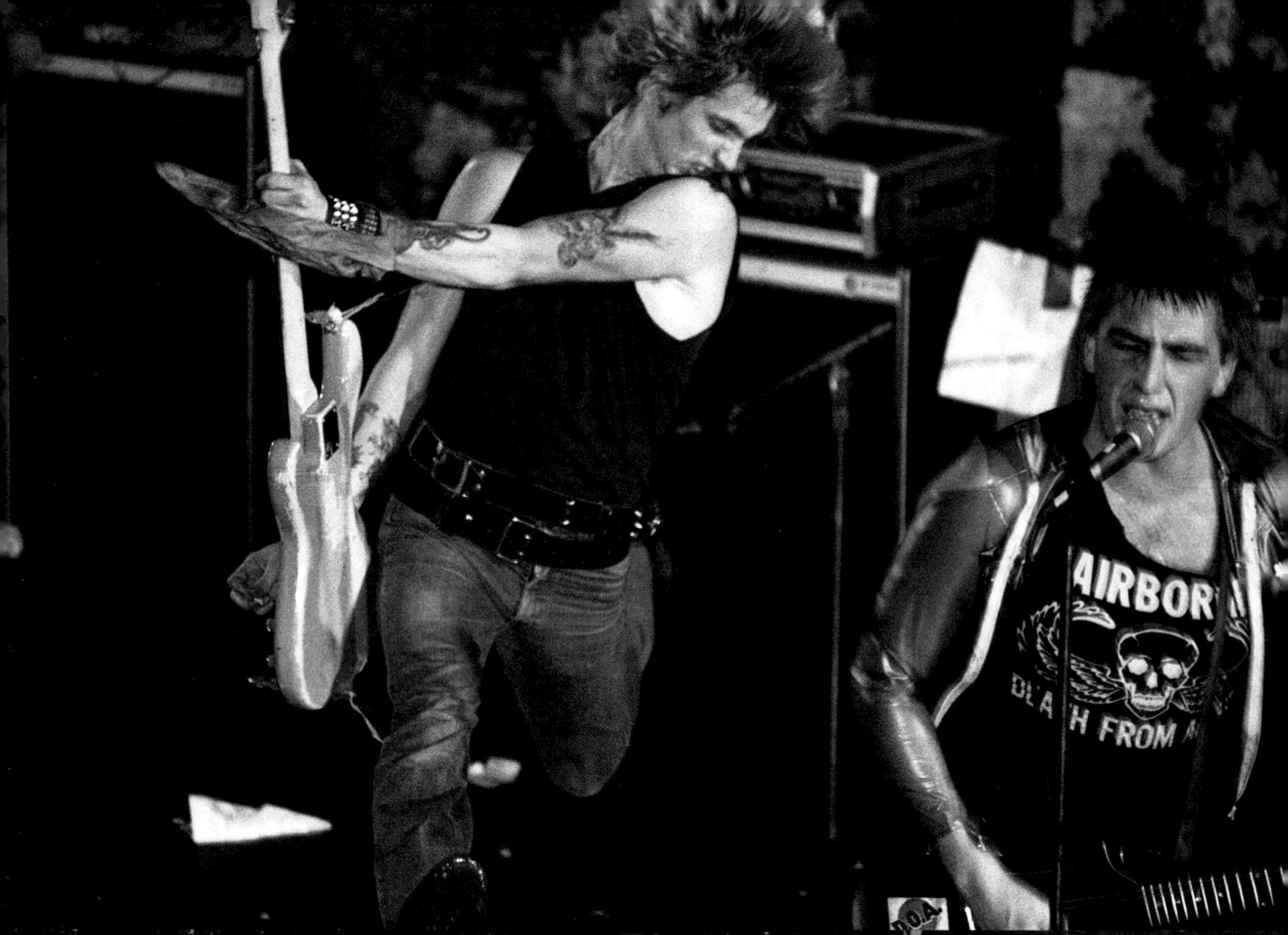

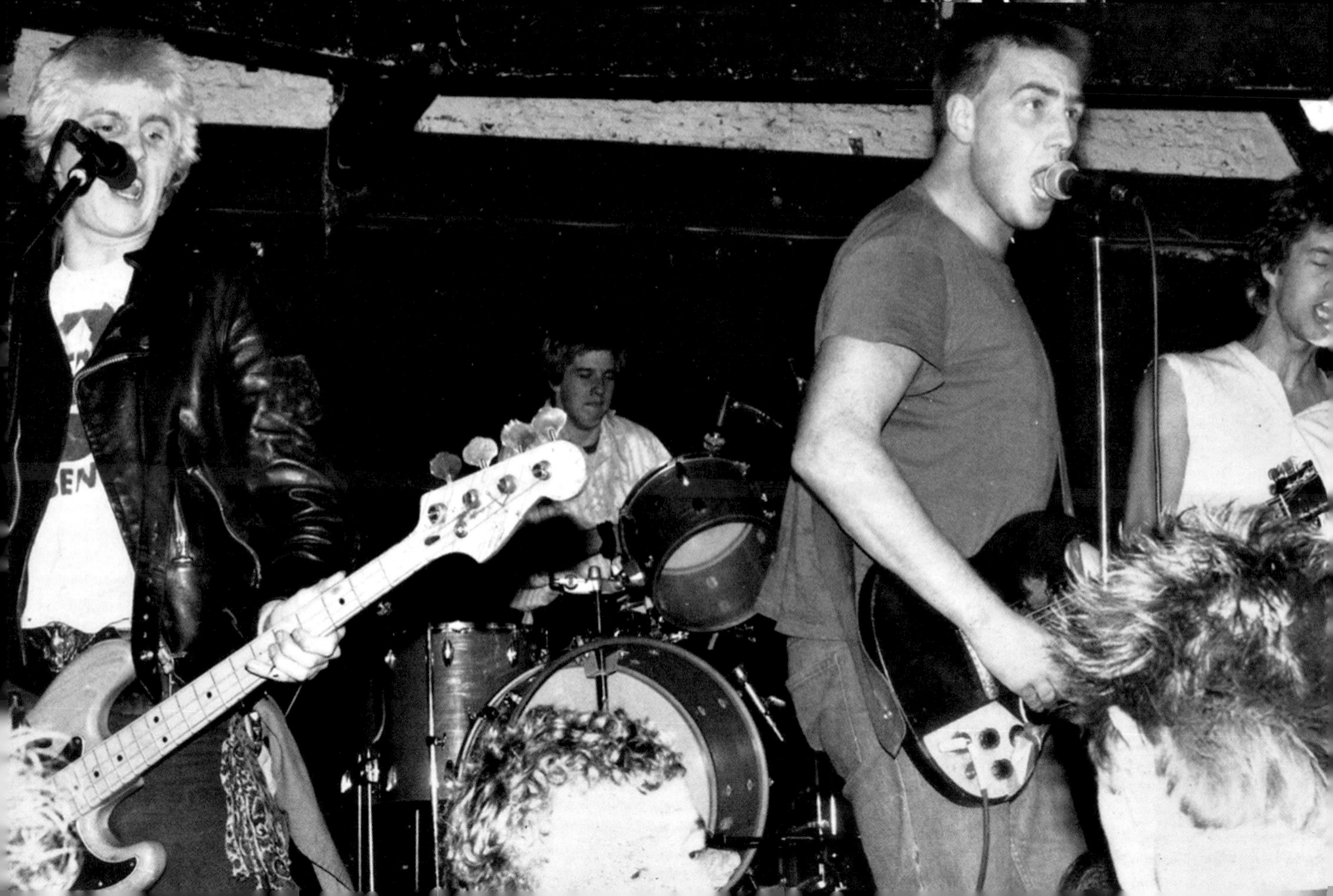

Two days after we finished recording our first album, *Something Better Change*, the tour started in Madison, Wisconsin, so we drove straight for two days and made the show with fifteen minutes to spare. It was July and as humid as fuck. After the Madison show, we were stuck in the fourth storey of a warehouse in Toronto for about ten days waiting for more shows. Tempers were almost as short as the money. The manager fought the roadie, the roadie fought the drummer (and they were brothers), the bassist fought the manager, and the roadie fought the bassist. I just called them all fuckin' idiots.

D.O.A. plus the Hot Nasties   8 P.M., JUNE 13th AT THE UNION HALL 120-17th AVENUE S.W. NO GLASS!!

On our first trip to Calgary, Randy kicked Chuck's hand and broke a bone. We taped a drumstick across his palm, and it killed him every time he hit the snare drum. So we played for only thirty minutes and some of the kids called us ripoffs.

We got invited to play this festival called Deep Wave. Teenage Head was getting popular, so some foolish promoters thought they would build a festival around them and some other hot-shots. They expected 10,000 and less than a 1,000 showed. Our set started out with a spaced-out hippie MC named Freewheelin' Frankie Avalanche introducing us as "Johnny Shithead and the D.O.A.s." Things were really starting to stink. We hammered out "The Enemy" and a couple of other songs, and when we got to "World War Three," Randy's bass crapped out. He tried smashing it in frustration, but it didn't break. I said, "Lemme try that!" I started smashing it, and it still wouldn't break, so Randy said, "Give me that piece of shit!" Then he chucked it about forty feet (twelve metres) across the stage toward the monitor board. The jackass monitor guy thought Randy was trying wreck his equipment and put Randy in a chokehold. I grabbed the monitor guy and squeezed his throat until he let go of Randy. Turned out our cheque for the show bounced. Fuck Deep Wave.

```
GET OUT OF MY LIFE
WHERE YOU AT
YOU'RE MAKIN' ME WEAK
A KNIFE IN MY BACK
BUT I'M BEGGINNING TO THINK

YOUR NEW WAVE'S SHIT
YOUR NEW WAVE'S SHIT    I'M GONNA GET SICK
AND I'M GONNA GET SICK
ALL OVER ... YOU

I NEVER NEVER WANNA BE LIKE YOU
I NEVER NEVER WANNA BE LIKE YOU
I NEVER NEVER WANNA BE LIKE YOU
I NEVER NEVER WANNA BE LIKE YOU

YOU SOUND SO STALE
YOU STUPID WIMPS
AND I'M BEGGININ' TO THINK
YA FUCKIN' STINK

YOUR NEW WAVE'S SHIT
YOUR NEW WAVE'S SHIT
AND I'M GONNA GET SICK
ALL OVER ... YOU

I NEVER NEVER WANNA BE LIKE YOU
I NEVER NEVER WANNA BE LIKE YOU
I NEVER NEVER WANNA BE LIKE YOU
I NEVER NEVER WANNA BE LIKE YOU

YA FUCKIN' JERKS
```

The Republicans held their National Convention in Detroit in 1980. Ronald Reagan was about to be anointed their presidential candidate, so local activists set up a protest show during the convention. D.O.A. and Toxic Reasons were invited to play. We were delighted to see that there were still some sane people in the Motor City, so we gladly accepted. In August it was stinkin' hot in Detroit, and the garbage men were on strike. There were so many rats running around, you needed name tags to be able to tell them from the Republicans. The protest show was at a small park in central Detroit with a stage set up on a flatbed truck. About 2,000 anti-Reaganites were there having a good time listening to the ever-excellent Toxic Reasons. D.O.A. hit the stage, and as we were playing, we saw a rather large contingent of people approaching the park from one of the side streets. In the distance it was hard to see what they were up to, but there was a lot of them. As they got closer, we could see they were waving American flags and holding placards with slogans that read We Love Ronald Reagan, America Love It or Leave It, and Commies Burn in Hell. It was the Pea-Brained Americans-for-Reagan chapter. Before we knew it, a riot started. We were still on stage playing when a phalanx of Detroit police burst onto the scene and tried to get between the two warring factions. We finished the song we were playing, then our manager yelled out, "Play 'Fucked Up Ronnie'!" We did, then we got the fuck out of there.

There are some things in life that you do, and you think this is the right thing to do, and you wonder why everyone doesn't get it. Well this is it for me: a Rock Against Radiation show on July 19, 1980, to protest against the nuclear arms race between America and the USSR. It was organized at Nathan Phillips Square right in front of city hall in Toronto, Canada's biggest city. It's not every day that they invite punk bands to do this kind of thing. D.O.A. headlined the bill supported by some notable Ontario bands, the Viletones, Forgotten Rebels, the Demics, Joe College, and the Rulers. It turned out that most of the Toronto bands had not bothered to bring their equipment. "Oh we'll just borrow D.O.A.'s gear 'cause we're too pathetic and lazy to bring our own." Now don't get me wrong, we are usually quite reasonable about helping out, but in this case our equipment was on its collective last legs. The Demics' manager asked Bob the roadie about using our gear and Bob told him, quite civilly, no. The manager then called D.O.A. "a bunch of rock stars." At that point Bob picked up a portable metal bike rack (that would hold about three or four bikes) and threw it at this pompous piece of shit. The manager ran for his life, and the Demics didn't play that night.

When we finally got up on stage, the punks that were the supporters of the Toronto bands in question started seig-heiling us and chucking shit. They just did not get it.

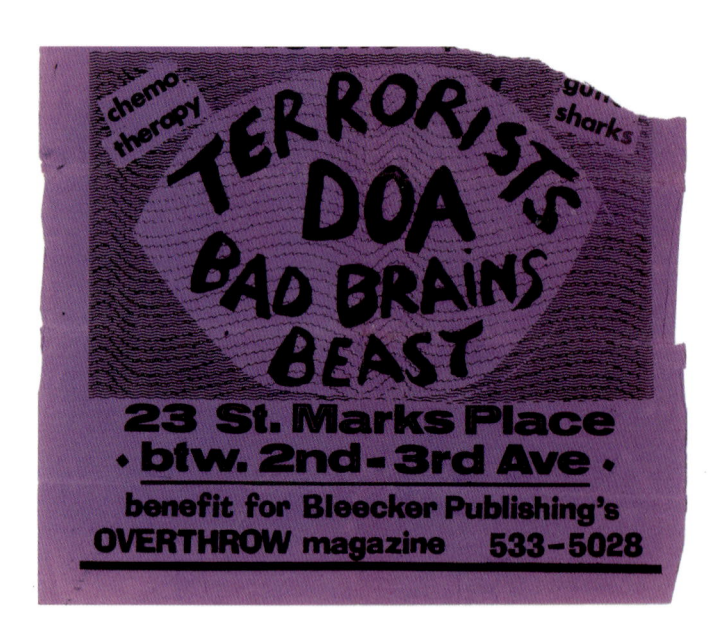

Our second time in New York, we played again with the amazing Bad Brains. There was only a curtain dividing the stage and backstage, and as the opening band started their set, Chuck set up his drums just on the other side of the curtain and started rocking out to a completely different beat. He was three times as loud as they were, so that was kind of the end of their set. That weekend, D.O.A. jammed with Steve Jones (Sex Pistols) at an after-hours club.

In October, we drove 1,400 miles from Vancouver to Los Angeles crammed into my Volkswagen Rabbit to do a show with Black Flag for $175. Our manager told us it would be a great career move. Four hundred people showed up early for the gig and tons more were on their way, so Chuck Dukowski (Black Flag's bass player) said, "Hey, we're going to do two shows, so we'll double your money." When the first show was over, the punks spilled onto the street; there were about 800 of them out there. A Los Angeles Police Department cruiser drove by and one of the punks chucked a beer bottle at it and hit the fender. The cop car stopped and a few more bottles smashed against it before it drove off. In short order, a few more cruisers drove through the heart of the action and got bombarded by bottles. The punks cheered and yelled—it was a pretty good time on a Wednesday night.

About fifteen minutes later, a police helicopter was hovering over the intersection and forty police cars had arrived and blocked off the street. A cop walked out into the middle of the now-blocked intersection and held a shotgun over his head. He did a slow 360-degree circle, just to make sure all the punks knew that the LAPD meant business. That must have been the signal to rest of the cops, because all hell broke loose. The police waded into the crowd, wildly swinging their billy clubs. The punks tried to scatter, but all the cop cars in the way made that difficult to do without taking a beating. The second show never happened. The next day, the L.A. papers read "Riot at the Whisky." It was the first L.A. rock riot since the Doors played there in 1966. Funny thing was, we had played with Black Flag three weeks before at the Hong Kong Café in L.A., twenty people had shown up, and Black Flag paid us eight bucks. I guess our manager was right.

Siouxsie and the Banshees plus special guests.. **D.O.A.**
california hall
wednesday november 26th

By this point, California had become our home away from home; if somebody had a good idea for a show, we would bomb down the I-5 and be in the Golden State in twenty hours. I think the waitresses at the Denny's in Yreka thought we were locals.

We got an offer to open up for Siouxsie and the Banshees at the California Hall in San Francisco. A couple of thousand people showed up. We had paid our dues in the Bay area; the crowd went nuts for our set. The Banshees had to wait an hour before they could go on after us. Our manager was grinning from ear to ear.

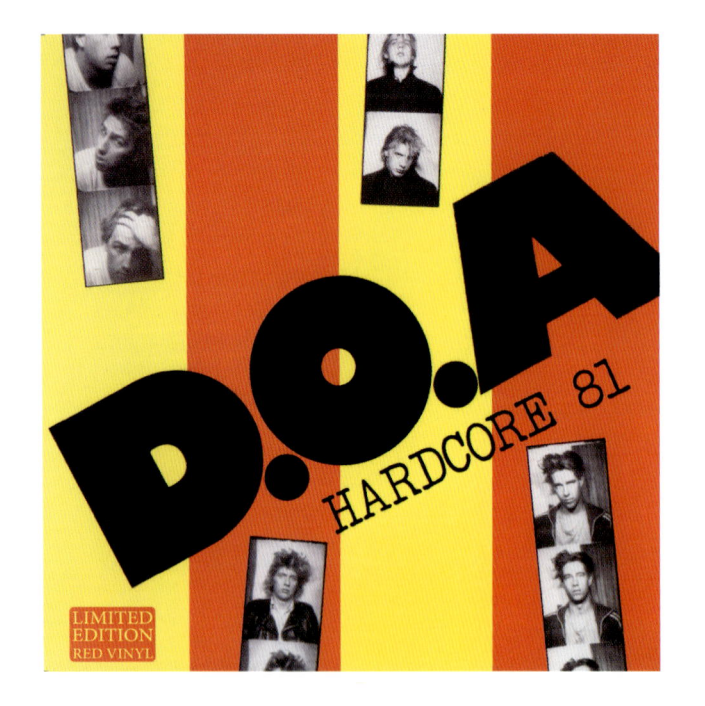

On one of our trips to California that year, we saw a magazine that talked about a new kind of punk. The writer (apologies, I can't remember the name) called it "hardcore." He said the most prominent examples of hardcore consisted of west coast bands like Circle Jerks, Black Flag, D.O.A., Dead Kennedys, and the Avengers. The bands were uncompromising, political, and definitely not slaves to fashion. When we got back to Vancouver, we were working on demos for our second album; our manager, Ken, proposed we title it either *Hardcore Plus* or *Hardcore 81*. We chose *Hardcore 81*.

After it was finished, we put together a festival called Hardcore 81 at a club called the Laundromat (later renamed Richards on Richards) and invited Black Flag and Seven Seconds up from the States to join in. It was a great weekend of bands. Rumour had it that the Vancouver police liked the idea so much that they rented an office across the street and clandestinely videotaped everybody who went in or out of the venue. Might as well hand it to them, keeping tabs on all the troublemakers at once.

THE NEIGHBOURHOOD BULLY IS AFTER ME.
WAVIN' HIS FINGER, LIKE A PISTOL.
FLAPPIN' HIS JAW, LIKE ADOLF HITLER

SLUMLORD, MY OVERLORD
SLUMLORD, I GOT NO CHOICE
SLUMLORD, YOU'RE REALITY

IT'S ALL LAID OUT LIKE A PRISON BLOCK
EACH LITTLE PEASANT, WITH THEIR PLOT
SLUMLORD, YOUR TITLE FITS THE DEED

SLUMLORD, MY OVERLORD
SLUMLORD, I GOT NO CHOICE
SLUMLORD, YOU'RE REALITY

SLUMLORD
SLUMLORD
SLUMLORD
SLUMLORD

SLUMLORD!!!

HARDCORE 81 TOUR

7TH ST. ENTRY
SAM'S 29 N. 7th St. Downtown Mpls. 332-1175

THE DAWNING OF A NEW ERROR...

D.O.A.

WEDNESDAY APRIL 22
Half-price Drinks

DESTROY TRADITION

X

WITH GUESTS

D.O.A.

THURS. JULY 2 • 8 PM

MacEwan Ballroom
University Of Calgary

YOU ARE INVITED TO A PRIVATE PARTY WITH D.O.A.

AND **REALLY RED** FROM TEXAS!
THE WRECKS FROM RENO HIGH!

AMERICAN LEGION HALL
RALSTON & 9TH RENO

MON NOV 2 8PM $5 DONATION PLEASE

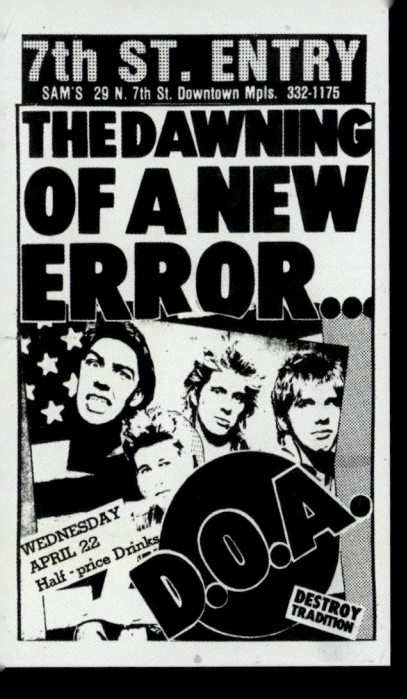

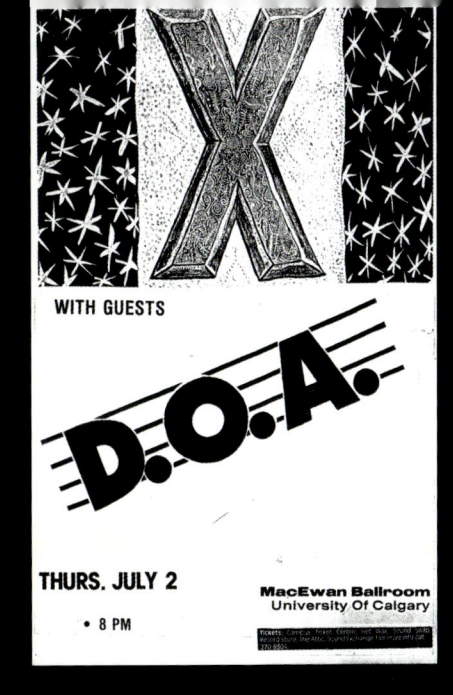

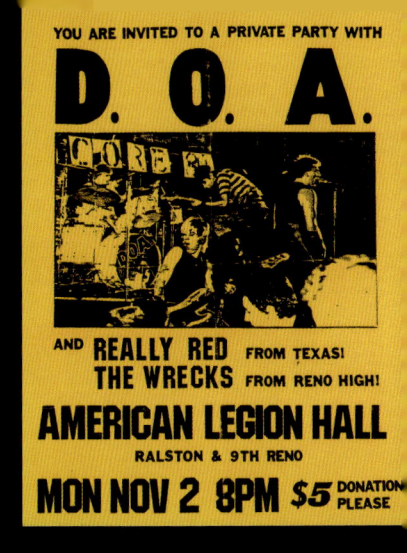

TUESDAY JULY 28

$4

D.O.A. FROM VANCOUVER B.C.
DESTROY TRADITION

PLUS!
TOXIC REASONS — F-OHIO
SECTION EIGHT — F-RENO
WHO SCREWED YOU? — F-MINN.

FACILITY BUILDING 9PM
2 4 RESERVATION RD
RENO

NO ALCOHOL

Ken booked the Hardcore 81 tour in a big loop around North America. The album and the tour helped push the term "hardcore" into the common vernacular and that's why D.O.A. is commonly called the godfathers of hardcore. We kicked the tour off in Seattle at the Gorilla Room, where I slipped off the edge of the stage during the encore and totally messed up my ankle. I ended up in a walking cast and had to sit on a stool to sing for the next five shows.

The 7th Street Entry (top left) was a bunker-type arrangement in Minneapolis. Hüsker Dü opened the show; they played *Land Speed Record* non-stop. They also played an intense version of "Statues." Most definitely incredible.

The gang from Reno (left, top right) was certainly on the wild side, and we became good friends with a lot of them. I phoned Cliff Varnell (the local promoter) and told him that we were bringing a band from Minneapolis with us called Hüsker Dü. Cliff misheard me, because Hüsker Dü had morphed into Who Screwed You? We had a good laugh about that with them! Our pals from Dayton Ohio, Toxic

The show at the Peppermint Lounge had been booked by Marshall Berle (the nephew of famed comedian Milton Berle). He pretty well bullshitted the club about our status: we ended up getting more dough than we ever thought possible for punk rock, and we also ended up with the biggest rider of booze we had ever seen in our lives. We had to play an early and a late show. I'm not so sure how good the first show was, as we had drained two-thirds of the rider before we started. The late show was pretty good because we had sobered up by that time. About halfway through the first show, Biscuits came out from behind his kit and flung a large glass pitcher of beer across the stage. It bounced and nailed this poor gal right in the noggin. It didn't make any sense at all.

At the Arcadian Hall, before we played we had to haul twenty old carpets from the attic to cover the beautiful hardwood dance floor so the punks didn't fuck it up. At the side of the stage was a stack of signs normally used to indicate to the seniors that usually danced there what kind of dance step to use. While D.O.A. played, Simon Snotface paraded out signs saying "Salsa," "Fox Trot," "Samba," and "Waltz." I guess they didn't have pogo and slam signs on hand.

EASTERN FRONT

SATURDAY JULY 25 — 11 AM to 6 PM — SUNDAY JULY 26

D.O.A.
FLIPPER
T.S.O.L.
THE LEWD
WAR ZONE
THE FIX
7 SECONDS
SIC PLEASURE
ANTI~L.A.

THE SLITS
SNAKEFINGER
THE OFFS
EARL ZERO
MIDDLE CLASS
THE WOUNDS
TOILING MIDGETS
TANKS

AQUATIC PARK BERKELEY — 3rd St & BANCROFT WAY

tickets available at bass

©PEPE MORENO

Wes Robinson, who promoted shows in Oakland, California, put together one of the great punk shows of all time at an outdoor park in Berkeley just across the I-80 from the Bay. The grass was completely worn out in front of the stage, so when the bands played fast songs, all the punks started a mosh pit and raised a dust storm. A lot of punks wore bandannas around their necks as a fashion statement, but now, when the dust got kicked up, the bandannas actually had a practical use. Dirk Dirksen, whom the punks loved to hate, came out to introduce D.O.A. The crowd got ready to gob on him and throw beer cans, when Dirk outsmarted them with a trusty umbrella which he opened to perfectly repel the punk's projectiles.

No1
REGENT STREET
CENTRAL ENTRANCE
THE
AGENT-GENERAL
FOR
BRITISH COLUMBIA

On our first trip to the UK, Alternative Tentacles Records released our 7-inch EP *Positively D.O.A.* It was named single of the week in the big English music mag *New Music Express*. It sold really well and helped pave the way for our 1984 UK/European tour. A key song was "Fucked Up Ronnie," which was about then-president Ronald Reagan. The song had morphed out of "Fucked Up Baby" on *Hardcore 81* and was originally a Skulls song.

We found out we were on a bill in London when we read about it in a UK music paper. So we phoned the promoter; we weren't actually on the bill at all—it was just wishful thinking on the writer's part. We talked our way onto the bill and organized three other shows in London.

About 3,000 people showed up for the concert. It had an electric atmosphere. Some Hell's Angels, who were friends of the Anti-Nowhere League, wanted to pound the crap out of us, but East Bay Ray from the Dead Kennedys happened along at just the right time and said, "It's alright, you can leave these guys alone. They're okay—they're just Canadians, that's all." Our set went over well. We also did three club shows in London; these were so-so, as D.O.A. was an unknown quantity in the UK at this point.

Below right, the first D.O.A. bootleg.

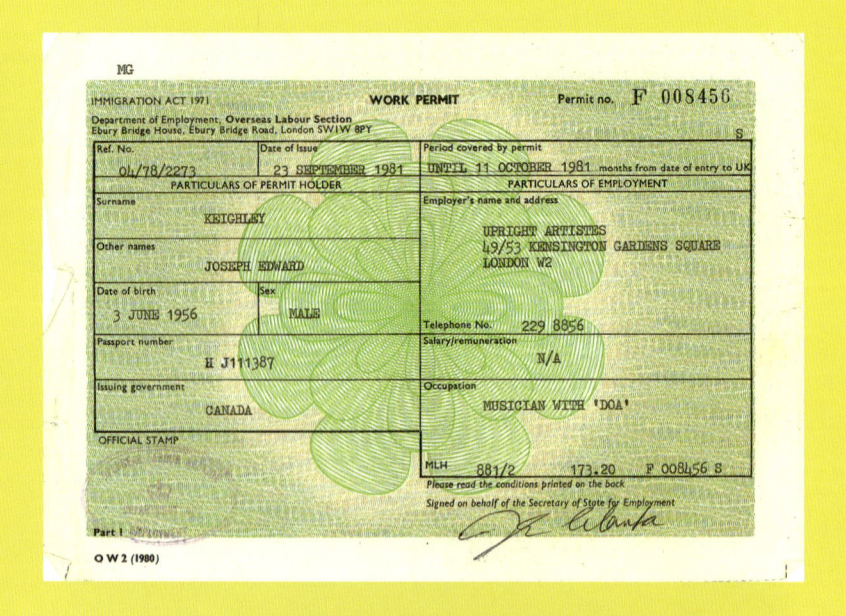

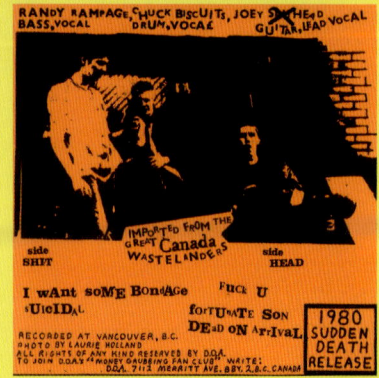

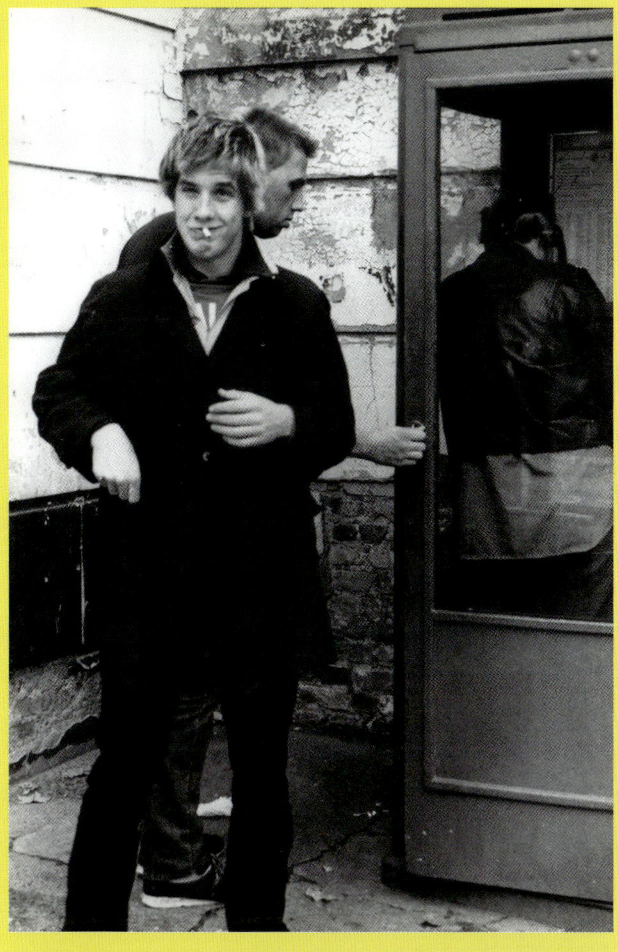

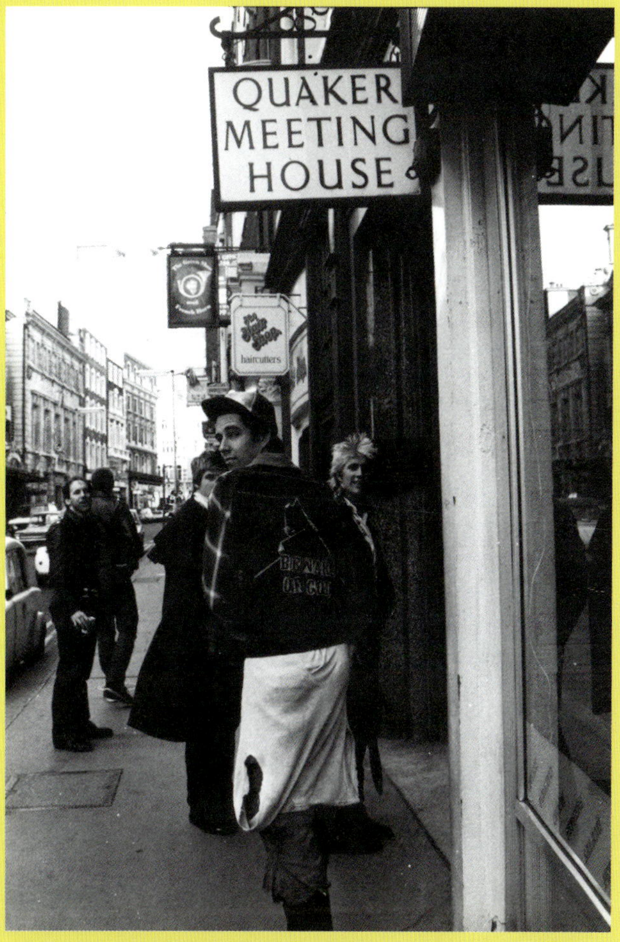
QUAKER
MEETING
HOUSE
haircutters

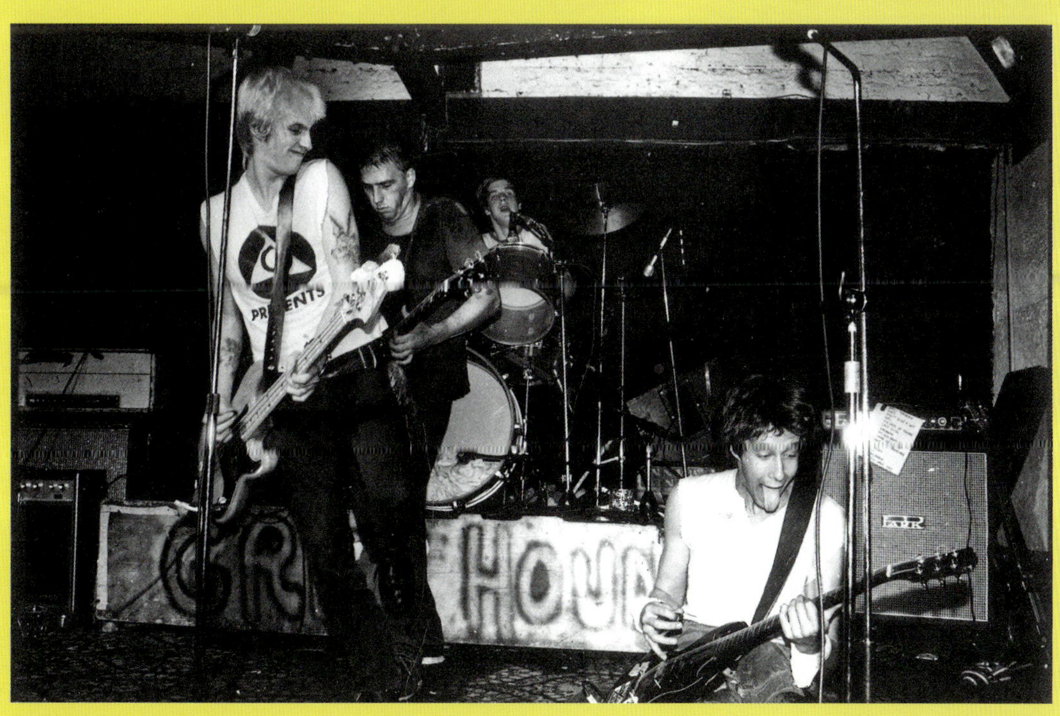
PRESENTS

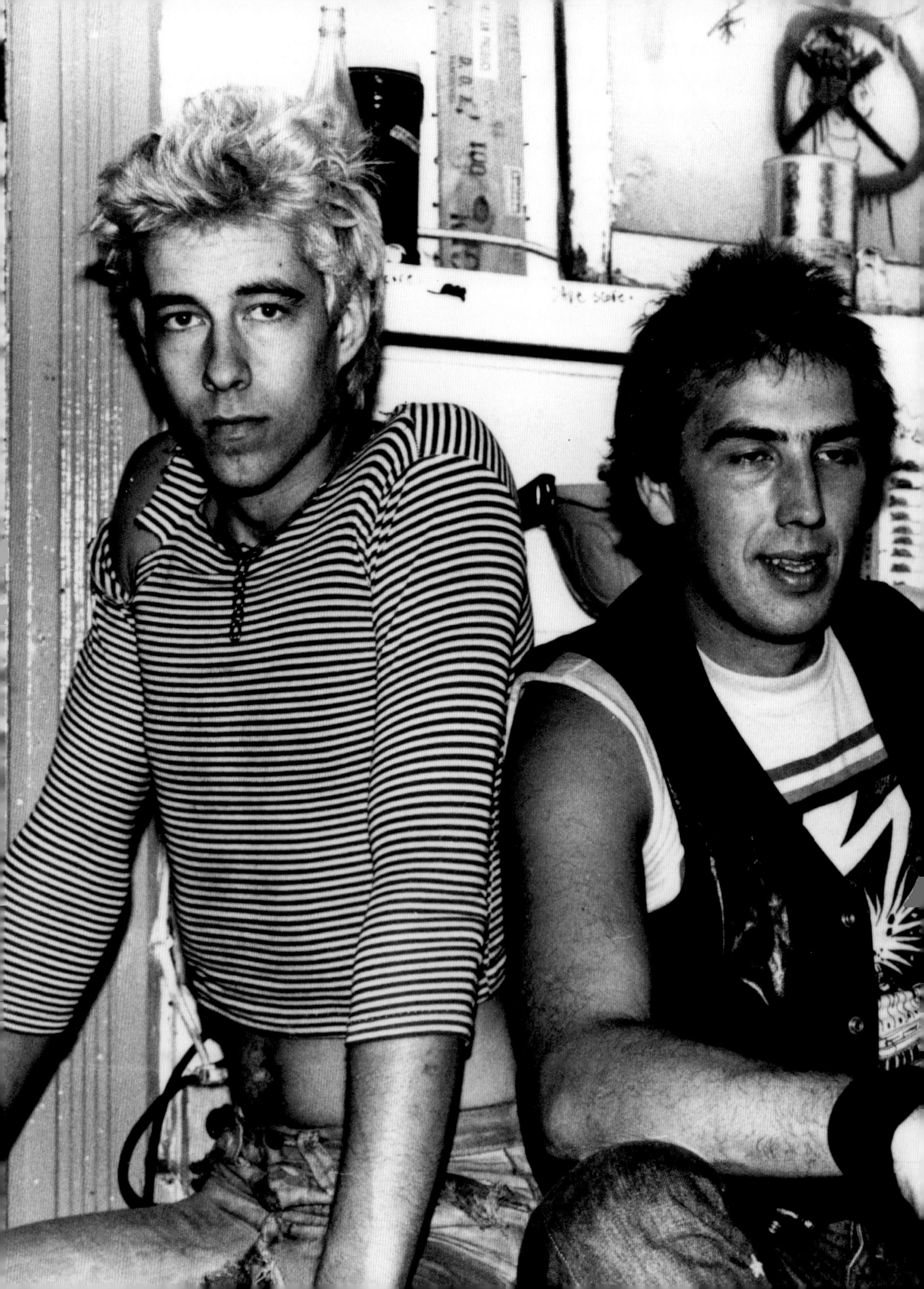

Chapter 3

1982–1983

ANARCHY RULES, OKAY!

Near the start of 1982, after four really successful years with D.O.A., Randy and Chuck each left the band. It was tough, but that's the way it goes sometimes. You couldn't make something as tumultuous as D.O.A. run along like hamsters on a wheel; there were bound to be fuck-ups along the way.

Dave, Ken, and I made the decision that the replacement for the rhythm section would be the formidable team of Wimpy and Dimwit on bass and drums. Dimwit, Wimpy, Gerry Useless (from the Subhumans), and I had been the "four amigos" growing up together in Burnaby, so it made sense to get at least three of the four of us back together again. After all, anything powerful and true relies on friendship and camaraderie—there's no stopping that.

We recorded the eight-song EP *War on 45* with producer Thom Wilson and entered a whole new phase. Our fourth amigo, Gerry Useless, had got himself into some real trouble as part of the Squamish Five. We did a benefit single, "Right to Be Wild," in 1982 and organized concerts to help with the legal fees. In 1983, our home province of British Columbia came within a whisker of a general strike, so we wrote and released the benefit single, "General Strike." At that moment, I think we became British Columbia's official protest band.

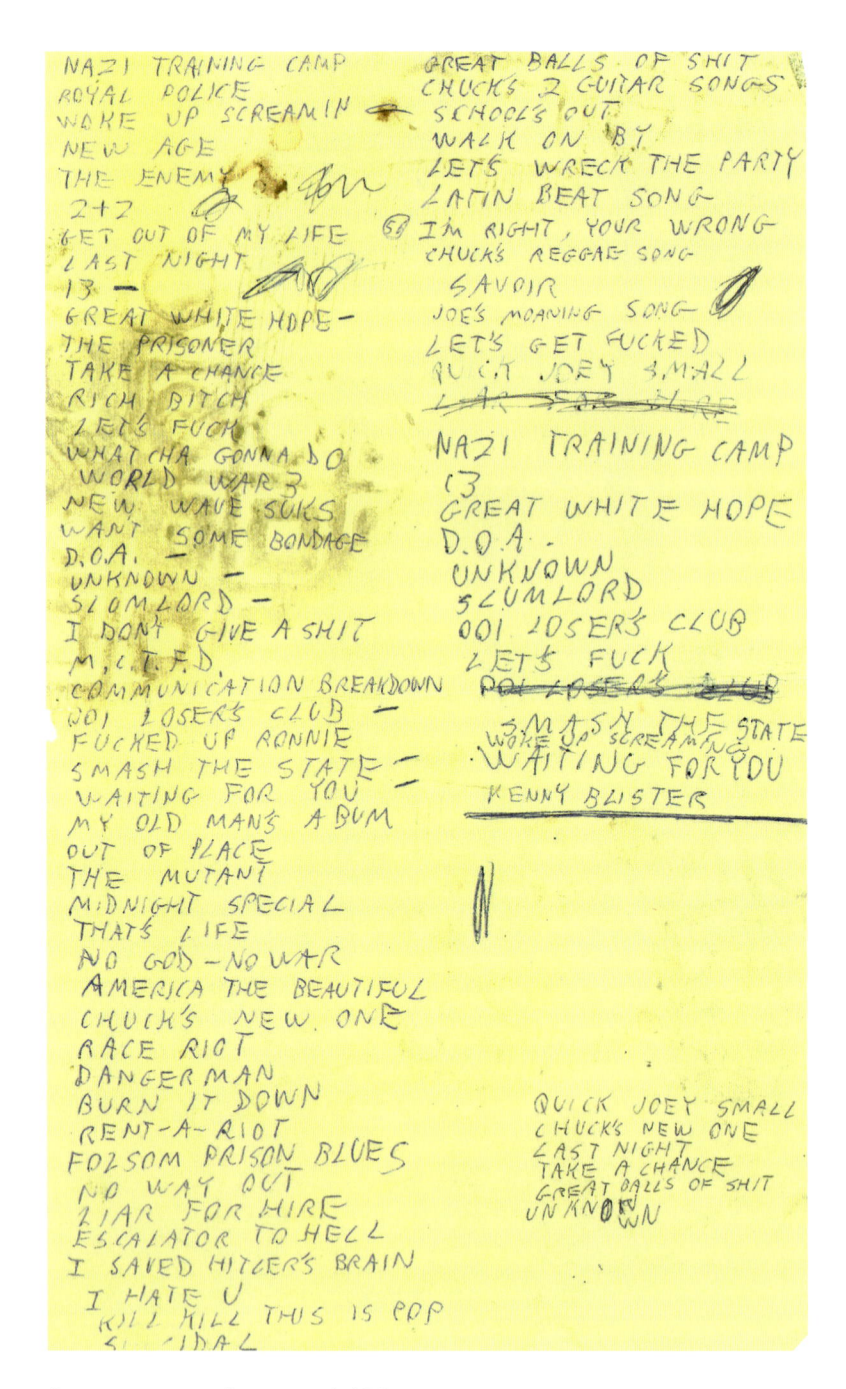

Our master song list ca. early '82.

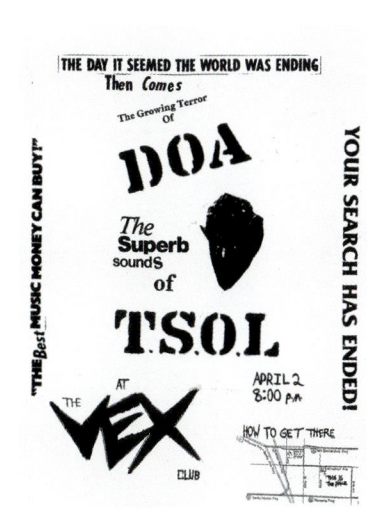

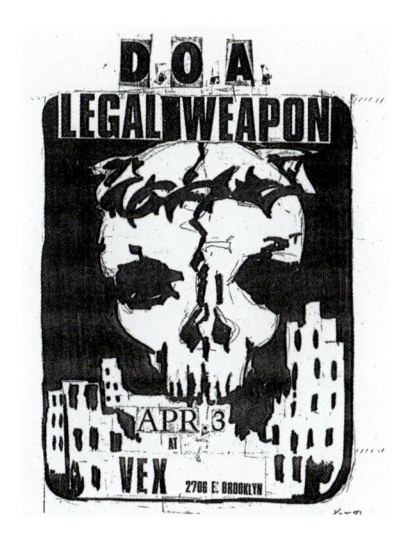

D.O.A. and our pals Personality Crisis went on a short tour of the Canadian Prairies

We played five California shows with T.S.O.L., two of them at the Vex in East L.A. The shows were good, but when we wanted to walk to the store for smokes, the club sent a bouncer escort, so us whiteys did not get beaten up and robbed before the show.

AMERICA THE BEAUTIFUL
J. KEITHLEY — PRISONER PUBLISHING

LOCK YOUR DOOR, LOCK IT TIGHT
IT'S THE NEW IMMORAL RIGHT
THEY WANT TO CLEANSE THE HOME OF THE BRAVE
FOR THE MASTER RACE OF THE U.S.A.
IT'S SO BEAUTIFUL
ON THE STREET, YOU WON'T KNOW THEM
LIKE A PACK OF WOLVES IN SHEEP'S CLOTHING
SPREADIN' WIDE, SPREADIN' FAR
NOT JUST ANOTHER FALSE ALARM
IT'S SO BEAUTIFUL

CHORUS
AMERICA — I'VE GOT MY BIBLE
AMERICA — I'VE GOT MY HANDGUN
AMERICA — ARE YOU READY
AMERICA — IT'S THE HOME OF THE BRAVE
AMERICA — AN' THE HOME OF THE SLAVES
AMERICA — ARE YOU READY

— REPEAT CHORUS

BEAUTIFUL, HOME OF THE BRAVE,
BEAUTIFUL!

AMERICA THE BEAUTIFUL

ED GACE, MANSON, NIXON TOO
A BOILING POT OF TASTELESS STEW

IT'S WHAT YOU ARE, IT'S WHAT YOU MADE
STRAIGHT FROM THE GOOD OL' U.S. OF A.

BY DAY A COP, BY NITE A TEACHER
ON SUNDAY A GOSPEL LEACHER

SO LOCK YOUR DOOR, LOCK IT TIGHT
HOPE THEY WON'T COME AN' GET YOU TONITE

AMERICA — THERE ARE NO SLAVES
AMERICA — HOME OF THE BRAVE
AMERICA — YOU CAN DIG YOUR OWN GRAVE
AND YOU WILL!!!

AMERICA — STARS AN' STRIPES
AMERICA — YA GOT NO GRIPES
AMERICA — THE TAKINGS RIPE

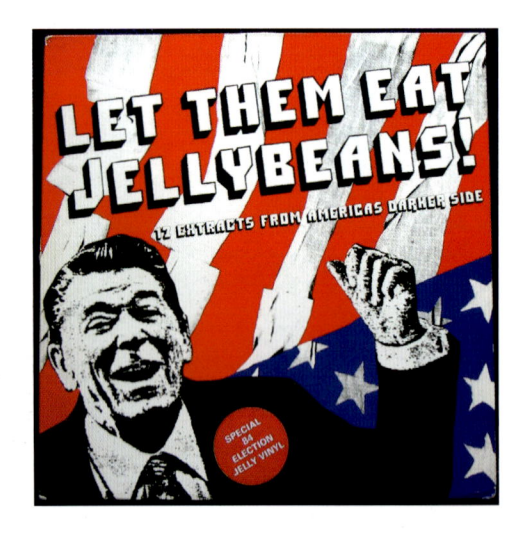

That April we did some recording with the new line-up at Mystic Studios in L.A. These tracks were never released, but a couple of the songs came out on a 7-inch bootleg.

Let them Eat Jellybeans! was released on Jello's Alternative Tentacles label, and the album opened a lot of doors for North American punk around the world. D.O.A.'s contribution was "The Prisoner."

NO WAY OUT   DEEP — NOBODY KNOWS
              MESS
              PUNCH — NO WAY OUTS
— LEAD — JOE
DOUBLE GUITAR BREAK — JOE   LEAD VOCALS
FIRST PART OF   IN CHORUS MAYBE
POUNDING "A"   REDONE, THEY CHANGE
DOWN THE CENTRE   IN PITCH EACH TIME

RENT-A-RIOT
                                    Mystic
VOCAL — AD-LIBS   spring 1982

RACE RIOT
LEAD GUITAR — IT'S GOTTA GO!! — FENDER'S GOTTA GO
THAT'S LIFE — PIANO IN CHORUS   RIGHT ON
              PROVIDING IT'S IN TUNE   — JOEY SHITHEAD
COCKTAIL SOUNDS ON INTRO INTRO
              BIG BASHUP BEFORE DRUM
LIAR FOHIRE   RECOVERING FROM PARTY SOUNDS ATEND.
DAVE'S GUITAR ON INTRO SHOULD GRADUALLY COME UP
DOUBLE VOCALS ON NOBODY WANTS YOU etc.?
LEAD GUITAR — JOE

AMERICA THE B.
VOCAL INTRO — SCRUB
DOUBLE HIGH GUITAR PARTS
MAYBE DROP HEYS EXCEPT FOR LAST 4
OVERDUB ANOTHER GUITAR ON LAST CHORD

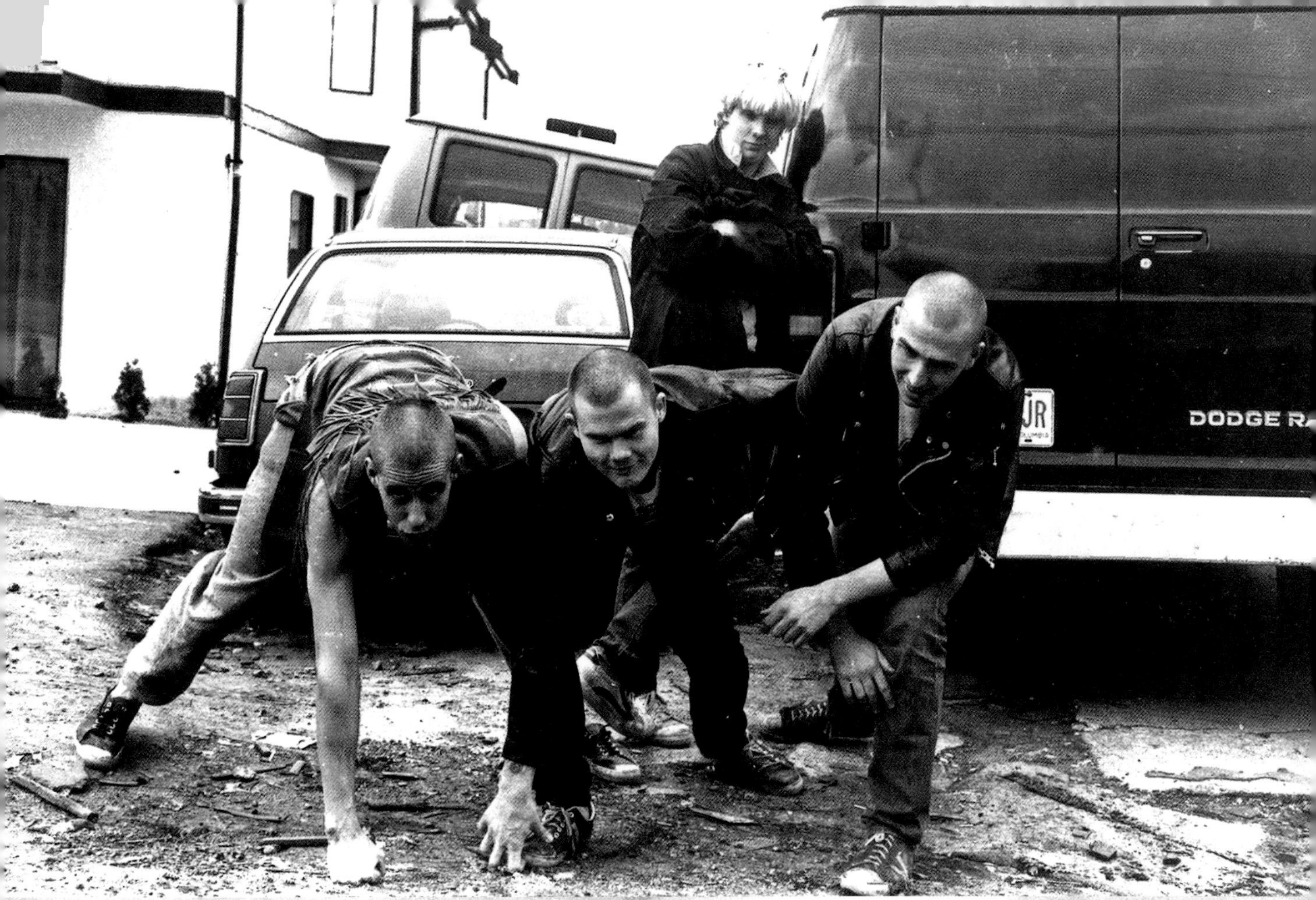
DODGE RA

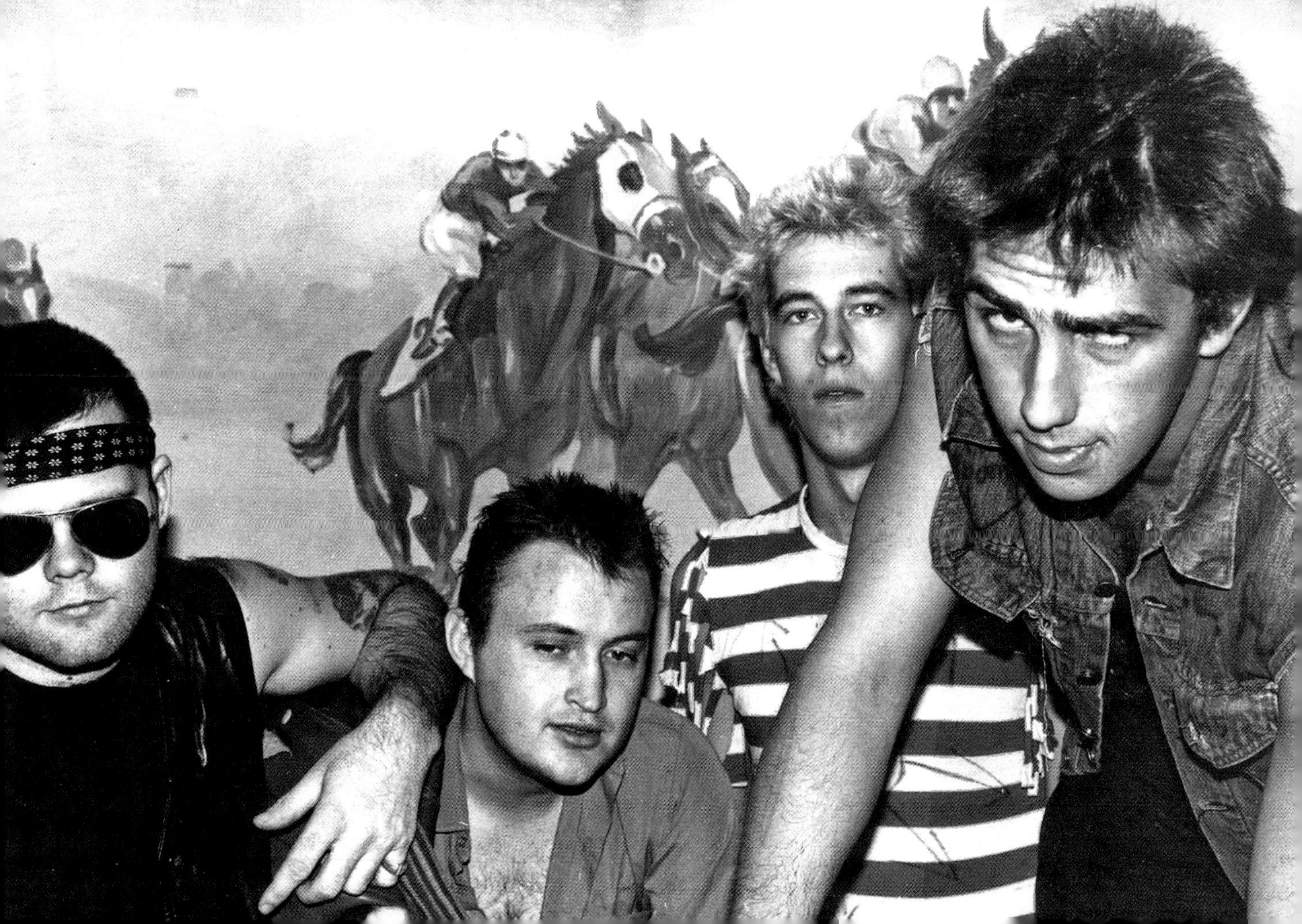

By this point Biscuits had quit D.O.A. and joined Black Flag. Dimwit took over on drums, and Wimpy (Subhumans) became our bassist. Our manager, Ken Lester, cooked up this crazy weekend: on July 15, we played at the On Broadway in San Francisco with M.D.C. and the Undead. We flew to New York and played with the Dead Kennedys and Kraut at the Paramount on Staten Island on Friday, July 16. Then we flew back to L.A. and played with Black Flag on Saturday, July 17. We were almost D.O.A.

The US version of *War on 45* was released in July '82 on Faulty Products, our new label. In late July '82, we recorded and mixed this in five nights (midnight to six a.m.) at Perspective Sound in L.A. Thom Wilson produced it. Shawn Kerri did the artwork.

We used a different cover for the Alternative Tentacles UK version. Our friend Clay Sampson, a First Nations artist, did the very appropriate artwork. As you can see (facing page), there was a variation in the tracks of the two releases.

POLICE COUNTY MORGUE
D.O.A.
8 GREAT TUNES! 8
WAR on 45
8 SONGS TO MARCH BY!
WE LIKE THE EIGHTIES
MARCH INTO THE 80's

TALK - ACTION = 0
THE SONGS...
SIDE 1
1. LIAR FOR HIRE (J. KEIGHLEY) 2:50
2. I'M RIGHT, YOU'RE WRONG (J. KEIGHLEY) 1:58
3. AMERICA THE BEAUTIFUL (J. KEIGHLEY) 2:20
4. LETS FUCK 2:17
SIDE 2
1. WAR (WHITFIELD/STRONG) 2:22
2. I HATE YOU (J. KEIGHLEY) 2:27
3. WAR IN THE EAST (RANKING TREVOR/D.O.A.) 4:25
4. CLASS WAR (DILS) 1:39
ALL SELECTIONS PUBLISHED BY PRISONER PUBLISHING (P.R.O.) EXCEPT * COPYRIGHT 1982 D.O.A.
CAST OF CHARACTERS...
D.O.A.: JOEY SHITHEAD (GUITAR, VOCALS) DAVE GREGG (GUITAR, VOCALS) DIMWIT (DRUMS, BASS, GUITAR) WIMPY ROY (BASS, VOCALS)
PRODUCER, THOM WILSON/D.O.A.
COVER ART, SHAWN KERRI
MANAGEMENT, KEN LESTER
BAR-B-QUE CHOIR: (ON 'I HATE YOU') PETER HASKELL, HEATHER HALEY, ANDREW MABEN, JOHN McADAMS, LISA Z., BENITA HARLOW, CARLA NELSON, RICHARD ZEIER, KEVIN CUTSFORD, AUDREY MOOREHEAD, MICHEL KERMIT.
CONTACT:
D.O.A.'s "MONEY GRUBBING" FAN CLUB AND MANAGEMENT c/o P.O. BOX 65896 STATION 'F' VANCOUVER, B.C. CANADA
ALTERNATIVE TENTACLES RECORDS

War on 45 D.O.A. War on 45
Holy Bible
Repent! You Fucking Savages! Repent!

VIRUS 24
TALK - ACTION = 0
Alternative Tentacles Records Ltd., 49 - 53 Kensington Gardens Square, London W2 4BA.
D.O.A.'s 'Money Grubbing' Fan Club & Management, p.o. box 65896, Sta. 'F', Vancouver, B.C., Canada
THE SONGS...
SIDE 1
2. UNKNOWN (C. BISCUITS) 2:28
3. RICH BITCH (J. KEIGHLEY) (FOR DI AND THE TWO MAGGIES) 3:01
4. LETS FUCK 2:17
SIDE 2
2. I HATE YOU (J. KEIGHLEY) 2:27
3.* WAR IN THE EAST (RANKING TREVOR/D.O.A.) 4:25
4.* CLASS WAR (DILS) 1:39
ALL SELECTIONS PUBLISHED BY PRISONER PUBLISHING (P.R.O.) EXCEPT *. COPYRIGHT 1982, D.O.A.
CAST OF CHARACTERS...
D.O.A.: JOEY SHITHEAD (GUITAR, VOCALS) DIMWIT (DRUMS, BASS, GUITAR) WIMPY ROY (BASS, VOCALS)
PRODUCER, THOM WILSON/D.O.A.
FRONT COVER, CLAY SAMPSON
BACK COVER, SHAWN KERRI
MANAGEMENT, KEN LESTER
BAR-B-QUE CHOIR: (ON 'I HATE YOU') PETER HASKELL, HEATHER HALEY, ANDREW MABEN, JOHN McADAMS, LISA Z., BENITA HARLOW, CARLA NELSON, RICHARD ZEIER, KEVIN CUTSFORD, AUDREY MOOREHEAD, MICHEL KERMIT.
SUPPORT YOUR LOCAL INDIAN ARTISTS
CLAY SAMPSON DESIGN STUDIO
ILLUSTRATION and DESIGN

The War on 45 tour was the first time we played in Montreal. In DC, we and Henry Rollins played at Ian MacKay's (Minor Threat, Fugazi) high school. It was also our first time in Nashville, so we sang outside the Grand Ol' Opry just to say "Yeah, we sang there!" The support band, Committee 4 Public Safety, were a surprise; punk rock but with weird country guitars none of us had ever seen before.

We always found Boston among the most out-of-control scenes, along with Orange County and San Diego. Our show at Cantones proved no exception. The place was fucking small; it should have held about 100 people. By the time Kill Slug got on, there were about 200 punks inside. When D.O.A. came on, they were standing on the tables it was so packed. We started playing and the crowd went off, breaking tables, ripping ceiling tiles out, and throwing chairs across the bar. It was a situation. The bar owner called the cops. About forty of them swarmed in and stopped the show after we had played three songs. The newspapers called it a "Punk Rock Riot," but the cops let us go and charged the bar owner with being over-capacity.

WAR ON 45 TOUR

THE CANADIAN INVASION OF
D.O.A.
ALSO APPEARING
POISON IDEA
PLUS!
THE FARTZ
AUG. SUNDAY 1
$5.50 ADVANCE
$6.50 AT DOOR
9:00 DOORS OPEN
AT THE
METROPOLIS
1 S.W. 3rd, PORTLAND
TICKETS AVAILABLE AT THE MET, SINGLES GOING STEADY,
PARK AVENUE REC., MUSIC MILLENNIUM — BOTH STORES

CLEAR AND DISTINCT IDEAS PRESENTS
SLAM-N-SWEAT '82
ALL AGES!
D.O.A.
FIVE BANDS
CODE OF HONOR
HÜSKER DÜ
REBEL TRUTH
WRECKS (RENO)
WEDNESDAY, 9:00
JULY 28TH
FOR INFO, CALL 447-0612
1025 9TH ST (BTWN J&K)
ODDFELLOWS BUILDING
$4.50 ADVANCE:
$6.00 AT DOOR
TOWER POSTERS 16TH & BROADWAY
TOWER POSTERS WATT & EL CAMINO
ZAPPLE RECORDS LOWER FREEBORN HALL UC DAVIS
THE BEAT RECORDS 5522 "H" STREET
MARKEE RECORDS 815 K STREET
AFTERMATH RECORDS 5527 HEMLOCK
ESOTERIC RECORDS 1716 BROADWAY

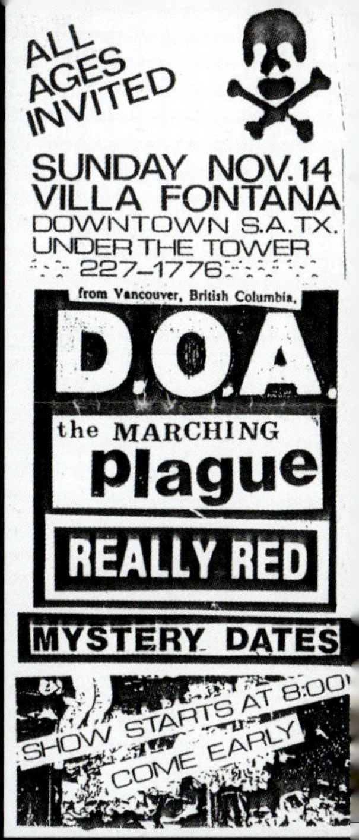

ALL AGES INVITED
SUNDAY NOV. 14
VILLA FONTANA
DOWNTOWN S.A.TX.
UNDER THE TOWER
227-1776
from Vancouver, British Columbia,
D.O.A
the MARCHING plague
REALLY RED
MYSTERY DATES
SHOW STARTS AT 8:00
COME EARLY

D.O.A
Top W. Coast PUNK
NOV 6
DELINQUENTS
TOXIC REASONS
ALL AGES O.K.
3 BANDS
$3 advance
$4 at door
SAT
BROOKWOOD HALL
5515 Wagoner-Ford

D.O.A
andi
Committee 4 Public Safety
NOVEMBER 7th
CANTRELLS

D.O.A.
WAR on 45
MARCH TO THE END
18 activist anti-war tracks
Brand New! Out Now!
MAR 16TH
P3 & Q's

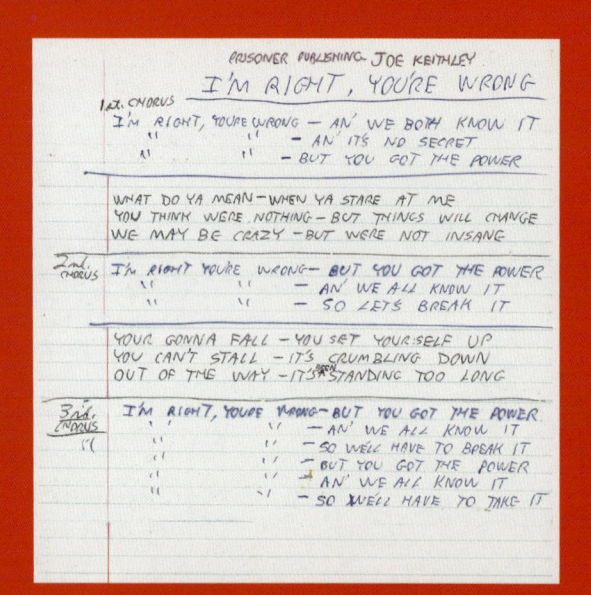

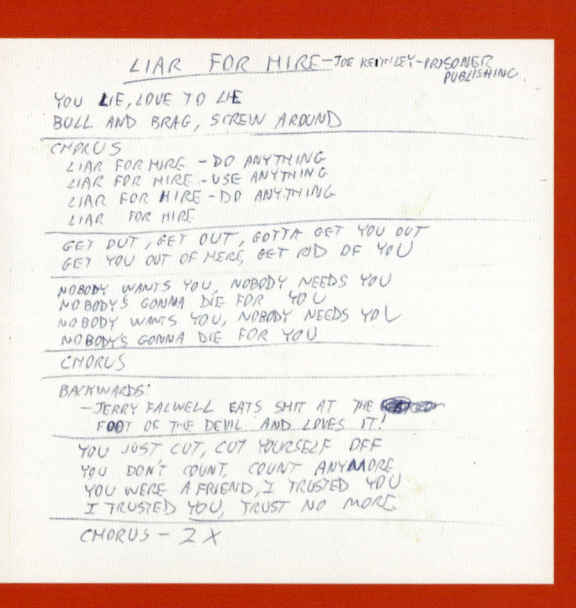

The Ukrainian Hall show in Hollywood with Black Flag was a weird one. Members of the Circle One gang bum-rushed the door, then punched out the merch guy and stole fifty Black Flag and D.O.A. T-shirts. We played with the Flag about twelve times, and it was always chaos, which made for great punk rock. It was also cool to gig with them as they went through their progression of singers. From Keith to Ron to Dez and finally Henry, they were all great! One of the top bands of all time.

On December 26, we started driving 3,000 miles (4,800 km) for an ill-fated New Year's Eve show in New York that never happened. We were dead broke, and the tour was heading to the deep south, the first time we had ever been there. Money was so low that we reduced our per diems (money for food, smokes, and beer) to two dollars each per day. Yikes!

We were desperate for a show, so our agent booked us into the Mudd Club. No guarantees, just a percentage deal. I helped put up the posters, took the money at the door and, of course, played that night. The Sluts from New Orleans opened, and they were great.

LETTER FROM GERRY

BE STRONG AND RESIST ALWAYS

Our situation would be quite bleak and much more difficult were it not for the love and strength of the many groups and individuals who have come forward and given their full support to us and to the issues raised by the charges against us. We owe a great deal of thanks to the feminist and anarchist communities in Vancouver and abroad, who responded to our situation immediately and unselfishly, and to our support group which is acting as a link between us and the community we are now isolated from.

We are also very grateful for the support we have received from the Vancouver punk community. Many punks have expressed solidarity with us, and D.O.A. has made a generous offer to raise money for our defence by releasing a fund-raising single, Fuck You/Burn It Down. all profit will be turned over to our defence group which, in turn, will use it as needed.

While we truly appreciate all these efforts made on our behalf, and are completely aware of their great value, we feel there is another form of support that should also be undertaken and will ultimately be beneficial not only to us, but to everyone concerned with real positive change. That form of support is action.

It's so easy to talk about how bad things are in the world today, and it's so hard to actually do something about them. A lot of people who were politically aware have given up on the idea of change through action or have adopted the attitude that, given time, civilization will eventually evolve by itself into some wonderful utopia. Given time by itself, however, civilization will almost certainly develop into an unconquerable police state or will wipe itself out entirely by atomic war or by poisoning the environment.

Each new day the pigs — the corporate state's brutal henchmen — are becoming more sophisticated and technologically advanced. These capitalist commandos are constantly being given a freer hand to deal out alleged "justice", while their viciousness and arrogance are surpassed by none. Their employers easily maintain a facade of democracy because they're surrounded and protected by a blind society. They will stop at nothing to ensure that their job is done; the job of waging war on oppressed people so they will never have a chance to seize what is rightfully theirs: control over their own lives. If the tide of the corporate industrialists' world-wide attack is not turned soon, we may well pass the point of no return.

The environment under attack

Environmentally, we teeter at the brink. Industrial development of the magnitude there is today threatens our very physical and mental existence. The industrialists see the natural world only in terms of exploitation for profit, and with the promise of jobs and low-priced products they lure us into seeing it in the same perverted terms. It's from this perspective that forests become lumber, mountains become minerals, rivers become electrical power, and pollution and all other forms of industrial devastation are deemed justifiable and necessary.

The persistence of this attitude much longer will inevitably lead to disaster. It's not just foolish of us to destroy the environment we depend on for our survival, it's also wrong, regardless of the reasons, for us to assume we have the right to destroy it. This planet, in its natural form, is perfectly capable of taking care of itself and all living creatures on it and, without human interference, could continue to exist in harmony for thousands of years. But instead of cherishing it for its infinite beauty and respecting it for its persevering strength, we continue to rape and plunder it on an incredibly massive scale.

This is the dangerous and unacceptable situation that exists today. It has become a vicious circle. The west beefs up its nuclear arsenal and the east responds accordingly and, in turn, the west again beefs up its nuclear arsenal and the east again responds. And so on and so on. The probable result of this escalating insanity should be clear to us all by now. The nuclear time bomb is ticking, and time is quickly running out.

If we really hope to stop this trend of destruction and oppression before it's too late, and bring about positive change on the earth, we must take a very close look at ourselves. Those of us who are men must realize that despite what we may think of ourselves, we continue to be highly oppressive and dominating. This is partially due to our refusal to acknowledge and embrace the so-called feminine aspects of our personalities such as compassion, sensitivity and tenderness. Instead, we deliberately emphasize the negative, so-called male tendencies of aggression, competitiveness and arrogance. It's no wonder that these same tendencies are so prevalent in the world around us. There appears to be a direct relation between those tendencies and the most serious problems we face today. Men have been the absolute rulers of practically all cultures throughout history. Obviously we are not as capable of making the right decisions as we would like to believe, and we must now ambitiously and wholeheartedly accept responsibility for, and work to remedy, this unacceptable situation immediately.

Sexism: a fundamental issue

Sexism is not a side issue. It is a fundamental one, and until this fact is recognized and dealt with, all our efforts toward positive change are hypocritical and sadly lacking. Throughout the world men continue to dominate women. Sometimes it's subtle and belittling; sometimes it's outfront and brutal. It's always degrading and damaging. Women are commonly believed to be less intelligent, less practical and less mature than men, and are expected to be subservient, meek and completely concerned with pleasing men through sexual appearance and activities. Women that are able to rise above this enslaving stereotype, through intense hardship and struggle, are generally considered to be macho or weird, and are loathed by the average man as well as some women. The pain and frustration that men cause women is very real, very deep and totally inexcusable, and men must learn to come to grips with their contemptuous attitudes towards women and permanently eradicate them from their consciousness.

Women also must take a close look at themselves, decide what they want to do in life and act on it, independently of male pressures and attitudes; taking strength from the true spirit of womanhood and remaining undaunted in the face of animosity and hatred. Unfortunately, little help can be expected from men towards these goals so women must develop and nurture their own methods of struggle and bases of support.

The spirit of revolt

Those of us truly concerned about the nightmarish quality of life today and have a real desire to do something about it, must first free our minds from state-conditioned modes of thought and awaken the spirit of revolt within us.

In the last 400 years, through wholesale slaughter and destruction, thousands of species of animals have been ruthlessly obliterated. This shameful practice continues today, and it is accelerating largely because of the increased scale and the advanced technological methods of current industrial activity.

Vast amounts of once wild and untamed land suffer the long-lasting or permanent scars of so-called progress. Power lines, roads, open pit mines, logging operations, mega farms and huge sprawling cities litter the landscape. There are few places left on the face of the earth where our consumer industrial society has not made its presence felt and, even in the least inhabited areas, the omnipresent shadow of nuclear devastation threatens.

Nuclear destruction: the ultimate terror

Nuclear devastation is the ultimate threat to the planet; the terror held in the hands of the ultimate terrorists. The trafficers of the technology of death would have us believe that the constant build up of nuclear arms is necessary to defend "democracy" against the evil intentions of unfriendly nations. In fact, the nuclear weapons/energy industry is a billion-dollar business and, like any competitive business, it must have constant demand for its products if it is to maintain high profits. If no such demand really exists, one must be artificially created through slick, aggressive propaganda campaigns even if it means creating a tense and hostile climate in which nuclear war is not only possible, but probable.

Only through a complete understanding of our dangerous and dismal situation and the causes behind it, and by adopting a radical outlook towards changing it — including the essential concepts of anarchism, feminism and environmentalism — can we hope to break the chains of oppression that bind us and this planet so completely. We are all in for the struggle of our lives — literally — and we must be prepared for much hardship and sacrifice. If we can maintain our courage and integrity, however, and continuously resist the enemy's efforts to destroy us we can still win the fight.

Now is the time to begin the long, difficult process towards creating real positive change and a free and respected earth. Now is the time for action.

Love and struggle,
Gerry

THE SPIRIT OF FREEDOM - CANNOT BE SUBDUED

D.O.A. RIGHT TO BE WILD

*Side A: **Burn It Down!** (J. Keighley) — (3:14)
Side B: **Fuck You** (G. Hannah) — (2:31)
*Published by **Prisoner Publishing/P.R.O./B.M.I.** ©1983
D.O.A. is: **Joey Shithead** (Guitar/Vocals); **Brian Goble** (Bass/Vocals); **Dave Gregg** (Guitar); **Dimwit** (Drums/Piano)
Producer: **Thom Wilson/D.O.A.**
Packaging: Apologies to **Roy Lichtenstein** and **Bianchi**
Thanx to **Ken** and **Dave Lester**
D.O.A.'s **"Money Grubbing" Fan Club** is still at POB 65896, Station "F", Vancouver, B.C. Canada

FREE THE FIVE

In the early morning, Jan. 20, 1983, just outside Vancouver, Canada, a small army of police arrested five people and charged them with a series of guerrilla-related political activities. The five — Gerry Hannah, Julie Belmas, Ann Hansen, Doug Stewart and Brent Taylor — face life in prison if convicted.

The charges include: bombing a controversial new hydro-electric development opposed by environmentalists; dynamiting the plant that's producing guidance systems for the first strike Cruise missile; and firebombing three pornography outlets distributing videos containing torture, mutilation and sexual violence against women. They also face conspiracy and weapons charges.

Although the five have no criminal records, they have been denied bail and may be held in prison up to a year awaiting the outcome of their trial. The prosecution has taken the unusual step of proceeding with a direct indictment, denying the accused a preliminary review of the evidence against them.

Gerry Hannah, as "Gerry Useless", a member of the punk band The Subhumans, wrote **Fuck You,** the song recorded by D.O.A. for this fund-raising record.

The other four arrested have been active for years in political activities, ranging from anti-nuclear organizing to setting up benefit concerts to tossing pies at pompous politicians.

Gerry grew up in Burnaby, a working-class suburb of Vancouver. When punk arrived in 1977 Gerry, along with several friends he'd grown up with, formed the early hardcore of the local scene. The Subhumans and D.O.A. were largely composed of people from this close-knit group.

With Gerry as bass player, The Subhumans released several records and played the punk circuit throughout North America. They also played political concerts including several anti-nuclear benefits, a fund-raiser for El Salvadorean guerrillas, a Rock Against Reagan show on Ronnie's inauguration, a Rock Against Racism concert for the Pontiac Brothers (Michigan prisoners on trial for allegedly killing KKK guards) and an anarchist smash-the-state concert.

To Gerry, punk was more than getting drunk, living on welfare and not caring about anything. He believed that punk could shake people out of their complacency; that people could learn, change and take action.

Gerry initiated Rock Against Radiation, an outdoor concert at which The Subhumans, D.O.A. and other popular Vancouver bands shared the stage to protest nukes.

He wrote such songs as the anti-nationalist **Oh Canaduh** and an attack on sexism, **Slave to My Dick. Slave** was recently named "a rock anthem for the '80s" by Creem magazine.

One reason Gerry was attracted to punk was its assertion that ordinary people can make music for each other; that musicians don't have to have years of training and be supported by callous promoters and corporate record labels.

Gerry and the other four understand that social change, as well, is made by ordinary people working together to take control of their lives. Change isn't conducted by "professional" organizers or experts; it's made by people showing compassion and cooperation, and standing against racism, sexism, ecological destruction and the terror waged against people and the earth.

David Spaner,
former manager of The Subhumans

SUPPORT THE FIVE

1) To contact Gerry, Ann, Brent, Julie or Doug directly write to them individually at Lower Mainland Regional Correctional Centre, Drawer "O", Burnaby, B.C. V5H 3N4, Canada. They'd all be happy to get a letter from you.
2) For a newsletter and up-to-date info on the case write to: **Free the Five Defense Group,** Box 48296, Bentall Station, Vancouver, B.C. V7X 1A1 Canada. Also, bands or people interested in doing benefits for the five should contact the Defense Group because there will be information kits, videos and support speakers available.
3) Donations should be sent directly to: Free the Five, Account #91740-1 c/o CCEC Credit Union, 205 E. 6th Ave., Vancouver, V5T 1J7, Canada.
4) For more info on the case to date check out: **Open Road,** Spring 83, $2, Box 6135, Station "G", Vancouver, B.C. V6R 4G5, Canada. Also: **Resistance,** Issues 4&5, send donations, Box 790, Station "A", Vancouver, B.C. Canada; and **Kinesis,** April 83, $1, 400 A West 5th Ave., Vancouver BC V5Y 1J8, Canada.

Right to be Wild!
D.O.A.
BENEFIT SINGLE
FREE THE FIVE
'EMERGENCY ISSUE'

The tour took us to Detroit on January 21. We had a show with the Angelic Upstarts at the City Club, and were sitting around the dressing room wondering what had happened to our pal Gerry Useless—nobody seemed to know. Then we got a phone call from our manager saying that Gerry and four others had been arrested by an RCMP tactical squad on the highway to Squamish, BC.

We wanted the Squamish Five (a.k.a. the Vancouver Five) to get a fair trial, so we decided to raise some money for their defence. We recorded a single with producer Thom Wilson called "the Right To Be Wild."

One side was the Subhumans' classic "Fuck You," and the flipside was a song I wrote called "Burn It Down."

BURN IT DOWN
J. KEITHLEY — PRISONER PUBLISHING

WELL, ALL THE PRISON WALLS
WE WON'T LET THEM STAND
I GOT TO BURN THEM DOWN

UP AGAINST THE WALL — THERE'S NO WAY
THEY WON'T MAKE ME GO — THERE'S NO WAY
WELL NO ONE JUDGES ME — THERE'S NO WAY
NOBODY WANTS THEM — NO WAY!

ALL THE PRISON WALLS — BURN IT DOWN
WE WON'T LET THEM STAND — BURN IT DOWN
I GOT TO BURN THEM DOWN — BURN IT DOWN
WELL NOBODY WANTS THEM

BURN IT DOWN
BURN IT DOWN
BURN IT DOWN

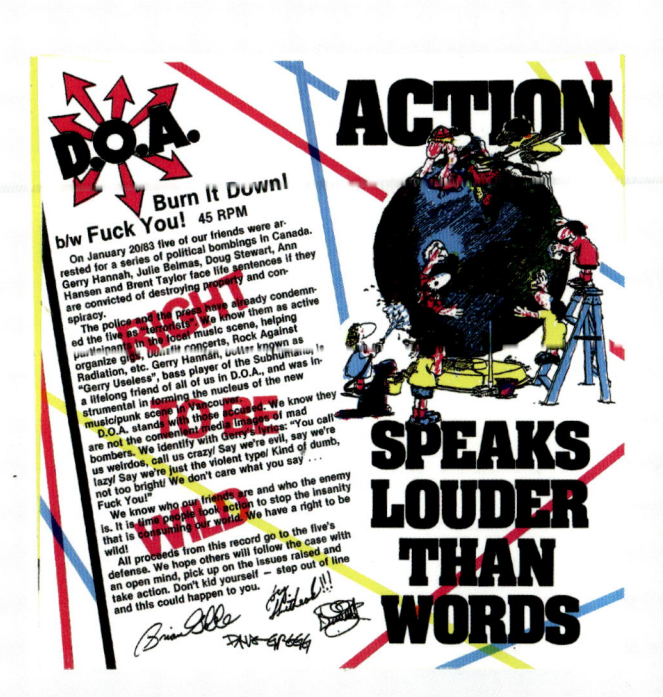

D.O.A.
RIGHT TO BE WILD
ALL PROCEEDS FROM THIS RECORD GO TO "FREE THE FIVE"
BURN IT DOWN / FU_K U

D.O.A.
Burn It Down! b/w Fuck You! 45 RPM

On January 20/83 five of our friends were arrested for a series of political bombings in Canada. Gerry Hannah, Julie Belmas, Doug Stewart, Ann Hansen and Brent Taylor face life sentences if they are convicted of destroying property and conspiracy.
The police and the press have already condemned the five without a trial. We know them as active participants in the local music scene, helping organize gigs, benefit concerts, Rock Against Radiation, etc. Gerry Hannah, better known as "Gerry Useless", bass player of the Subhumans, is a lifelong friend of all of us in D.O.A., and was instrumental in keeping the nucleus of the new music/punk scene alive.
D.O.A. stands with our friends. We know they are the conscience needed in this sick mad bombers. We identify with Gerry's words: "You call us weirdos, call us crazy! Say we're evil, say we're lazy! Say we're just the violent type! Kind of dumb, not too bright/ We don't care what you say — Fuck You!"
We know who our friends are and who the enemy is. It is time to take action to stop the insanity that is consuming our world. We have a right to be wild!
All proceeds from this record go to the five's defense. We hope others will follow the case with an open mind, pick up on the issues raised and take action. Don't kid yourself — step out of line and this could happen to you.

ACTION SPEAKS LOUDER THAN WORDS

OTHER BRAINLESS PRODUCTION
D.O.A.
Euthanasia
Spores
SAT. APRIL 2ND
AT THE UNION HALL
DOORS DO NOT OPEN UNTIL 8.30
BE THERE OR BEWARE
CITR-FM 102 and Georgia Straight present
SHOWCASE '83
D.O.A.
LOS POPULAROS
I, BRAINEATER
Fri. March 11
U.B.C. SUB Ballroom All Ages Welcome
Doors: 8 p.m. Come Early. Advance tickets: $5 AMS Members; $6 All Others; Available at AMS Box Office; Zulu Records; Odyssey Imports. Information: Call 228-2711. Produced by AMS Concerts
CLEAR & DISTINCT IDEAS PRESENTS
D.O.A.
SOCIAL UNREST
3 STOOGES
THE AUTHORITIES
FRIDAY OCT. 7
8:00 $4.50 advance
ALL THE UNUSUAL LOCATIONS, AFTERMATH RECORDS, THE BEAT • ESOTERIC RECORDS, ALL TOWERS • TICKETRON, NANCIE'S IN AUBURN & PLACERVILLE, IN DAVIS: BRENDAN 753-1736
CLUB MINIMAL
$6.00 AT THE DOOR
FOR INFORMATION CALL: 453-8503
3747 W. PACIFIC AVE. • SACRAMENTO (OFF 12TH AVE. WEST)
D.O.A.
VANCOUVER, B.C.
MINOR THREAT
D.C.
WHITE CROSS
RVA.
JUDICIAL FEAR
NORFOLK
BENNY'S
THUR JUN 9
611 W. MAIN ST.

We played with the Ramones five times over the years, and they always rocked like fuckin' crazy. They changed my life and many others' with their innovative style and humour. It was always an honour to be on the bill. Joey, Johnny, and Dee Dee—you're all sorely missed.

It was incredible to open for one of our idols, Iggy Pop. We did two nights and as usual the Igster was on fire. He was very cool hanging out with us, really down to earth.

July 1 was a great show that raised money for the Squamish Five defence fund. We also found the solution for out-of-control men at the concert: all the security were women. They were able calm everybody down and prevent fighting in the mosh pit and the hall. By this point, Dimwit had quit, and Ned "Peckerwood" James (Verbal Abuse) took over on drums.

We did several more Vancouver Five benefit shows in 1983.

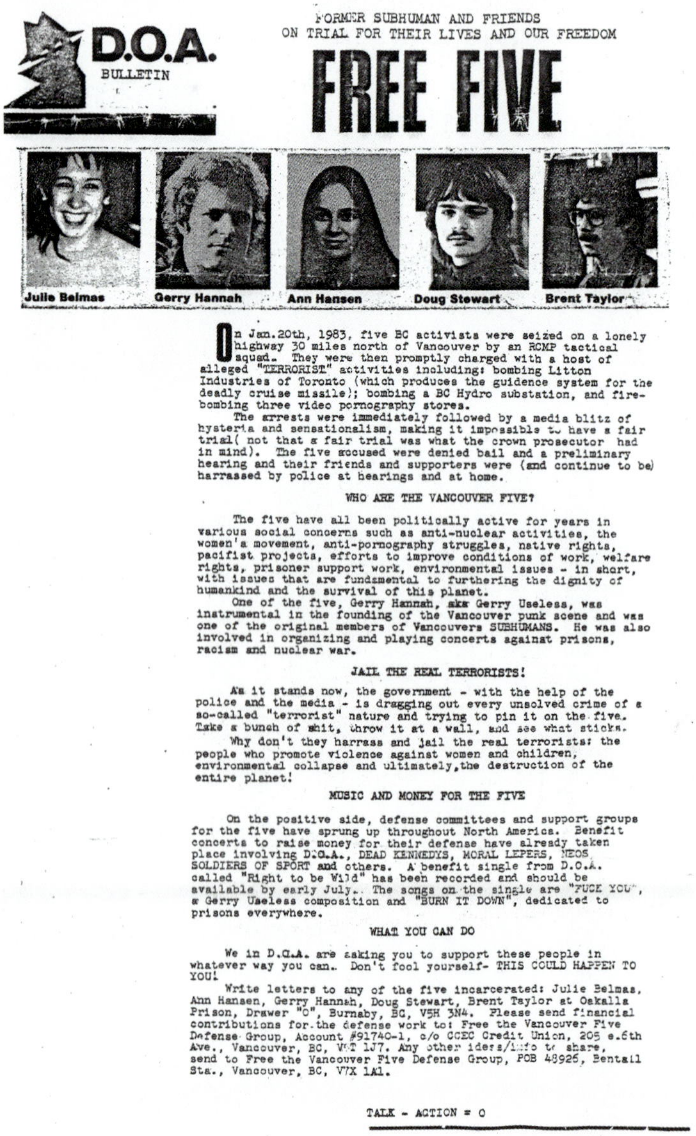

KCMU welcomes
$ five
D.O.A.
Right to be Wild!
GO HOME !
D.O.A.
spluii numa
fastbacks
HOLY WAR CADETS
all ages
METROPOLIS
2nd & Washington
Saturday 9pm
NOV 26

CITR FM 102 and THE GEORGIA STRAIGHT PRESENT
LIVE!
UNBELIEVEABLY
AT U.B.C.
D.O.A.
MORAL LEPERS
DANCE FUNK RHYTHMS
BILLY SHEARS
POP-ROCK! EX-SCISSORS
OCTOBER 14
FRIDAY
A.M.S. MEMBERS $6.50 ADVANCE AT A.M.S. BOX OFFICE.
FREE D.O.A. SINGLE WITH $7.50 ADVANCE TICKET AT ZULU, ODYSSEY, RAVE
D.O.A.
RIGHT TO BE WILD
BURN IT DOWN
SUB BALLROOM U.B.C.
DOORS 8PM. COME EARLY.
INFO: CALL 228-2711
PRODUCED BY A.M.S. CONCERTS
ALL AGES WELCOME

ONE NIGHT TO FREE THE 5
D.O.A.
M.D.C.
TOXIC REASONS
SLUGLORDS
TRIAL BY MEDIA
Video on The Five
D.O.A.
RIGHT TO BE WILD
BURN IT DOWN
Benefit single out NOW on
Records
OCT. 8
SATURDAY
On Broadway
435 BROADWAY, S.F.

SUNDAY, OCT. 30
HALLOWEEN HI-JINX
8PM
XXX
SO YA WANTA SEE SOMETHING REALLY SCARY!
WITH
D.O.A.
BILLY SHEARS
THE RATZ
FROM PORTLAND
AND WATCH OUT!! TODDZILLA
ALL AGES. $5
$1 OFF WITH COSTUME
DOOR DECISION FINAL
STALAG 13
ASK A FRIEND FOR ADDRESS OR GO TO ZULU RECORDS

IAN STEIN PRESENTS
THE DAWNING OF A NEW ERROR...
D.O.A.
M.D.C.
TOXIC REASONS
SLUGLORDS
SAT. OCT. 8, 1983
ON BROADWAY
THEATRE NIGHTCLUB

OUT NOW!
D.O.A.
RIGHT TO BE WILD!

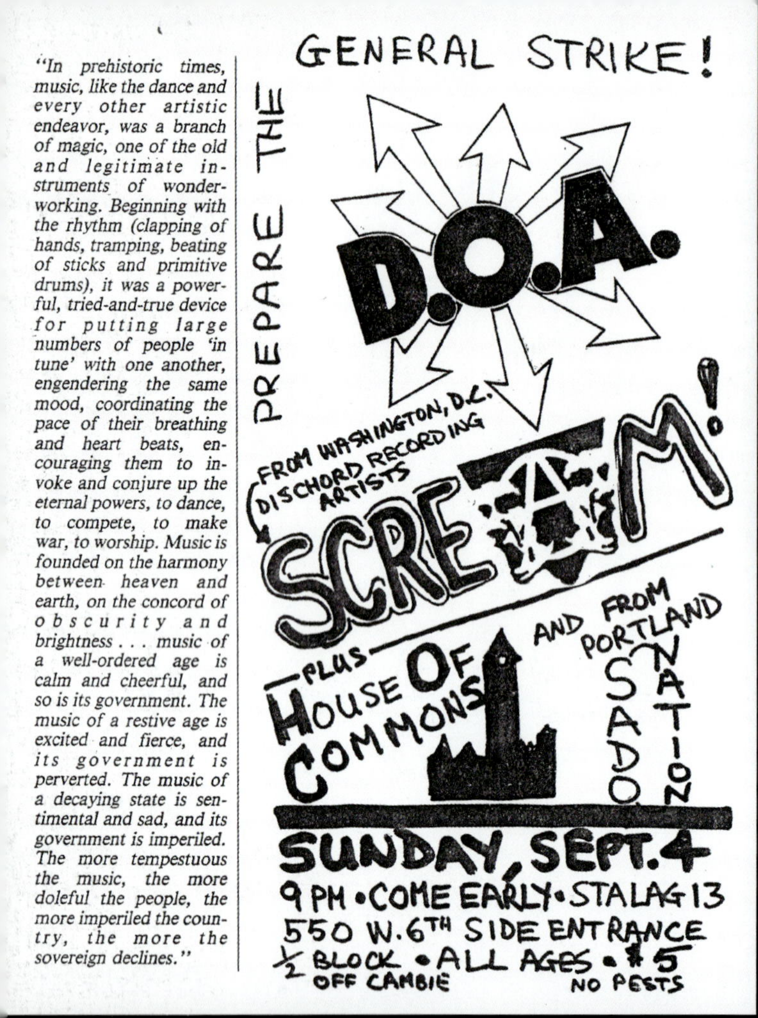

> "In prehistoric times, music, like the dance and every other artistic endeavor, was a branch of magic, one of the old and legitimate instruments of wonder-working. Beginning with the rhythm (clapping of hands, tramping, beating of sticks and primitive drums), it was a powerful, tried-and-true device for putting large numbers of people 'in tune' with one another, engendering the same mood, coordinating the pace of their breathing and heart beats, encouraging them to invoke and conjure up the eternal powers, to dance, to compete, to make war, to worship. Music is founded on the harmony between heaven and earth, on the concord of obscurity and brightness... music of a well-ordered age is calm and cheerful, and so is its government. The music of a restive age is excited and fierce, and its government is perverted. The music of a decaying state is sentimental and sad, and its government is imperiled. The more tempestuous the music, the more doleful the people, the more imperiled the country, the more the sovereign declines."

PREPARE THE GENERAL STRIKE!

D.O.A.

FROM WASHINGTON, D.C. DISCHORD RECORDING ARTISTS

SCREAM!

PLUS HOUSE OF COMMONS AND FROM PORTLAND SADO NATION

SUNDAY, SEPT. 4
9 PM • COME EARLY • STALAG 13
550 W. 6TH SIDE ENTRANCE
½ BLOCK OFF CAMBIE • ALL AGES • $5 • NO PESTS

LIMITED EDITION 1000 COPIES

D.O.A.

GENERAL STRIKE b/w THAT'S LIFE

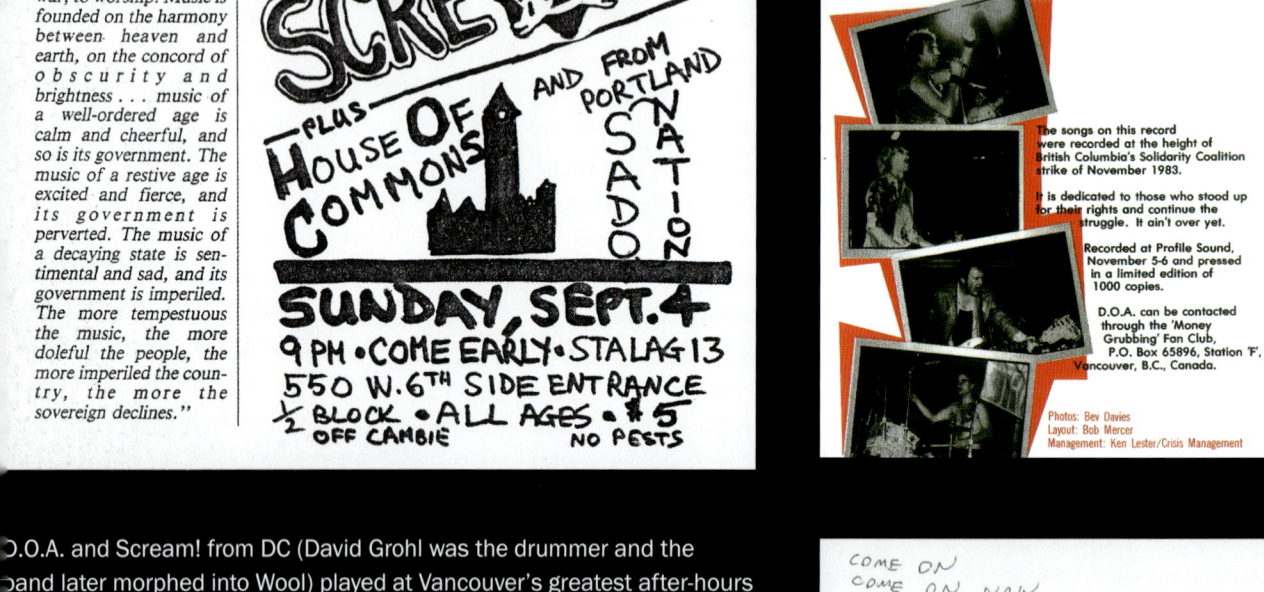

The songs on this record were recorded at the height of British Columbia's Solidarity Coalition strike of November 1983.

It is dedicated to those who stood up for their rights and continue the struggle. It ain't over yet.

Recorded at Profile Sound, November 5-6 and pressed in a limited edition of 1000 copies.

D.O.A. can be contacted through the 'Money Grubbing' Fan Club, P.O. Box 65896, Station 'F', Vancouver, B.C., Canada.

Photos: Bev Davies
Layout: Bob Mercer
Management: Ken Lester/Crisis Management

D.O.A. and Scream! from DC (David Grohl was the drummer and the band later morphed into Wool) played at Vancouver's greatest after-hours warehouse, Stalag 13. The show was part of our General Strike awareness campaign.

Premier Bill Bennett (Social Credit Party) had brought in a number of draconian measures aimed against union members and the working poor that brought British Columbia to the verge of a general strike. Dave Gregg and I sat down one afternoon at Fort Gore and wrote the song "General Strike." We decided to put it out as an "Instant Crisis" single. We recorded it at Profile Sound on November 5th and the single was out a week later.

Here's a rough sketch of the "General Strike" lyrics Dave and I wrote that day (right).

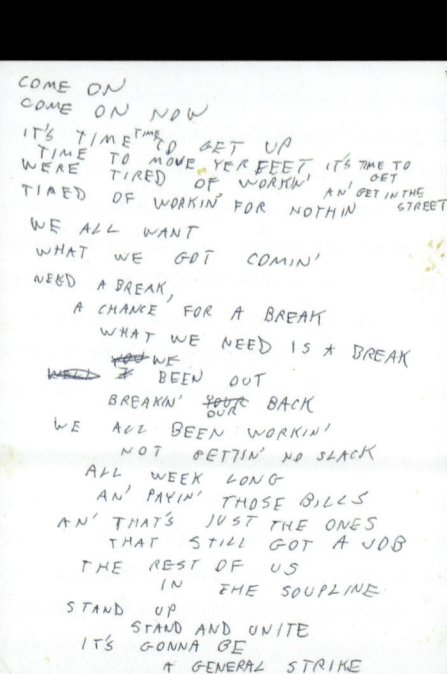

COME ON
COME ON NOW
IT'S TIME TO GET UP
TIME TO MOVE YER FEET IT'S TIME TO
WE'RE TIRED OF WORKIN' AN' GET IN THE
TIRED OF WORKIN' FOR NOTHIN' STREET
WE ALL WANT
WHAT WE GOT COMIN'
NEED A BREAK,
A CHANCE FOR A BREAK
WHAT WE NEED IS A BREAK
WE'VE BEEN OUT
BREAKIN' OUR BACK
WE ALL BEEN WORKIN'
NOT GETTIN' NO SLACK
ALL WEEK LONG
AN' PAYIN' THOSE BILLS
AN' THAT'S JUST THE ONES
THAT STILL GOT A JOB
THE REST OF US
IN THE SOUPLINE
STAND UP
STAND AND UNITE
IT'S GONNA BE
A GENERAL STRIKE

PRESS RELEASE

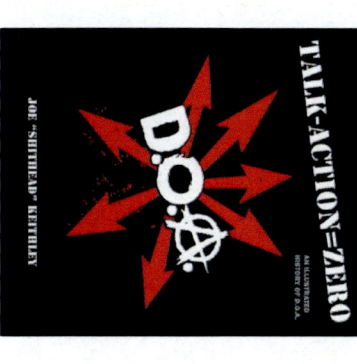

TALK – ACTION = ZERO
An Illustrated History of D.O.A.
By Joe "Shithead" Keithley

A SPRAWLING VISUAL HISTORY OF THE SEMINAL PUNK BAND D.O.A.

Includes a free download of classic D.O.A. tracks.

Market:	Music
BIC Code:	AV
Report Code:	NP
Published:	16 June 2011
Extent:	224pp, 25.4 x 20.3 cm
Illustrations:	150 Full-Colour and B/W photographs
Binding:	Paper
ISBN:	9781552523965
Price:	£17.99
Available for Sale:	UK, Ireland & Europe

The punk band D.O.A., established in 1978, is considered one of the founders of hardcore punk, alongside such other seminal groups as Black Flag and Minor Threat. Their raw, melodic sound, which drew comparisons to the Clash and the Ramones, has always been matched by the band's acute political sensibility; known for its uncompromising and outspoken anarchist viewpoints, D.O.A. has been active on behalf of many issues, including anti-racism, anti-globalisation, freedom of speech, women's rights and the environment. Its slogan, "Talk – Action = Zero," refers to the importance of artists and others who need to "walk the walk" when it comes to their politics.

After more than 30 years, D.O.A. remains as active as ever, touring

KEY SELLING POINTS:

- Joe Keithley is considered as Canada's godfather of punk.
- Includes a free download of D.O.A. tracks.
- D.O.A. has recorded 13 studio albums, including *Talk – Action = 0*, which was released in 2010.
- D.O.A. tour almost constantly, including dates in Europe.
- Includes an introduction by Joe Keithley and vintage photos, posters, handwritten lyrics and tour schedules that span over 30 years.

MARKET:

- Music

recording regularly (its 13th studio album was released in 2010); its fan base now spans three generations.

This large-format book is a sprawling visual history of the group by lead singer/guitarist Keithley – made up of vintage photographs, posters, handwritten lyrics, and other various ephemera – that offers a visceral glimpse into the hardcore life of one of the hardest-working punk bands in the business.

The book also includes an introduction by Keithley, a foreword by Greg Hetson of the Circle Jerks, and a free download of classic D.O.A. tracks.

Also available from Turnaround:
I, Shithead   9781551521480   £12.99

For more information, please contact Georgie Lord at georgie@turnaround-uk.com or on 020 8829 3031.

Joe Keithley is the founder of D.O.A. He has long been an activist, including as a candidate for the Green Party, and is the founder of Sudden Death Records. He lives in Vancouver with his wife and their three children. His autobiography, *I, Shithead: A Life in Punk* (Arsenal Pulp Press, 2003 – available from Turnaround) has been translated into French, German, and Italian.

Published by **ARSENAL PULP PRESS**

Distributed by **TURNAROUND** (visit www.turnaround-uk.com)
Unit 3 Olympia Trading Estate, Coburg Road, Wood Green, London, N22 6TZ
T: 020 8829 3000   F: 020 8881 5088   Mnemonic: Turn   E: orders@turnaround-uk.com

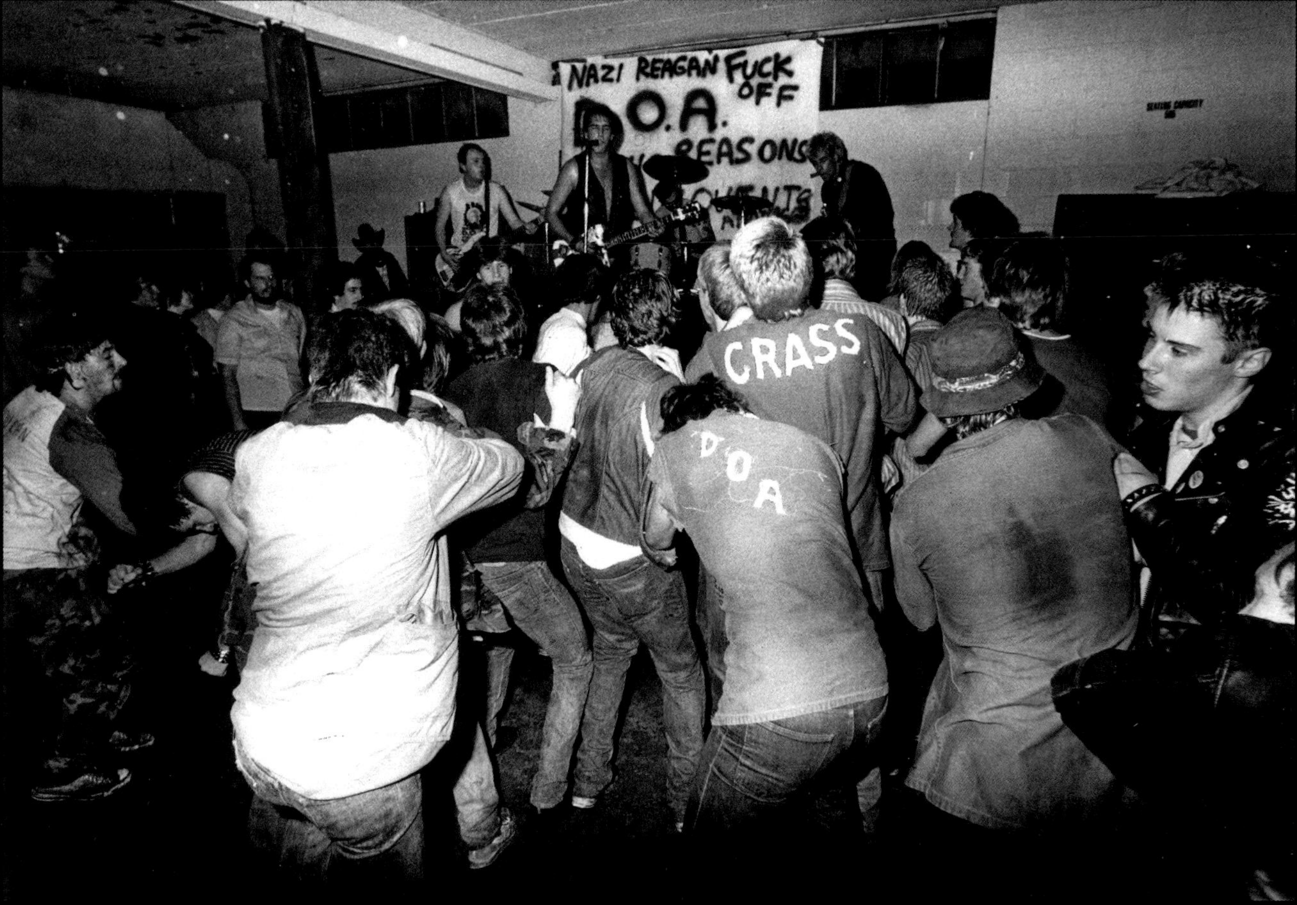
NAZI REAGAN FUCK OFF
REASONS
CRASS
DOA

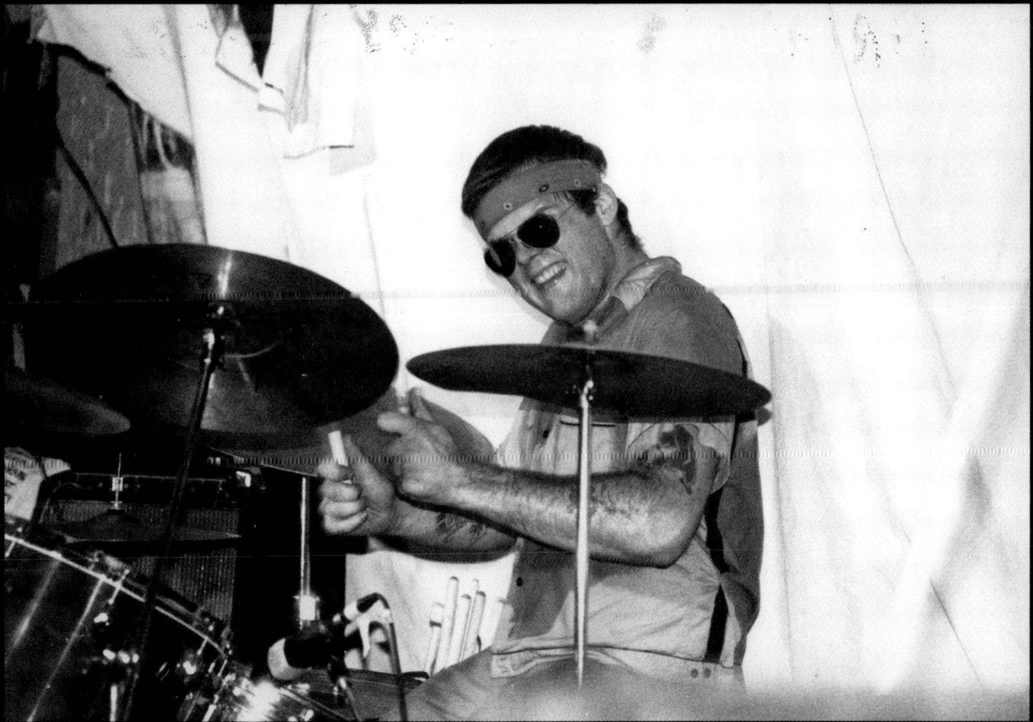

BLOODY BUT UNBOWED

These were the busiest years we had yet experienced. In '84, Alternative Tentacles Records (in London) released *Bloodied But Unbowed*. So we organized our first European tour. We were introduced to a whole other level of politics we had not seen or experienced in North America. Our eyes were opened to the Euro world of squats and activism. Squatters would take over abandoned buildings and turn them into productive centers that included art and performance venues, workshops, and living space. At the end of the first European tour, we recorded at the BBC in London for a "John Peel" session, which we turned into the *Don't Turn Yer Back on Desperate Times* 12-inch EP. We also pulled off a full North American tour that year. Halfway through '84, we let Greg James go, and Dimwit came back as our drummer. And we started recording a new album.

In 1985, *Let's Wreck the Party* was released, so we began an intense tour (unofficially named the Endless Tour, Part One and Part Two) which lasted seven-and-a-half months. Between May and December, we played 132 gigs in 105 different cities in thirteen different countries on two different continents. We travelled half way around the world, from Anchorage, Alaska, to Warsaw, Poland, Miami, Florida, and Sundsvall, Sweden. We also played in England, West Germany, Belgium, the Netherlands, Denmark, Norway, Italy, France, and Switzerland, all within about two months. And toured Canada for a month and spent four months in the States. We covered 63,000 miles, 40,000 of them in vans, and it took us nine different vehicles to pull it off. After all of that, we arrived back home exhausted and broke, par for the course.

Chapter 4

1984–1985

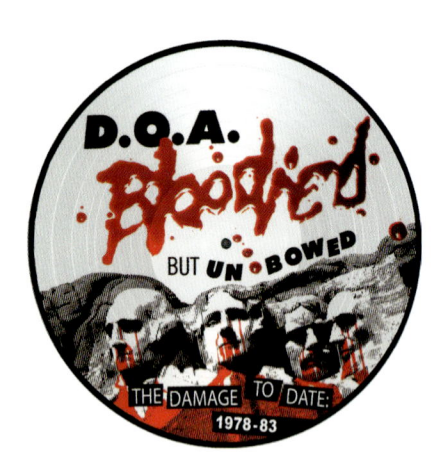

In late 1983, we combined tracks from *Something Better Change, Hardcore 81,* and a couple of early singles. There is a slight track variation between the American and the UK releases. At the start of 1984, Alternative Tentacles released *Bloodied But Unbowed* in the UK and Europe. It was a perfect setup for our first major European tour.

We toured across Canada to raise enough dough to get there. The concert at the church on rue Berri was legendary in Montreal.

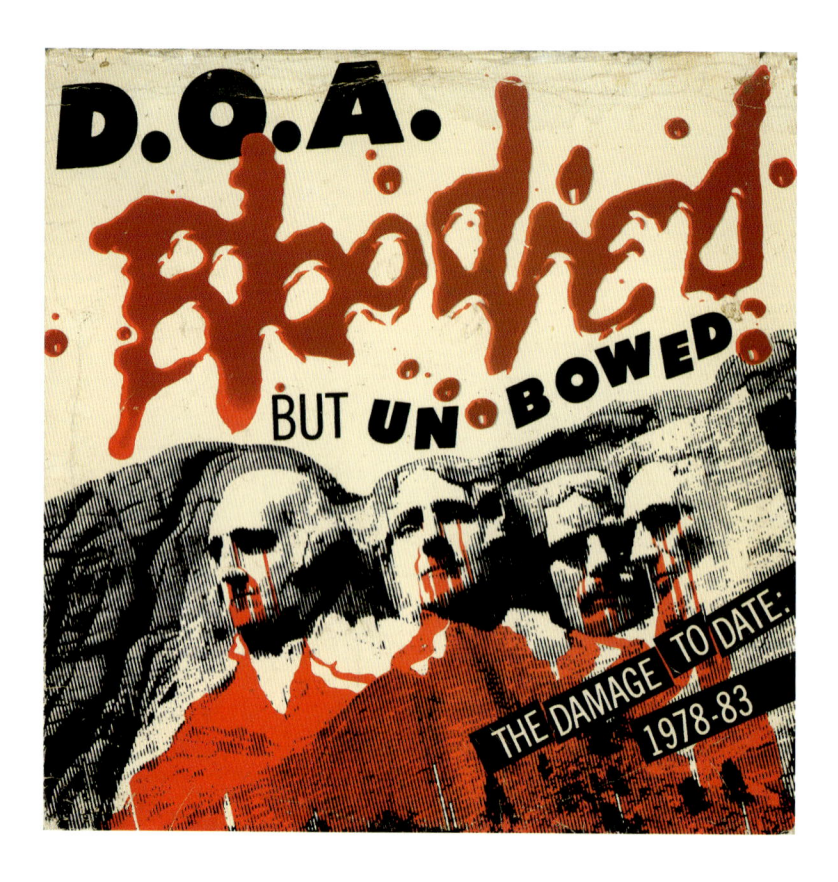

86

FEBURRY · 7 · 8 PM

D.O.A.

the Nils — no policy — SCUM

1767 BERRI · THE CHURCH

FREE DOA SINGLE

D.O.A. BURN IT

DOA Book Chronology : Joe

Feb 13
leave for UK 9:05 pm, stop Manchester
JOE diary on a scrap of paper "Toronto Feb 13/84
13 shows 5,000 miles after "D.O.A. go away, welfare day" we watched the wardair flight attendant drop kick our guitars down the luggage chute and are waiting to go"

Feb 14
arrive Gatwick, 10:30 am
JOE diary on a scrap of paper "Catshit Int. Feb 14/84 Madis Grisl Happy valentine day terra firma. We are placed in airport purgatory. Met mark from pittsburg. Coffee is working its magic on the 2 dinners & 4 breakfasts that I ate!!"
Feb. 14th arrive at Gatwick- oh yeah Wardair touches down at Manchester for an hour- Dave ate four dinners and three breakfasts-

Feb 15
first gig in London; UK to Feb 24

Feb 16
Tues. 16th - Feb. 100 Club

Feb 18
gig in Colne Justine
the stage consisted of a 4x8 piece of plywood on top of milk crates with Ned in a pit behind us- the P.A. was turned on its side- so the horns pointed into your belly- pitiful-

Feb 22
Level 3 in Swindon

Feb 23
Trinity Hall, an old church Old Market Bristol Toxic Shock, the English Subhumans played   WENT TO — ROADIE LOCKED KEYS STONEHENGE — IN THE VAN. ROAD!

Feb 24
The next day Fri. 24th onto the Carribean [?] Club in Reading

Feb 29
the ambulance centre in Southwash , it was a benefit for the 5 and for this jailed Japanese anarchist

MARCH

Mar 1
THURS go to Amsterdam

Mar 2
Groningen "Simplon" Club. THURS. Billed as "punkweekend konsert, Canadese hard-core punk"

Mar 3
SAT Leiden
JOE diary on a scrap of paper "March 5th Finally something to wright about   DIGGING
Went to a bar - a hockey game the Milky Way"   CRAWLING WATER

Mar 7
Copenhagen WED Ungdomshuset, Copenhagen the youth centre.   SQUAT/ + ROWDY
YES FRONT SEATING POSTERS

Mar 10
Rotterdam (SAT)

Mar 13
AMSTERDAM Paradiso TUES

Mar 15
Thurs. March 15 Welligen's squat- great gig- real enthusiastic- Gary left that nite back to - or maybe it was at Paradiso- with Dave from Brighton- too bad- he was good to have along.

LAURA
JOE
DAVE
WIMPY
PECKERWOOD
LESTER
IAN BONEHEAD

Mar 16
Hanover Germany FRI
March 16th the gig - with Beton (cement) Combo not bad

Mar 17
BERLIN Germany SAT the Pankehallen on the Panke river- a huge warehouse
BERLIN WAR TOUR FANATICS

Mar 18
Sun. 18th March- 2nd day in Berlin. A secret gig that nite our payment was as much alcohol as we could drink. Sic Pleasures
Club poster for ALTER BAHNHOF club; Mike Thulke presents "D.O.A. Death On Arrival" with opening act KINDER ONE NAHMEN

EASTER
SMOKED STEAM TRAIN
TICKING COP ON AUTO SKODA

Mar 20
Tues NAHGOLD! Juggencentern

Mar 21
Friburg WED marked GARY GOES

OMNIBABA
TAKING PASSPORT
RACISTS

Mar 22
Date Thurs. 22nd Bochum Lester quit at the hotel in Berlin- said I wasn't enjoying myself nor was he

Mar 23
Homburg ticket stub, 10DM, says open house konzerte the Sporthalle in Homburg

Mar 24
Bremen SAT at KULTURZENTRUM SCHLACHTHOF E.V. 9 DM
the youth centre was called the Slaughterhouse   SCHACHTHOF

Mar 25
Bielefeld SUN   5 KURT VONNEGUT

Mar 26
Stuttgart 80% on MON
An interview by SEAN in LAST RITES fanzine, No. 7 from Illinois (Chicago) :
"Joey: We did a total of 30 gigs in 50 days starting with 8 in England, then up North and West doing 5 gigs in Holland at a couple of squats. In Germany, we did 12 gigs which were pretty good for the most part, but there was a lot of fighting between people at various times..."

Mar 27
Kemptom Tues.March 27th

ON TRAIN CAPITALIST

Mar 28
Vienna WED

Mar 29
ZAGREB Yugo Thurs

Mar 30
great hall- 1,000 people- probably the best gig of the tour in my mind Llubjiana, Yugo FRI

Mar 31
a socialist centre Milan SAT at Centro Sociale Leoncavallo, with support acts
CRASHBOX, C.C.M., RAPPRESA, and GLIA
VW VAN BREAKS DOWN / SAY GOODBYE TO LAURA

APRIL

Apr 1
fly to London

THURS 9:40 A.M. VICTORIA STATION
MARCH 1st.
10 HOUR TRIP TO AMSTERDAM
THURS. 1st
FRI 2nd. GRONINGEN - "SIMPLON"
SAT. 3rd LEIDEN
SUN 4th - OFF
MON 5th - OFF
TUES 6th - TRAVEL TO COPENHAGEN
WED. 7th - COPENHAGEN
THUR 8th -
FRI 9th - TRAVEL TO ROTTERDAM
SAT. 10th - ROTTERDAM
SUN. 11 - OFF
MON 12 OFF
TUES 13 AMSTERDAM - "PARADISO"
WED. 14 - OFF
THURS 15 - OFF
FRI 16 - HANOVER GERMANY
SAT. 17 - BERLIN GERMANY
SUN. 18 - OFF
MON. 19 - HOF ?
TUES. 20 - NAHGOLD?
WED. 21 - FRIBURG GARY GOES
THUR 22 - OFF
FRI 23 - HOMBURG?
SAT. 24 - BREMEN
SUN. 25 - BIELEFELD

BLOODIED BUT UNBOWED TOUR 1984

1. D.O.A.   NEW WAVE SONG
2. I'M RITE   SLUMLORD
3. AMERICA   WAITING FOR YOU
4. FUCKED UP   THE ENEMY
5. BURN IT DOWN   I HATE U
6. SINGIN'   GENERAL STRIKE
7. W.W.3   THAT'S LIFE
8. CLASS WAR   WRITING'S ON THE WALL
9. FRONTIER   PRIVATE HELL
10. 13   MURDER IN HOLLY
11. SINISTER SEASON   KILL THE M,
12. RICH BITCH   TAKIN' CARE O' B,
13. LET'S FUCK
14. OUR WORLD   13 U.S. MARINE CORPS
15. D.O.A.   WHATCHA GONNA DO
16.
17. LIAR FOR HIRE
18. RACE RIOT
19. WAR IN THE EAST
20. WAR
21. FUCK YOU
22. PRISONER

THE ENEMY
TAKIN CARE O' B.

SLUMLORD
THAT'S LIFE

NEW WAVE SONG

Poster 1 (D.O.A.)

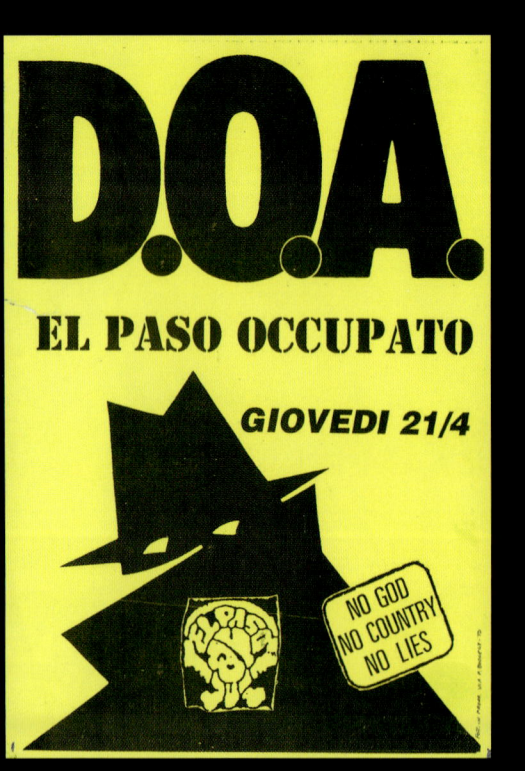

"CHARLIE, YOU BETTER BE GOOD. IT WASN'T EASY GETTING IN HERE, YOU KNOW."

D.O.A.
FROM CANADA

+ BETONCOMBO & UPRIGHT CITIZENS

17.3.84 PANKEHALLEN 20:00 Uhr 10.-

Flyer

BENEFIT FOR ANARCHIST PRISONERS

AT THE AMBULANCE STATION 306 OLD KENT ROAD, SOUTHWARK S.E.1

TUBE. Elephant and Castle
BUSES FROM TUBE. 53, 63, 21, 141, 177,
WEDNESDAY 29th FEBRUARY 1984 8pm-12pm

BANDS:

D.O.A. Vancouver band who put out a benefit single for the Vancouver 5: Fuck You (by Gerry Hannah - one of the Vancouver 5) b/w Burn It Down.
MICHAEL BELBIN Political Poet.
THE HAPPY END 15-piece Revolutionary band
& ANARCHIST VIDEOS £1 ENTRANCE

THE VANCOUVER 5 are five young Canadians who have been framed on a variety of charges in 1983 relating to a series of bombings across Canada during the previous year. The bombings included a controversial power station in British Columbia, a factory in Toronto making parts for the Cruise Missile and three Porn Video Emporiums in the Vancouver area. All 5 are pleading not guilty and have been in prison since January 1983.

K. OMORI a Japanese anarchist under penalty who was convicted of the bombing of a government building on flimsy evidence. He is due to be hung early this year. An appeal against this sentence is now before the the Japanese courts

All Enquiries: Anarchist Black Cross,
c/o 121 Bookshop, 121 Railton Road, London SE24. Tel: 01-274 6655 2—6pm.

Poster 2

D.O.A.
EL PASO OCCUPATO
GIOVEDI 21/4

NO GOD NO COUNTRY NO LIES

To get to Berlin we had to enter and drive for about six hours through the old East Germany. The East German border guards were tough, but they let us through. We drove past the Berlin Wall and into the heart of West Berlin. We were all really excited. The show was at an old warehouse with glass skylights called the Pankehallen. At first the gig seemed normal, but as D.O.A. started playing, a bunch of would-be fascists outside started throwing bricks and rocks up toward and then down through the glass skylights. The projectiles came crashing onto the audience inside. Then these goons bum-rushed the door. An out-and-out riot broke out between the fans inside and the jerks who had burst their way in. The gig organizers were ready for this; they brought out a selection of bats and clubs and chased these geeks out the door and down the street. Between songs we all looked at each

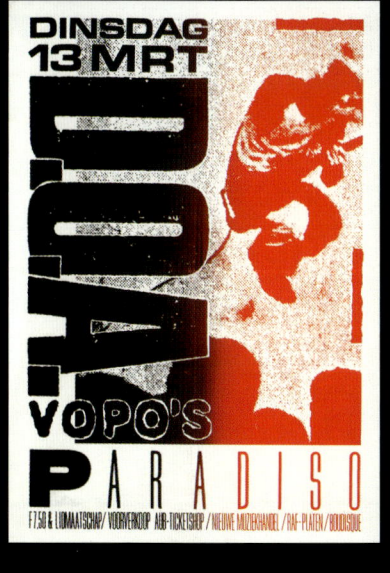

Some birdbrain was at the front of the stage at the arena in Vienna during our set and was really trying to fuck with us. Smashing the mike into our teeth, throwing the monitors around, that sort of thing. Finally, he threw a full pint of beer into Wimpy's face. I lost it; I threw my guitar across the stage to our roadie, Luxury Bob, and I jumped off the stage, put the geek into a headlock, and chucked him out the door. When I got back on stage, the whole crowd cheered. The next day we caught the train to Yugoslavia.

Leoncavallo was the last show of the European tour. We took the train after our two shows in Yugoslavia (Zagreb and Ljubljana). On the train, we had been temporarily arrested by the Yugoslavian police, and by the time we arrived in Milano, we were exhausted. The show was huge, about 3,000 people—punks and activists came from all over northern Italy. When we played, there were three giant mosh pits going on simultaneously.

EUROPEAN TOUR 1984

After the Milano show, we flew to London and recorded four songs at the BBC with the legendary DJ John Peel. This session later turned out to be the *Don't Turn Yer Back* EP.

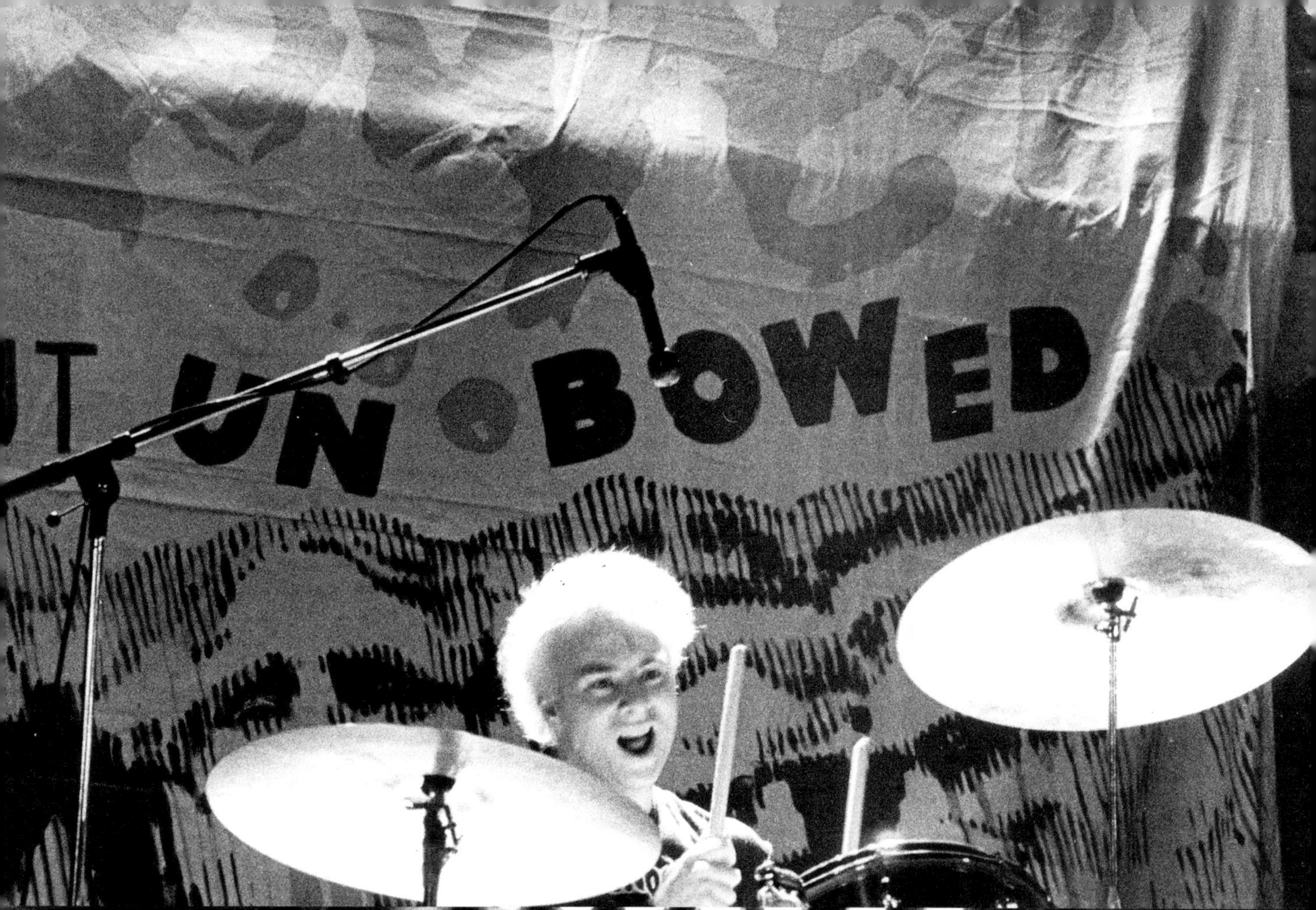
UT UNBOWED

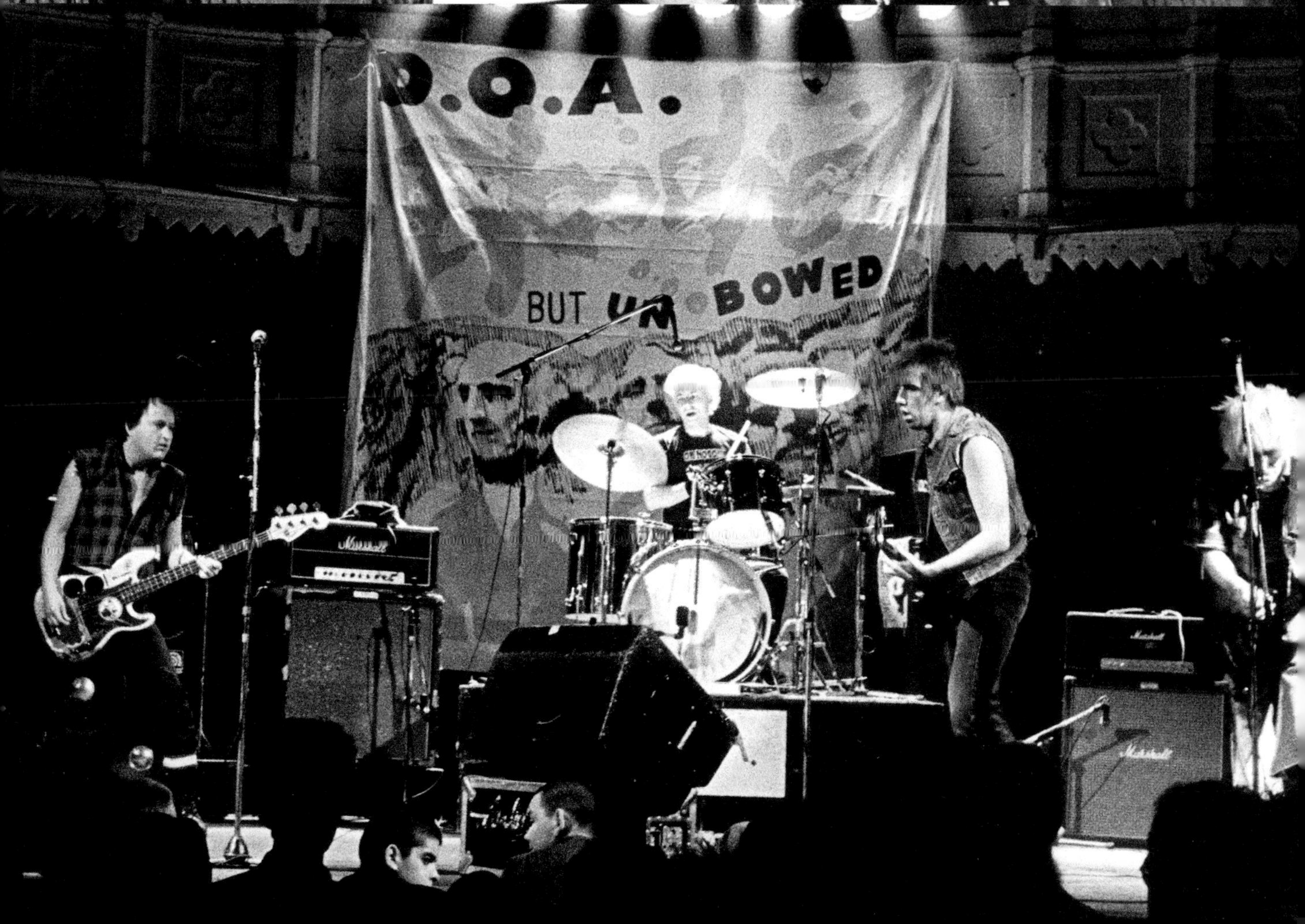
D.O.A.
BUT UNBOWED

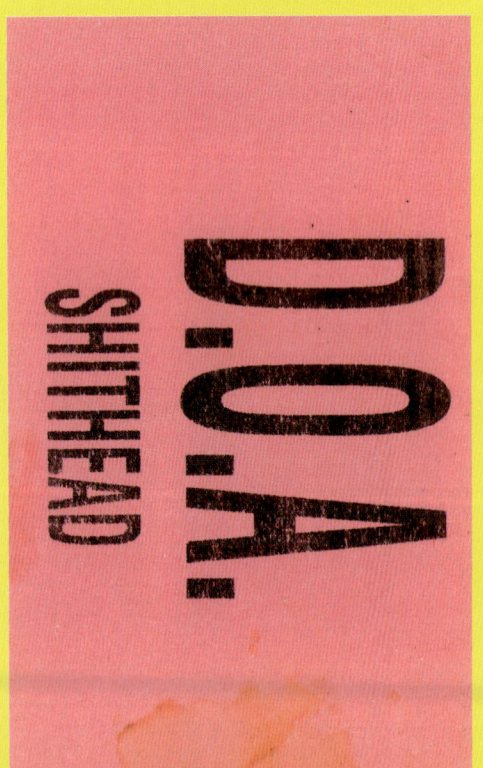

After Europe we toured our way back across Canada to Vancouver. Jesus Bonehead (Dayglo Abortions drummer) organized a show at the O.A.P. Hall. If you call that organizing. There was no one watching the back door, and he had inattentive fifteen-year-old girls taking the entrance fee at the front door. Bonehead never paid us in full; surprise, surprise.

WELCOME HOME
D.O.A.
with Guests
MAY 4th • 8PM
NEW YORK THEATRE
639 COMMERCIAL DR.
TIX VTC/CBO, Woodwards, Eatons & Usual Outlets
Produced by Perryscope

D.O.A.
AUTOMATIC SHOCK
Dayglow Abortions
MAY 11th O.A.P. HALL
1600 GOVERNMENT STREET
ADVANCE TICKETS $5 / DOOR $6
Tickets at Lyle's & Mezzrow's
PRESENTED BY
• CFUV •

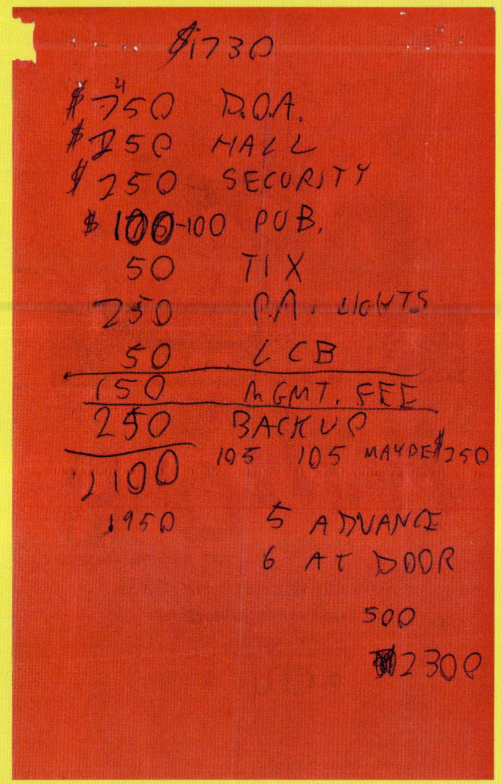
$1730
$750 D.O.A.
$250 HALL
$250 SECURITY
$100-100 PUB.
50 TIX
250 P.A. LIGHTS
50 LCB
150 MGMT. FEE
250 BACKUP
2100 105 105 MAYBE $250
1950 5 ADVANCE
6 AT DOOR
500
2300

We played a huge show at the Olympic Auditorium in L.A. The Exploited had had all their gear confiscated by the police in Spain, so they arrived with nothing. We loaned them our gear for the gig.

(Left). This was another anti-nukes benefit in Vancouver, Rock Against Radiation, with Female Hands and Device.

We liberated those red, white, and blue Conservative Party of Canada posters and made them into something that had some actual value—D.O.A. posters (facing page).

The scene in San Diego (facing page) was in a dead heat with Orange County and Boston for the most out-of-control. On the outskirts of Sacramento we played with Abrasive Wheels; why do these English bands always play their fucking songs twice?

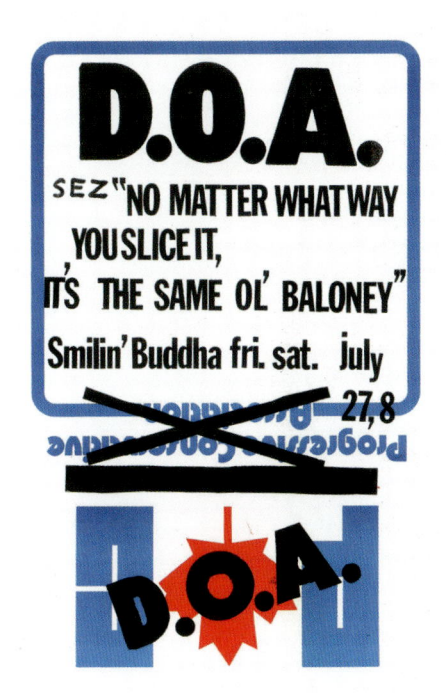

Previous to the show with Johnny Rotten's PIL (Public Image Ltd.) we had covered our guitars and amplifiers with silver mylar (a bright shiny material). Dimwit, now back behind the kit for D.O.A., had silver drums as well. With any kind of lighting at all, the audience got the reflection coming right back at them. We said we were the only band that was really serious about putting the metal back in heavy metal.

Mr. Ed Banger proudly presents
D.O.A.
YORK THEATRE
639 COMMERCIAL DRIVE
KICK out the JAMS!
NO MEANS NO
HOT SPIT DANCERS
CHAINSAW Running
FRI. SEPT. 7
7 PM. step lively!
Tickets; $6.50 adv. $7.50 at the door. Available at Zulu, Black Market, Oddessy, Collectors, and Cabbages n Kinx.
All ages welcome!

THIS MONDAY D.O.A.!!!
MONDAY SEPT. 17 INDIAN CENTER 120W. 1300S.
D.O.A.
7SECONDS
RAUNCH
THE UNWANTED
STENCH
$6 ADV. . 7AT THE DOOR
Mr. Shithead incites fans and fuzz alike.
$6.00
TICKETS AVAILABLE AT RAUNCH
375 WEST 400 SOUTH
532-6592

4 Bands from all over North America!

Canada's D.O.A.

DIE KREUZEN
Milwaukee, Wisc.

OFFENDERS
Austin, TX.

SHANGHAI DOG
Vancouver b.c.

FRIDAY 1.21
VILLA FONTANA
SHOW STARTS 8 PM
ALL AGES
Tickets $6 door / 4.50 advance at HOGWILD RECORDS

NEW YEARS EVE

HEAR THE BELLS KNELL... THE FUTURE IS HERE
THE FUTURE IS NOW!

D.O.A. 1984
i, BRAINEATER

$6 AT DOOR

INDUSTRIAL WASTE BANNED
FIRST AID
+
DEATH SENTENCE

COME EARLY
DEC. 31   8 P.M.   AT STALAG 13
6th + Cambie

Let's Wreck the Party came out on Alternative Tentacles UK. Unfortunately there was a screw-up with the printer, and the first run came out with a tiny front cover. Ken Lester pretty well shit his pants when he saw the small version!

the night D.O.A. played club soda wednesday, march 13

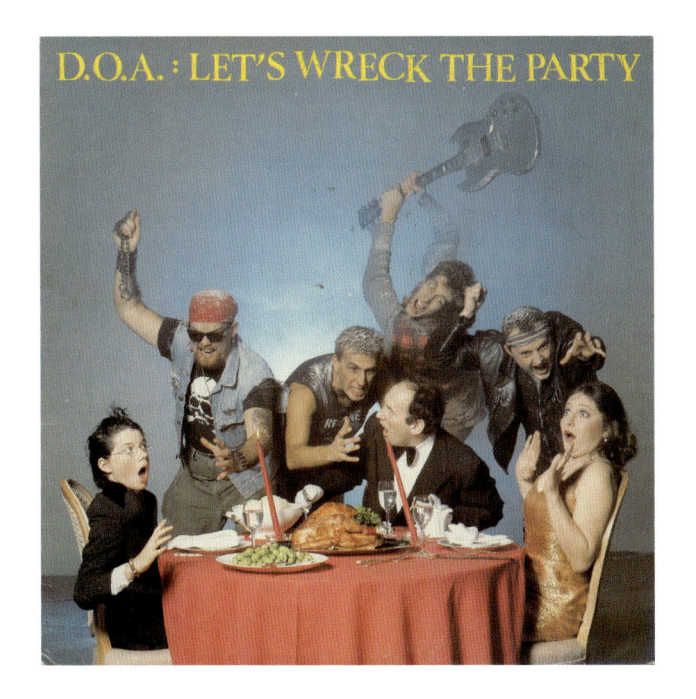

Cover of the US release and drawings by Shawn Kerri of *Let's Wreck the Party*, before and after: an early record cover concept.

At the Vancouver release party for *Let's Wreck the Party*, Brian "Too Loud" McLeod joined us on stage (he broke one of my SG guitars that night too). Club Soda was the kind of place that hated D.O.A., so it made for a tumultuous evening.

101

D.O.A. MAY 85 **D.O.A.**

LET'S WRECK THE PARTY!!!

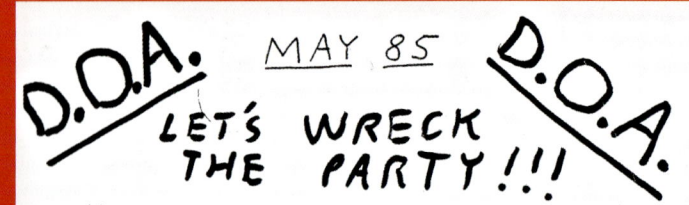

HELLO FRIENDS + MONEY-GRUBBERS

IT'S BEEN A BATTLE, TOOTH + NAIL ALL THE WAY, AN UP-HILL FIGHT. BUT WE'VE FINALLY CLEARED THE DECK, PUT THE TANK IN GEAR AND WE'RE READY TO ROLL.

THE OPENING ROUND OF SHELLS, DESIGNED TO GO STRAIGHT TO THE SOFT UNDERBELLY OF THE ENEMY, EXPLODES AS THUS. D.O.A.'s BRAND NEW ALBUM "LET'S WRECK THE PARTY" ON ALTERNATIVE TENTACLES. IT'S A TWELVE GUAGE SHOTGUN BLAST THAT CONSISTS OF:

SIDE 1: OUR WORLD / DANGERMAN / RACE RIOT / SINGIN' IN THE RAIN / DANCE O' DEATH / GENERAL STRIKE

SIDE 2: LET'S WRECK THE PARTY / SHOUT OUT / MURDER IN HOLLYWOOD / THE WARRIOR AIN'T NO MORE / NO WAY OUT / TRIAL BY MEDIA

Well Jesus H. Christ - that's that - phew!

THEN COMES THE CRUSHING DEFEAT AND MERCILESS ROUT THAT WE'VE BEEN WAITING TO UNLEASH. - THE CITY BY CITY BATTLEPLAN. WE'VE WON THE COUNTRYSIDE, NOW IT'S TIME FOR THE REBELS TO TRIUMPH AND STORM THE CITIES, NOW SET WATCHES AND WE'LL MEET AT THESE COORDINATES:

FRI. MAY 10th - ROCK GARDENS, 410 5th AVE. IN SEATTLE with THE FASTBACKS + NO MEANS NO
SAT. MAY 11th - PINE St. THEATRE IN PORTLAND with NO MEANS NO + 69 WAYS INFO: (503) 230-0661
MON. MAY 13th V.F.W. HALL ASHLAND, OREGON INFO: (503) 488-0980

1ST
I HATE YOU
SINISTER SEASON
FUCKED UP RONNIE
THE FRONTIER
SINGING IN THE RAIN
WWIII
WAITING FOR YOU
WHATCHA GONNA DO?
I'M RITE YER WRONG
AMERICA
  GENERAL STRIKE
D.O.A.
RICH BITCH
LET'S FUCK
PRISONER
WAR IN THE EAST
WAR
13
SCUMLORD
— LIAR FOR HIRE
  BURN IT DOWN
— CLASS WAR
  FUCK YOU
  THAT'S LIFE.

2ND

Our set list, more or less, for '85.

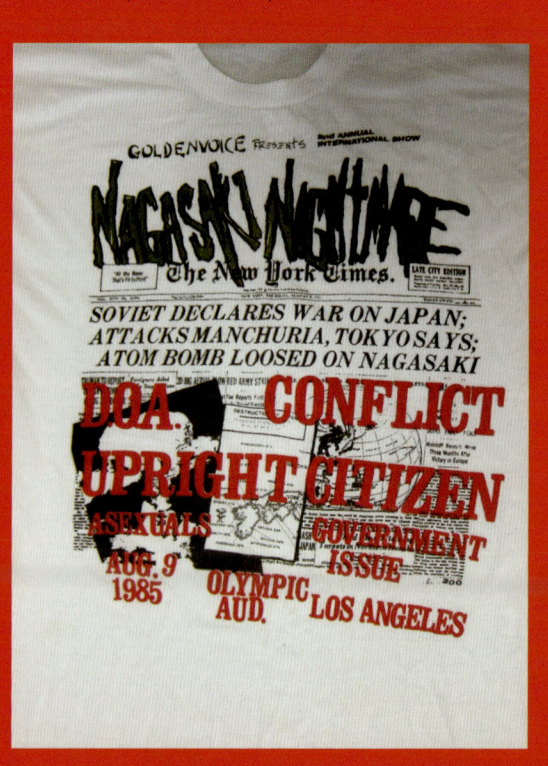

THURS. MAY 16th CLUB CULTURE SANTA CRUZ with RIBSY, STARK RAVING MAD + UGLY AMERICANS INFO: (408) 737-8650
OOPS!!! ALSO ON WED. MAY 15th. D.O.A. WILL DO AN IN STORE AT ROUGH TRADE RECORDS IN SAN FRANCISCO SO COME AN' B.S. WITH D.O.A. - CAUSE WE GOT PLENTY TO GO AROUND!
FRI. MAY 17th. SACRAMENTO with CIRCLE JERKS + FASTBACKS INFO: (916) 444-3133
SAT. MAY 18th THE STONE IN SAN FRANCISCO with DICKS, FRIGHTWIG + FASTBACKS
SUN. MAY 19th SKATE PLUS IN RENO with DICKS, JACKSHIT, FASTBACKS + UGLY AMERICANS
MON. MAY 20th CLUB LINGERIE IN HOLLYWOOD with DICKS
FRI. MAY 24th. PHOENIX INFO: (602) 263-5190
SAT. MAY 25th. SAN DIEGO with G.B.H.

NOW, FOR A POPULIST VICTORY WE NEED EVERY WOMAN, MAN + CHILD, SO STAND UP + BE COUNTED

ROGER, OVER + OUT!!!

Above, one of our newsletters, mailed out semi-frequently to all the members of our Money-Grubbing Fan Club.

The Nightmare in Nagasaki fortieth anniversary concert was held on August 9, 1985, at the Olympic Auditorium. D.O.A., Conflict, Upright Citizens, and Government Issue played.

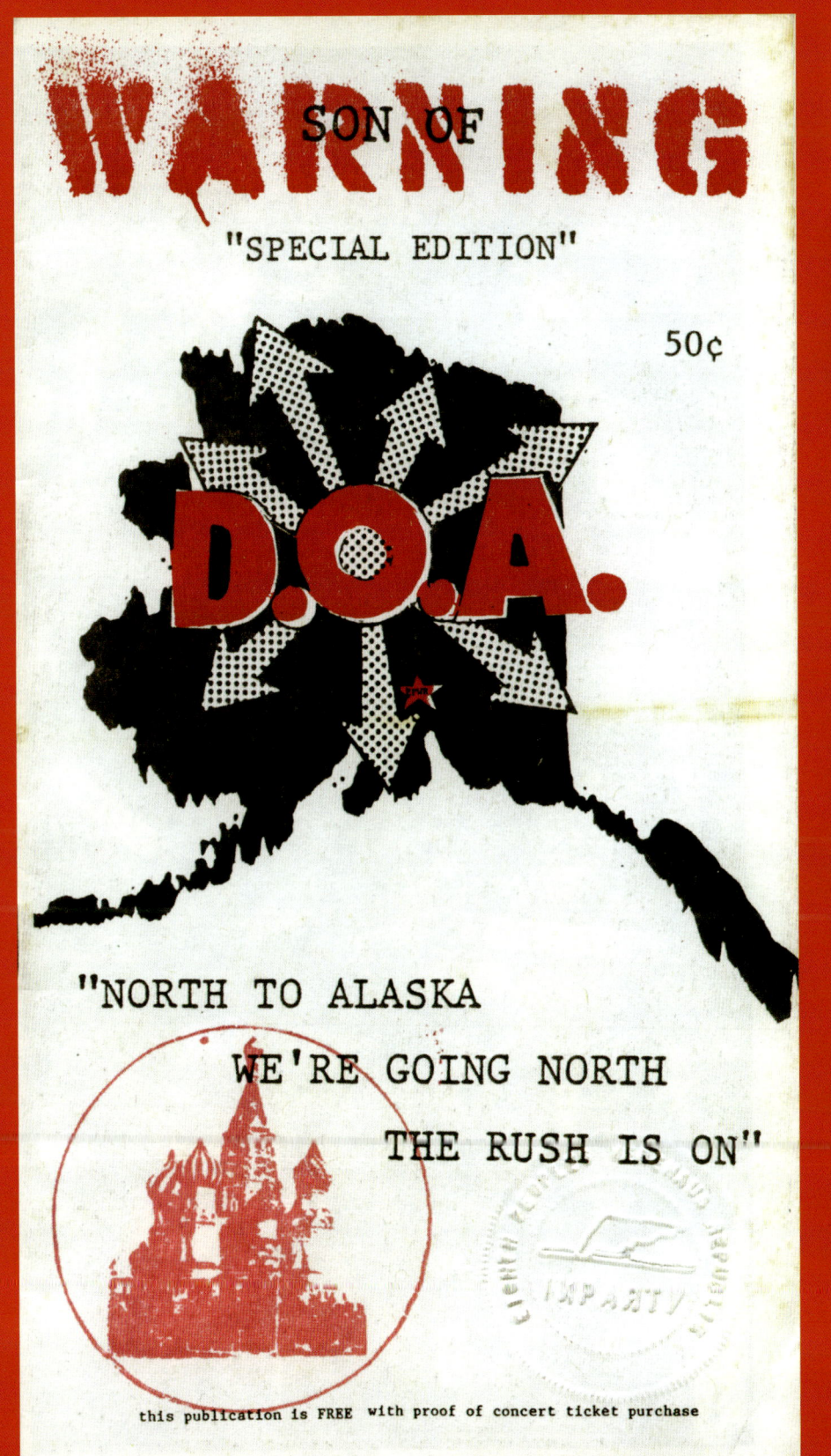

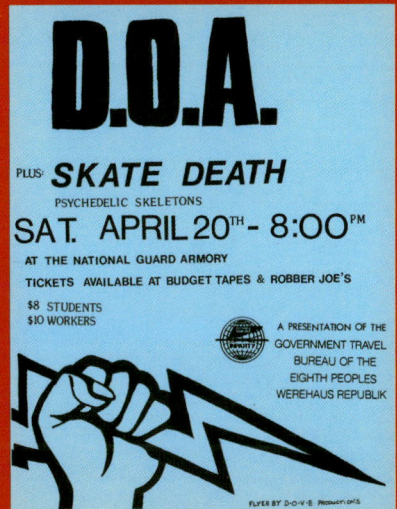

North to Alaska! North, the rush is on! We had a great time in Alaska, staying at a warehouse in Anchorage where the concert promoters lived. They had declared themselves to be the Eighth People's Republic and were no longer part of the United States. They issued "passports" to all travellers (including D.O.A.) who entered their republic. An all-around cool idea. Hey, Sarah Palin, watch out, you traitor!

Joe with Johnny Ferreira and Brian "Too Loud" McLeod

Hutch mixing D.O.A. in Poland.

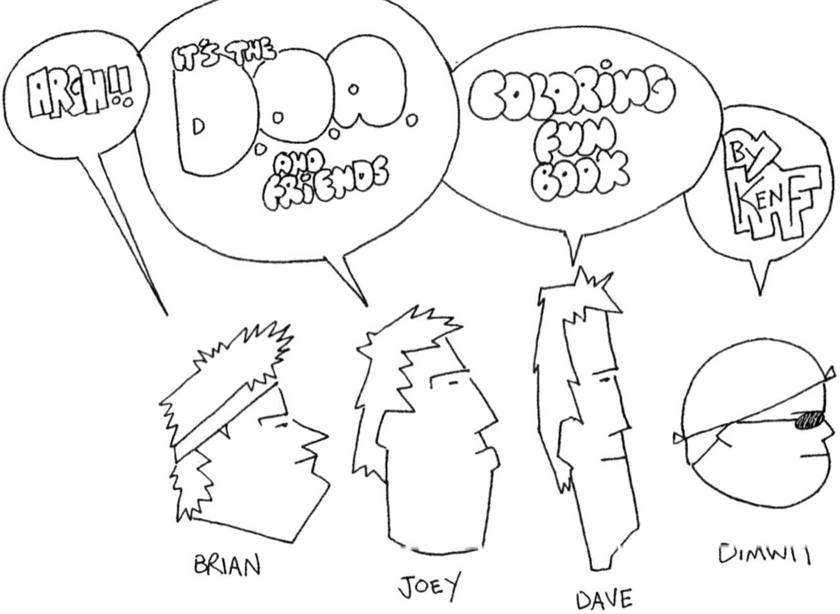

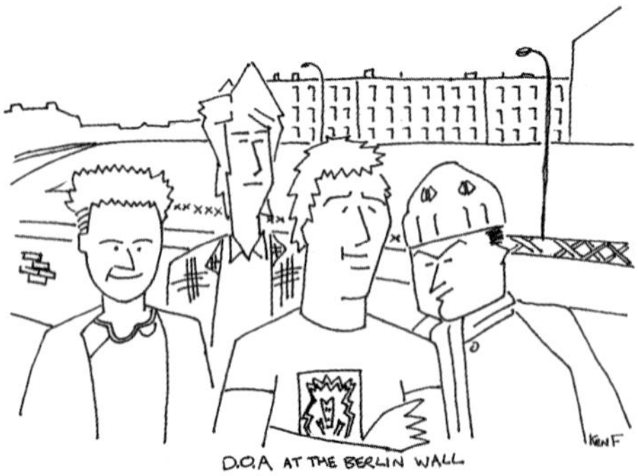

D.O.A AT THE BERLIN WALL

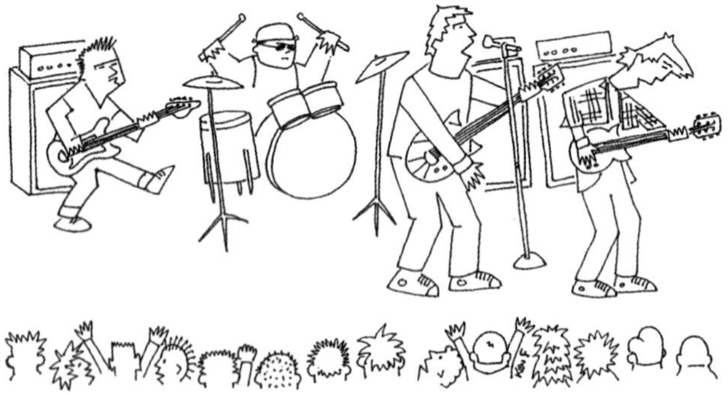

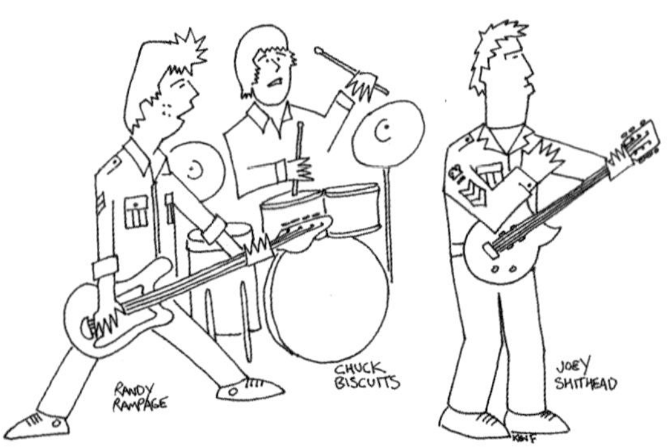

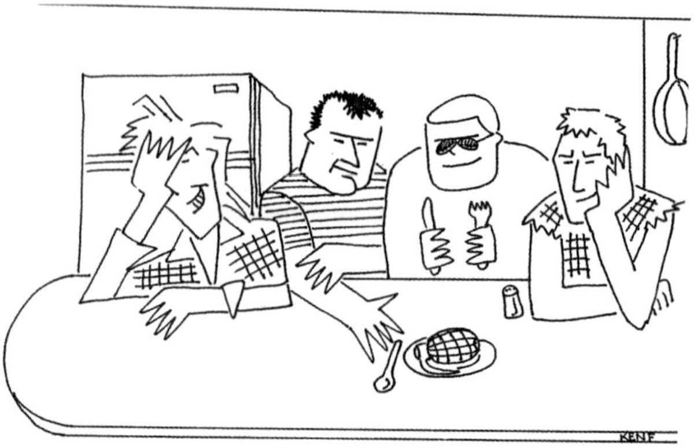

D.O.A.
from Vancouver B.C.
and **the DICKS**
SAT. JUNE 15th
at — THE MIAMI —
3930 CASS, tel: 831-3830

PRICE $6
for more info call: 832-266

FROM CANADA PRESENTS

D.O.A.
SAT. APRIL 20TH

GORILLA GARDENS
ROCK THEATRE
410 5th ave. s.
tel. 340-0404
8:00 p.m.

D.O.A.
NO MEANS NO
FAST BACKS
ITCHY BROTHER
MAY 10 FRI
$6.00 ADVANCE
$7.00 AT DOOR

Clear & Distinct Ideas Presents

D.O.A.
Tales of Terror
FAST BACKS
CIRCLE JERKS
PROBLEM FISH

FRIDAY, MAY 17TH
7:30 PM
CREST THEATER
1013 K STREET, SACRAMENTO
INFORMATION: 444-3133

Advance Tickets At:
Bass, Ticketron, Tower,
Record Factory, The Beat,
Dimple Records,
Aftermath Records,
Esoteric Records, Spirit
Records

THE HARDEST WORKING BAND IN SHOW BUSINESS

D.O.A.
FROM VANCOUVER B.C.
NO MEANS NO
69 WAYS

SAT MAY 11 9PM
$5.50 ADVANCE ALL AGES $6.50 DOOR
Tickets at Bass, 2nd Ave. Records, Music Millennium INFO/CHARGE 228-1805

PINE STREET THEATRE
SE 9TH & PINE

Wednesday, June 12TH

D.O.A.
DICKS
A.O.D.
MEIN KAMPF

8 P.M.
all ages!

They're fighting for your future!
$6.00 AT DOOR
FOR MORE INFO
CALL → 434-2255

DANCELAND
4066 Shawano Ave., Green Bay
(6 Miles West of Green Bay)

US SUMMER TOUR 1985

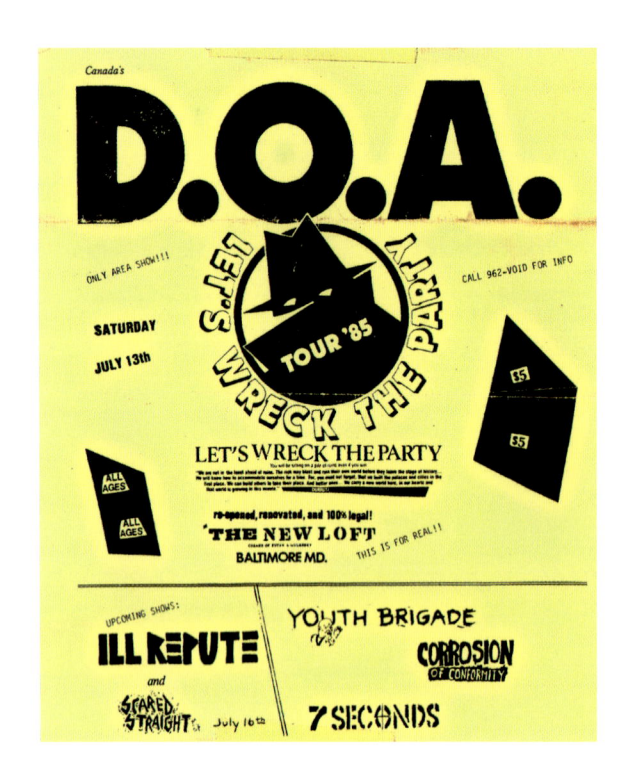

We hung a large D.O.A. banner (20 by 10 feet / 6 by 3 metres) from the roof of a four-storey building so people could see that the show (with Soul Asylum) was going on from a long way away. I stood there and admired it, then walked off to get a cup of coffee. When I got back, the banner was gone. Some jerk had stolen it. We later found it stashed in a dumpster. This is the same banner that was on the ceiling of the Cactus Club in San Jose for years.

We played at the WUST Radio Hall in DC; while we were in the middle of our set with Government Issue, the radio hall manager waved me over to the side of the stage and discreetly said, "Somebody just came in here with a gun. But don't panic and don't alarm the audience." Fuckin' great! I said to myself, I'm probably the number one target up here.

We discovered after the show that somebody had stolen our front and back licence plates from the van. We had ten more days touring on the eastern seaboard, so we just drove around without plates. "Licence plates! We don't need no stinking licence plates!"

BRING BACK THE FUTURE TOUR 85
D.O.A.

$16

Rätschlag

THE BEAT

Down Syndrome

BILL LEVIN PRESENTS

Father's Day Mondo
All ages welcome!

...wson's Lake — 6707 Westfield Blvd.
Sunday, June 16, 12 noon
featuring

.A. Toxic Reasons Articles Of Faith
...dolion   Primales   Mathbats
...ortion
    Latex   Sloppy
    Novelties   Seconds
        THE DICKS

Tickets: $10 Advance — No day of show
Tickets available at Karma, Blocks & all Ticketmaster locations, and Modern times, & 2nd Time Around.
— No Bottles or Cans Permitted —

PERRYSCOPE presents THE ONLY SUMMER APPEARANCE OF...
D.O.A.

AND FROM RE...
7 SECONDS
WITH REGGAE
REDEMPTION
SUNDAY, AUGUST 4
NEW YORK THEATRE
639 COMMERCIAL
TICKETS: VTC/CBO, ZULU, ODYSS...

DOOR: 6:30 SHOW 7:30 AN ALL AGES GIG

REDMAN PRODUCTIONS PRESENT
A Layborday Blowout With
D.O.A

GOVERNMENT ISSUE
JUST BACK FROM A WEST COAST TOUR
DAG NASTY

WUST Radio Music Hall
8 & V St's N.W.
Saturday August 31, 1985
Doors open at 7:30 pm
$7 at the door

C.I.A.

CONCERTPROMOTION IM AUFTRAG DER MUSIKER.

Kontakt:
Bodo Jacoby & Michael Blume
Vaalser Straße 319
5100 Aachen
Tel.: 0241 - 86640 oder
0241 - 871576

concertinformation + concertinformation + concertinformation

D.O.A. & FRIGHTWIG

So. 29.09 Hamburg - Markthalle
Mo. 30.09 Berlin - Quartier Latin
Di. 1.10 Frankfurt - Batschkapp
Mi. 2.10 Tübingen - Jugendhaus
Do. 3.10 München - Alabamahalle
Fr. 4.10 Zürich - Rote Fabrik
Sa. 5.10 Lausanne - Dolce Vita
So. 6.10 Freiburg - Cräsh
Mo. 7.10 ~~Köln - Stollwerck~~
Di. 8.10 Aachen - Ritz
Mi. 9.10 ~~Bochum - Zeche~~
Do. 10.10 ~~Bremen - Römer~~

Dear Bill,
this Dates are more clear than the dates from the Poster.
Not sure are the gigs in Köln, Aachen and Bremen, but we give you as soon as possible the exactly informations about this.
It's may be possible that we can arrange two gigs more for the 29 and 30 of october in Bielefeld and Kempten.
Greetings

Our German and Swiss tour during two-and-a-half months in Europe, sixty shows in all. One of the highlights was a D.O.A., Sonic Youth, and Frightwig concert in Munich, Germany, in the middle of Octoberfest.

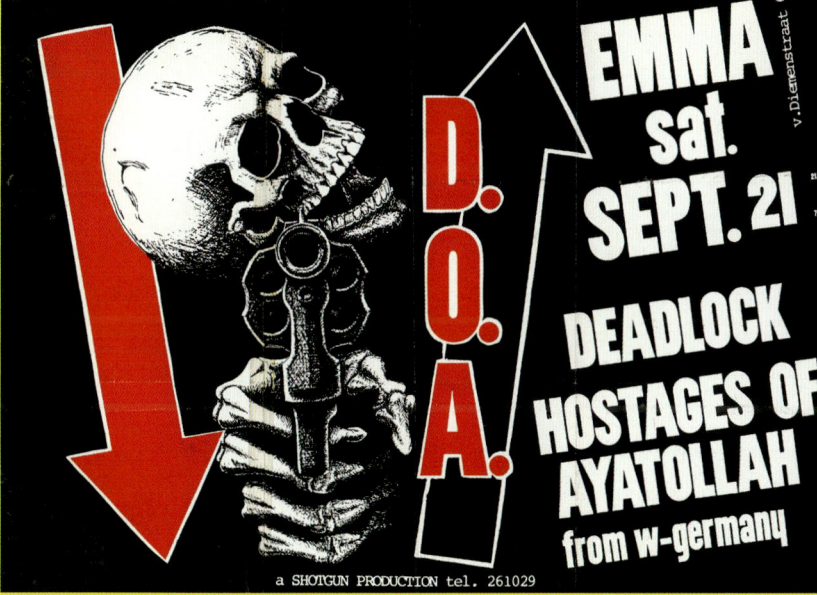

A big crowd showed up for our show in Zurich—there were punks from Switzerland, Germany, France, and Italy. Frightwig's drummer, Cecilia, sometimes went to the front of the stage to sing, leaving me to fill in on drums. Cecilia totally aggravated this one drunken punk. They wrestled over the mike and when Cecilia let go of it, the guy pulled it with such force it broke his nose. The enraged punk wanted to have it out with Cecilia. As I was drumming, I signalled frantically to our German roadie, Bernie, to stop this geek. Bernie ran across the stage and smashed the guy in the face so hard he flew off the stage backward about fifteen feet (five meters). After that, we called him "One Punch Bernie, the German Boxing Champ."

EUROPEAN TOUR 1985

in concerto

D.O.A.

& supporters:
UPSIDE — Bring Back the Future — From Canada
stigmathe — TOUR '85
AGTM — ORE 2

MERCOLEDI 6

CINEMA ASTRA di S. GIOVANNI LUPATOTO (VER)

AUTOGESTIONE — X INFO: 045-43452
COLLETTIVO DISUMANO — UPDUK — ROMANO

Setlist:

- World War III — Let's Wreck / Tits / 001
- Class War — No Way Out / Burn It Down
- America — Great White Hope / New Wave Sucks
- Race Riot — I Don't Give A Shit / Great White Hope / Woke Up Screaming
- Whatcha Gonna Do? — Rich Bitch / Let's Fuck
- I'm Wright Your Wong — Waiting For You
- Enemy
- Fucked Up Ronnie
- War in the East
- War
- Slumlord
- I Hate U
- Singin in Rain * 13
- D.O.A. * Green Beret
- Liar * 2' Training Camp
- Let's Fudge
- The Prisoner

- **29.09.** Hamburg-Marktha
- **30.09.** Berlin-Quartier Lat
- **01.10.** Frankfurt-Batschka
- **02.10.** Tübingen-Clubha
- **03.10.** München-Alabamaha
- **04.10.** Zürich-Rote Fabr
- **05.10.** Lausanne-La Dolce Vi
- **06.10.** Freiburg-Crä
- **08.10.** Bielefeld-A.J
- **09.10.** Bochum-Zec
- **10.10.** Bremen-Schlachth

D.O.A.

SPECIAL GUEST:

FRIGHTWIG

Dead On Arrival
(CANADA)

FRIGHTWIG
(NEW YORK)

ZAT. 28 SEPTEMBER
HET BOLWERK
KERKGR. 8 SNEEK TEL. 05150-18707

ENTREE	F 7,50	ZAAL OPEN 21.00 UUR
V.V./C.J.P.	F 6,--	1ste BAND BEGINT 21.30 UUR

V.V. : POPEY-JOURE/PLATENHUIS-BOLSWARD/BOLWERK-SNEEK/
LOOPER-SNEEK/DISK LEEUWARDEN/PAKHUIS-HEERENVEEN

ORGANISATIE: ST. DARK INC. I.S.M. HET BOLWERK

D.O.A.
LET'S WRECK THE PARTY

Tourleitung:

D.O.A. "Let's Wreck The Party"

Back in North America, we picked up our van, "the Blue Bullet," which was parked in the Bronx, and drove up to Canada for four shows. The day after we played in Ottawa, the Blue Bullet's engine blew up. We sold off the van for a miserable pittance and flew back to Vancouver. Just before we left Europe, our van "Galloping Gertie" also had major engine problems, so we had to sell it for next to nothing as well. Seven-and-a-half months of touring and we arrived home dead broke. Fuckin' great!

DOA: one reason to jump and scream!
BULLWINKLES
presents:
Tuesday, November
26
1. JOEY "SHITHEAD" KEIGHLEY (GUITAR & VOCALS)
2. DAVE GREGG (GUITAR & VOCALS)
3. BRIAN "SUNNY BOY" ROY GOBLE (BASS & VOCALS)
4. DIMWIT (DRUMS)
THE Amazing
D.O.A.
is back!
from Vancouver
$10 COVER
FREE RECORD!!
D.O.A.
WITH
OCTOBER CRISIS
&
iDioT SavaNt

Clear & Distinct Ideas Presents
D.O.A.
THE DICKS
DIE KRUETZEN
POLKACIDE
FRIDAY DEC. 6
THE FARM
1499 POTRERO San Francisco
ALL AGES
Advance Tickets At:
BASS & ROUGH TRADE
INFORMATION; 431-1326
8:00 PM

THE OTHER SIDE presents at CITY GARDENS
1701 CALHOUN ST. TRENTON NJ
(609) 392-8887
NO ALCOHOL SHOWS
ALL SHOWS 6-10pm
SUN DEC 29
Circle Jerks (LA)
AND
D.O.A.
LET'S WRECK THE PARTY
(CANADA)
plus BODIES IN PANIC (NJ)
SAVAGE SILENCE (NJ)
SUN JAN 5
T.S.O.L. (LA)
AND
MARGINAL MAN (DC)
SUN JAN 12
A VERY SPECIAL EVENING WITH
plus SNAKEFINGER
Advance Tickets on Sale Now
(SF) THE RESIDENTS'
the residents
SUN JAN 19 - MEGADETH (CALIF)
SUN JAN 26 - DESCENDENTS
SAT-JAN 18 - JOE JACKSON - 21 and over - 8:30pm - TIXS ON SALE NOW

soundproof presents
fri. dec. the 13th
an all ages gig!
D.O.A
the return of...
no means no
slow
little ratskulls
viking hall 828 e. hastings

NO WAY OUT

THE LINE IT FORMED
FROM THE LEFT TO THE RIGHT
ANYBODY LEFT INSIDE
WAS NOWHERE IN SIGHT

YOU'VE HAD YOUR CHANCES
YOU'VE HAD YOUR TIME
NOW QUIT WASTIN' WHAT'S LEFT
AND GET IN LINE

NOBODY KNOWS, NOBODY CARES
THAT THE WORLD'S GOIN' NOWHERE
NOBODY KNOWS, NOBODY CARES
THAT YOUR ALL GOIN' NOWHERE
CAUSE THERE'S
NO, NO, NO, NO WAY OUT

THE PARTS MADE FOR YOU
IT'LL FIT NICELY
ONE SIZE FITS ALL PRECISELY

NOW YOUR A MAN
A MAN FOR ALL AGES
IN YOUR ONE SIZE FITS ALL CAGES

(CHORUS)

WHAT YOU DO, YOU DO IT FOR ME
CAN'T YOU SEE THAT NOTHIN'S FOR FREE
YOU'LL FIT IN, THAT'S THE WAY IT WILL BE
IT'S SO PLAIN, IT'S OBVIOUS TO ME

NO, NO, NO, NO WAY OUT !!!

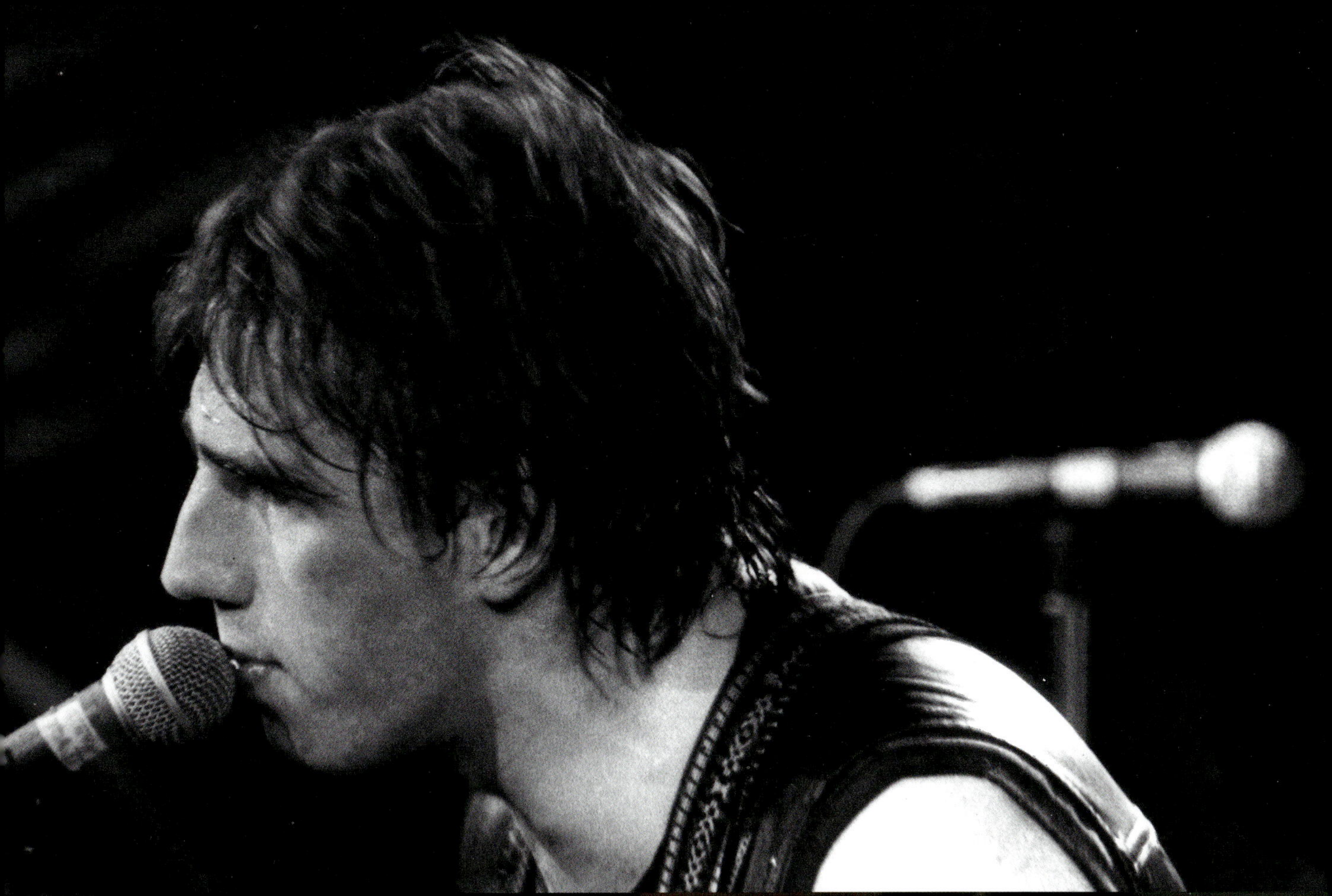

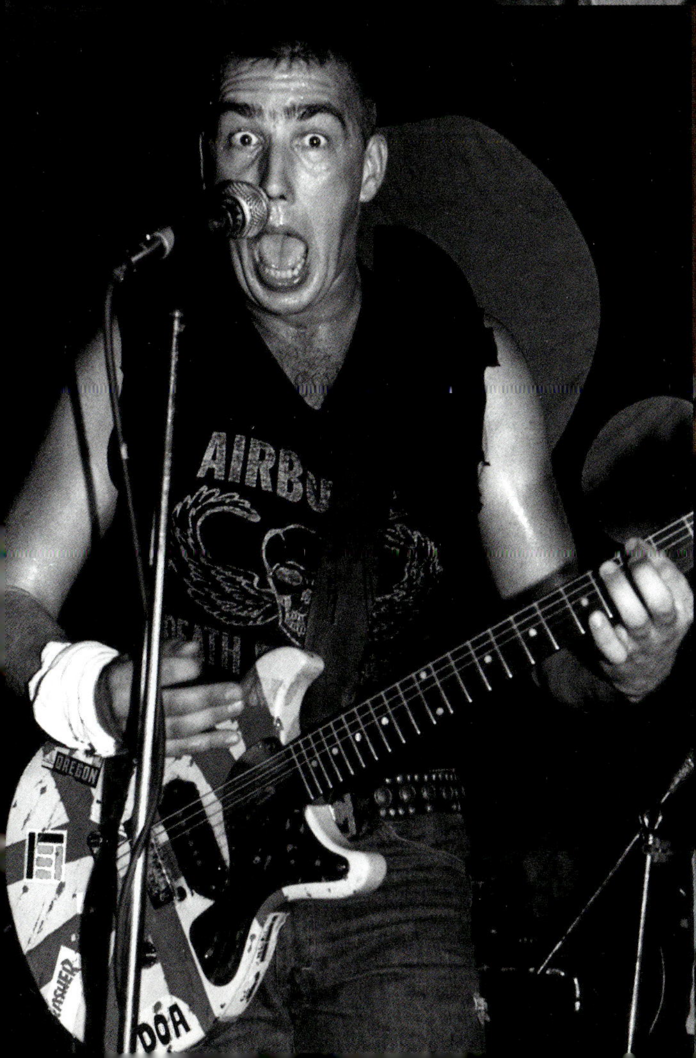
OREGON
DOA

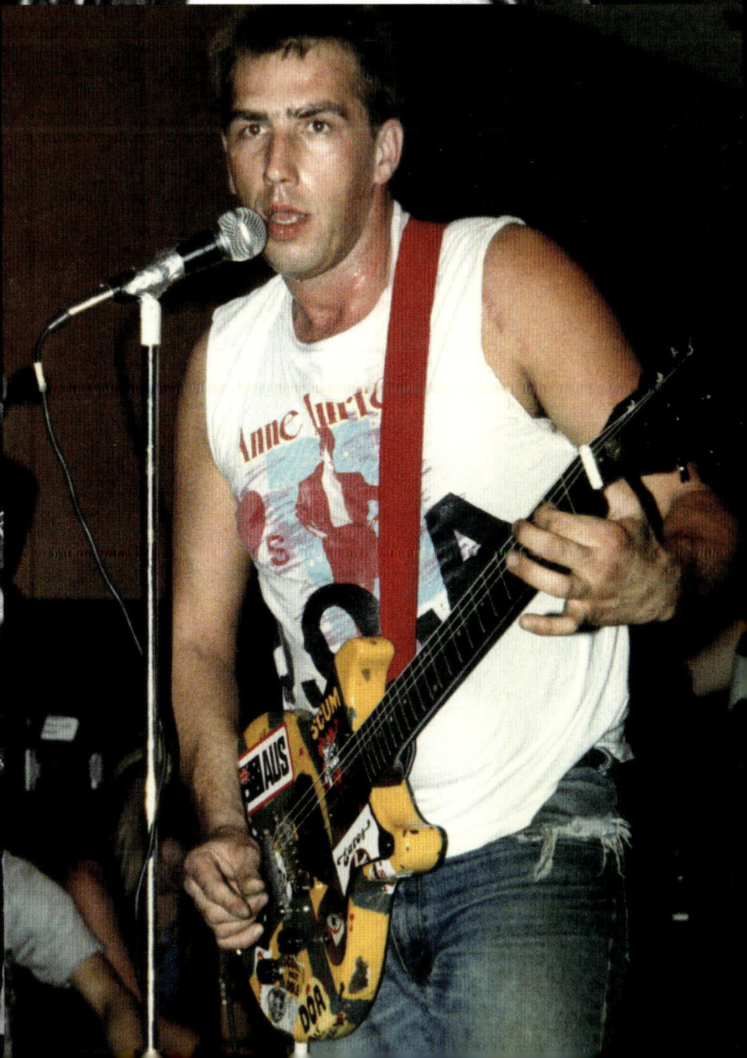
SCUM
AUS
DOA

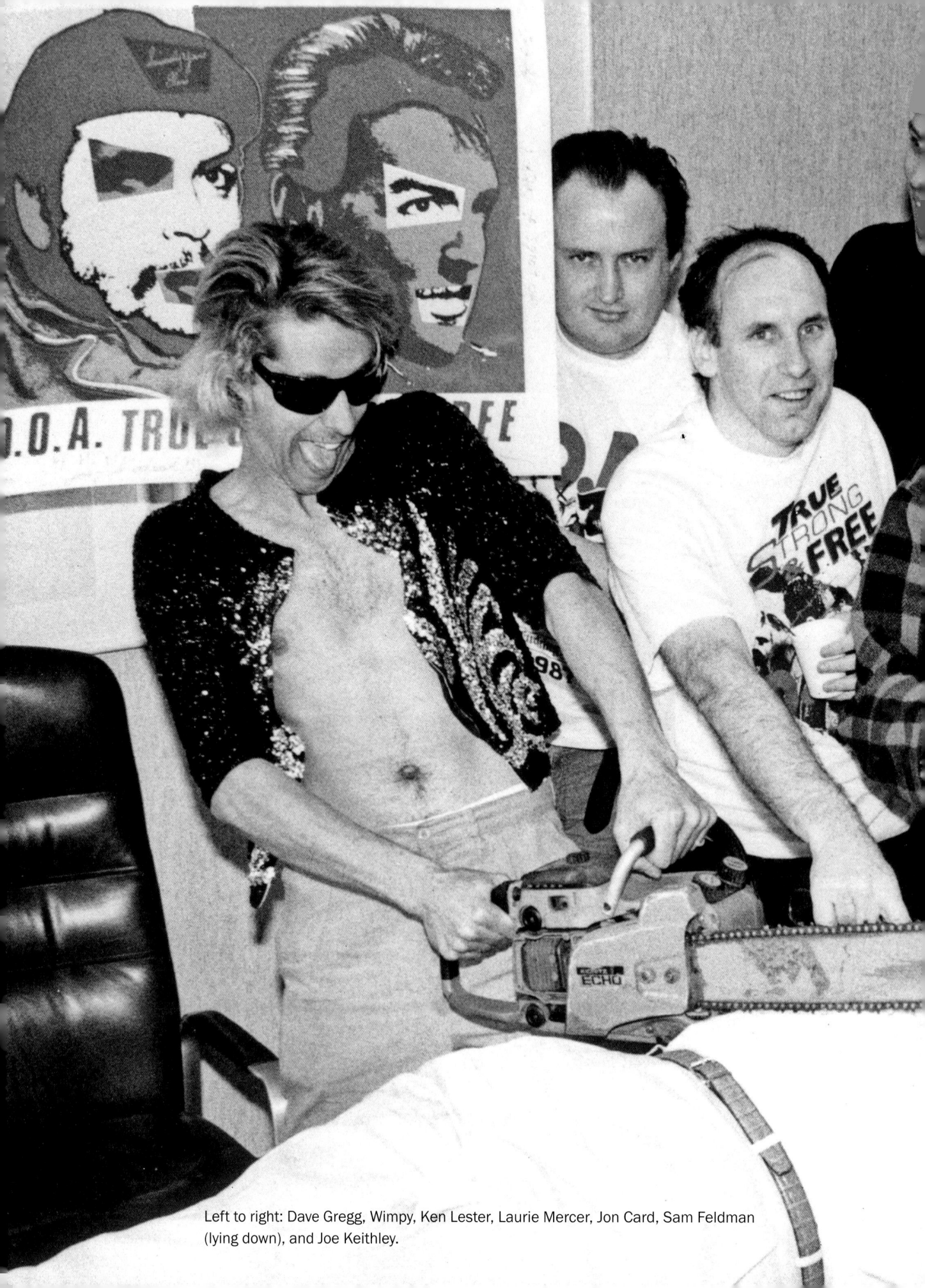

Left to right: Dave Gregg, Wimpy, Ken Lester, Laurie Mercer, Jon Card, Sam Feldman (lying down), and Joe Keithley.

Chapter 5

1986–1988

IT'S READY TO EXPLODE

In 1986, powerful drummer Jon Card came on board, and we recorded the album *True (North) Strong and Free*, released in 1987. We had signed to a new label after a monster show in New York City. That album spawned the "Taking Care of Business" video, in which D.O.A. played hockey with Randy Bachman as coach. This spawned our real hockey team, the D.O.A. Murder Squad, which, in turn, spawned a new musical subculture: Puck Rock.

We did a lot of cool benefits for causes such as saving the rain forests, buying an ambulance for Soweto in South Africa, preventing the eviction of poor folks in Vancouver's downtown eastside, and lobbying for free university education. Toward the end of 1988, we were stuck in a horrible record deal; it was time for a shake-up. Dave Gregg left and was replaced on guitar by Chris Prohom. Ken Lester, our manager, left as well. It was time to reorganize and reinvigorate.

D.O.A.'s only 12" single for clubs: *It's Ready To Explode.*

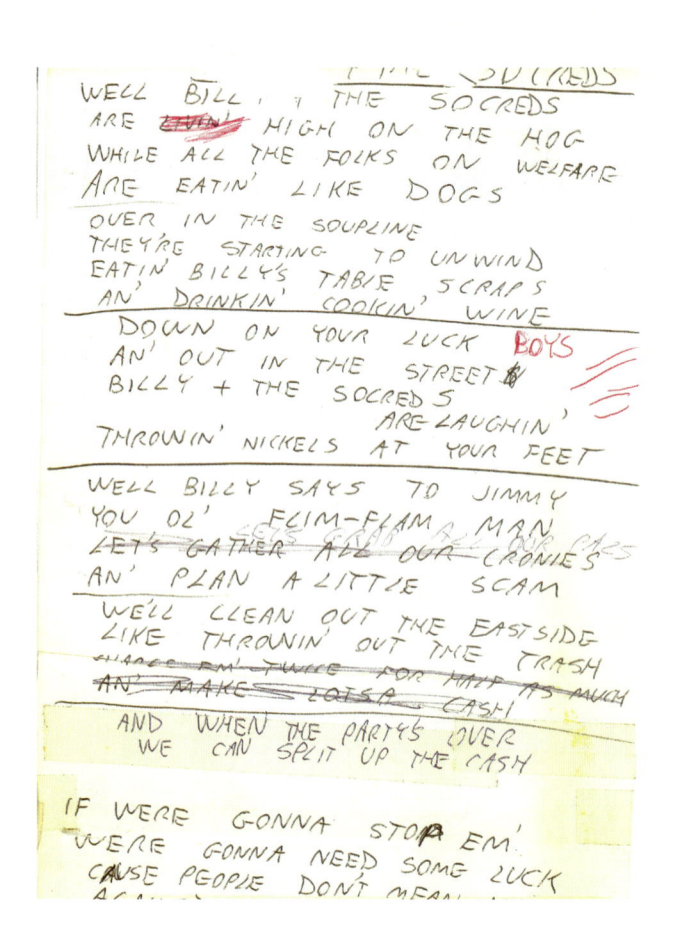

The Stein Valley was the last remaining unlogged watershed in south western British Columbia. In the mid '80s this magnificent forest was in danger of being turned into lumber and toilet paper by logging companies. A group of activists asked D.O.A. to play an anti-logging benefit. On May 17 we arrived in the tiny town of Lillooet, BC, to do the show. We were greeted by a line-up of fifty logging trucks and loggers who were protesting against D.O.A.'s protest show. We received various verbal and phone threats claiming "blood will be spilled" and "let's chainsaw 'em" if the show went ahead. The show did—and we survived. Through the efforts of many activists, the valley was not logged.

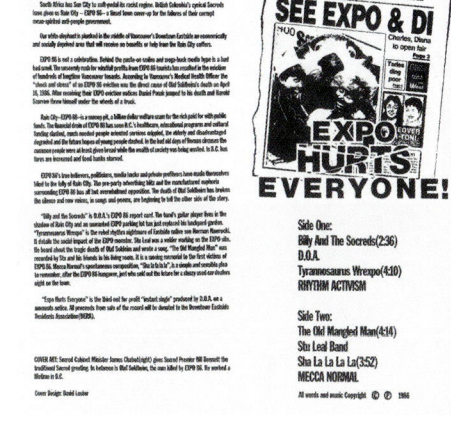

Vancouver hosted a World's Fair called Expo 86. At first it seemed the six-month exposition would be an interesting event, but to make room for the tourists, hotel and rooming house owners started throwing long-time tenants out just to increase profits. A lot of people had nowhere to go; one old guy, Olaf Solhein, committed suicide (by jumping out his window) after getting evicted. People in the city were outraged. We released this 7-inch benefit EP, *Expo Hurts Everyone*, on May 8, 1986.

PETE SEEGER · ARLO GUTHRIE
With D.O.A. And Other Performers To Be Announced
IN·AID·OF·EXPO·EVICTEES

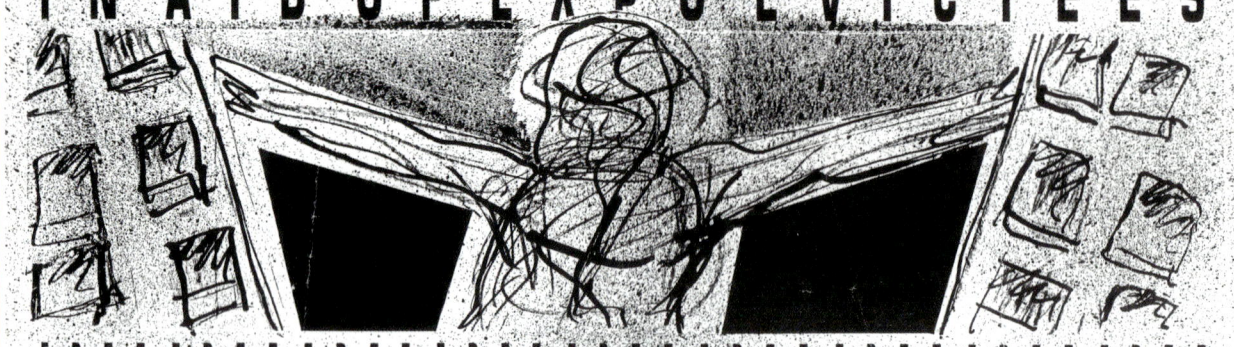

FREE FREE FREE FREE FREE FREE FREE FREE FREE
SUNDAY, MAY 25, 2-6 PM, MALKIN BOWL (STANLEY PARK)
SPONSORED BY THE CITY OF VANCOUVER & VANCOUVER FOLK FESTIVAL SOCIETY & VANCOUVER PARKS BOARD. MORE INFO: FOLK FESTIVAL OFFICE 879-2931

From left to right: Pete Seeger, Arlo Guthrie, Stu Leal, Wimpy, Joe, Dave Gregg.

From left to right: Dave, Joe, and Jim Green.

Vancouver activist Jim Green and the Downtown Eastside Residents Association (DERA) organized a benefit show for the homeless evictees from Expo 86. D.O.A. played a semi-acoustic set because the Vancouver Parks Board said our music would scare the animals at the nearby zoo and our fans might trample the fauna in the park (both statements were at least partially true). After D.O.A. played a rousing set, Pete Seeger and Arlo Guthrie put on a wonderful performance. The event raised $10,000 for the evicted.

A short time later, we had a weekend of shows at the Smilin' Buddha in Vancouver. We presented DERA with a cheque from the proceeds of the *Expo Hurts Everyone* EP sales.

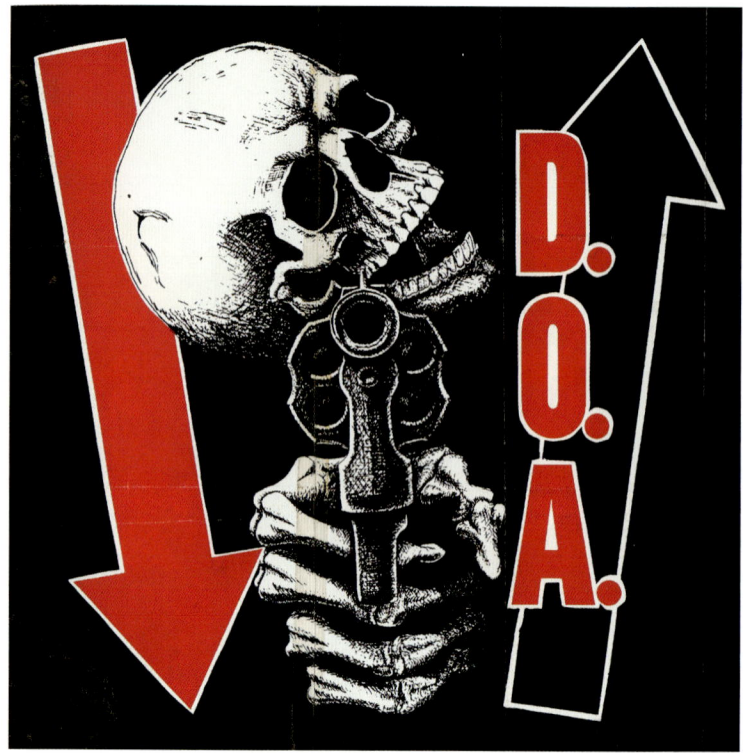

In 1986 we started using this design for T-shirts, and later on, for poster and album art. Anthony Kiedis wore a white version in the Red Hot Chili Peppers' "Under the Bridge" video. This came about because Jon Card and Wimpy played golf with Kiedis and Flea one day in L.A. No word on the Chilis' handicaps, but I suspect Jon Card won the tournament.

D.O.A. - "TO HELL AN' BACK" - D.O.A.

-JUNE 86- -COMMUNIQUE-

"It took us a long time to get to the bottom an' we ain't stoppin' there!!"

George Wainborn could'nt stop 'em; Polish and German border guards could'nt stop 'em; angry loggers could'nt stop 'em; riots in L.A. and Frankfurt could'nt stop 'em; not even Tyrannosaurus Wrexpo could stop 'em!

-Out of adversity comes strength hope and humour-

D.O.A. - READY TO GO - With a fresh set o' tunes, a new drummer - He's John Card, he used to belt it out for S.N.F.U. and Personality Crisis - and a new album in the works.

As time has gone by they've become more and more incontainable. The megadecible minstrels have been branded "PUNK - HEAVY METAL" - "HARDCORE" - "HARDROCK"!!! But always lookin' to break down any new barrier, they've now had the handle of "FOLK" tossed their way, following their recent appearence with Pete Seeger and Arlo Guthrie. Well I guess D.O.A.'s been the electronic folk music of the eighties all along anyways.

Well on the heels of the overwhelming successful concert in Stanley Park that raised money for the EXPO Evictees - D.O.A. goes, " To Hell an' Back" to the less than glamorous surroundings of the lower eastside. Right back where they started, back to the Smilin' Buddha. Right back to the heart of a community that's struggling to survive under the bloated weight of EXPO.

When? Welfare weekend of course! Friday June 27th and Saturday the 28th. Tickets are $5.00. On the Saturday nite, Jim Green from D.E.R.A. will be there to receive the proceeds from the benefit E.P. "Expo Hurts Everyone" from D.O.A. and friends in a special cheque bouncing to the moon ceremony. Crisis music for Crisis times.

All this on the eve of D.O.A.'s summer "To Hell an' Back" ramble through the U.S.A., 22 dates in 35 days. Firing right across the continent to <u>Milwaukee, July 4th,</u> sweeping through the midwest out to New York to headline at the Ritz, July 14th, in a show sponsored by the New Music Seminar. Then swingin' through the Eastern Seaboard and marching on down to the sea, by way of Atlanta. Then cutting back through the heartland, to arrive home August 6th.

Jesus, by then it'll be time for them to finish recording their 5th album.

- Ah... ever onward and downward!

- more later.....

TO HELL AN' BACK

WE DRIVE AT NITE, DRIVE AT NITE
GO RIGHT PAST YA AND A CLEAR OUTA SIGHT
TAKE THE DARK PASSAGE THROUGH THE EMPTY NITE
HIT THE HI-WAY, YEAH WITH ALL OF OUR MIGHT
LIKE A FREIGHTTRAIN ROLLIN' DOWN THE TRACK
WE'LL KNOCK RIGHT OVER AN' GIVE YA A WHACK
YEAH WE'RE DRIVIN' TO HELL AN' BACK

LIKE A WAR LIKE A WAR
GOTTA PUSH AHEAD, LIKE WE DONE IT BEFORE
YOU KNOW THE COUNT AN' I KNOW THE SCORE
YEAH GETTIN' READY FOR THE FUN IN STORE
GOT NO TIME TO GET UNPACKED
GIMME SOME ROOM, GIMME SOME SLACK
YEAH WE'RE DRIVIN' TO HELL AN' BACK

YEAH WE'RE DRIVIN', YEAH WE'RE DRIVIN'
KEEP ON DRIVIN' TO HELL AN' BACK

PUSH IT TO THE LIMIT, PUSH IT TO THE LIMIT
IT'S A NEW FRONTIER, CAN'T WAIT A MINUTE
GOT SOME ROOM I GOTTA ADMIT
SO CLIMB ON BOARD, AN' GET ON IT
HOLDIN' BACK AN' THINGS ARE BLACK
IT MUST BE TIME, TO LOSE THE PACK
YEAH WE'RE DRIVIN' TO HELL AN' BACK

WE DRIVE AT NITE, DRIVE AT NITE
BLAST RIGHT PAST YA AN' A CLEAR OUTA SIGHT
TAKE THE DARK PASSAGE ...

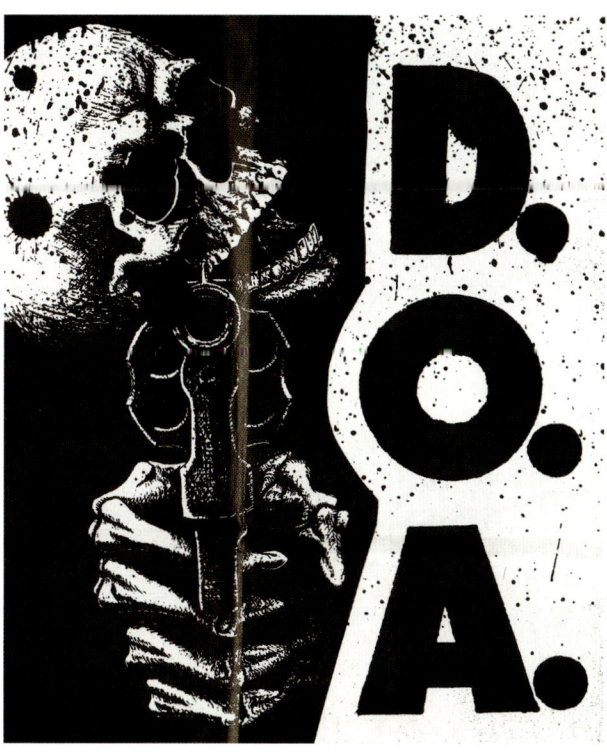

While on our To Hell 'n' Back tour with No Means No, Dave Gregg pulled a Hendrix with his Strat at the On Broadway in San Francisco.

The Outhouse was just outside Lawrence, Kansas. It was an indestructible cinderblock building in the middle of a corn field, so you could not bother anybody. The first thing you did when you got there was coat yourself with insect repellent or be bitten alive. I don't even want to think what happened to the kids who went out and had sex in the cornfield. Because it was in the middle of the field, they charged admission by the car load. We played there about six times, and it was one of the best venues anywhere.

CYCLONE PRODUCTIONS PRESENTS:
VAN.BC.
FRI. JULY 18
D.O.A.
+
CORROSION OF CONFORMITY
FROM N.C.
ALSO...
"Dress Up and Die!"
NJ's Skulls
W. PHILLY's
SERIAL KILLERS
GIRARD BALLROOM
6th & GIRARD AVES
8:00 PM
ALL AGES

Anne Murray
D.O.A

CLUB RED
PRESENTS
mon. JULY 7
D.O.A.
WITH
NO MEANS NO
FROM VANCOUVER B.C., CANADA
204 S. Fifth
Champaign Ill
Champaign Urbana Golf Core
INFO: 359-9468 John/Paul
367-7005 Josh
$4.00 Donation
BE THERE EARLY (7:00) OR YOU'LL MISS IT!! OVER BY 10:30
Alternative Anything
AT THE REQUEST OF THE CHAMPAIGN POLICE NO ALCHOHOL WILL BE PERMITTED AT CLUB RED OR ON ITS PROPERTY
COME ON, HELP US OUT HERE

(250)
SEC ROW SEAT
GA GA 253
ALL AGES
DOOR
ADULT $5.00
NO REFUNDS OR EXCHANGES
D.O.A.
PRESENTED BY KJHK AND REDLINE
THE OUTHOUSE
ALL AGES/THR NITE
JULY 31 '86 9PM
TAX INCLUDED
ADULT $5.00
ALL AGES
GA GA 253
SEC ROW SEAT
ADULT $5.00
DOOR
ALL AGES
GA GA 253

PROFILE RECORDING ARTISTS

D.O.A.

PERFORMING SONGS FROM THEIR NEW ALBUM
"TRUE (north) STRONG & FREE"

SPECIAL GUESTS

RANDY BACHMAN & DENISE McCANN

DUANE O'KANE PRODUCTION
& OXFAM CANADA PRESENT

WARNER/REPRISE RECORDING ARTISTS

54-40

DEATH SENTENCE

ARTISTS AGAINST APARTHEID

FRIDAY NOV. 14th

COMMODORE BALLROOM

DOORS OPEN: 8 PM, TICKETS $8
TICKETS AVAILABLE AT ALL
VTC/CBO TICKET OUTLETS

ALL PROCEEDS GO TO
OXFAM CANADA TO AID
ANTI-APARTHEID PROGRAMS
IN SOUTH AFRICA

Design: David Lester/Get To The Point Graphics

OXFAM and Duane O'Kane Productions Present:

ARTISTS AGAINST APARTHEID BENEFIT CONCERT

Featuring:

DOA
54-40
Randy Bachman
&
Denise McCann
Death Sentence

COMMODORE BALLROOM 870 Granville

FRIDAY, November 14   8 P.M.

Tickets: $8.00 at all VTC/CBO Outlets
Further Information - Call OXFAM - 736-7678

All proceeds to OXFAM projects in South Africa.

Apartheid was still the rule of law in South Africa, so we did our bit to help out against that bullshit. D.O.A. gave more than 200 benefit shows over the years for various just causes, but this was probably my favourite. The money from the show was given to OXFAM, which bought an ambulance for the people in Soweto, South Africa.

At this all-ages show in Victoria, BC with No Means No, a bunch of goons attacked the kids in the audience. Boy, were they surprised when the punks fought back. It spilled out onto the street. The punks tore apart a nearby picket fence and used the lumber to chase away the goons, who had their collective tails tucked firmly between their legs.

CFUV 105.1 F.M. PRESENTS:

D.O.A.

WITH GUESTS:
NOMEANSNO
AND
MISSION OF CHRIST

SATURDAY, DECEMBER 6 1986
FERNWOOD COMM. CENTRE
1240 gladstone
8:30 PM

TICKETS: $10 ADVANCE
$12 DOOR

AVAILABLE AT LYLES, CATAPULT & MEZZROW'S

MINORS WELCOME

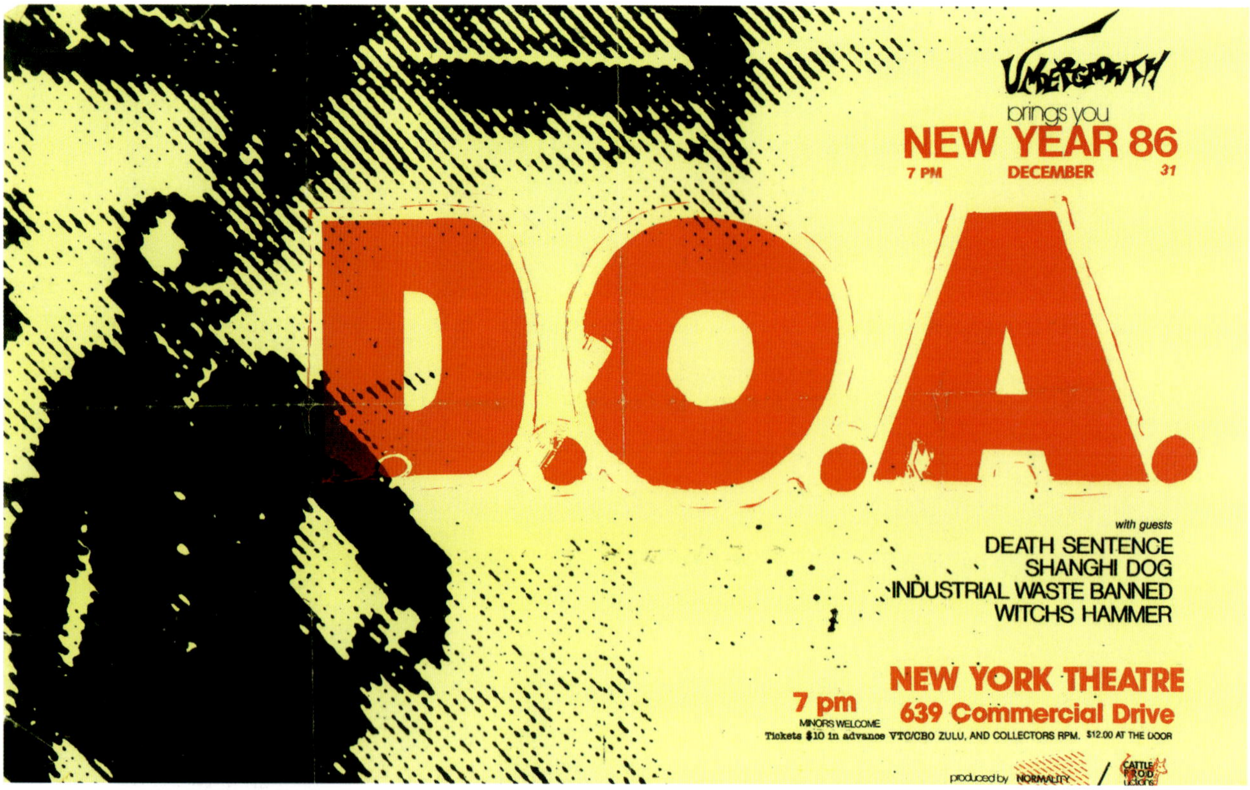
brings you
NEW YEAR 86
7 PM DECEMBER 31
D.O.A.
with guests
DEATH SENTENCE
SHANGHI DOG
INDUSTRIAL WASTE BANNED
WITCHS HAMMER
NEW YORK THEATRE
7 pm
639 Commercial Drive
MINORS WELCOME
Tickets $10 in advance VTC/CBO ZULU, AND COLLECTORS RPM. $12.00 AT THE DOOR
produced by NORMALITY / CATTLE PROD uctions

MARKS

THE TOWN PUMP PRESENTS
D.O.A.
TRUE NORTH STRONG & FREE
FEBRUARY 12
THE
TOWN PUMP
GASTOWN·683·6695

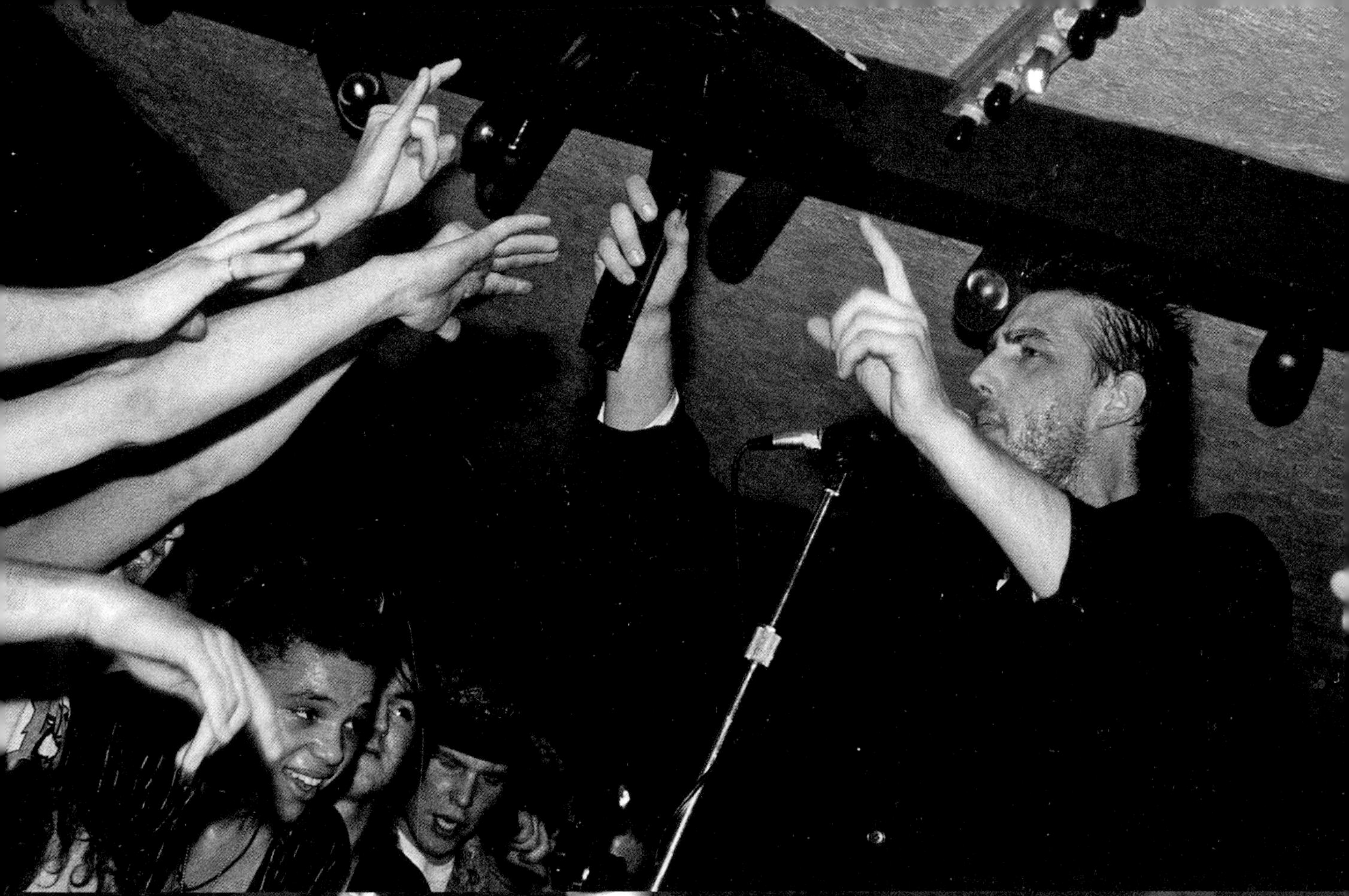

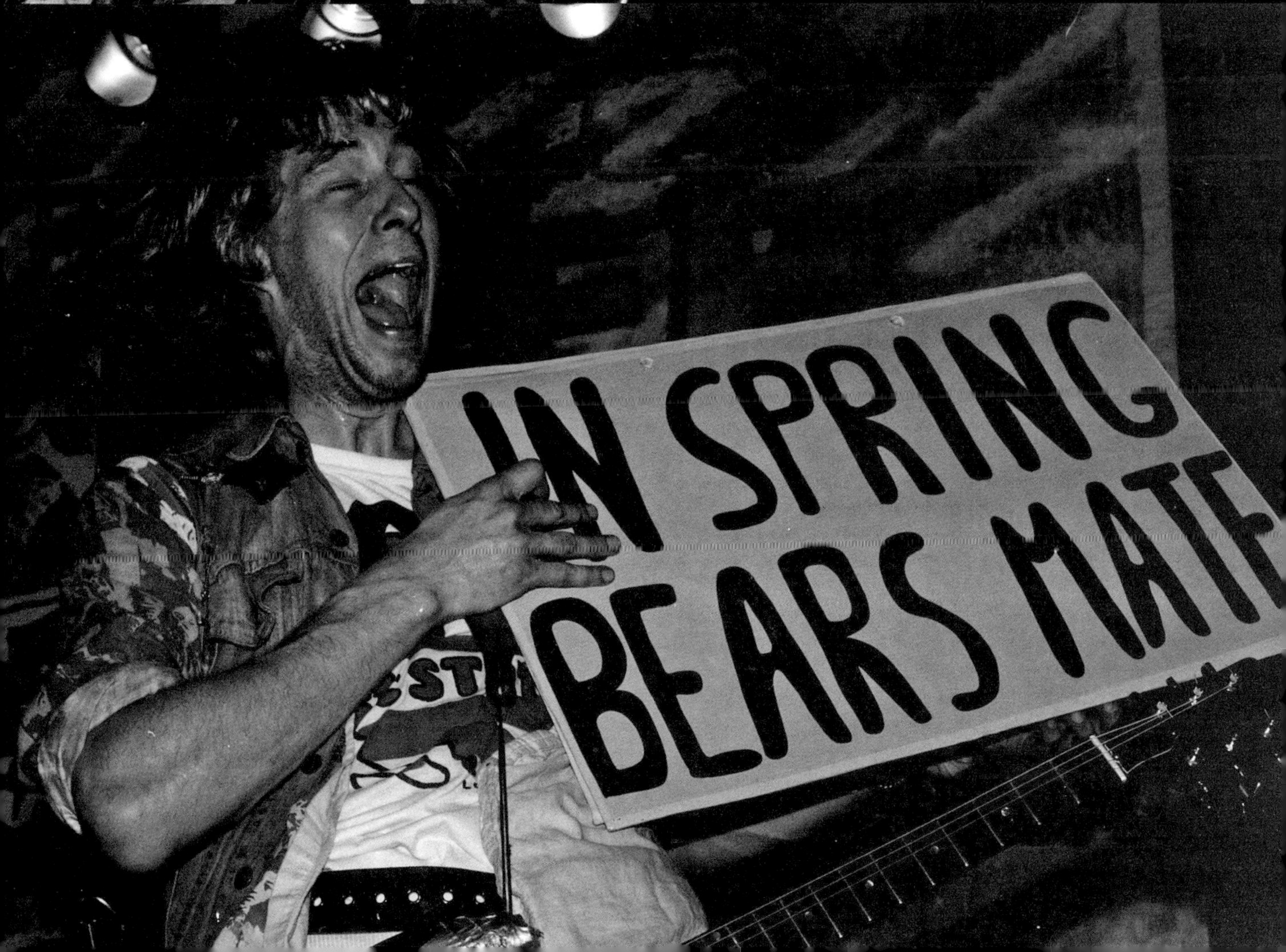
IN SPRING
BEARS MATE

In the fall of 1986 we played at the New Music Seminar in NYC and were signed to a record deal with Rock Hotel/Profile Records. *True (North) Strong & Free* was recorded in the later part of 1986 at Profile Studios (no connection to Profile Records) and was co-produced and engineered by Cecil English. It was released February 10, 1987.

For the *True (North) Strong & Free* tour, we purchased an old school bus and painted it red. The name plate on the front of the bus read "Miss Piggy," and we found out why it earned that nickname. Over the next sixteen months, it broke down repeatedly and bankrupted the tour. The shirt below was designed by our friend Iain Ross (Curious George). It seemed prophetic with the flames coming out of the back of the bus.

We made a tour brochure (facing page) which was mailed to every member of the Money-Grubbing Fan Club.

D.O.A.'s NEW ALBUM: "TRUE(north), STRONG & FREE"

IT'S THE DAWNING OF A NEW ERROR. . . D.O.A. HAS risen and roared from the Great White Wastelands creating the album we were all hoping for. Last Fall, the dreaded axe-murderers tore into Vancouver's Profile Studio with a vengeance. The result is D.O.A.'s self-produced "True(north), Strong & Free."

THIS TIME, D.O.A. WANTED AN ALBUM THAT REFLECTED the primal scream of their live show. TSF is forged in sweat and tempered with a ragged diamond hard spirit. It's an album about survival and determination, never giving up. D.O.A. launches a musical insurgency, with topical songs, beer-belly humour and power chords ripping the living heart of Hardcore Rock out of the hands of cynical idolmakers, technicians and businessmen.

"TRUE(NORTH), STRONG & FREE" CHISELS AWAY THE sugar-coating and exposes the spineless formula rock that is clogging up the airwaves. D.O.A. is like acid burning through the stagnation of current shlock-rock. The screams we hear herald a new Rock Renaissance, an outburst of truly creative energy. Rock outlaws are tearing up the pop-culture musical rule books again and D.O.A.'s intense new album is in the thick of the fight.

D.O.A. NEVER TAKES THE PRESSURE OFF. THEY ARE REAL Canadian Hockey Rock: an aggressive offence, a brutal defense of ideas and relentless non-stop action. TSF opens with **To Hell An' Back** hammering home the spirit and resolve needed to defeat adversity and return stronger, again and again. Then comes the true Canuck national anthem, **Takin' Care of Business**, Bachman-Turner Overdrive's classic, renovated with humour and respect, by fans (BTO was the first major Rock band the D.O.A. guys ever saw.) **Bullet Catcher** chronicles the fate of those who work for the Masters of War. **Endless Sky** celebrates vision and hope. **Ready To Explode** was inspired by Manu Dibango's African song "Dangwa." D.O.A.'s mechanical royalties for this song will be donated to the African National Congress to fight apartheid in South Africa.

SIDE 2: BEGINS WITH ANOTHER SLICE OF CANADIANA, **Lumberjack City**, and ends with **51st State** where "all the stars are overweight." In between is the difficult to get D.O.A. classic, **Nazi Training Camp**, on an album for the first time, updated for the flag wavin' fools" who will have their flags "tagged to a body bag." Next is **None But the Brave**, D.O.A.'s only real love song. **Power Play** is about the evil that ravages us all.

"TRUE(NORTH), STRONG & FREE" IS AVAILABLE ON VINYL and cassette and will be D.O.A.'s first Compact Disc. It is likely **Takin' Care of Business** b/w **Ready To Explode** will be released as a 12" 45 for radio play.

Jon Card

D.O.A.: THE NEW CREW, SCHOOL BUS & TALES OUT OF SCHOOL

YOU CAN'T MISS D.O.A. ON THE ROAD THIS YEAR. THEY'LL be driving a big bright black and red school bus. The new face on stage is drummer **Jon Card**, formerly of the legendary Personality Crisis and SNFU fame (he drums on the latter's recent album: "If You Swear, You'll Catch No Fish"). Winnipeg's **Mike Lambert** is the new Road Manager. He has worked with MDC and M.I.A. on previous tours and has promoted the bulk of his hometown's decent alternative gigs. Roady this trip is **Chris Crud** who toured Canada with the Enigma's and the U.S. last year with No Means No.

SHOWMAN, JON CARD APPEARS AS RUFUS LEE KING IN **Mr. Nausea's (Dave Gregg)** fuck band the **Groovaholics**, a unit which features credible renditions of 70's Disco chestnuts, freaking out those critics who can't believe hardcore guys who first proclaimed "Disco Sucks" can now pack dance floors and earn beaucoup bucks pumping out funk and disco grooves. Some people aren't even laughing.

D.O.A.'S FRONTMAN, JOEY "SHITHEAD" KEIGHLEY, JUST got married for the second time. He's finished putting together an album for the Polish band **Dezerters**. Joe met the band when D.O.A. toured Poland and brought their tapes to the West. The album should be released on the Maximum Rock 'n' Roll label this summer. D.O.A. bass player, **Brian Goble**, has just become a father. Joe and Brian are working on the title cut and soundtrack album for **Terminal City**, a movie to be shot in Vancouver this summer and released later this year. All the D.O.A. guys and **Jello Biafra** are slated for appearances in the film.

CRUSADE '87 D.O.A. TOURS AMERICA

THE GUYS IN D.O.A. ARE IN GREAT SPIRITS, VERY CONFident and excited about their new album and developing new band projects. They feel there is a huge hole in the musical spectrum begging for inspired, committed rockers of all styles. Bands that push everything to the limit.

CRUSADE '87 IS THE FIRST PHASE OF D.O.A.'S EVANGELical onslaught supporting "True(north), Strong & Free" and their belief that not everyone is going along for the yuppie, soft-cock, big-hair, pseudo-rambo, reaganite approach to music and life. D.O.A. intends to keep on screamin' as long as it hurts. Topical content and gutsy effort are their own reward. The band will be experimenting with a stage show as large as the venues and their financial resources will allow. They have three new backdrops, including a Haida-style Raven, symbol of creativity and trickery—warning "followers" to examine all ideas for themselves and not follow "leaders" or "stars." If time permits the Raven will have an 8'x8' screen for appropriate projections in its body. Crusade '87 will see D.O.A. perform all the songs from the new album and revive some fave raves not seen in recent years.

REMEMBER THE LAST TOUR? THE FURIOUS SCHEDULE, including the Gruel-a-thon, continuous gigging for 7 months. D.O.A. played 133 shows in 105 different cities, in 13 countries on two continents. They travelled from Anchorage, Alaska to Warsaw, Poland, halfway around the world. They used 9 trucks (two blown engines and multiple blown tires), 11 planes, 19 trains and six ferries to travel 70,000 miles, or well over 2.5 times around the globe. Over 60,000 people saw the band live in Canada, U.S., U.K., Holland, Denmark, Sweden, Norway, Germany, Poland, Switzerland, Italy, France and Belgium.

"NO ONE CAN DO IT ALONE," DAVE GREGG HAS POINTED out. "There is a community of kindred spirits out there—people who make it possible for a truly popular culture to exist."

D.O.A. PLAYED BENEFITS RANGING FROM 10,000 PEOPLE at an anti-Expo concert in Vancouver, where the guys co-billed with Pete Seeger and Arlo Guthrie, to an anti-apartheid concert headlined by D.O.A. which raised $10,000 and purchased a fully equipped ambulance to be used in the South African township of Soweto. At that concert BTO's Randy Bachman joined D.O.A. for a rendition of "Takin' Care of Business." In playing with Seeger and Bachman D.O.A. seems to have found the lost chord that can unite diverse musical styles around an issue. Getting folkies, punks and rockers together is no mean feat.

FOLLOWING CRUSADE '87 D.O.A. HOPES TO PULL OFF their most ambitious fantasy-to-date—an experimental intense-a-thon, a Rock'n'Roll Circus/Carnival. Three busloads of friends, bands, musicians, poets, performers, politicos, comedians, etc. who will descend on your community for a week or so presenting a multi-media event that those attacked will never forget. D.O.A. wants to break down the boundaries of what is possible and broaden participation in an activist vision that cynics don't believe can exist. D.O.A. is saying all of us should be inspired to live our own lives, not just dress up in the current style or join a group for a few hours of entertainment. The Rock'n'Roll Circus is looking for cities to victimize. If you think your city or campus has a 1,000 plus capacity hall and the potential interest to support an intense-a-thon write D.O.A. c/o Crisis Management, Ltd.

CRUSADE '87: D.O.A.'s U.S. TOUR (so far)

March
10-PROVIDENCE, R.I.-The Living Room
11-NORWALK, CT.-Anthrax
12-BALTIMORE, MD.-Channel One
13-NEW YORK, N.Y.-The Ritz
14-TRENTON, N.J.-City Gardens
15-PHILADELPHIA, PA-Club Pizazz
16-WASHINGTON, D.C.-930 Club
17-PITTSBURGH, PA-Electric Banana
18-
19-DAYTON, OH-Gilly's
20-CINCINNATI, OH-Bogarts
21-DETROIT, MI.-Token Lounge
22-CHICAGO, IL-Metro
23-MILWAUKEE, WI.-Cafe Voltaire
24-MINNEAPOLIS, MN.-First Avenue
25-
26-
27-MORGANTOWN, W.V.-Underground
28-RICHMOND, VA.-Rockitz
29-RALEIGH, N.C.-Brewery
30-ATLANTA, GA.-Metroplex
31-

April
1-GAINESVILLE, FL.-American Legion
2-
3-TAMPA, FL.-Ft. Homer Armory
4-MIAMI BEACH, FL.-Cameo Theatre
5-
6-
7-ATHENS, GA.-THE UPTOWN
8-BIRMINGHAM, AL-THE NICK
9-DALLAS, TX-THEATER GALLERY
10-HOUSTON, TX-
11-AUSTIN, TX-THE RITZ
12-
13-
14-TUCSON, AZ-NINO'S
15-PHOENIX, AZ-MASON JAR
16-SAN DIEGO, CA-
17-LONG BEACH, CA.-FENDERS
18-OXNARD, CA.-OXNARD COMMUNITY CENTER
19-
20-SAN JOSE, CA.-STAGE COACH INN
21-
22-SAN FRANCISCO, CA-THE MAB
23-SAN FRANCISCO, CA-THE MAB
24-SACRAMENTO, CA-CLUB CAN'T TELL
25-ARCATA, CA-THE DEPOT
26-RENO, NV.-
27-
28-ASHLAND, CA-
29-BEND, OR-
30-

May
1-SEATTLE, WA./TACOMA, WA.
2-PORTLAND, OR.-

D.O.A. CONTACT ADDRESSES

1. "MONEY GRUBBING" FAN CLUB
2. CRISIS MANAGEMENT, LTD.
3. .001 LOSERS' CLUB

Write all those c/o:
P.O. Box 65896, Station "F,"
Vancouver, B.C., Canada. V5L 4B6.

1. THE "Money Grubbing" Fan Club is a general contact address. Send $1. U.S. with each letter to get notification of D.O.A. gigs in your area. Mail Order catalogue, Discography, Family Tree sheet or personal correspondence with D.O.A. guys.
2. Crisis Management, Ltd. handles D.O.A.'S business and legal affairs, as well as, requests for interviews, personal appearances, special projects, Circuses, videos, movies, etc.
3. The .001 Losers' Club costs $15. U.S. per year to join. See article in this newsletter for details.

PROFILE/ROCK HOTEL RECORDS
740 Broadway, 7th Floor
New York, N.Y. 10003

Info on new D.O.A. releases, 45s, EP's, tapes, Compact Discs, etc. They service radio and TV stations with promo records, videos, etc. and provide basic bio material, [illegible] and review copies for fanzines and other media.

BANDWAGON ENTERTAINMENT
Att: Andy Somers
Box 5125, F.D.R. Station
New York, N.Y. 10150

Handles D.O.A.'s concerts and club bookings.

.001 LOSERS' CLUB

IT HAS SIMPLY BECOME TOO EXPENSIVE TO MAILOUT D.O.A. newsletters and info packets for free via the "Money Grubbing" Fan Club. [illegible] the MGFC will be a contact address. Letters containing $1. U.S. will get a Mail Order price list, a discography, a D.O.A. family tree, etc. if requested. Letters and questions will be forwarded to the band members for reply. Addresses will be added to the mailing list but a postcard will only be mailed when D.O.A. is coming to your area.

INSTEAD OF THE MGFC, D.O.A. IS STARTING THE .001 Losers' Club to keep fans informed. For $15. U.S. per year .001 Losers will receive: three newsletters a year, an autographed picture, access to special issue records or "instant singles," stickers and assorted gig posters when available, first dibs on novelty merchandise, political diatribes, etc., updated press kit information, promo posters, etc., notification and access to the first copies of new releases and test-pressings. You'll get a membership card, and when possible, guest list and party privileges and full access to the intense-a-thon, Rock'n'Roll Circus. The first 100 people to sign up for .001 Losers' Club will be able to get the "Che/Elvis" limited edition silkscreen for $10. U.S.

Design: David Lester/Get To The Point ▶ Graphics

"CHE/ELVIS" SILKSCREEN

IN THE LATE 50'S, REVOLUTIONARY icons, Che Guevara and Elvis Presley, ascended the international charts together. They were fresh air in a conservative decade strangling in the grip of the Cold War and the shadow of the Atomic Bomb. Each, in their own way, represented hope and vitality, opening up the future, taking Rock & Revolution in directions no one could predict.

"CHE/ELVIS," A 25" x 31", 4 COLOUR, limited edition (270) silkscreen, signed and numbered by the artist, David Lester, is available from D.O.A. Mailorder for $20.(U.S.) Charter members of D.O.A.'s new .001 Losers' Club can get it for only $10.(U.S.)

THE DAWNING OF A NEW ERROR...

D.O.A. TRUE STRONG & FREE

Thanks to Bev Davies and Alex Waterhouse-Hayward for the Photos.

D.O.A. MAIL ORDER

WRITE TO D.O.A.'S "MONEY GRUBBING" CONTACT Address for a list of available Mail Order merchandise. Send $1. U.S. to cover postage, etc.

ON THE TOUR, D.O.A. WILL HAVE A RANGE OF NEW T-shirt designs, beer mugs, bandanas, bumper stickers, two colour stickers (12 different designs to a packet), and the "Che/Elvis" silkscreen. All at the usual inflated tour prices, but. . .you don't have to wait 6 weeks for the wrong order. Retailers interested in bulk orders should contact Crisis Management, Ltd. for details.

D.O.A.

THE DAWNING OF A NEW ERROR... SPRING 1987

FINDS D.O.A., AS ALWAYS, TRUE, STRONG & FREE, PART of a real Rock Renaissance, an intense

NEW ALBUM OUT

THEY ARE READY TO EXPLODE, DRIVING THEMSELVES TO HELL AN' BACK, demolishing NAZI TRAINING CAMPS of all types, menial, musical or physical, while refusing to be BULLET CATCHERS in anybody's POWER PLAY. D.O.A. leaves LUMBERJACK CITY in the 51st STATE for

U.S. TOUR DATES

SEARCHING FOR THE ENDLESS SKY OF THE LAST FRONTIER. In the classic tradition of Rock & Revolution, D.O.A. is making a

"CHE/ELVIS" PRINT

AVAILABLE TO ALL THOSE SPIRITS INTERESTED IN TAKIN' CARE OF BUSINESS and breaking down the barriers to Freedom. NONE BUT THE BRAVE (and even some of us cowards) are invited to make the one in a thousand

.001 LOSERS' CLUB

A GREASE COVERED, PIMPLE POPPING, SWEAT DRENCHED, howling reality.
READ ON. . .

INSIDE

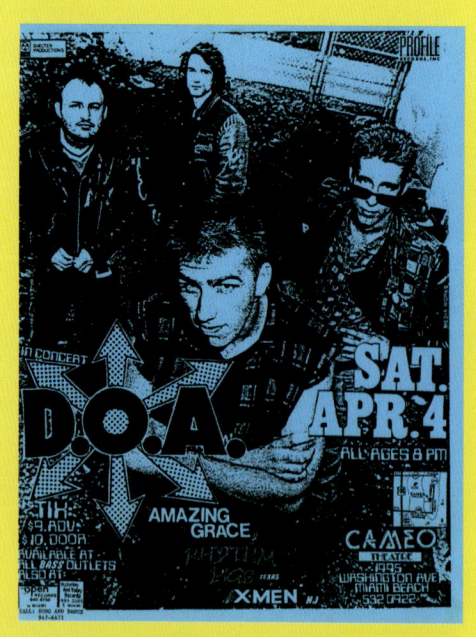

We should have known better than to book an April Fool's Day show in Gainsville, Florida; there wasn't a whole lot to gain. The promoter tried to stiff us until our 300-lb (180 kg) buddy Ed Pitman (Toxic Reasons) joined the negotiations.

When we arrived at the Cameo Theater to play our first-ever show in Miami, we heard a kid had been stabbed at the theatre that day. The cops wanted to cancel our show, so I forked over some cashola to the two that were on scene. They took the cash, casually hung out, and the show went on. That night, our tour manager, Mike Lambert, was sleeping in Miss Piggy as the night watchman when some gangbangers tried to get inside. They probably would have killed Mike and taken all the gear, but he scared them off with a baseball bat.

TRUE STRONG & FREE

D.O.A.

ACROSS CANADA 1986

"D.O.A. is the best hardrock band in the world."

"D.O.A. kicks ass.
D.O.A. is a lot of fun and deadly serious. The very thing that pulled us all out of a slumber in the first place. The beast is alive, praise the lord..."

D.O.A.
WITH:
OUTCRY
TUESDAY
MARCH 24
4:00 PM
ALL AGE SHOW

FIRST AVENUE & 7th St entry
The Downtown Danceteria

A VINTAGE FABULOUS WALLY PRINT FROM WALLY INDS

We started using this design for posters and T-shirts after Dave Lester combined Che and Elvis.

Punk rock poster design 101: use icons to attract attention to your show, especially ones that kick ass.

ROCK ON!

WED. SEPTEMBER 30th

THE TOWN PUMP

66 WATER

$6

D.O.A.

THE SCRAMBLERS

THE SICK ONES

RANDY RAMPAGE   ZIPPY PINHEAD

BRAD KENT   BENNY DORO

JUNE 1, 87

IMMEDIATE NOTIFICATION + PLUG DEPT.

BRIEF NOTES FROM THE FORCES ONGOING WAR DIARY...

BELIVE IT OR NOT, D.O.A. VENTURE'S INTO THE WILDS OF SURREY, TO SHOOTER'S CABERET IN NEWTON — LEST YOU READ SOMETHING INTO A NAME, FLAK JACKETS ARE NOT REQUIRED. THIS FORAY WILL HAPPEN MON. JUNE 8th...

ALSO UPCOMING IN MORE FAMILIAR ENVIRONS, D.O.A WILL BE BLASTING IT OUT AT THE LUV-A-FAIR, THURS. JUNE 11th. OPENING UP WILL BE THE NEWLY FORMED "TIN GOD" RISING UP FROM THE ASHES OF SHANGHAI DOG — TIN GOD ARE MIKE GRAHAM (SHANGHAI DOG, SUBHUMANS) DOUG ANDREWS (SHANGHAI DOG) BRUCE WALTHER (SOLDIERS OF SPORT) + KEN MORRISON (CELEBRITY DRUNKS)

ALSO ON THE BILL, DIRECT FROM HUMBOLDT COUNTY, CALIFORNIA — AGENT 86 — I DON'T KNOW IF THE CHIEF WOULD APPROVE, BUT THERE YOU HAVE IT!

MORE LATER...

P.O. Box 65896, Station F,
Vancouver, B.C., Canada V5L 4B6

Cool show at Graceland in Vancouver with the Beatnigs (who later became the Disposable Heroes of Hiphoprisy) in support of free speech in El Salvador. The eclectic bill raised a bunch of dough for the people's radio station.

Ken Lester came up with the idea to have non-stop performances on the main stage and side stages, and to throw in a bunch of booths as well—a couple of years before Lollapalooza started. He called it the Intens-i-thon.

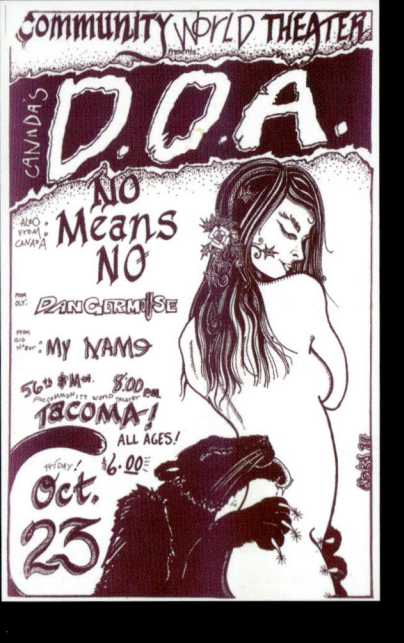

The Jockey Club in Newport, Kentucky had a fabulous history as the centre of nightlife in the Midwest's wide open Sin City back in the 60s. Patrons included Elvis, Frank Sinatra, and Marilyn Monroe, who were entertained by greats like Chubby Checker and Chuck Berry. By the time the punks took it over in the '80s, the club's ceiling was falling down, there were holes kicked through the walls, and the bathrooms smelled like they hadn't been cleaned in thirty years. But what a place to play! D.O.A. played there ten times, which may have been the record for out of town bands.

NMN — TALK – ACTION = A GOOD DINNER PARTY

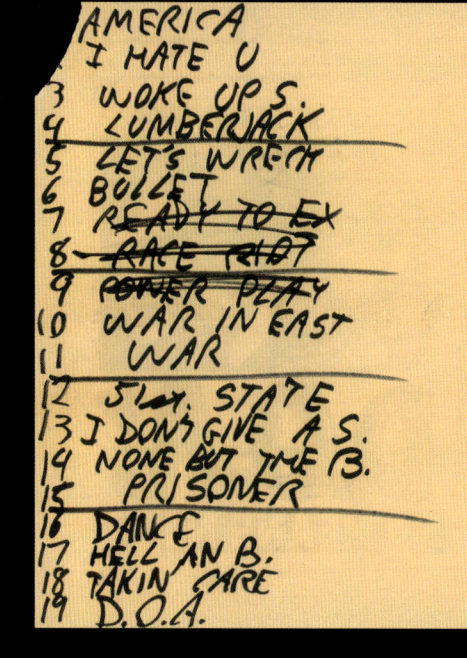

Setlist:
1. AMERICA
2. I HATE U
3. WOKE UP S.
4. LUMBERJACK
5. LET'S WRECK
6. BULLET
7. READY TO EX
8. ~~RACE RIOT~~
9. ~~POWER PLAY~~
10. WAR IN EAST
11. WAR
12. SL.. STATE
13. I DON'T GIVE A S.
14. NONE BUT THE B.
15. PRISONER
16. DANCE
17. HELL AN B.
18. TAKIN CARE
19. D.O.A.

D.O.A. / NO MEANS NO TOUR DE FORCE:
UPDATE, CANADIAN DATES & VENUES

Canada's rock'n'roll crusaders, D.O.A. and their amazing tour-mates NO MEANS NO, are moving into striking position for their winter assault on the Great White Wilderness. The two-fisted Tour de Force has just wrapped-up a whirlwind hard rock juggernaut which saw the Canuck double-threat knock-out audiences in 29 U.S. cities in 32 days. The tour overcame harsh weather conditions and vehicle breakdowns to show American audiences what Canada's rock'n'roll renaissance is all about. D.O.A. and NO MEANS NO play different brands of music but the spirit, commitment and intensity of their performances and musical visions turned sceptics into believers everywhere the tour stopped to play.

D.O.A., wild as ever, is fast expanding their audience appeal, featuring fantastic new material from their most recent album "TRUE(north), STRONG & FREE". Unfortunately, this new D.O.A. album is still only available as an import in Canada while the band's U.S. label, Profile/Rock Hotel, are negotiating a Canadian distribution deal for their entire catalogue. Even so, "TRUE(north), STRONG & FREE" has become D.O.A.'s best-selling album ever on the basis of U.S. sales alone.

D.O.A.'s video for "Takin' Care Of Business", off the album, should show-up on MuchMusic and other video outlets starting this week. It shows D.O.A. performing live on stage and on the ice engaging the evils of the world in a hilarious non-stop Hockey Rock action. B.T.O.'s Randy Bachman even shows up as D.O.A.'s hockey coach.

Hopefully, "TRUE(north), STRONG & FREE" will be available in Canada soon. At least, before the release of D.O.A.'s next album which they will begin recording as soon as they get back to Vancouver around Dec. 14. NO MEANS NO is also slated to begin work on their next album for Alternative Tentacles as soon as they touch bases in their hometown of Victoria.

D.O.A.'s and NO MEANS NO's Tour de Force dates and venues in Canada are:

Nov. 24—Halifax,N.S.—Pub Flamingo
25—Fredericton,N.B.—Monsignor Boyd Family Centre
26—Quebec City,P.Q.—Club Grand Derangement
27—Sherbrooke, P.Q.—TBA
28—Ottawa, ON.—Porter Hall, Carleton University
29—Montreal, P.Q.—Cafe Campus
Dec. 1—Toronto, ON.—Diamond Club
3—London, ON.—Mingles Tavern
4—Hamilton, ON.—Bannisters
5—Guelph, ON.—UniCentre, University of Guelph(2 shows)
7 & 8—Winnipeg, Man.—West End Cultural Centre
9—Regina,Sask.—Student Union, University of Regina
10—Saskatoon,Sask.—TBA
11—Edmonton,AB.—Dinwoodie Lounge,University of Alberta
12—Calgary,AB—Westward Club
18 & 19—Vancouver,B.C.—The Venue—Welcome Home Gigs

— 30 —

D.O.A. + NO MEANS NO
SPECIAL SHOW! WEDNESDAY OCTOBER 28TH
CLUB LINGERIE · SUNSET BLVD. AT WILCOX · 466·8557 · 21 + OVER!

TOUR DE FORCE

A forty-date North American tour with our good pals No Means No, one of my favourite bands of all time.

D.O.A. with John Wright in Moncton.

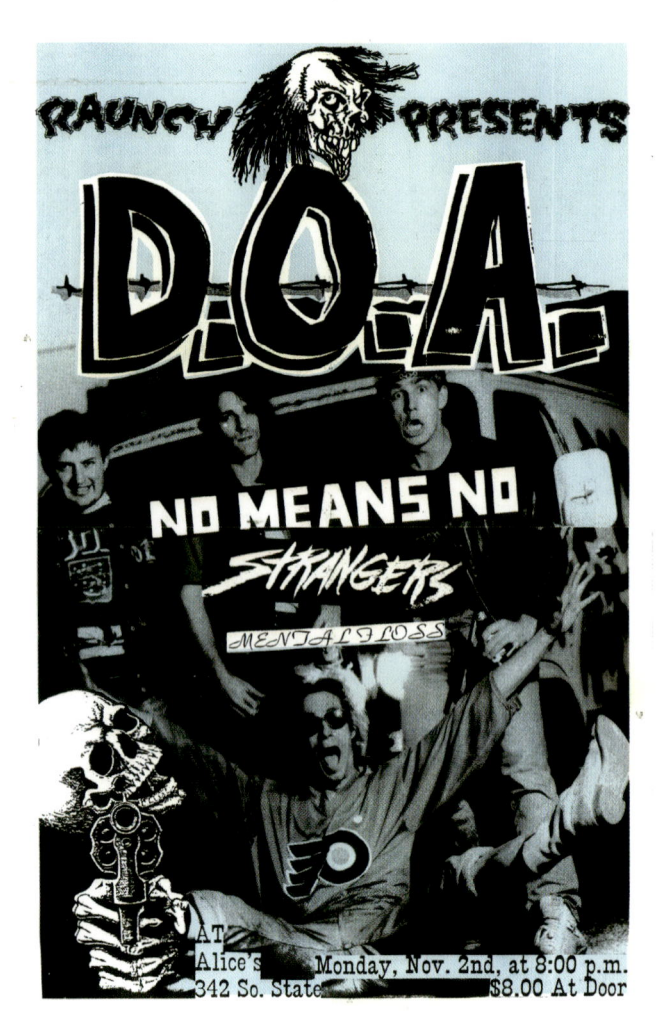

We played in the Mormon capital of Salt Lake City at Alice's Restaurant. Like Arlo Guthrie's song said, "You can get anything you want at Alice's Restaurant." Apparently the locals did, as Alice's was busted that day for stacks and stacks of drug sales over the previous six months. When we arrived for sound check, there were TV news crews all over the place filming the goings-on. While we played, a huge TV camera guy was filming us and Alice's patrons for the eleven o'clock news. The guy was in the way, so I tried to hipcheck him and his camera off the stage, but he stood his ground.

When we got back to Halifax to start the Canadian leg of the tour, Jon Card was hospitalized for a non-stop nose bleed, so John Wright (No Means No) filled in on drums in Halifax, Moncton, and Quebec City. John is a great drummer, so the sets were fun and on the adventurous side.

TUE. NOV. 10TH
THE NIGHT BEFORE VETERAN'S DAY - NO SCHOOL & WORK
at BROWN JUG (FORMERLY 1ST STOP)
1155 BROWN ST. - DAYTON
THE DAWNING OF A NEW ERROR...
Design: David Lester/Get To The Point ▶ Graphics
D.O.A.
NO MEANS NO & THE OBVIOUS
9pm $6 ADVANCE $7 DAY OF SHOW
18 years & up with ID!!

D.O.A
NO MEANS NO
MUDD HELMUT
MONDAY NOV. 16TH
ALL AGES
YOU KILL ME
Hey Kids SHOW STARTS AT 9:00 SHARP BE THERE OR I'LL KILL MYSELF... HA HA HA HA HA HA
ROCKITZ

UNE COLLABORATION CKRL-MF, LE D.J. ET LES PRODUCTIONS SANS NOM
FETONS LEUR RETOUR D'EUROPE !
D.O.A.
JEUDI LE 28 NOVEMBRE
20.30 HRES AU
CAFÉ DE LA BAR BOURSE
139, rue ST-PIERRE, QUÉ.
LUC MARTINEAU + FAMILY
326 RUE DOLBEA
QUEBEC CITY P.
CANADA
ALBUM D.O.A.
"LET'S WRECK THE PARTY"
GRATUIT !
POUR LES DEUX CENTS
PREMIERS BILLETS,
GRACIEUSETE
DE LE D.J.
LE D.J.
$10.00 BILLETS CHEZ: LE D.J., CAFE DE LA BOURSE
VINYL, 664 rue St-Jean
ECONO-DISQUES, 234 rue St-Joseph e.

D.O.A
&
NO MEANS NO
TRUE STRONG & FREE
D.O.A.
au GRAND dérangement
jeu. 26 nov.
30, ST-STANISLAS, VIEUX-QUEBEC
INFO: 692-3000
21 H.

D.O.A.
NOMEANSNO
Sound Garden

GRACELAND
1250 Richards St. (alley)
WEDNESDAY FEBRUARY 24

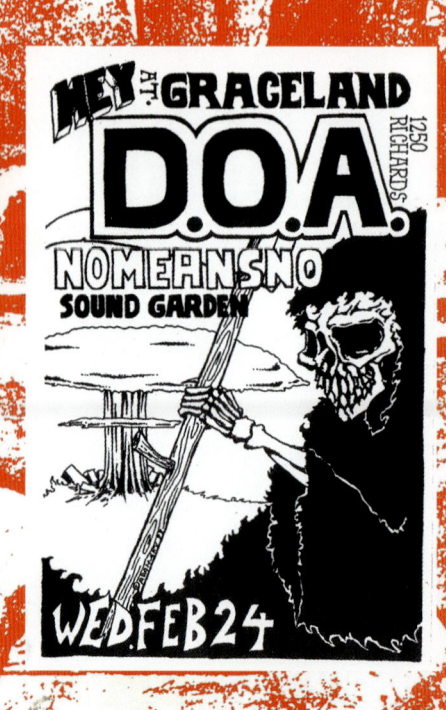

Jon Card with Hutch, our long-time sound man.

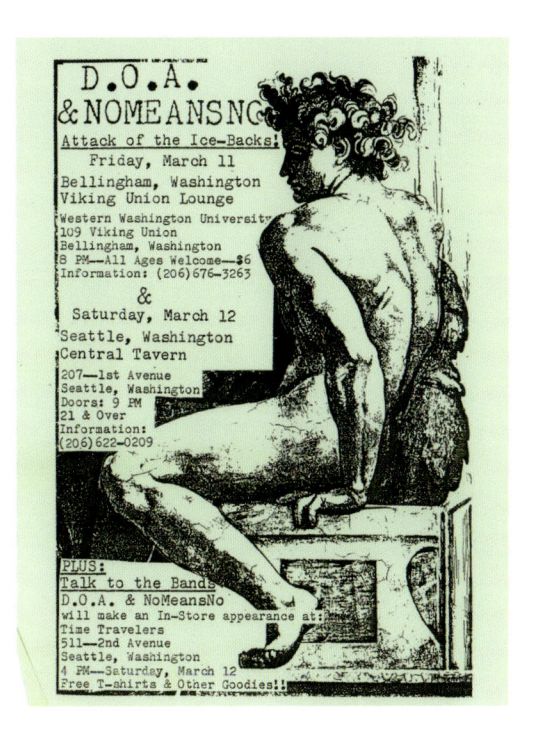

On our way to a weekend of gigs in Washington State, Miss Piggy broke down again, so I had to trudge across a soaked farmer's field to get help. The show at the Central was cool; Kim Thayil (Soundgarden) came out to shoot the shit backstage.

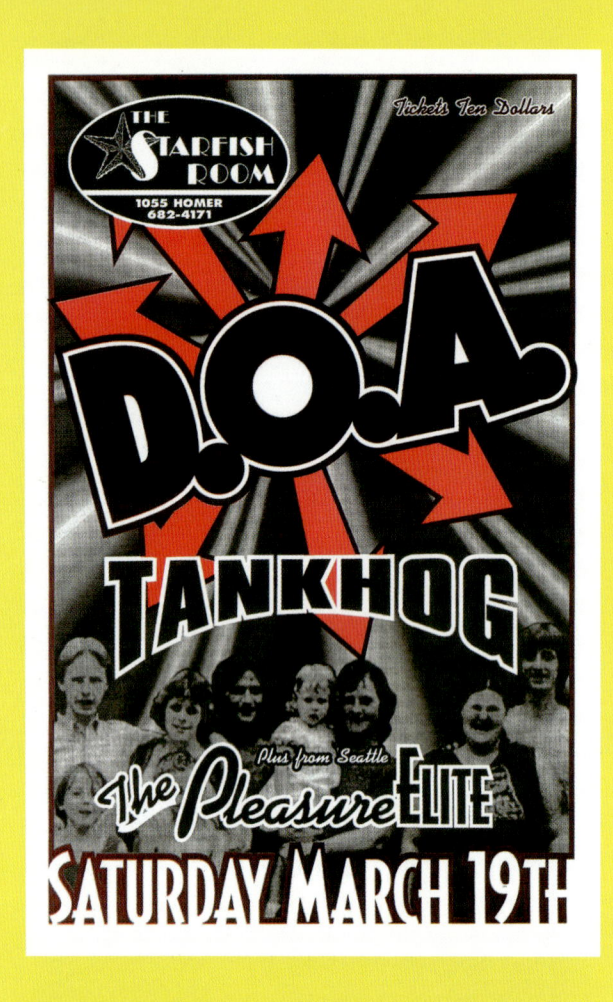

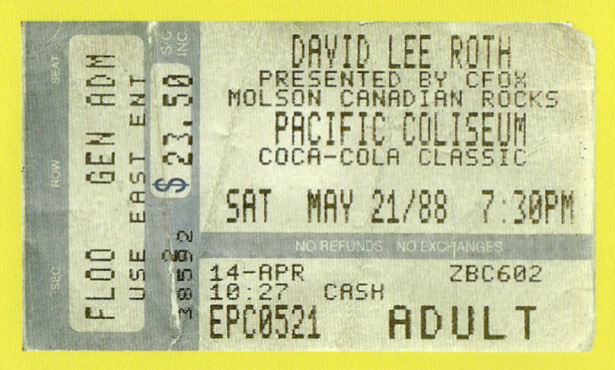

In Vancouver at the Starfish Room (formerly Club Soda, and previously the Quadra Club) and a May Day show in Vancouver with Sister Double Happiness (Gary and Lynn from the Dick's new band).

David Lee Roth had played in Vancouver the year before, when promoter Bruce Paisley had pranked Ken Lester, saying we could get on the bill. The next year, Paisly called again offering the same spot—Ken told him to piss off, but this time he was serious. Poison was supposed to open, but their guitarist had broken his leg. We got to the Coliseum, hung up our backdrop, and stood back to admire it ... but it looked the size of a postage stamp. When we got up to play, the Poison fans with their poodle-dog haircuts started booing us and throwing coins. Between songs, Dave picked up the change and said, "I have eight bucks, fuckers!" Some of the 16,000 people actually dug us. After our set, I ran into David's road manager; he was a real dipshit. We exchanged some words and then I shoved him. He called over some security goons who escorted me to the dressing room and then threw all of D.O.A. and our entourage out of the Coliseum while David Lee Roth was still on stage. Ahhhh ... you gotta love show business.

Three simultaneous concerts were held across Canada to oppose Prime Minister Brian Mulroney's proposal for a Free Trade agreement with America. We saw the treaty as a sell-out by Canada's big businesses. We wanted Fair Trade, not Free Trade.

Viva La Revolution! Bastille Day at the mighty Commodore in Vancouver (top right).

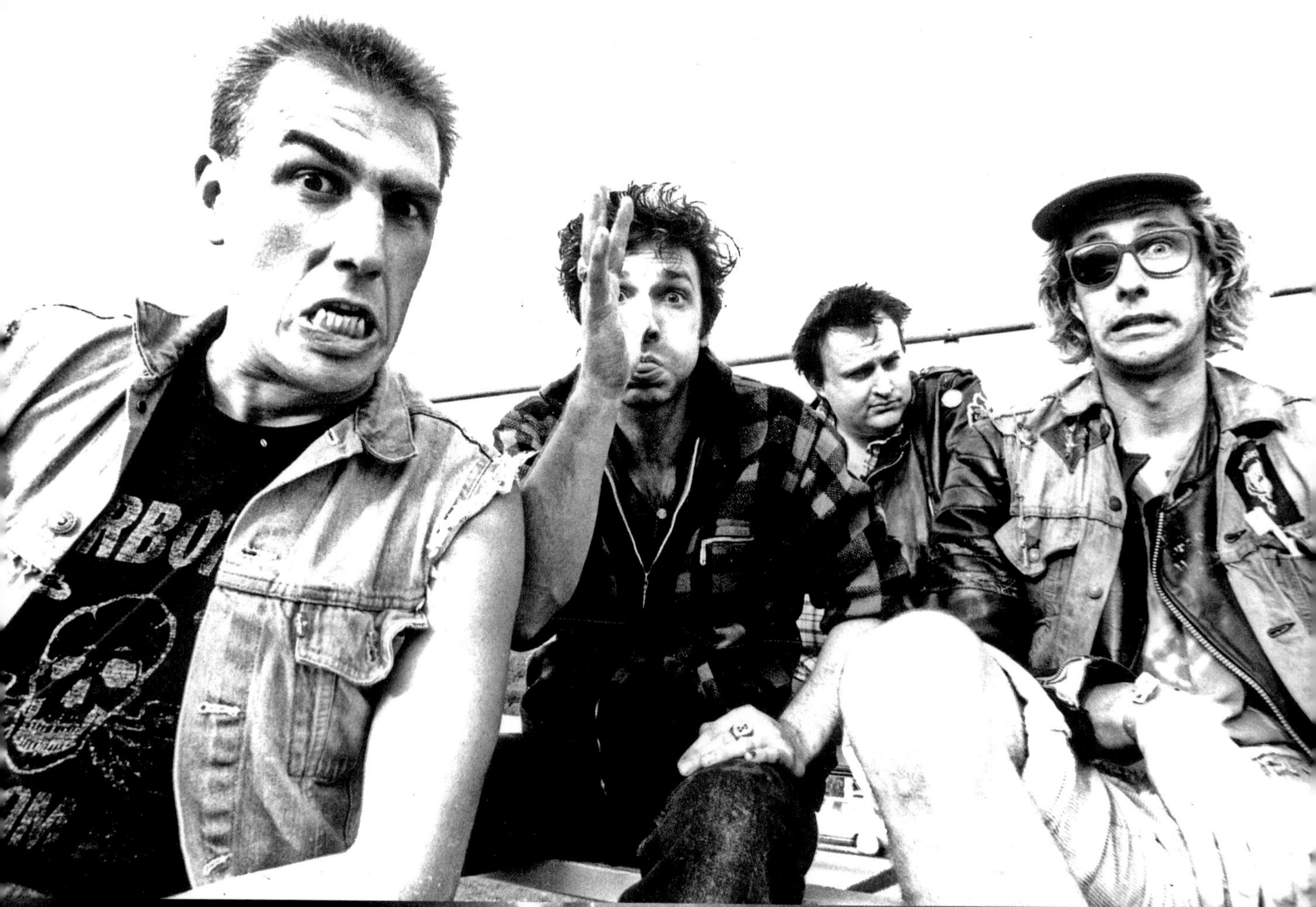

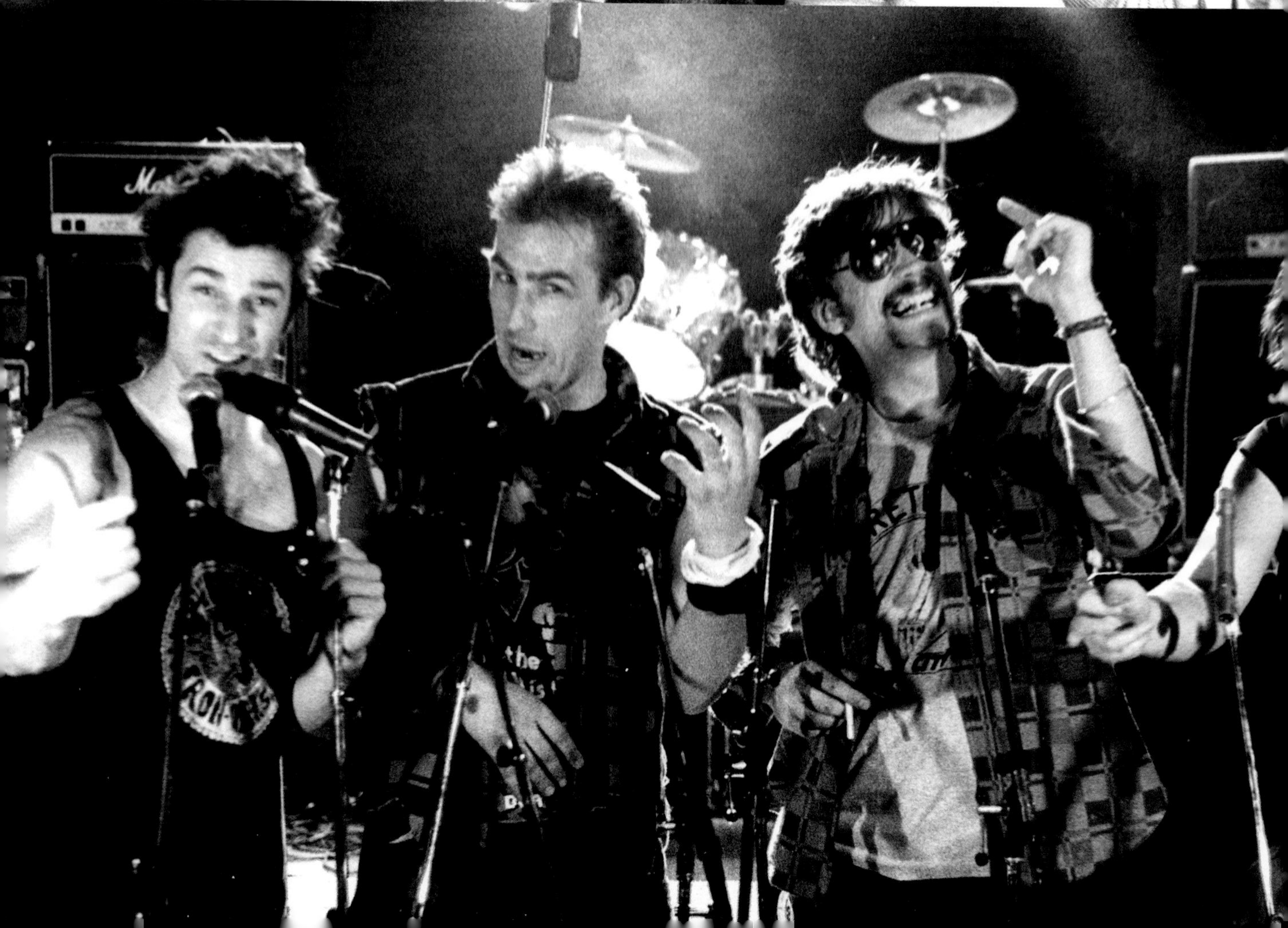

Cecil English and I were producing the Vampire Lezbos' album at this time, so we added them to D.O.A. shows in Vancouver and New Westminster.

2001 LOSER'S CLUB

D.O.A.

the outlaws are back

special guests
FROM KAMLOOPS
DESPERATE MINDS
FROM SPOKANE
VAMPIRE LEZBOS   ALL AGES

SAT. SEPT. 24 8 P.M.
THE PARAMOUNT
652 COLUMBIA
NEW WEST.
info: 526-8675

THEY'VE ALL RAVED!
SO LOOK OUT!

D.O.A.

WITH
BRUNO GERUSSI'S
MEDALLION
also SPOKANE'S
VAMPIRE LEZBOS

WED. SEPT. 28
TOWN PUMP
66 WATER

A benefit show in Missoula, Montana to build a skate ramp for the locals. Part of a twenty-show tour around North America.

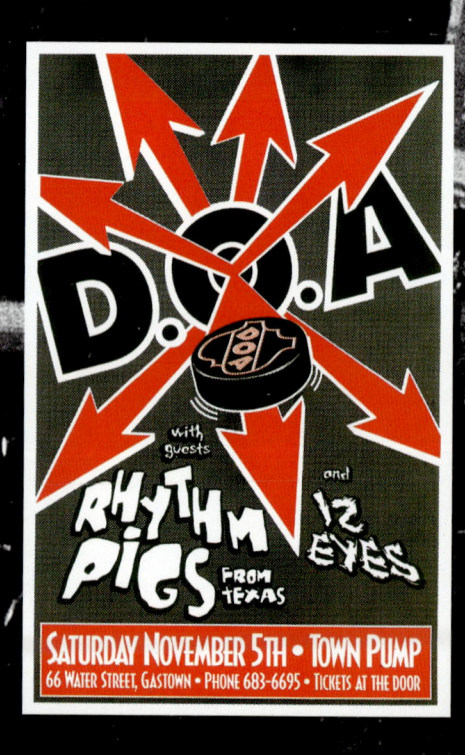

ROCKIN' RUDY'S presents...
MEGADECIBEL MINSTRELS
D.O.A.
SKATEBOARD BENEFIT

TOP HAT
TUESDAY JULY 19 5:30 PM SHARP
TICKETS $5.00 ADVANCE / $6.00 DOOR

ALL AGES/ IF IT'S TOO LOUD, YOU'RE TOO OLD

Everybody in D.O.A., except Jon Card, loved this poster. The Salt Lake City promoter had taken the cover of *War On 45* and put in "the Book of Mormon" where it previously read "the Holy Bible." Jon had been raised as a Mormon so he did not appreciate this, but we did, and every chance we had we went into hilarious pseudo preacher rants!

RAUNCH PRESENTS
D.O.A.
WIND OF CHANGE   INSTED
SAT. DEC. 17TH 8:30 PM
$6.00 AT THE DOOR
SPEEDWAY CAFE
505 WEST 500 SOUTH 532-5733

D.O.A.
with guests
RHYTHM PIGS FROM TEXAS and 12 EYES
SATURDAY NOVEMBER 5TH • TOWN PUMP
66 WATER STREET, GASTOWN • PHONE 683-6695 • TICKETS AT THE DOOR

THE HARDEST WORKING BAND IN SHOW-BUSINESS
D.O.A.
WITH
SKULL AND DEATH MIDGET
ALL AGES
DEC. 6
PINE ST. THEATRE
FROM CANADA:
D.O.A
WITH
FROM L.A.
SCREAMING SIRENS
FROM NEW ORLEANS:
DASH RIP ROCK
AT: CLUB LINGERIE
WED. DEC. 14TH
SUNSET AT WILCOX
466-8557
21

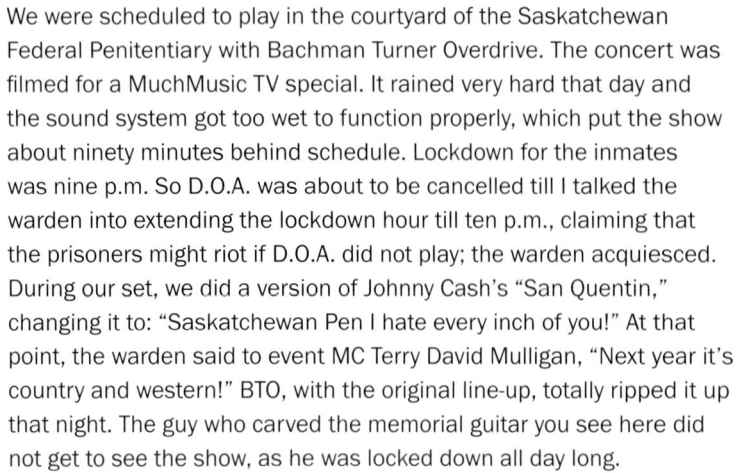

Randy Bachman rocking out with D.O.A. at the Edge in Vancouver.

We were scheduled to play in the courtyard of the Saskatchewan Federal Penitentiary with Bachman Turner Overdrive. The concert was filmed for a MuchMusic TV special. It rained very hard that day and the sound system got too wet to function properly, which put the show about ninety minutes behind schedule. Lockdown for the inmates was nine p.m. So D.O.A. was about to be cancelled till I talked the warden into extending the lockdown hour till ten p.m., claiming that the prisoners might riot if D.O.A. did not play; the warden acquiesced. During our set, we did a version of Johnny Cash's "San Quentin," changing it to: "Saskatchewan Pen I hate every inch of you!" At that point, the warden said to event MC Terry David Mulligan, "Next year it's country and western!" BTO, with the original line-up, totally ripped it up that night. The guy who carved the memorial guitar you see here did not get to see the show, as he was locked down all day long.

We were invited to play a political event called Refuse and Resist in NYC. It had a very good cross-section of bands, plus celebrities like Susan Sarandon. The whole event had a great spirit and was a little surreal.

We did a benefit show, organized by my brother Jef, for striking White Spot restaurant workers. It was also the last time Dave Gregg would play for D.O.A. The evening had a lot of emotion.

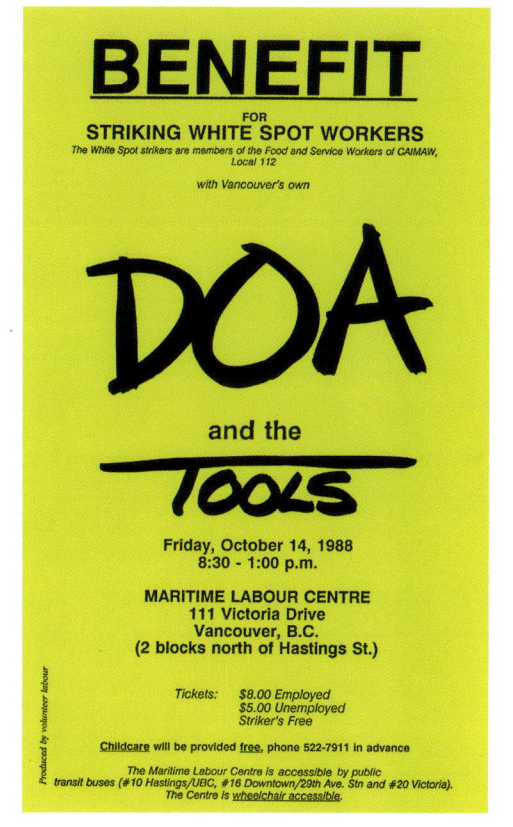

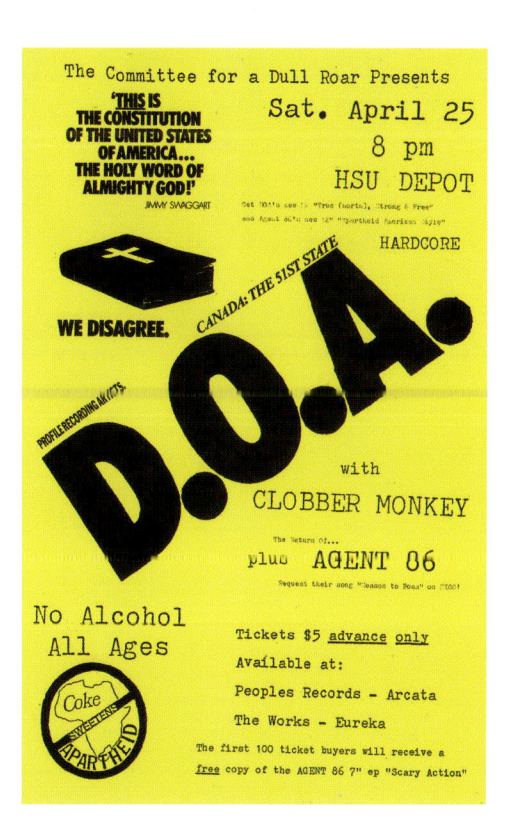

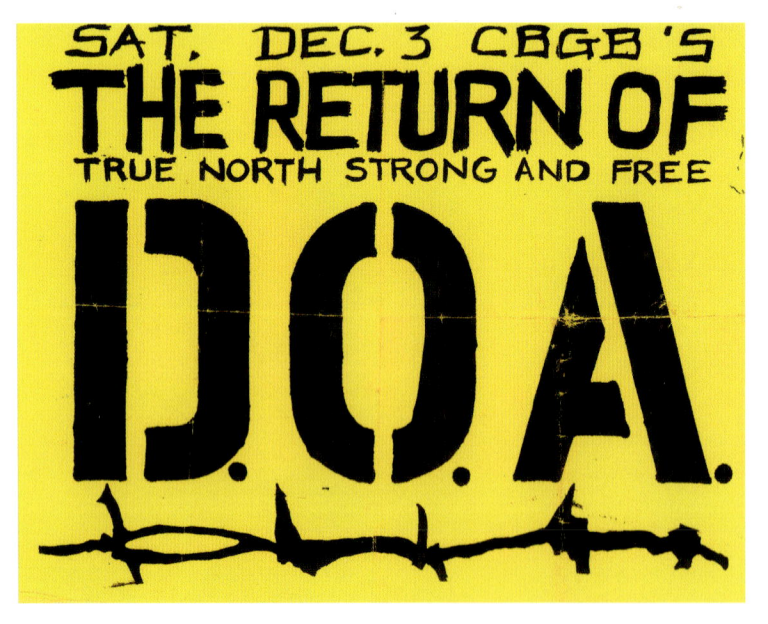

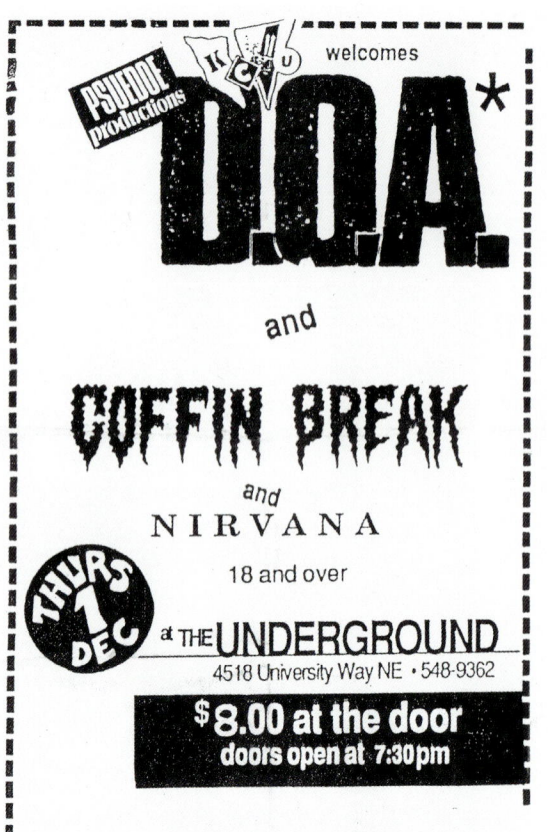

At this show in Seattle, Coffin Break was very good, as was Nirvana. This was Nirvana's second show ever.

Contrary to popular belief, D.O.A. never did play CBGBs back in the early days. We were actually banned from the joint after our roadie Bob spraypainted "RELIGION SUCKS D.O.A. RULES" over a mural of Jesus Christ, a Lower Eastside landmark. So this Dec. 3rd, 1988 show was the first time we played there.

At right is the cover of a promo book that we were handing out at the time, looking for a new record deal.

D.O.A.

the GUN is LOADED

The Dirty Dozen are: D.O.A., C.O.C., and D.R.I., after their 1990 concert in Munich.

THE END

We got a new manager in 1989, Laurie Mercer. I appeared in my first movie, *Terminal City Ricochet*. We signed to a new label in L.A. and recorded the album *Murder*, released in 1990. From my involvement with *Terminal City* came a great collaboration with our old pal Jello Biafra—*The Last Scream of the Missing Neighbors* album, also released in 1990. We worked with Terry Jacks and Bryan Adams to help raise money and awareness to stop the pollution coming from BC's pulp and paper mills. We hadn't been to Europe in five years, so we went and played a crazy two-month long tour over there. We also recorded a great live DVD, *The End,* in San Francisco (on which Jello has a guest spot). But after a rough summer tour in '90, I had had enough. I wanted to spend more time at home with my wife and our two small kids, and it seemed like the band was going around in circles. At the end of 1990, we broke up. After going at it so hard for almost thirteen years, it felt like it was time to call it quits.

Chapter 6

1989–1990

In the Strait of Georgia (the waterway between the mainland of British Columbia and Vancouver Island), there is a testing ground at Nanoose Bay where the Canadian and US navy practice firing torpedoes and various other weapons. Activists from the area invited D.O.A. to the nearby city of Parksville (on Vancouver Island) to play a benefit show called Peace Fest Rock. The idea was to stop ships with nuclear weapons from entering BC waters. When we arrived at the venue about four p.m. (the doors were due to open at seven p.m.), the well-intentioned activists did not have the stage built or the PA set up. So we used our muscle and brain power to get the stage built and the PA up and running by seven. There was only one hitch: we had wired the power for the PA directly into the arena's 220 power system (it takes a lot of power to run an entire arena). While we weren't looking, one of the PA crew rewired the power incorrectly, so there was no grounding for the PA, which means you can get a hell of a shock from it. As soon as our guitarist Chris Prohom tested his microphone, the building's power supply ran through his body! He fell face first and collapsed on his guitar. We picked him up and carried him into one of the dressing rooms. He was as white as a ghost, and it took us about two hours to convince him to get back up on stage and play that night.

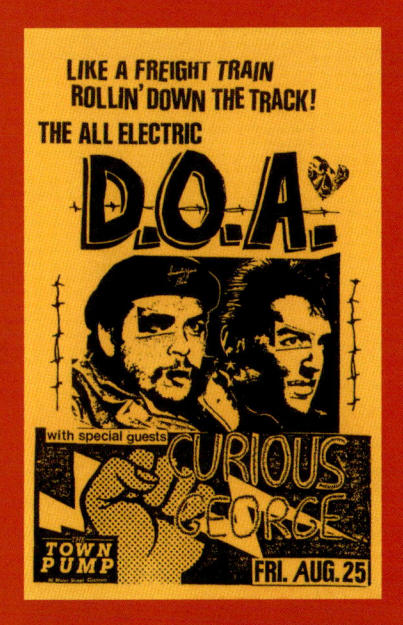

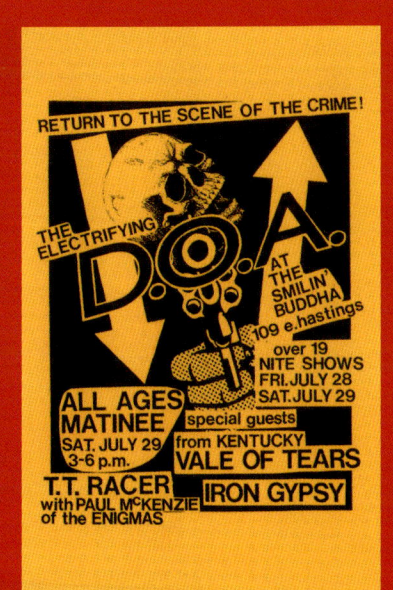

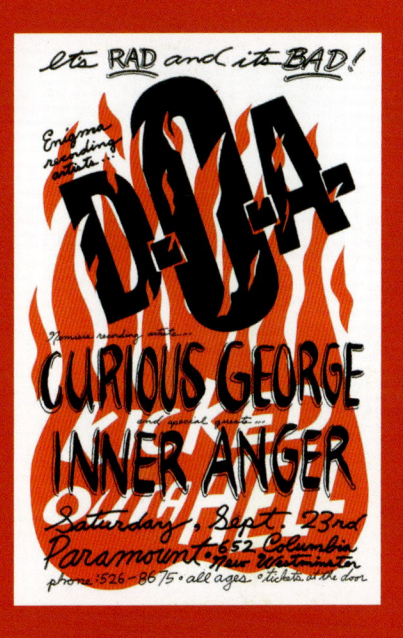

A return to the scene of the crime: This was the last time D.O.A. or any act of note would play the Smilin' Buddha. It was kind of sad—this was where punk rock really found its way in Vancouver. The Buddha was run by Lashman and Nancy, who had a way of making the punks feel at home when they entered (well, usually anyways...). Now, their son Robbie was running Vancouver's oldest nightclub—right into the ground. I didn't think the Buddha could get any scuzzier, but it had! There was a dead pigeon lodged in the ventilation system (with the lower half sticking out), which had been there for months, all the tables and chairs were broken or barely gaff-taped together, and the place had not been cleaned in the last five or six years. Adios to Lashman, Nancy, Igor, Steve, and the Smilin' Buddha—we miss ya!

A benefit show for End the Arms Race (left). Around this time, we occasionally billed ourselves as Drunks On Acoustic, an acoustic show with plenty of imbibing. This went on for about a year, until too many people said "Hey, you guys really changed your direction, man! Far out!" This was also the show that writer Michael Turner seemed to base the beginning of his book *Hard Core Logo* on.

161

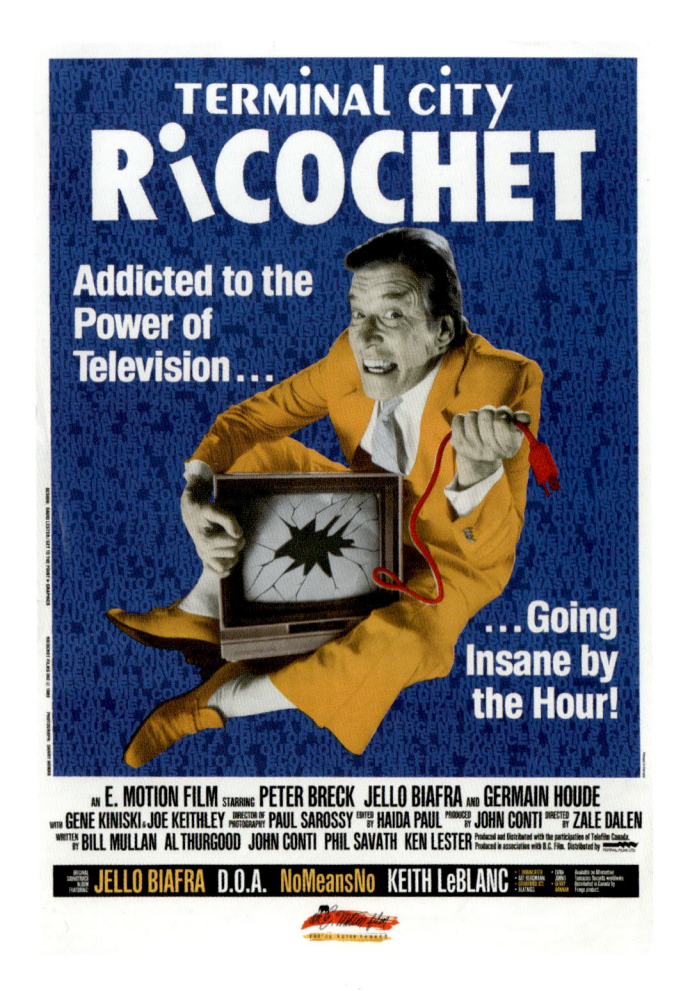

The underground movie *Terminal City Ricochet* has a great soundtrack. Ken Lester was involved with the film and urged us to record a song with Jello Biafra for it, so we came up with "That's Progress." Although not a cinematic triumph, the movie has some highlights. It was a lot of fun to make and the cast included Jello, me, and local wrestling legend Gene Kiniski. We all played cops in a futuristic world. Until recently the movie had been hard to find, but is now available on a double DVD from Alternative Tentacles. The DVD includes another movie I am in: *The Widower*. Gene (RIP) and I became friends during filming and he appeared in D.O.A.'s video for "We Know What You Want" from the *Murder* album.

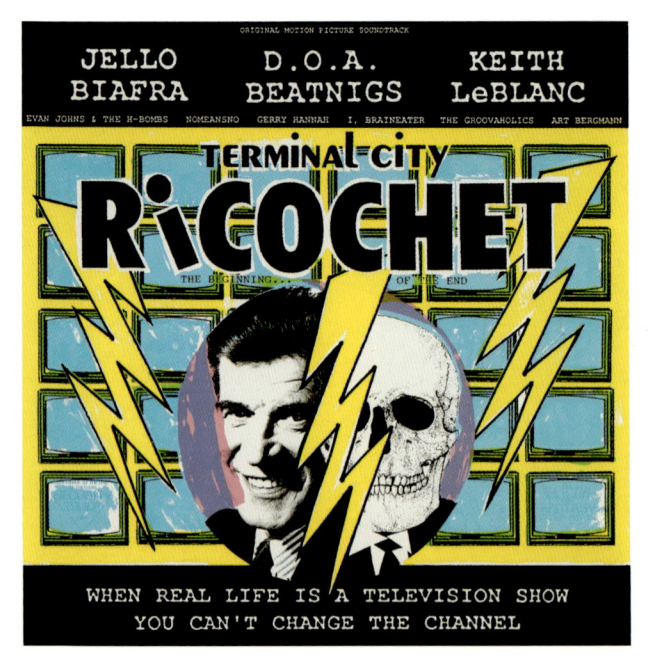

Since the arrival of Europeans, forestry has always been a huge part of British Columbia's economy. One sector of this industry is the production of pulp and paper. A number of scientific studies showed that the effluents (waste byproducts) from pulp and paper that were being spewed into our air and dumped into our waterways were having a disastrous effect on people's health and the environment. Cancer rates were rising, fish and shellfish were mutating, and so on. Dale Wiese, a friend and local musicologist, informed me that Terry Jacks (pop star from the '60s and '70s) was helping out a local organization called Environmental Watch that was fighting pulp and paper industry pollution. D.O.A. teamed up with Terry and recorded a version of his song "Where Evil Grows." We also helped put together a two-night benefit concert; both were at the 86 Street Music Hall and featured D.O.A. and Bryan Adams. An odd combo, for sure, but the publicity helped force the industry to clean up their act. Perhaps the oddest moment was Bryan and I performing a duet of the classic "Stand By Me."

The "Where Evil Grows" benefit single came out only on cassette. It was later added as an unlisted track to the *Murder* album.

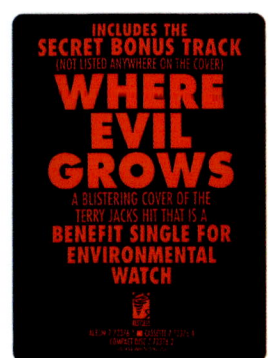

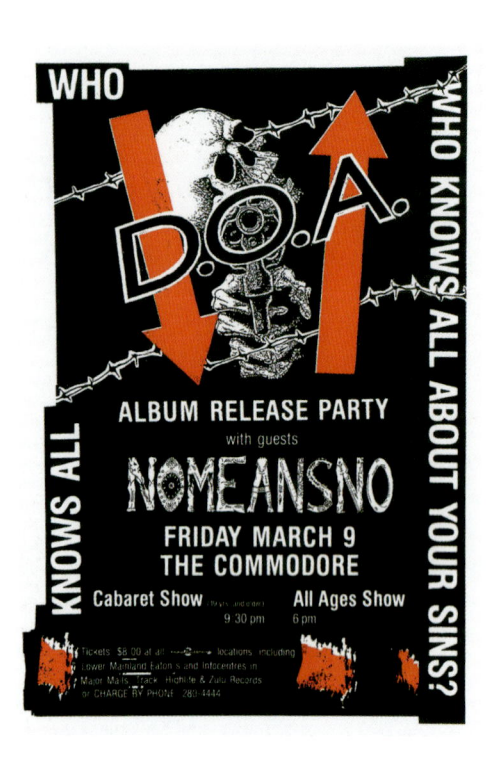

Our new manger, Laurie Mercer, booked us a nineteen-date tour across Canada to coincide with the release of the *Murder* album and the "Where Evil Grows" single. At a show in Winnipeg, there was a small bar underneath the cabaret where we played. At this bar a couple of patrons got in an argument about a drug debt. The first guy ran upstairs into the cabaret with his nemesis in hot pursuit. Just as the two of them were about to have it out, the first guy smashed off the large end of a beer bottle and rammed the jagged end into the other guy's eye. The bleeding guy staggered near the D.O.A. T-shirt booth looking like he was going to lose his eye. Our merch guy/road manager Jay Scott saw what was happening and managed to stop the bleeding with the use of about ten D.O.A. T-shirts. We later dubbed the beer bottle gouging "The Winnipeg Handshake."

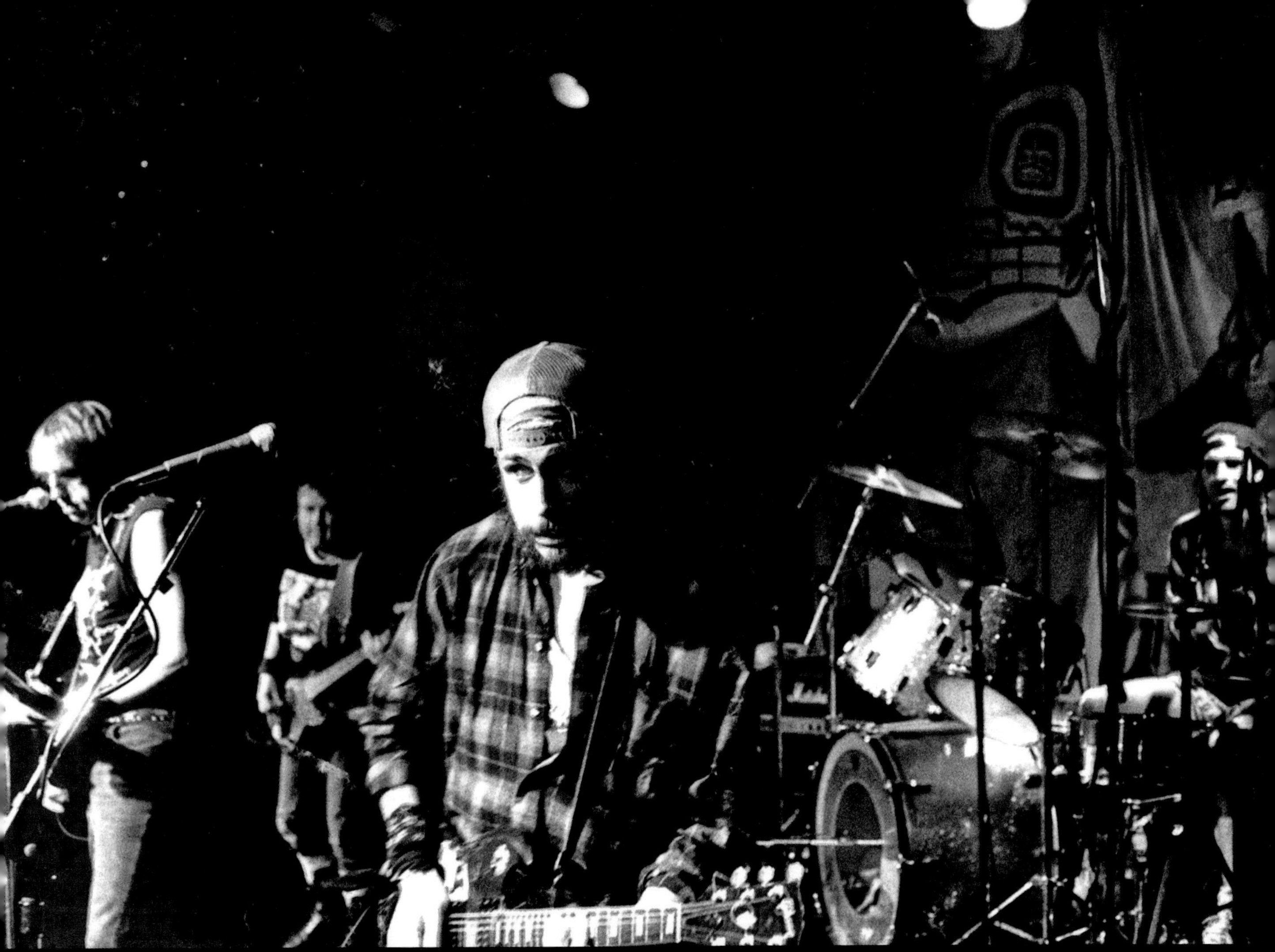

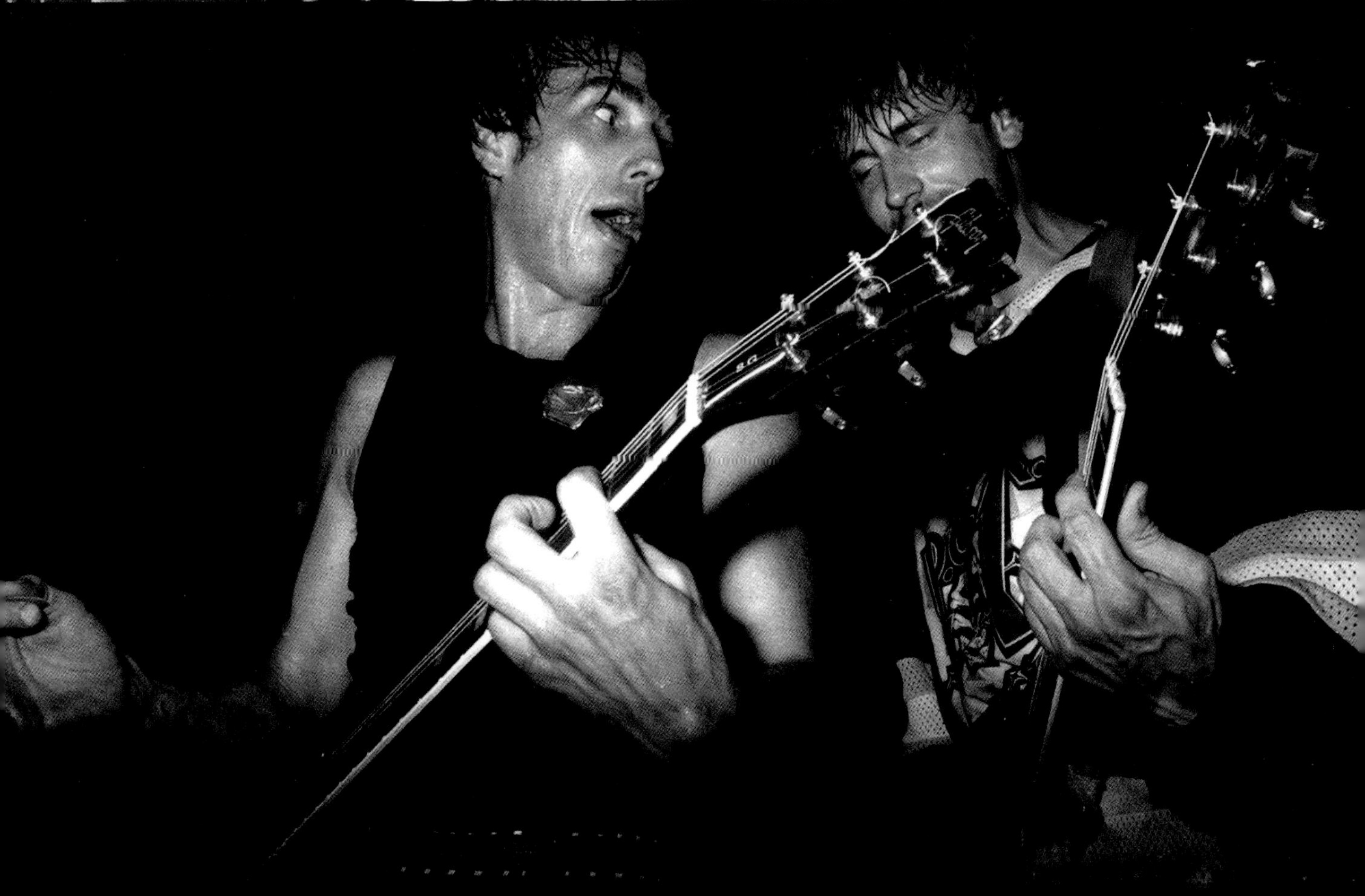

This album grew out of recording "That's Progress" for the *Terminal City Ricochet* movie soundtrack. It had gone so well that me and Jello decided to make an extended EP for release on vinyl and CD. Side A consists of five songs of the usual length. But Side B was just one track, fourteen minutes long. "Full Metal Jackoff" went on to become a big song all over Europe, where people had the endurance for its unending snarl. The song consists of three different riffs; we worked out how to play each of these riffs, but didn't have an arrangement. Before we recorded it with Cecil English at Profile Studios, we had time for only one rehearsal. Jello cued us with three different hand signals as to which riff should be played. The rehearsal went very well, so we recorded it in one take, with no edits. I thought Jon Card's right arm was going to fall off from the almost continuous eighth-notes on hi-hat cymbals for fourteen minutes. *Last Scream* turned out to be our best-selling album.

Mercer booked a tour in Europe for the release of *Murder*. We did a show on May 25 in a little village in the newly independent Slovenia, about a mile from the Italian border. We had to drive up about five miles of winding roads through vineyards to find the outdoor show. At the site for the venue, we found a basketball court, a makeshift stage, three little kids, and two grandmothers. We were in the middle of nowhere, and collectively asked, "Who the fuck booked this?" But when we came back from dinner there were 1,000 punks ready to raise hell. Great bands and a great show. After the show, we drove back down to the hotel. Wimpy had been drinking wine all night long, and as soon as we stopped, let forth the biggest Technicolor yawn I had ever seen.

```
20 MAR '90 19:36 PAPERCLIP AGENCY NL 31 80 232762              P.1/4
```

```
TO:      SL Feldman&Associates Att L. Mercer    Paperclip Agency
FAX NO:  +1 604.732.0922                        P.O. Box 1519
FROM:    Ruud Berends                           6501 BM  NIJMEGEN
RE:      DOA Dates                              the Netherlands
DATE:    03-20-1990                             phone +31.80.239322
                                                fax +31.80.232762
                                                tlx 20010 pms nl att. paperclip
------------------------------------------------
Dear Laurie;                          Update send to:
As promised the latest update:       -Roadrunner-England-Mark Palmer
April 1990                           -Alternative Tentacles-Bill Gilliam
Mon  9   Fly in to London / UK       -Enigma Records Int.-Karina Eichmann
Tue 10   Off/Hutch arrives           -Several DOA-fans.
Wed 11   The Dove - Ipswich / UK
Thu 12   Edwards VIII - Birmingham / UK    4 pages fax
Fri 13   Take Two - Sheffield / UK         ************
Sat 14   Bridge - Hebden / UK
Sun 15   Venue - Edinburgh / GB
Mon 16   Riverside - Newcastle / UK
Tue 17   Dutchess Of York - Leeds / UK (Or replacing show i.r. poss. do
         bill with No Means No)
Wed 18   Poly Technic - Portsmouth / UK
Thu 19   James St. Labour Club - Newport / UK (Poss. show with N.M.N. a
Fri 20   Fulham Greyhound - London / UK   L.S.E.
Sat 21   t.b.a.
Sun 22   Netwerk - Aalst / B
Mon 23   off
Tue 24   t.b.a.
Wed 25   De Melkweg - Amsterdam / NL
Thu 26   Atak - Enschede / NL
Fri 27   De Vlerk - Rotterdam / NL
Sat 28   Patronaat - Haarlem / NL
Sun 29   t.b.a.  Arnhem
Mon 30   Kling Klang - Wilhelmshaven / D
May Tue 1  Day off at Wilhelmshaven / D
Wed  2   Loppen - Kopenhaven / DK
Thu  3   Stadt Hamburg - Malmö / S
Fri  4   t.b.a.
Sat  5   Fagersta - Rockborgen / S
Sun  6   Cafe Q - Gavle / S
Mon  7   off
Tue  8   Markthalle - Hamburg / D
Wed  9   Bad - Hannover / D
Thu 10   TU - Mensa - Berlin / D
Fri 11   EX - Berlin / D
Sat 12   AJZ - Bielefeld / D
Sun 13   Live Station - Dortmund / D
Mon 14   Rose Klub - Köln / D
Tue 15   Batschkapp - Frankfurt / D
Wed 16   Schwimmbad - Heidelberg / D
Thu 17   Jugendhaus - Kempten / D
Fri 18   Crash - Freiburg / D
Sat 19   Festival - Saint Quentin / FRANCE
Sun 20   off
Mon 21   Theaterfabrik - München / D
Tue 22   OJC Konkret - Hohenems / A
Wed 23   U-4 - Wien / A
Thu 24   ?  - Zagreb / YU
Fri 25   Festival - Hum / YU
Sat 26   Cinema Alcione - Milano / I
Sun 27   Fabrica - Bologna / I       2 MORE ITALIAN G
Mon 28   Macchia Nera - Pisa / I
Tue 29   Hiroshima Mon Amour - Torino / I
Wed 30   off
Thu 31   L'Usine - Genève / CH t.b.c.   2 SWISS GIGS
June Fri  1  Kaserne - Basel / CH
Sat  2   Le Sax Cafe - Pontarlier / F
Sun  3   Centre Culturel Marc Sangnier - Metz / F   4 FRENCH
Mon  4   Theatre Dunois - Paris / F
Tue  5   Le Truc - Lyon / F
Wed  6   travel/Off
Thu  7   ? - London / UK   → LAST SHOW
Fri  8   fly home

Best regards

Ruud Berends
```

9 U.K. GIGS
1 BELGIAN GIG
5 DUTCH GIGS
1 GERMAN
1 DANISH
4 SWEDISH
11 GERMAN GIGS
1 FRANCE
1 GERMAN
2 AUSTRIAN GIGS
2 YUGOSLAV
2 ITALIAN

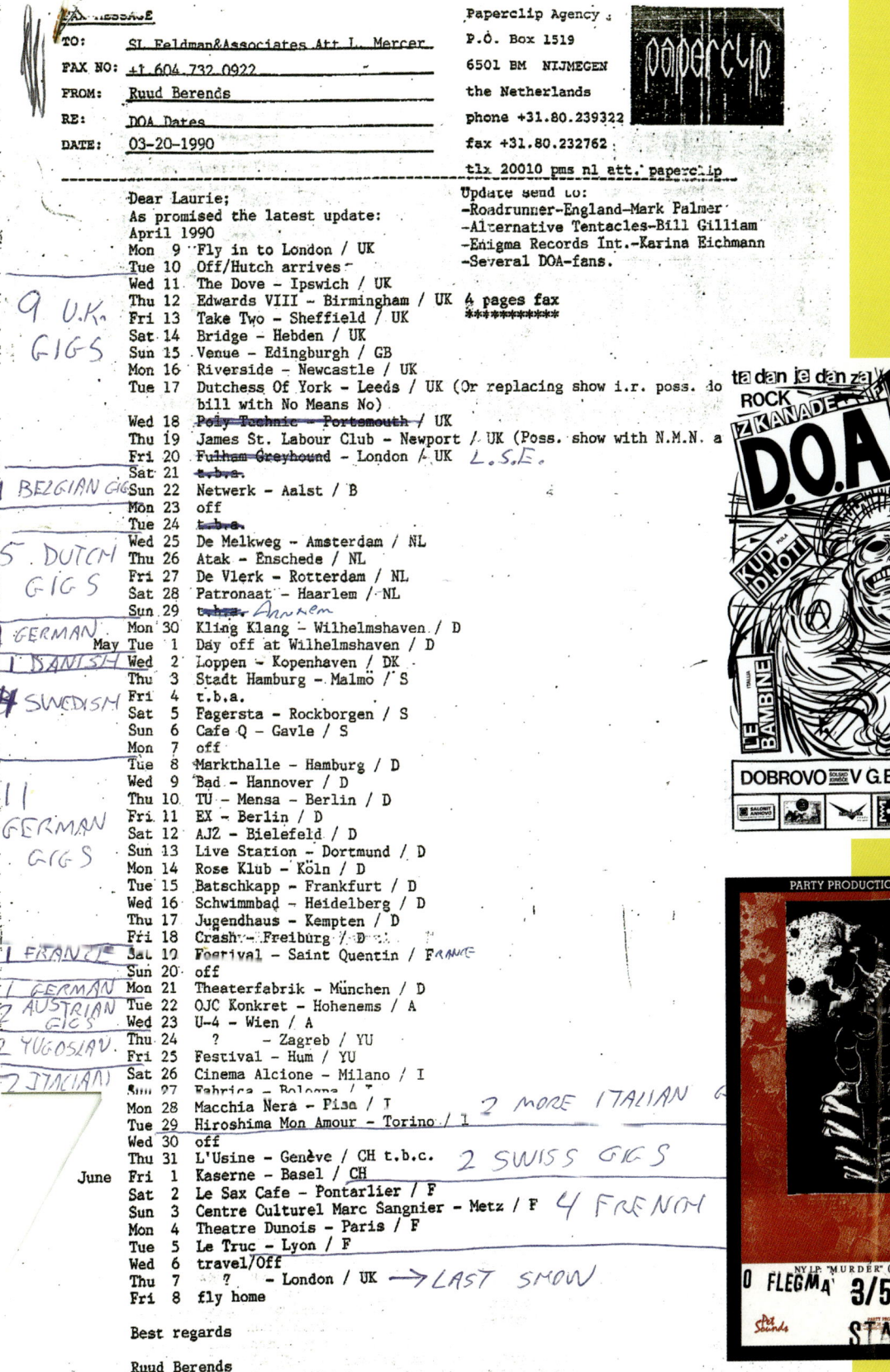

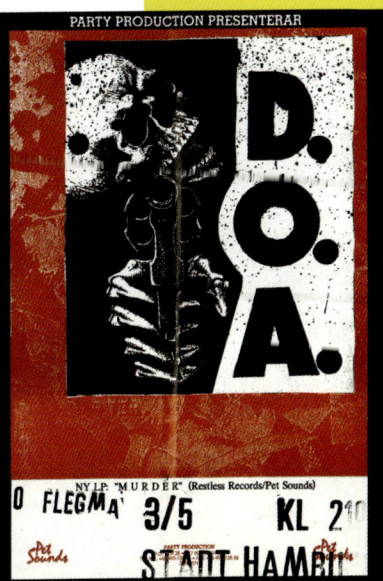

After playing Winnipeg we got held up at the US border at North Dakota. They wouldn't let our guitarist Chris across and the border guard threatened several times to seize Reid Fleming (our famous white tour van). We eventually got across, but without Chris, and did the show that night as a three-piece.

Madison was the first stop of our twenty-date US summer tour with Negazione, a great and powerful band we knew from Italy. The show was terribly promoted and poorly attended, so at the end of the night the promoter had no dough to pay us. Let's just say I was pissed off. As we were leaving town, I realized that the promoter had told us they were having a keg party. So we went to the party and took the keg as payment.

At our stop in Milwaukee, we saw a spray painted van that had been burned to a crisp in the parking lot behind the venue. I asked the promoter what had happened. "Oh yeah, that was the Exploited's van. Some skinheads lit it on fire while they played their set." We kept a guard in our van for the entire show.

A boat cruise on Lake Michigan along Chicago's "Gold Coast," with a bunch of drunken punks. Better get the life preservers out! We did a short sound check when the ship was docked. Wimpy showed us how to play the Gilligan's Island theme, and we morphed Herman's Hermit's "Sea Cruise" into "Booze Cruise," ooowee ooowee baby. By the time the cruise was in full swing, we were playing Booze Cruise just fine. Not so sure about the Gilligan's Island theme-song, though ... "Now sit right back and enjoy a tale, a tale of a fateful trip ..." Man overboard!

Back in one of our favourite towns, Dayton, Ohio: It should have been a great show. But unfortunately I got into a fight with a brain-dead fuckwit. The show was going great, but the fuckwit decided he was going to punch and elbow everybody he could in the mosh pit. He was the type of fool who started to make hardcore punk shows a lot less fun than they used to be. After I repeatedly tried to verbally settle the guy down, the idiot finally smashed Chris Prohom in the teeth with a mike stand. I had had enough. With my guitar still on, I reached into the pile and started pummelling him in the head. But I had broken one of D.O.A.'s cardinal rules, which is: when dealing with fuckwads, get them with your boots. So this guy balanced on top of the moshing crowd and got in a couple of glancing blows to my face while wearing a bunch of rings on both hands. My face got pretty cut up. The next day I woke up and drove around Dayton by myself to do some thinking. I phoned my wife to talk about it and decided it was time to break up the band. Not immediately, but soon.

D.O.A.
- All Ages
plus **ADRENALIN O.D.** and Loose
Thursday Aug 16th
at the Pipeline
9pm • $7
All Ages

By this point, Negazione flew back to Italy and the last few dates of the tour were cancelled. We played one last show in New Jersey with the kick-ass Adrenaline Over Dose (A.O.D.), but before the show we sought out the famous Tube Bar (where the "My Name Is Red" prank tapes were recorded). We came back to the venue an hour late and drunk as skunks. Funny thing is, to this day people still say it was a great show.

Brian Thalken (Authorities) and Joe hangin' at the Tube Bar.

Al, the bartender at the Tube Bar.

We decided to do one final tour down the west coast. At various points on this trip the road crew consisted of: John Wright (No Means No), Chi Pig (SNFU), Chris Crud, and Craig Bougie. This tour included the one and only show we ever played in Mexico— at Iguana's with L7 in Tijuana.

While in San Francisco we recorded a live DVD, produced by Dirk Dirksen, with a guest appearance by Jello.

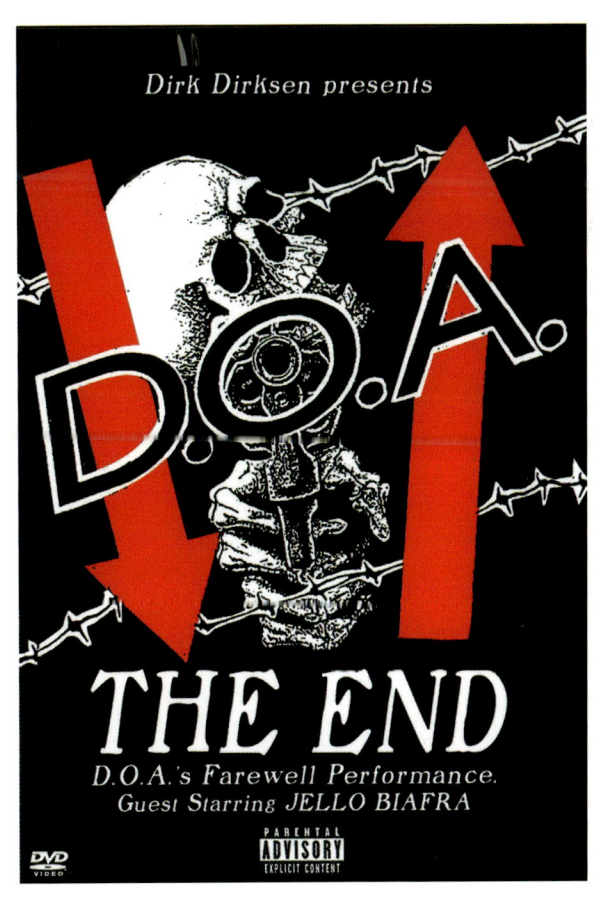

The last American show was in Seattle at the OK Hotel. John Wright had warned me that the flywheel cover of my chainsaw was broken. During the show, I picked up the chainsaw, fired it up, and the tip of the ring finger on my left hand got ripped off by the flywheel. I dropped the saw, went backstage, cursed, and smashed a half dozen beer bottles against the wall. I could not believe my own stupidity. I finished the show as best as I could just singing.

BOOMTOWN

BOOMTOWN - 4X

IT'S HARD TO SAY, HOW IT GOT THIS WAY
WHAT I WANNA KNOW, WHEN DOES IT END
WELL THEY SQUEEZE YOU DRY, THEN THEY LET YOU DIE
AN' THEN JUST THROW YA AWAY
WELL THE JOBS WERE THERE, BUT THEY AIN'T NO MORE
NOW YOUR STARIN' AT A CLOSED FACTORY DOOR
AND THE BANKER, HE DON'T GIVE A DAMN
HE'D WALK RIGHT OVER A DYIN' MAN

BOOMTOWN - WELL THEY SET YOU UP
                JUST TO KNOCK YA DOWN
BOOMTOWN - YOUR GONNA GET TURNED
                UPSIDE DOWN

IT COMES AN' GOES, YEAH YA NEVER KNOW
WHEN IT'S YOUR TURN FOR, DESOLATION ROW
GOT NO TIME TO THINK, WHEN YOUR FEELIN' SORE
AN' THE GRASS AIN'T GREEN ANYMORE
A REVOLVING DOOR, THAT YOUR BOUND TO MEET
SHOVIN' PEOPLE, RIGHT OUT IN THE STREET
TO A NIGHTMARE, THAT KEEPS COMIN' ROUND
JUST HOLD ON AN' TRY NOT TO DROWN

BOOMTOWN - WELL THEY SET YOU UP
                JUST TO **SMASH** YOU DOWN
BOOMTOWN - WELL YOUR GONNA GET
                YOU'LL GET MOWED DOWN
BOOMTOWN - WELL YA GOTTA SMILE
GOTTA SMILE - YEAH BETTER NOT FROWN
BOOMTOWN - WELL, KEEP IT TO YOURSELF
SHUT YOUR MOUTH - YEAH SHUT-UP AN' SIT DOWN

EVEN IF YOU TRY, YOUR GONNA CRY
CAUSE YOU WON'T, MAKE ENDS MEET
CAUSE THE BOOMTOWN, WILL LET YOU DOWN
IT NEVER COMES THROUGH WITH THE GOODS

BOOMTOWN - WELL THEY SET YOU UP
        YEAH JUST JUST TO CUT YA DOWN
BOOMTOWN - WELL GONNA GET
        YEAH YEAH GONNA GET TURNED UPSIDE DOWN

D.O.A

FESTIVAL
DU
DEVENIR 90

DI CALCIO

Marshall
FESTIVAL
DU
DEVENIR 90

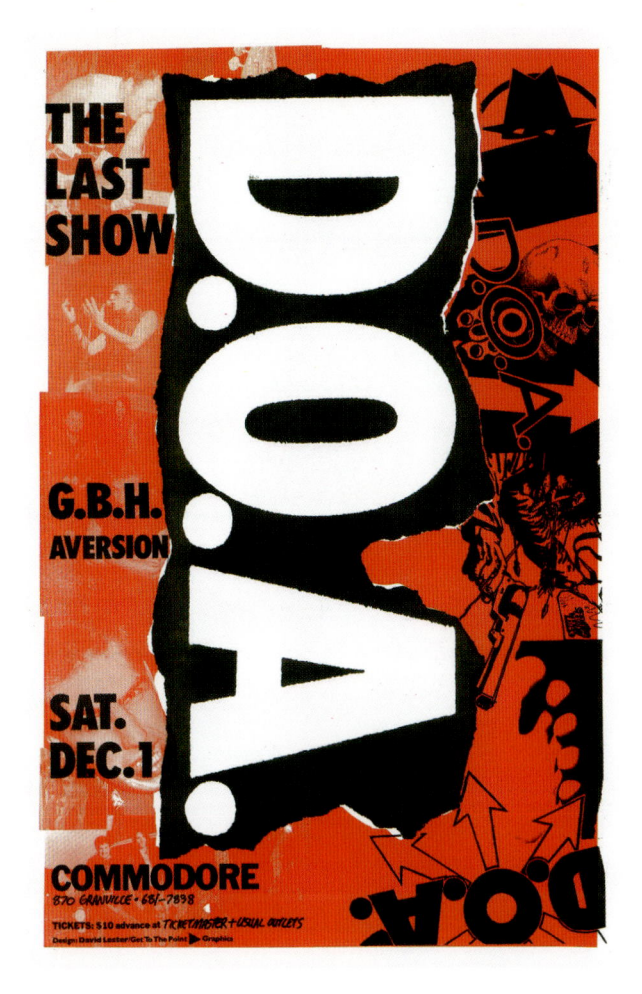

In Vancouver we had one last show booked at the Commodore with the ever powerful G.B.H. About 1,500 friends and fans showed up, and it was so jammed, you could not move.

One more time now! The Final Final show.

We recorded this live album in 1990 at Club Soda in Vancouver with Cecil English producing. This was the first time we used the slogan "Talk Minus Action Equals Zero"—not to be confused with the studio album released in 2010 called *Talk – Action = 0*.

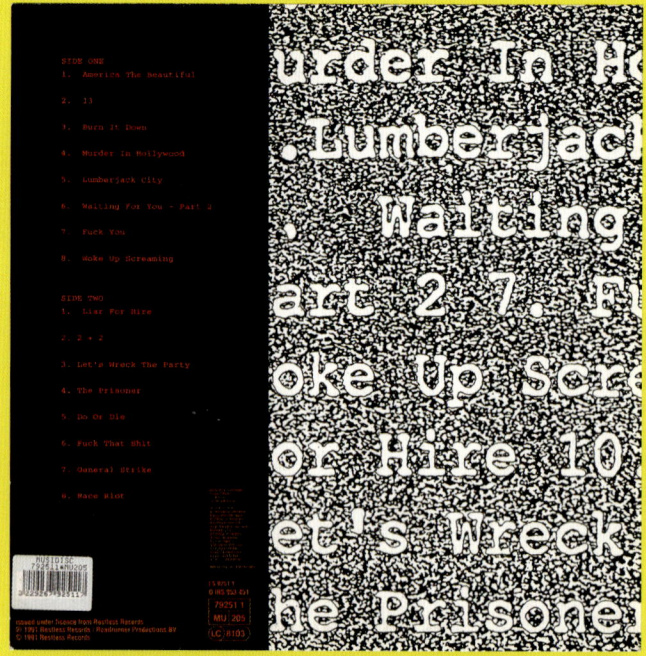

Joe and Canada's greatest athlete, wrestler Gene Kiniski (RIP), on the set of *Terminal City Richochet*.

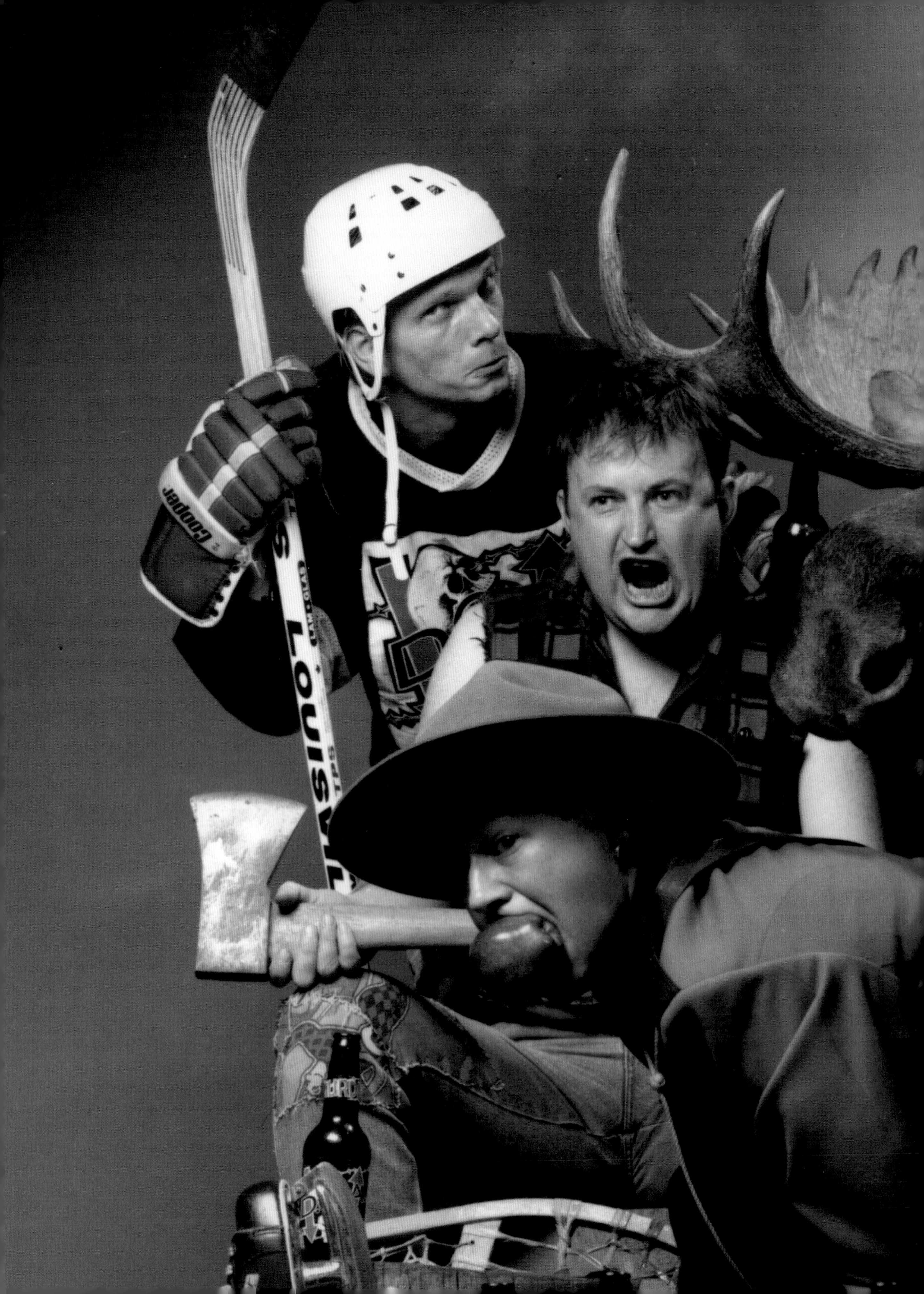
Cooper
LOUIS
TPS

Chapter 7

1991-1994

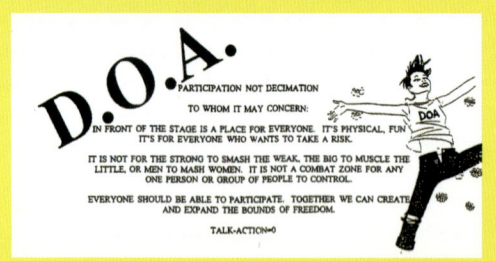

RESURRECTION

We're getting the band back together, man! Yeah, just like the Blues Brothers: "Tonight, One Night Only, the Fabulous D.O.A.s!" We had been broken up for about twenty months, and in that time I had started and disbanded a rock band called Instinct and worked at BCIT, a post-secondary polytechnic in Burnaby. When a journalist asked me why we were getting back together, I said, "'Cause I don't think there's any other band on the planet who does what we do." There was no other band that combined humour and politics while blowing your lid off with ear-splitting riffs.

We came back as a three-piece; Wimpy, new drummer Ken Jensen (formerly of Red Tide), and me. I felt really, really good about the band again. Having one of my best friends, the extraordinarily talented Mr Wimpy Roy, and the effervescent and energetic young Ken Jensen on drums, put it over the top. We immediately set to writing a stack of new songs and wanted to record an album. But our financing fell through, and the album seemed doomed until Jello came up with the dough and saved the album and Profile Studios at the same time. Jello also came up with *31 Flavors of Doom* as the album title, but I gave it a twist and thus *13 Flavours of Doom* was begat! We got our pals John Wright (No Means No) and Brian Who Else to produce and engineer that slab o' vinyl.

It felt like we had turned a corner. In 1993 and '94, we did two hugely successful tours of Europe, went to Australia and New Zealand for the first time, recorded and released another album, *Loggerheads*, on Alternative Tentacles, which was well-received, made a couple of singles—and it was all cool. But it came to a grinding halt on January 29th, 1995, when Ken Jensen died in a house fire. Dimwit had died from an overdose five months earlier, and my old buddy Stubby Pecker (who played bass briefly with D.O.A. in 1980) had also recently passed on. Rarely does life turn out the way you plan it. We still had a lot of spirit, but it had been taking a beating, that's for sure.

BEN-CORE PROMOTIONS PRESENTS
ALTERNATIVE TENTACLES RECORDING ARTISTS
THEY'RE BACK
★CANADA'S FINEST
D.O.A.
MON.
JANUARY
17th
plus special guests
SMOKIN' SHE-PUNK from VANCOUVER
CUB
AND
WRONG WAY RIGHT
LIVE At The
Hurry!
$6.00
VERY limited tix. Avail.
DOORS AT 7:00PM
$1.25 DRAFTS
SHOW
8:00
LAtin SocialCenter..
609 S.LINCON ST. STOCKTON
(2 BLKS. EAST OF I-5 OFF CHARTER)
Advance tickets available at
— Replay Records —
(Lincoln Center in Stockton)
ALL AGES

D.O.A. MURDER SQUAD!
it's not a band it's a hockey team!

benefit hockey for the food bank bring $2.00 or some food

D.O.A. vs. Highland Echo sun. feb. 24 8:30 p.m.
trout lake arena 16th. & Victoria

D.O.A. vs. C.F.O.X. mon. march 11 10 p.m.
50 E. 30th. near main st. riley park arena

HE'S BACK!
JOE KEITHLEY'S INSTINCT
WITH GUESTS PAGAN FRENZY
SAT. NOV. 2
the TOWN PUMP
66 Water St., Gastown
683-6695 / 681-2222

The D.O.A. hockey team was the champion of the Vancouver Media Hockey League (VMHL).

While D.O.A. was D.O.A., I formed a rock band called Instinct; we didn't last that long, but did play in Vancouver a couple of times.

AF MAGAZINE

Vancouver's alternative fortnightly

Sept 18-Oct 2 1992 — FREE

- Blade Runner
- Spies in Canada
- Fringe Reviews
- Chainsaw Kittens
- Fishbone
- Show Biz Giants

D.O.A. Crawls from the grave

The dead want to live.

Return of the Living Dead

Interview by Josephine Ochej

Is Chainsaw A Verb?

By Dave "Not Goth" Barber

To launch D.O.A.'s comeback, we booked a four-day kickoff tour at John Barleycorn's in Vancouver. It felt good to play as a three-piece again, as some of my fave bands, like Hendrix and ZZ Top, were three-pieces. After the Vancouver show, we left straight away for Edmonton. It was all going well till the van (Reid Fleming) started chugging out. Whenever you're on tour, vehicle problems always seem to happen in the middle of nowhere! Well, this was no exception. We couldn't get the speed up over thirty mph (forty-five km/h). That turned our sixteen-hour drive to Edmonton into about twenty-two hours, and we barely got to the show in time. We tried replacing the transmission, but when that didn't work, we left roadie Iain Ross with the van and took a $300 cab ride to make the Calgary show. We finally concluded that the exhaust pipe was blocked, so Iain and I got a hack-saw and cut a big hole in the tailpipe. The van ran great after that, but it was as loud as about five Harleys revving their engines. The Sunday we headed home, every time we pulled up near a church in a small town, we revved the engine, honked the horn, and waved our beers out the window.

Independents '92: a real cool event put on by Big Todd (RIP) in one of my fave stops: Kamloops, B.C.

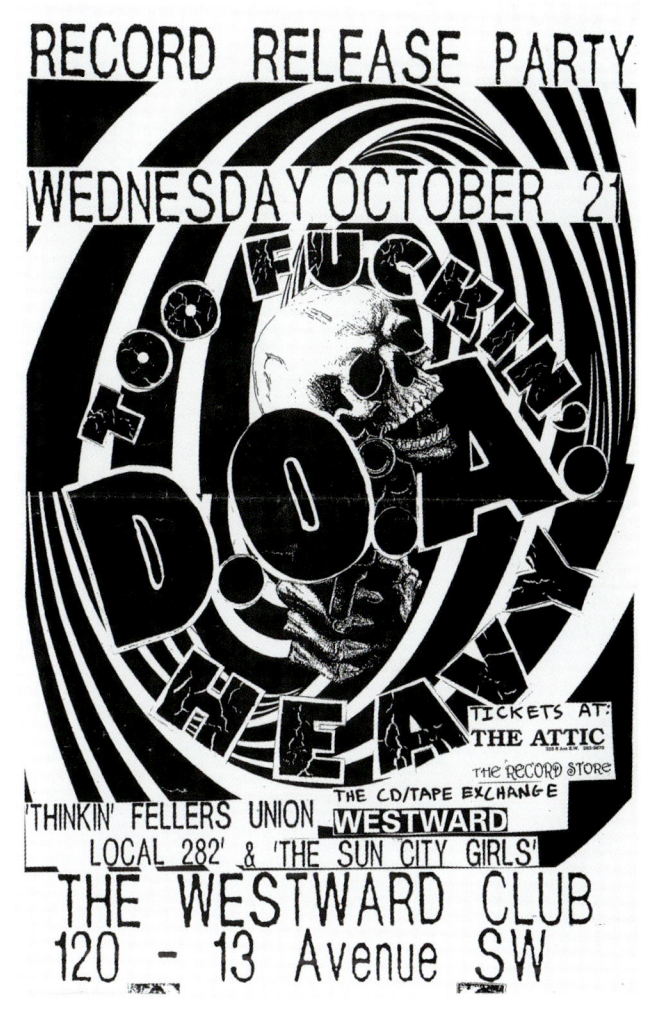

We were already recording a new album, but we didn't have a title yet, so we used the title of one of the new songs: "Too Fuckin' Heavy." The tour was cool, as we had Mr Wrong (Rob Wright from No Means No) as support every night. I've never seen one guy be as loud and powerful as Rob was; he played a ton of songs that would make up the bulk of NMN's next album. The middle of the tour turned out to be a gruel-a-thon, when we played Toronto, Berlin, London (England), and Montreal in about five days. Too Fuckin' Heavy indeed.

D.O.A. and Mr. Wrong Canadian Tour 1992

Date	City	Gig / Promoter	Guarantee	Bonus	Merch	Synopsis
Oct-20	Start					
Oct-21	Calgary	Westward/Wes Hegg	$1,	0.00		kinda lame
Oct-22	Saskatoon	Legion/ CFRN Radio	$1	0.00		good
Oct-23	Winnipeg	Spectrum/Mark Riddell	$	0.00		good
Oct-24	Winnipeg	" " " "	$	0.00		good
Oct-27	Berlin	BID/ Silke		0.00		the best
Oct-28	London, UK	The Grand/Bill Gilliam	$	0.00		great
Oct-30	Montreal	Foufounes/Paget Williams	$	0.00		good
Oct-31	Toronto	Lee's Palace/ Shaun McD.	$	81.00		excellent
Nov-01	Guelph	Trasheteria/Tony Spencer	$	$0.00		lame
Nov-02	London	Electric Banana/ Scott		83.00		ok
Nov-04	Waterloo	Phil's/David Atkinson	$	$0.00		ok/lame
Nov-05	Ottawa	Zaphod/Eugene Haslam	$	$0.00		good
Nov-06	Sudbury	Townhouse/Bernie		$0.00		ok
Nov-07	Thunder Bay	Crocks & Rolls/Frank	$	$0.00		great
Nov-08	Winnipeg	West End CC/David McK.		$0.00		good
Nov-09	Saskatoon	B&W Club/Jason Wettstein		$0.00		rip off
Nov-10	Regina	Channel One/John Vancise		$0.00		great
Nov-12	Edmonton	Bronx/Oliver Friedmann		$0.00		good
Nov-13	Calgary	Republik/Victor Choy		240.00		excellent
	Total	Total		704.00	$1	great!

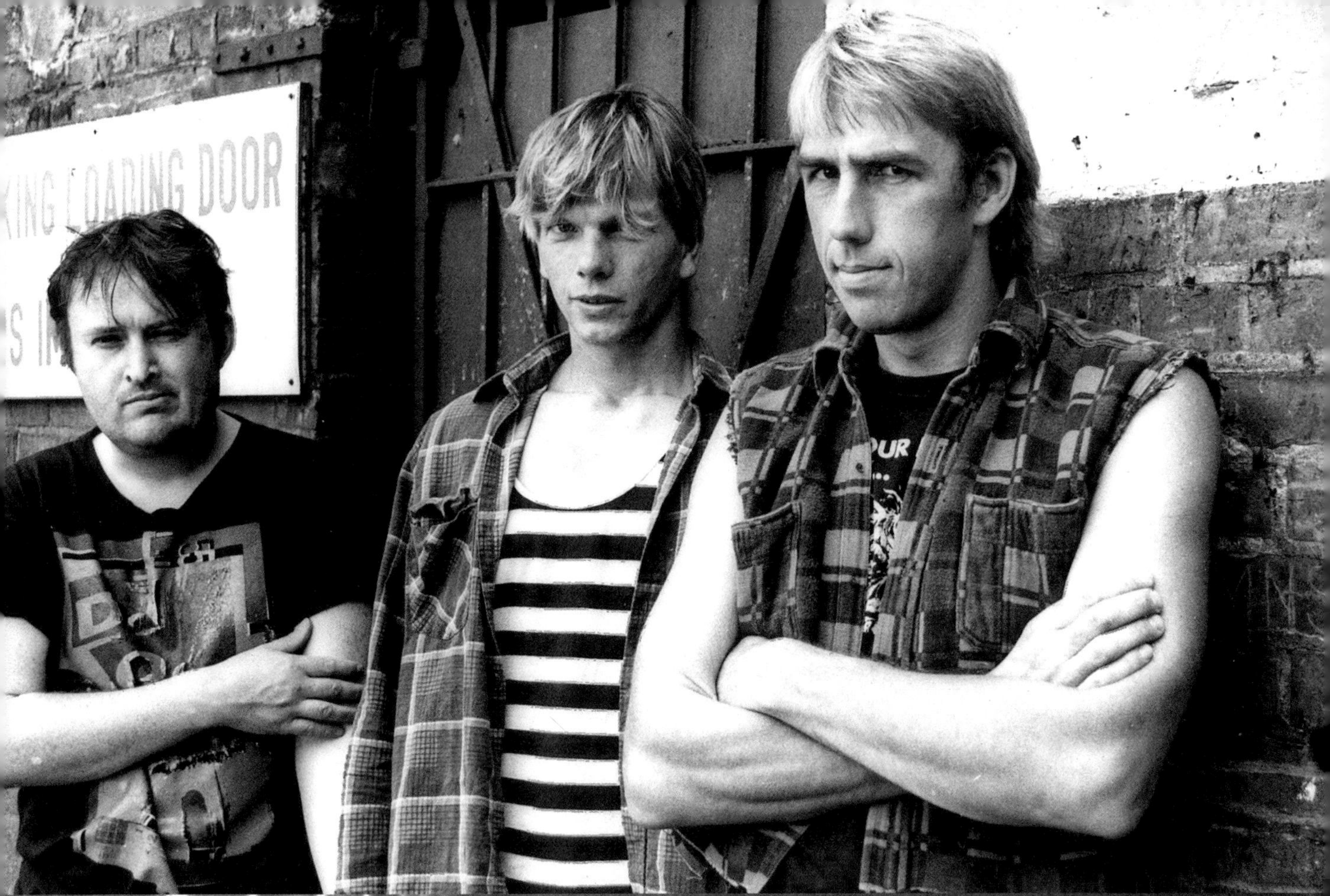
LOADING DOOR

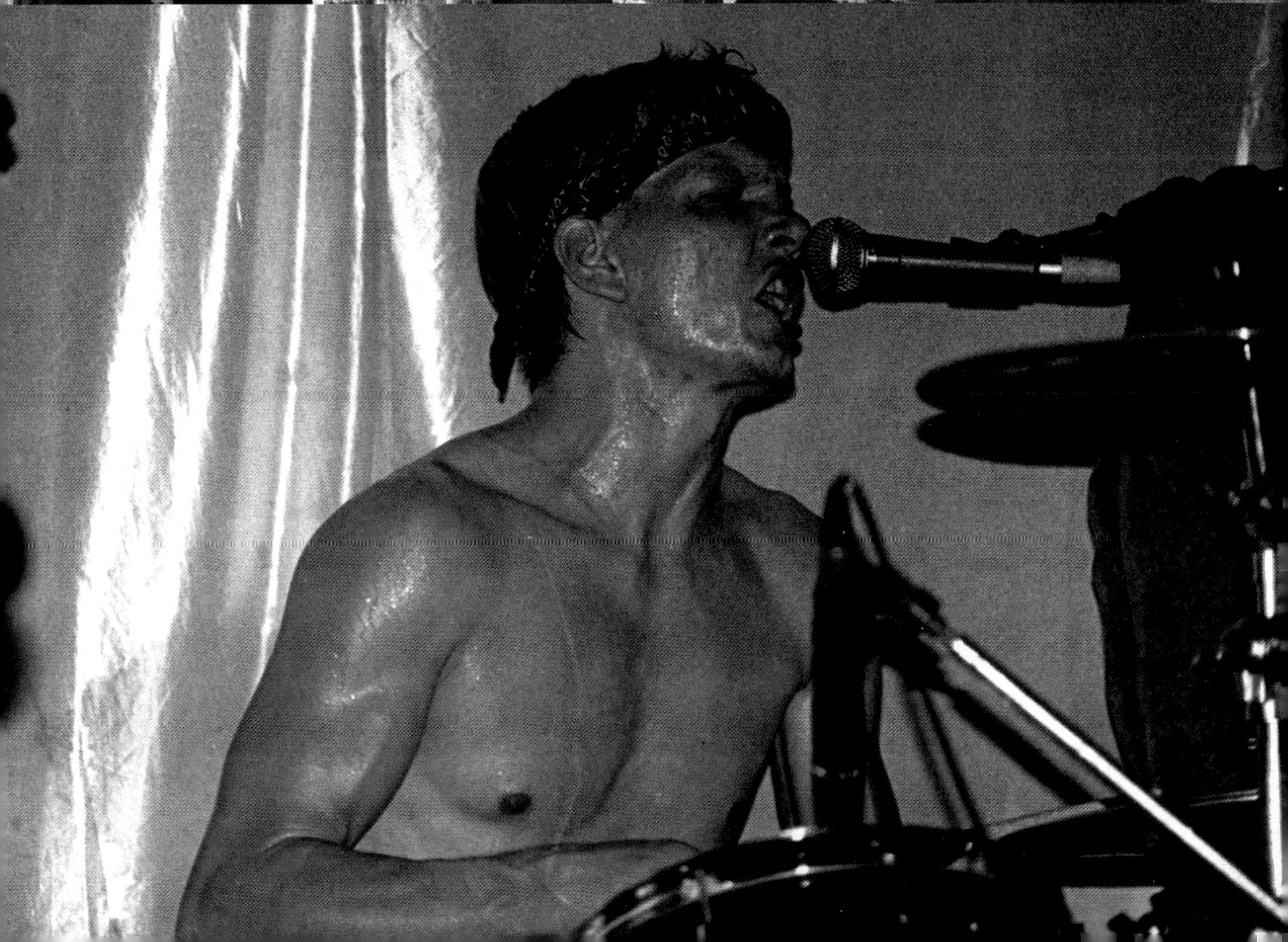

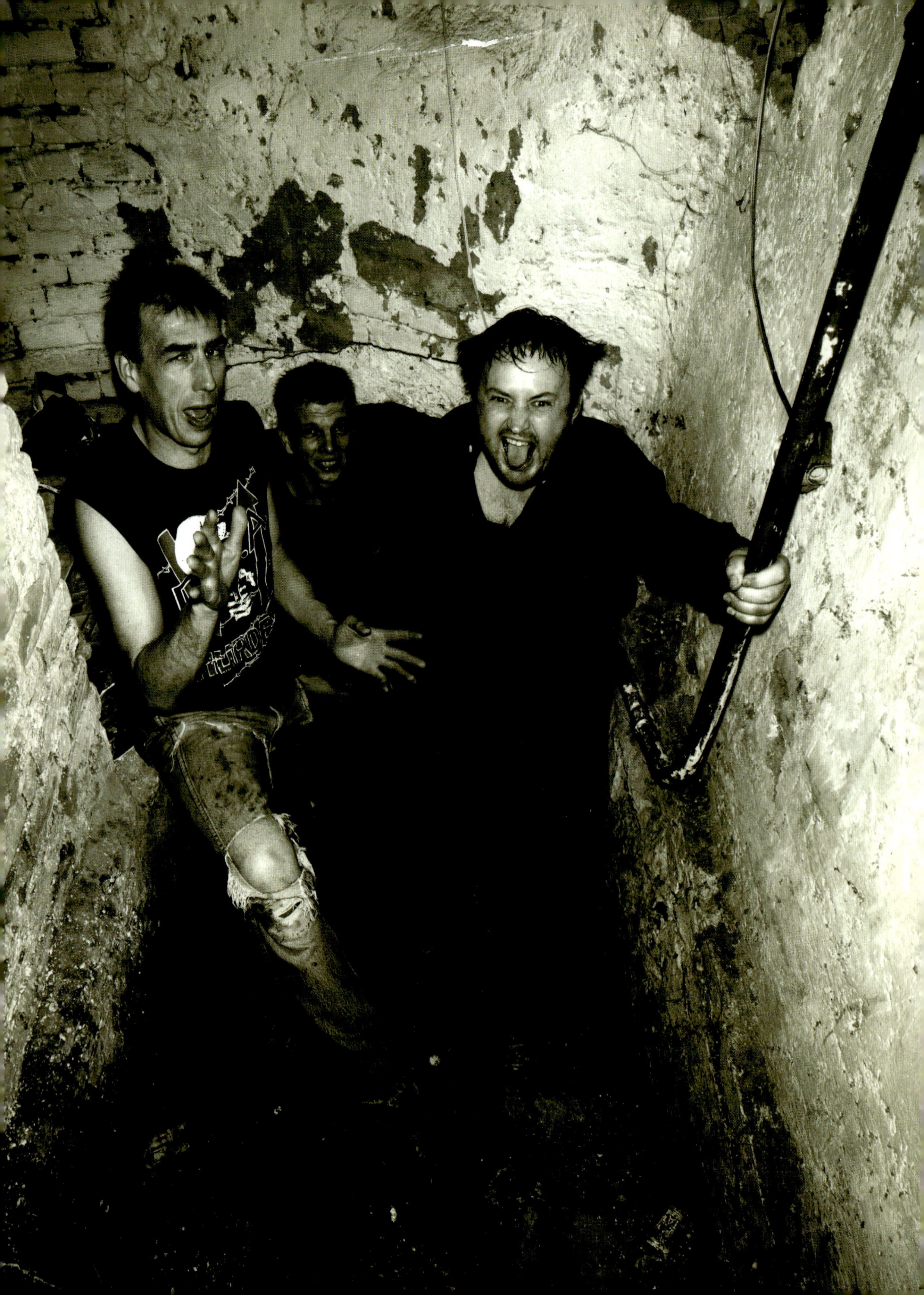

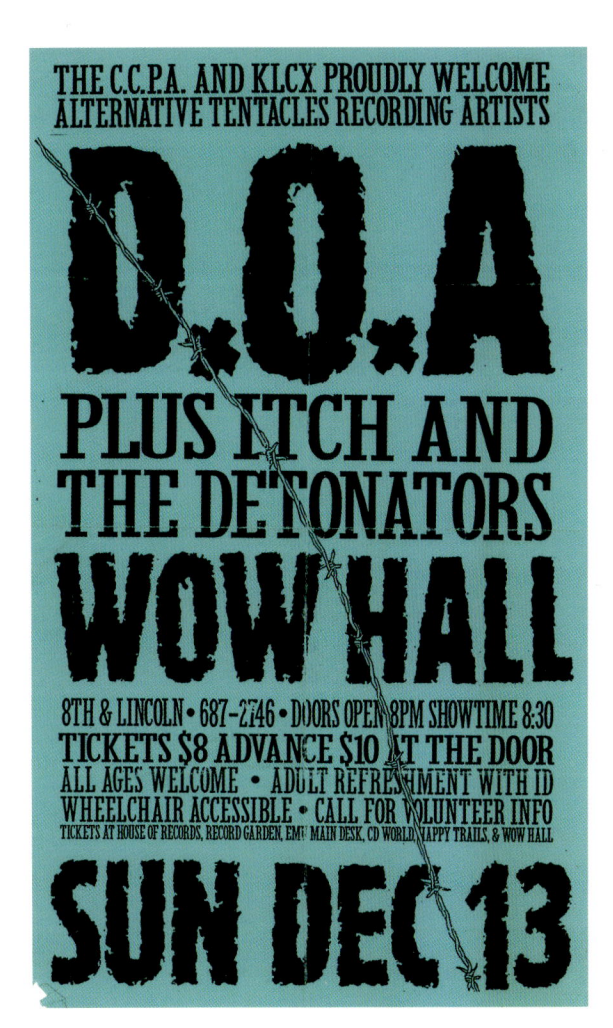

Eugene, Oregon—the anarchist's lair—where all the fun kind of trouble starts.

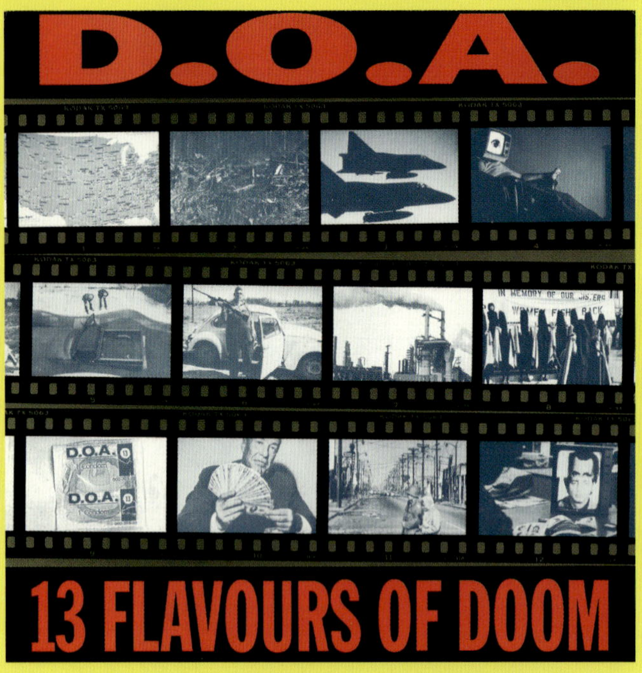
D.O.A.
13 FLAVOURS OF DOOM

ALREADY DEAD
DEATH MACHINE
BOMBS AWAY
THE LIVING DEAD
I PLAYED THE FOOL
TOO FUCKIN' HEAVY
HOLE IN THE SKY
HEY SISTER
USE YOUR RAINCOAT
LEGALIZED THEFT
BEATIN' ROCK'N'ROLL TO DEATH
TIME OF ILLUSION
PHANTOM ZONE

13 FLAVOURS
D.O.A.
OF DOOM

GREENPEACE

ALREADY DEAD

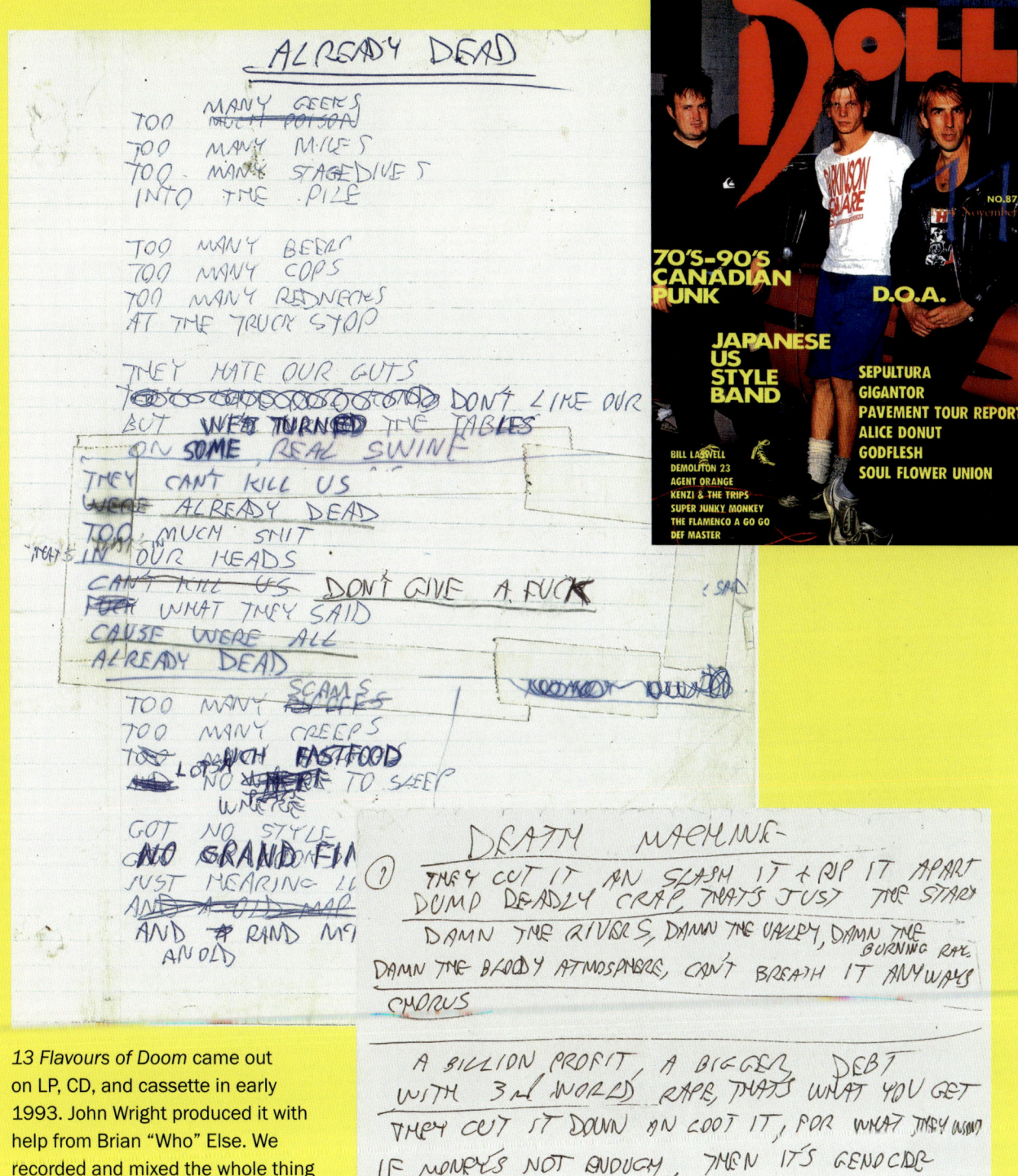

TOO MANY GEEKS
TOO MANY MILES
TOO MANY STAGEDIVES
INTO THE PILE

TOO MANY BEERS
TOO MANY COPS
TOO MANY REDNECKS
AT THE TRUCK STOP

THEY HATE OUR GUTS
DON'T LIKE OUR
BUT WE TURNED THE TABLES
ON SOME REAL SWINE

THEY CAN'T KILL US
WE'RE ALREADY DEAD
TOO MUCH SHIT
THAT'S IN OUR HEADS
CAN'T KILL US DON'T GIVE A FUCK
WHAT THEY SAID
CAUSE WERE ALL
ALREADY DEAD

TOO MANY SCAMS
TOO MANY CREEPS
TOO MUCH FASTFOOD
LOTSA NO WHERE TO SLEEP

GOT NO STYLE
NO GRAND FINALE
JUST HEARING
AND RAND MC
AN OLD

13 Flavours of Doom came out on LP, CD, and cassette in early 1993. John Wright produced it with help from Brian "Who" Else. We recorded and mixed the whole thing in seventeen days. Thanks to Profile Studios, John, and Jello Biafra, we were once again on our way with a cool new album.

DEATH MACHINE

① THEY CUT IT AN SLASH IT & RIP IT APART
DUMP DEADLY CRAP, THAT'S JUST THE START
DAMN THE RIVERS, DAMN THE VALLEY, DAMN THE BURNING RAIN
DAMN THE BLOODY ATMOSPHERE, CAN'T BREATH IT ANYWAYS

CHORUS

A BILLION PROFIT, A BIGGER DEBT
WITH 3rd WORLD RAPE, THAT'S WHAT YOU GET
THEY CUT IT DOWN AN LOOT IT, FOR WHAT THEY WANT
IF MONEY'S NOT ENOUGH, THEN IT'S GENOCIDE

CHORUS

AS I WALK THROUGH THE VALLEY OF DEATH
AND I WHAT WHAT, WHAT IS LEFT
IT RIPS ME, RIPS ME APART
DEATH MACHINE, TEARS OUT MY HEART

D.O.A
WE COME IN PEACE...
USA

ENGRAINED

GLOCKSEESTR. 35 · 3000 HANNOVER · 0511-18774

7.4. GLOCKSEE

At the old Boat Race pub in Cambridge, England, the walls were decorated with pictures of the rowing teams that had whipped arch-rivals Oxford, but the audience was UK punk all the way. One bloke kept trying to charge the stage and grab my mike for some sort of mindless Oi! Oi! Oi! routine. I warned him to back off repeatedly, then finally smashed him in the chest with the sole of my boot as hard as I could. Luckily he had had about twenty beers—he hit the deck hard. After the show, he told me what a great bloody gig it was. Funny, he kind of looked like the guy on the poster.

We finished the UK tour in Newcastle, then were supposed to catch the ferry to Norway for our Scandinavian tour. But the ferry we were supposed to catch from the north of England did not run till summer, which our booking guy had sadly not checked out. So a twelve-hour ferry ride to Oslo, Norway, became a thirty-hour driving and ferry odyssey through the UK, the Netherlands, Germany, Denmark, and Sweden.

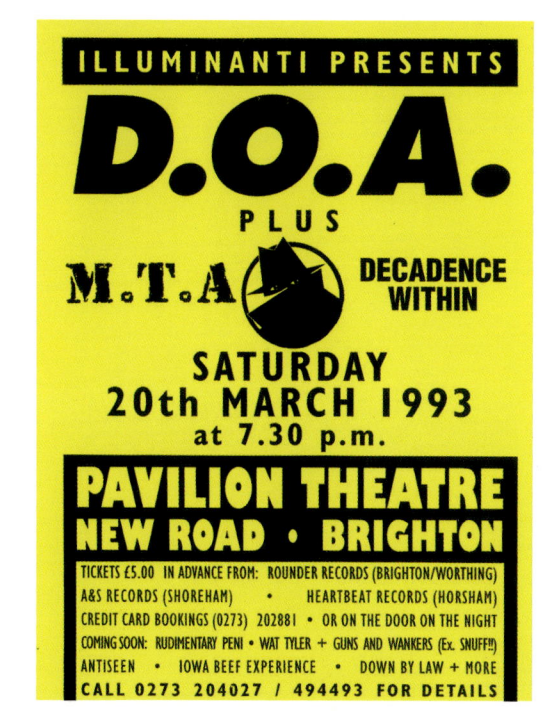

EUROPEAN TOUR 1993

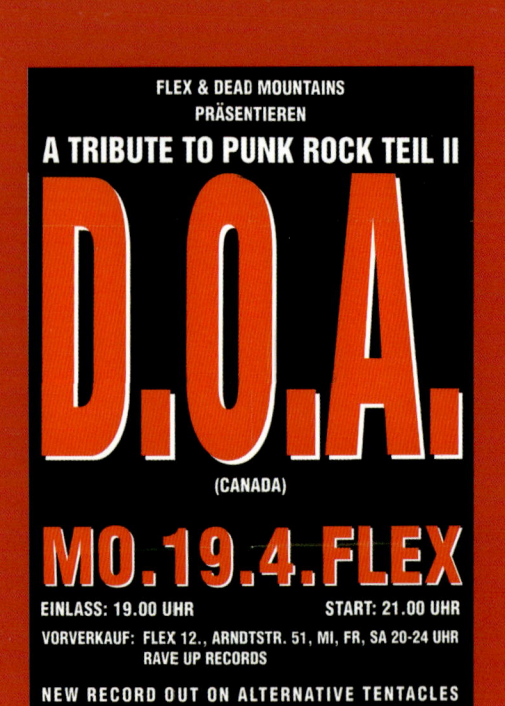

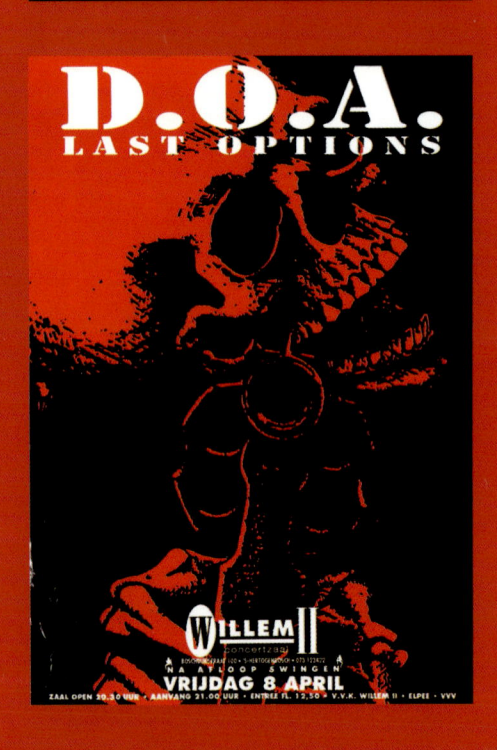

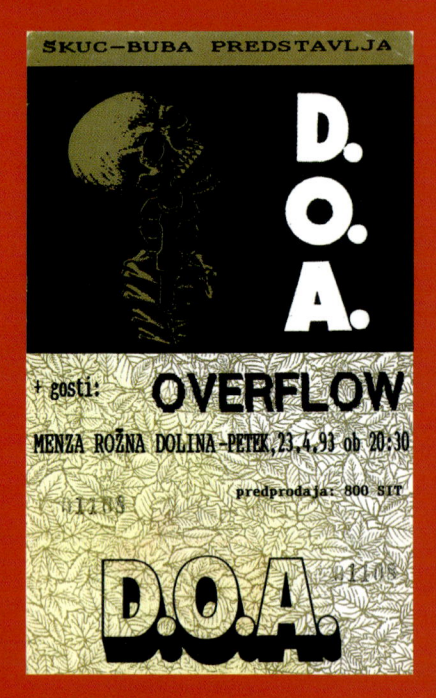

We had two good shows in Austria, but the way they referred to D.O.A. on the posters was rich. After those shows the unofficial title of the tour became: "The Men of Action Do a Tribute to Punk Rock."

About 1,500 punks bent on destruction showed up at the university in Ljubljana, Slovenia. It was complete fucking chaos! By the time we were finished, the front of the hall, which was constructed entirely of glass, was smashed to bits. I put down my guitar and went to grab my anvil case, which had all of our passports and all the cash from the tour. It was gone! Shit! My stomach formed a knot that a fucking fisherman could not undo. Our roadie Booza (RIP) took charge of the stage and I ran over to the merch booth. Ken Jensen had the anvil case in his safe keeping. After the D.O.A. show, the authorities banned punk rock at the university.

On the last song of an encore, Ken Jensen accidentally stabbed himself in the eye at the end of a drum roll. It was serious—he was in a lot of pain and blood was coming out of his eye. We weren't sure what to do. After a while, we decided to drive on to Berlin. Ken and I found a hospital the next morning and he got some "free" treatment. We played a huge show that night at SO36 in Berlin, and then Ken passed out. We cancelled a Stuttgart show the next day so that he could recuperate. For the rest of the tour, on doctor's orders, Ken could not read, watch TV, or do anything with his eye, so he would just lie down on the van's bunk, smoke cigarettes, and wait for the next show.

In Euskadi for the first time (above), I was doing my Reverend Joe Shithead bit and pulled out the D.O.A. silver cross. Both me and the cross got covered in beer in a hurry as the locals got hostile. Then somebody in the audience pulled out a lighter and tried to burn the cross. Holy Christ! That was a REAL revelation! After that, I always wrapped the cross in newspaper and set it on fire; thanks, Euskadi punks!

Almost level with the Po River that runs through the centre of Torino, Italy, there are some brick cavern-type structures where the king used to house his cavalry. The local anarchists had taken over the old horse barns and started putting on shows there. That was cool, but shit, you know sometimes rivers have a mind of their own and go where the fuck they want to after it really rains. And Torino is a lot like my hometown, Burnaby—lots of Italians and even more rain. So the day before the Radio Blackout Benefit, the river rose about twenty feet (six meters) and flooded the venue. As we arrived for the show, the anarchists were still wheel-barrowing the sand out of the hall. While we played, the ceiling water continued to drip through. Wimpy, not wanting to die from electrocution, stayed miles from his mike stand.

Before our show in Madrid, the organizers told us not to leave any valuables in the van, as they would be ripped off, so we emptied everything into the venue. Shit, it was like being back in Vancouver again!

After the show waaaay out on the wild west coast of Spain in Santiago De Compostela, we had to haul ass to get to France. Our roadie Booza took to passing ten to fifteen cars at a time on the horrible winding roads.

ZâR & Katakomb présentent...

D.O.A.

GONOKOX

Vendredi 7 mai

Salle Louis Jouvet

Rue Albert Dupuis
Rouen Les Sapins

Ouverture des portes 19 h

Prix des places : 50 balles

1 conso gratuite aux adhérents ZâR & Katakomb

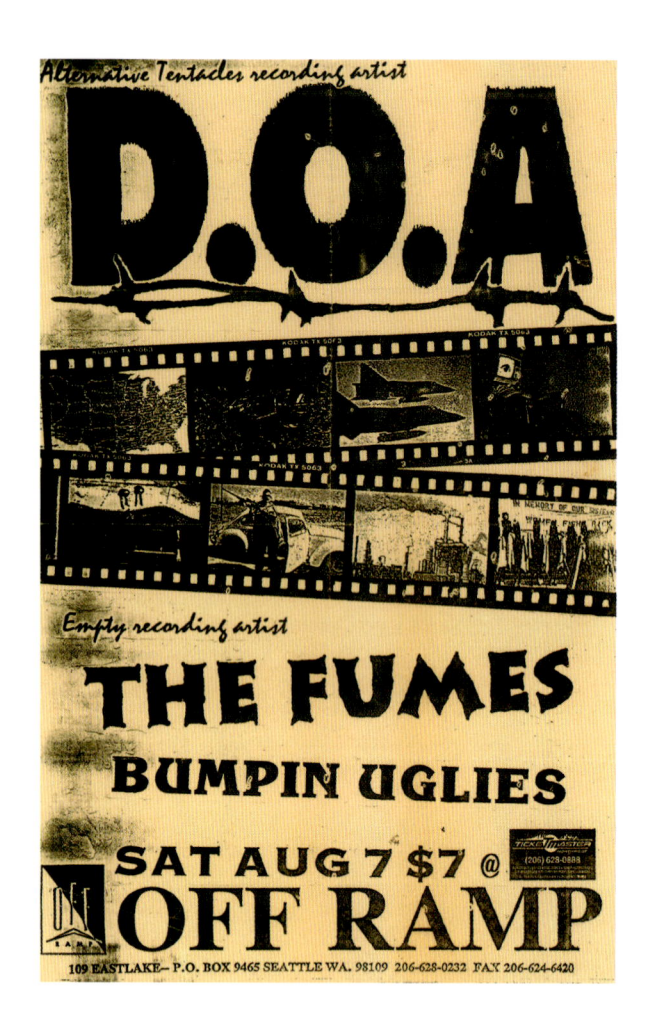

The Only Thing Green

You must have heard by now, it's time to go green
Get on the band wagon, it helps to be seen
But it's not a simple job, saving the Earth
So start with lip service, you know what it's worth

Time to clean up, the profits are high
Make a quick buck, let the B.S. fly

The only thing green in the colour of their money
Politicians and businessmen on the band wagon
They don't give a damn, they're liars and they're phoney
The only thing green is the colour of your money

There's lots of opportunity with the environment
And if you lie enough, you might become president
They make it friendly, they make it clean
But the crap they leave will never disappear

It's good for the Earth, it's good for the sky
Just count the cash, sell the lies

The only thing green in the colour of their money
Politicians and businessmen on the band wagon
They don't give a damn, they're liars and they're phoney
The only thing green is the colour of your money

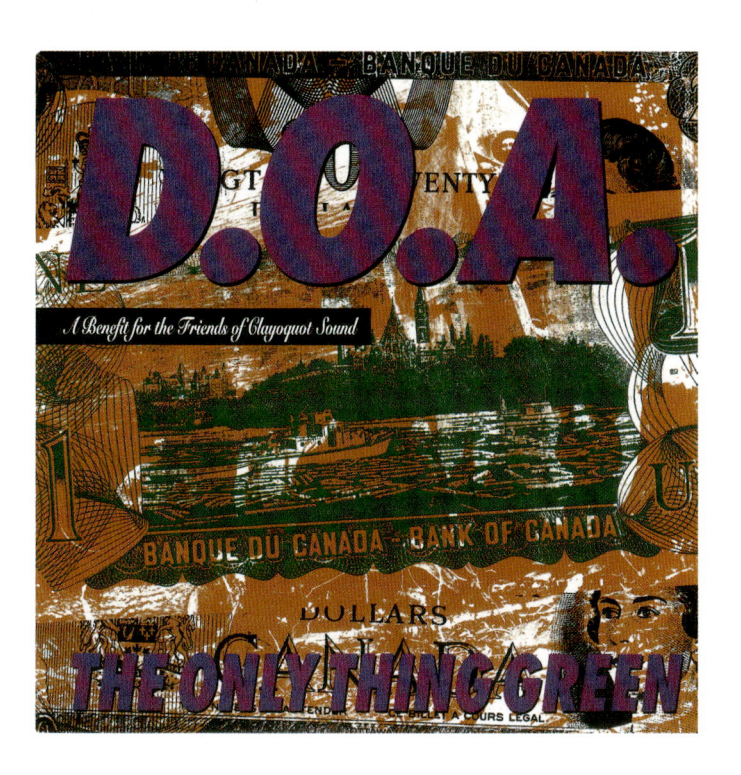

"The Only Thing Green" was a benefit single released in the fall of 1993 to help stop the clear-cutting of the old growth forest in Clayoquot Sound on British Columbia's Vancouver Island.

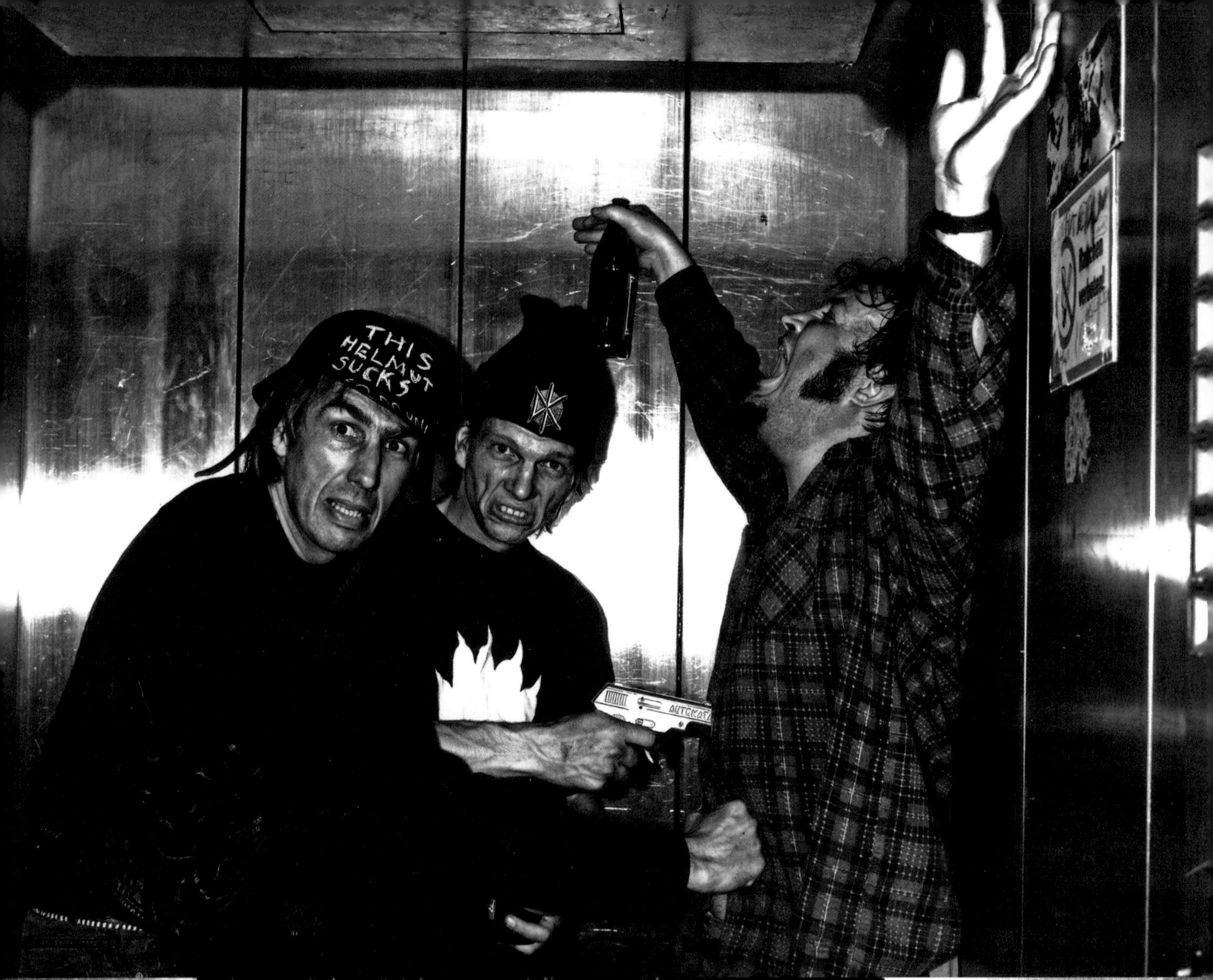
THIS
HELMUT
SUCKS

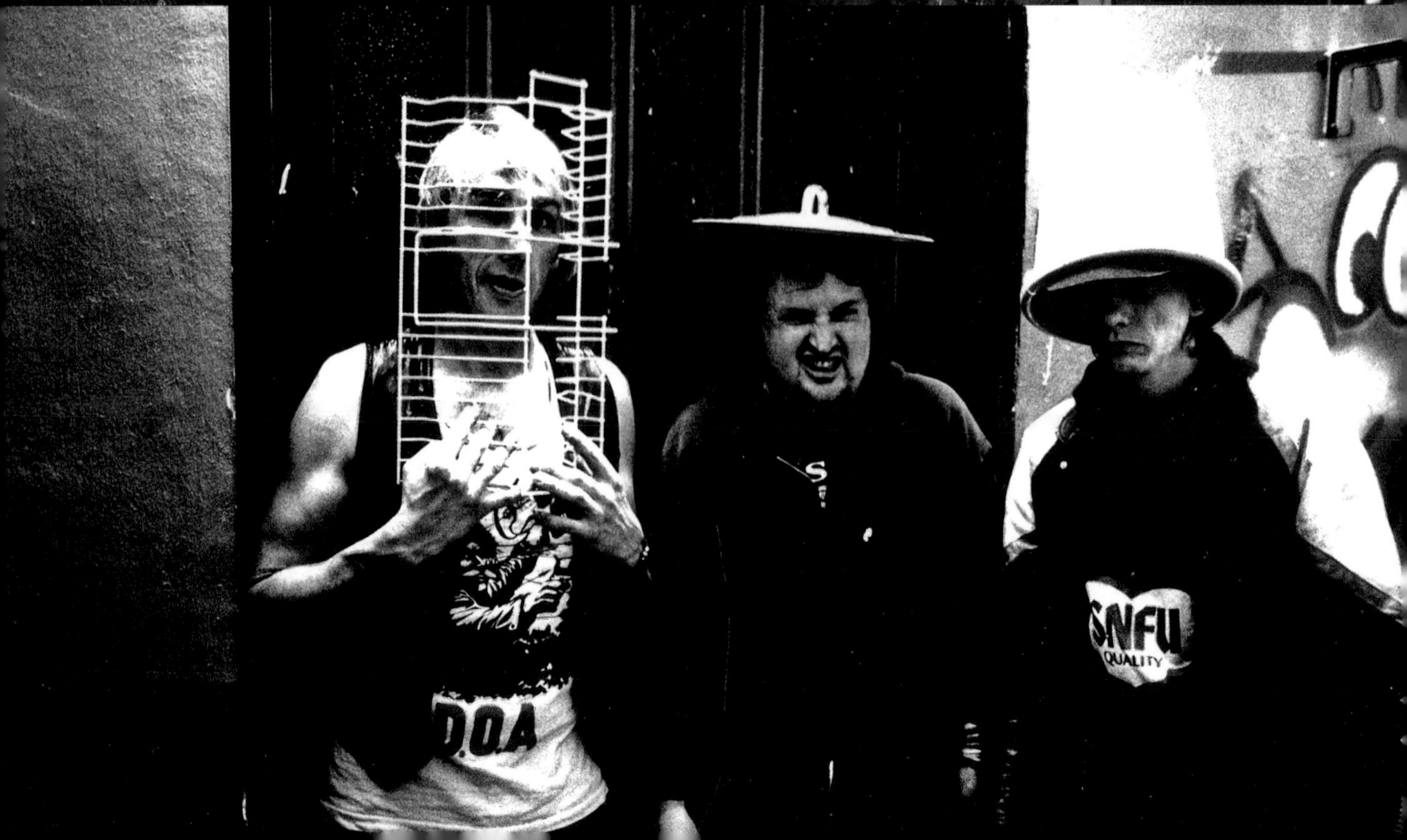
D.O.A
SNFU
QUALITY

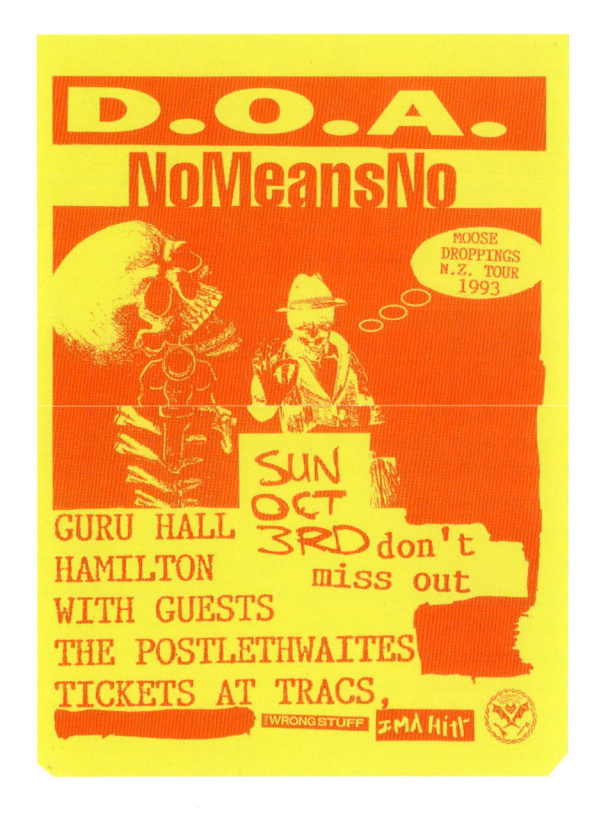

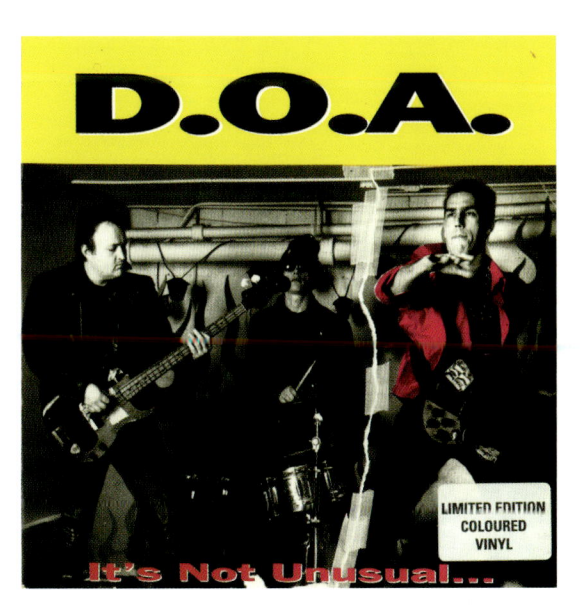

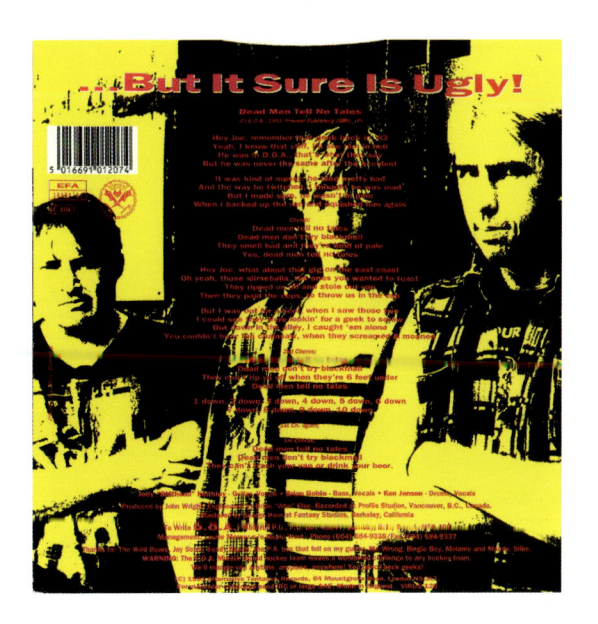

On our first trip to Australia and New Zealand, the gigs were great, the people were great, but then we got ripped off by the promoter at the end of the tour.

One morning Craig Bougie (tour soundman) and I were standing on the street in front of the backpacker's hostel where we were staying in Sidney. A beer truck drove by. The driver hadn't closed the back gate of his lorry, and a keg rolled off the truck and nearly crushed Craig. We grabbed it, took it upstairs, iced it down, and had our suds supply for the next week or two.

We did a ten-day European tour to promote the upcoming *Loggerheads* album and the "Not Unusual" single.

Gilman Greet in Berkeley was one of the coolest shows back in the day.

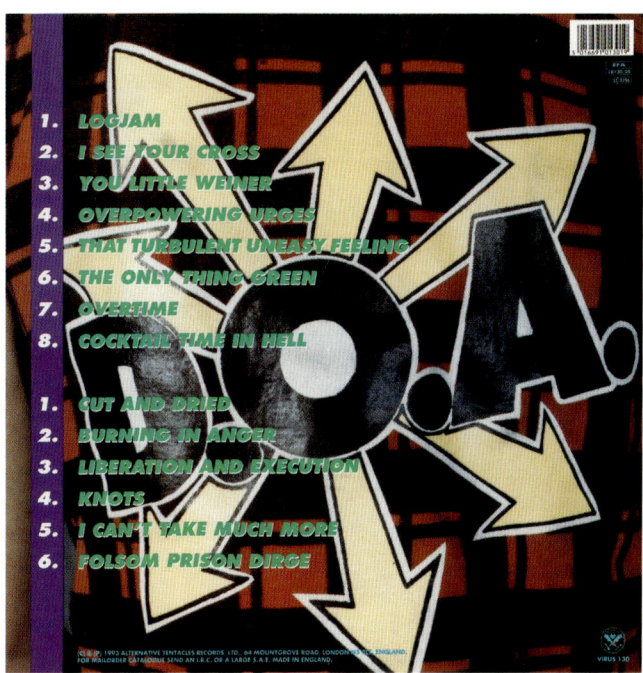

After the success of *13 Flavours of Doom,* we started working on a slew of new songs right away. Again we got John Wright to produce and Brian "Who" Else to engineer. It came out strong, and Ken Jensen came up with a couple of cool songs. D.O.A. was definitely running at full throttle. We had the album release party in Vancouver.

We started off the European tour with our first trip to Ireland. The show in Cork went well, but Dublin got cancelled, being Easter Good Friday, and we couldn't even get a pint of Guinness! Once we got past the British Army checkpoint for Northern Ireland, we played in Belfast. Good show and a tough bunch of kids there.

We stopped at the famous squat called EX in Kreuzberg, Berlin.

In Zaragoza, I sang with the opening band Parasito as they performed D.O.A.'s "Burn It Down." It was fun, but the strangest version I had ever heard!

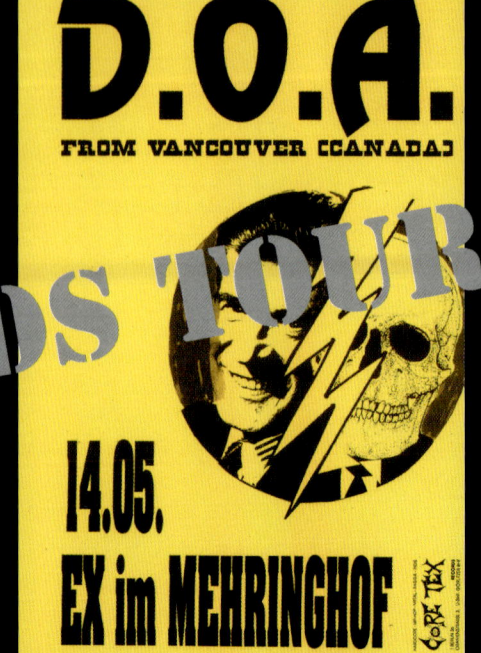

LOGGERHEADS TOUR

INDIPENDENCE DAY
Prepariamo il corteo del 14 settembre a Milano!
sabato
14 settembre
MAU MAU
domenica
15
D.O.A.
al Centro Sociale
Leoncavallo

D.O.A.
Nine Nine Nine
TOXIC YOUTH
in concerto
Venerdì aprile 22
dalle ore 23
in via Salomone 71
tram 12 / bus 66
Centro Sociale
LEONCAVALLO

ZâR & KATAKOMB présentent
STILL ANGRY
D.O.A.
LE SAMEDI 9 AVRIL
A LA GARE MARTAINVILLE
(ROUTE DE LYONS)
19 h 50 balles
1 conso gratuite aux adhérents ZâR & Katakomb
location : Katakomb, Mur du Son, Rose Bonbon, fnac
renseignements : 35 07 38 10

Producciones ZAMBOMBO, Bar Berlín y A. M. UTOPIA Presentan:
DESDE CANADA, 1978 - 1994 , Y TRAS 16 AÑOS DE PUNK Y ACTIVISMO:
D.O.A.
+ PARASITOS
DOMINGO 17 ABRIL
20 PM
700 Pts
UTOPIA
C/ LUIS DEL VALLE

D.O.A. (KANADA) **+ PANIKOS** (GRIECHENLAND)

11.5. RHENANIA 10,-

The next night we played at the Txitxarro in Euskadi near San Sebastian. Great show, but at the end of the night, Booza was packing up the van and took his eye off my Gibson SG guitar. Somebody pinched it and took off down the hill from the club. We searched and searched the area, but it was gone. I sat down and cried. I bought that guitar in 1975, and pretty well every song I had ever written was composed on it. A no questions asked monetary reward was circulated, but to no avail. Booza always said that I would get it back, but I was not so sure; this was the third time it had been stolen. But sure enough, about six months after the tour, I got the guitar back with a letter of apology. In 2002, when we were back in Euskadi, the promoter actually introduced me to the guy who had stolen the guitar, who told me he felt great shame and apologized, which I accepted.

```
LAST SET
W/ KEN JENSEN
DEC 31/94

E TO C / E TO D
13
I'M RIGHT / YOU'RE WRONG
DEATH MACHINE
2+2
BEHIND THE SMILE
AMERICA
UNCHAINED / LOST TIME
LITTLE WEINER
LET'S WRECK
LIVING DEAD
ALREADY DEAD
ONLY THING GREEN
LEGALIZED THEFT
SLAVE TO MY DICK
THE PRISONER
```

The hall for this show was right on the Rhine River in Cologne, Germany. The crowd was beserk: people were swinging off the lights and just generally fucking things up. While we played, the PA got hit by a mosh pit wave and as it started to topple, I caught the stack with my left arm and pushed it upright. I kept waving frantically to the sound crew to come over and prevent a re-occurrence, but they were so busy partying that they just thought I was egging the crowd on and waved back at me! I kept my eye on the PA stack and caught it a couple of more times that night.

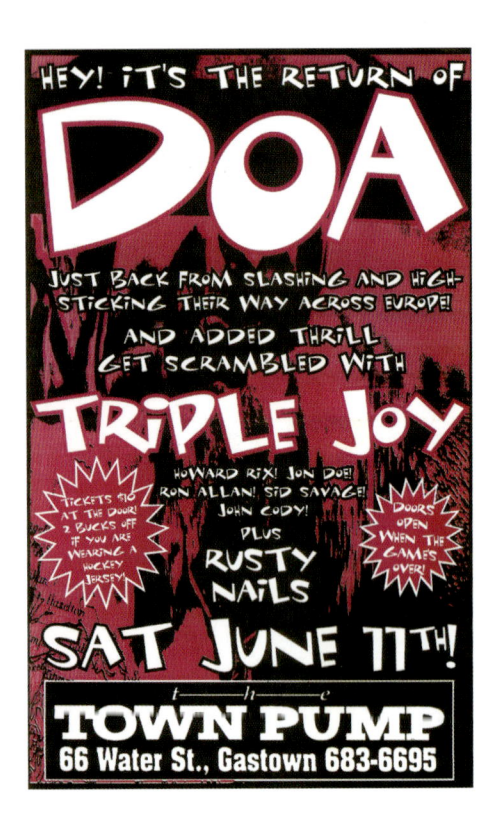

Back in Vancouver, the Canucks beat the New York Rangers in game six of the Stanley Cup final the night of June 11. Rangers fans were allowed into our show, but only if they turned their jerseys inside out.

Rock & Twang was an incredible outdoor show in Rossland, BC. The stage was at the bottom of the ski hill. There were bales of hay near the stage to soak up the water in case it rained. Punks started throwing hay around during the Smalls' set. "That looks like fun," I thought, until we got up there and they started chucking hay at us. The city boys soon discovered that hay also contains rocks and dirt.

D.O.A.

THE DAWNING OF A NEW ERROR

D.O.A. MINI-TOUR, FALL 1994

10/13 - LOS ANGELES, CA - The Roxy or Los Palmos Theater	10/23 - FORT WORTH, TX - Mad Hatter's
10/14 - SAN FRANCISCO, CA - Great American Music Hall	10/24 - KANSAS CITY, KS - The Grand Emporium
10/15 - LOS ANGELES, CA - Orange County or UC Long Beach	10/25 - LAWRENCE, KS - The Bottleneck
10/16 - TUCSON, AZ - Downtown Performance Center	10/26 - ST. LOUIS, MO - TBA
10/17 - PHOENIX, AZ - Boston's	10/27 - SIOUX CITY, IA - Cattle Club
10/19 - ALBUQUERQUE, NM - Golden West	10/28 - DENVER, CO - TBA
10/20 - SAN ANTONIO, TX - Wacky's	10/29 - SALT LAKE CITY, UT - Cinema Bar
10/21 - AUSTIN, TX - Emo's	
10/22 - HOUSTON, TX - The Abyss	

Check local listings for venue confirmation where necessary

13 FLAVOURS OF DOOM
13 Song CD/MC/LP

LOGGERHEADS
14 Song CD/MC/LP

THE ONLY THING GREEN
2 Song 7" (Clayoquot Sound benefit single)

I got some tragic news on September 27th, 1994: Our old drummer and one of my best friends, Dimwit, had OD'd. Wimpy, Gerry Useless, Dimwit, and I had been the four amigos in high school. When Dimwit passed away, a piece of me died inside. We put on a tribute show at the Commodore with a great lineup of talent. We did a somewhat faithful reunion of our first real rock band, Stone Crazy, with Wimpy, Brad Kent, me, and Terry (Tankhog) filling in for Dimwit on drums. Miss you like crazy.

COMMODORE BALLROOM
DECEMBER 28, 1994
AN EVENING WITHOUT DIMWIT

FEATURING:
The Four Horsemen
The Modernettes
Stone Crazy
Frank Frink 500
Bottom Feeders
Jim Cummins

Doors 8:30
Show 9:00
Tickets at all Ticketmaster outlets, Track Records, and Groove Music
Charge by phone 280-4444

Ken "Dimwit" Montgomery played with all the above acts at one time or another. Proceeds from this concert will go to erecting a park bench in his memory.

A Perryscope/Randall Thomas Carpenter Co-Production

On January 29, 1995, I was just sitting down to watch the Super Bowl when the phone rang. It was Tom Holliston (No Means No), who told me that Ken Jensen had died in a house fire. I was in shock. Wimpy, Tom, and I met at Ken's house in East Van. It was hard to believe that Ken was gone. Overcome by smoke, he had hit his head and died of smoke inhalation. Jensen was a real fun, top-notch friend.

A cigarette falling into a couch at a party had caused our friend and drummer to die. As in many old houses in East Van (and elsewhere), there was no smoke detector. We decided to put on a couple of awareness/benefit shows around the issue. Our manager Laurie Mercer and friends organized a show at the Commodore, and Bob Dog (Dog Eat Dogma) got an all-ages show going at the New York Theatre in East Van. These shows raised a bunch of dough for the Carnegie Community Centre and bought a bunch of smoke detectors for folks that needed 'em. Around Easter '95, my pal James McLean (October Crisis/Courage Artists) organized two benefit shows for D.O.A. in Toronto to replace our equipment that had been destroyed in the fire. Many thanks to everybody who helped out.

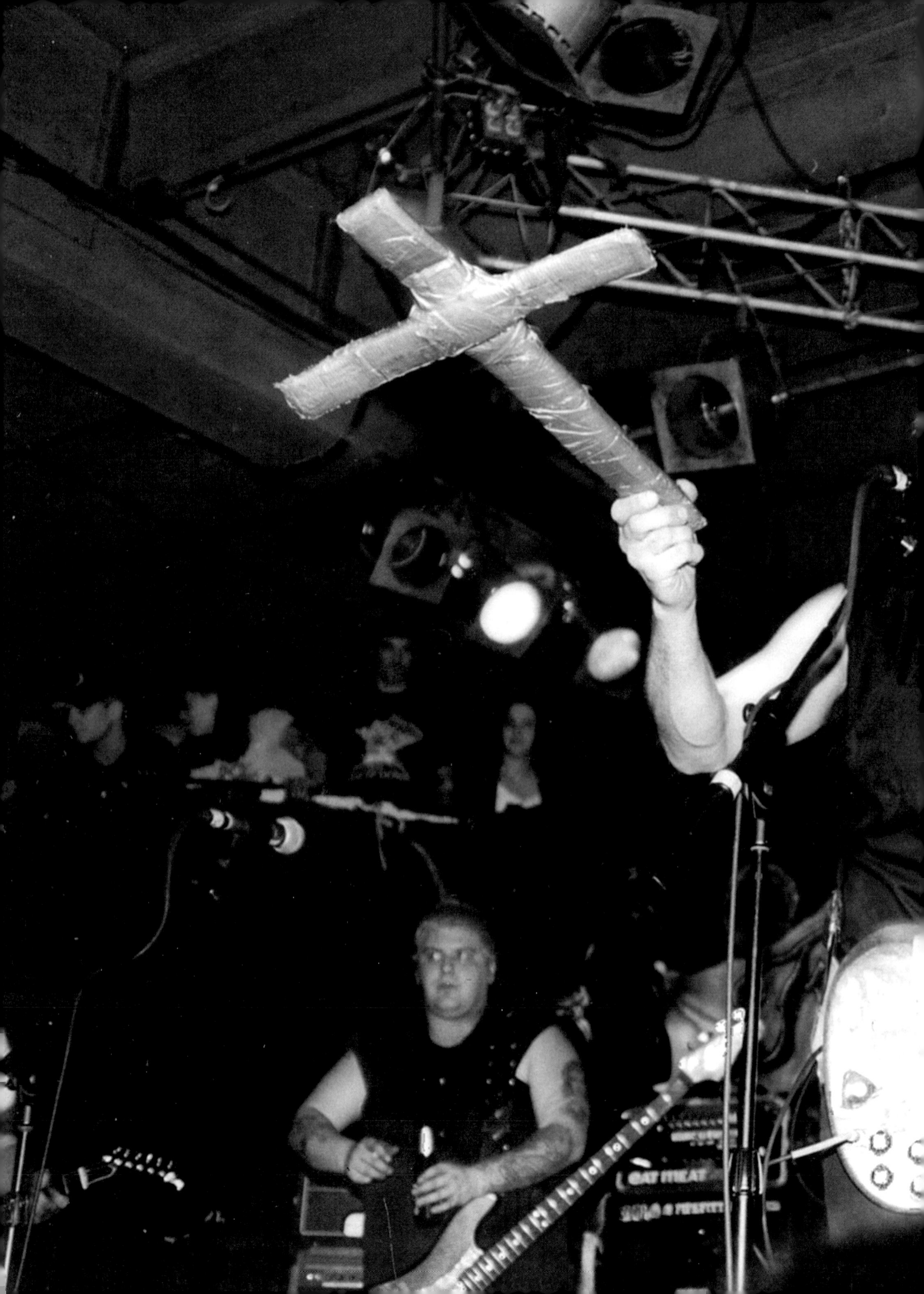

Chapter 8

1995-2000

Our merch catalogue.

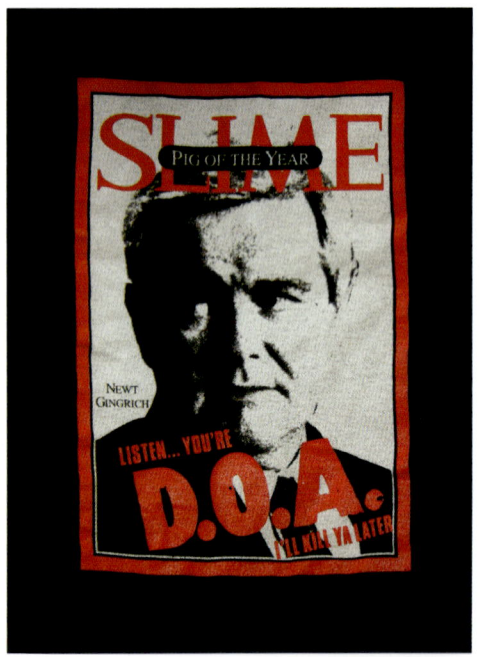

BRING BACK THE FUTURE!

After Ken died, we were devastated. We took the demo tapes out of the ruined house and played them for John Wright. We had been working on these songs for a follow-up to *Loggerheads*. John graciously agreed to play on the album, *the Black Spot*, which was released on Laurie Mercer's new label, Essential Noise. We got a new drummer in Brien O'Brien (from Curious George and Chrome Dog) and added the illustrious Ford Pier on second guitar. The tours, riots, and fuck-ups continued around the world till the end of '96, when Wimpy and Ford both left. This was a fucking drag, for sure, but with friends like that, I understood; revolution is constant.

Brien and I started making demos for a new album; he drummed, I sang, played guitar, and bass. There was no record company, no lineup—it was not fuckin' good! It was time to spread out, so at the urging of our soundman Bob Cutler, I started doing spoken word. That was cool, just keepin' it real, man! I also entered provincial politics; I ran for the Green Party in Burnaby and in the election I finished ahead of the leader of the BC Conservative Party in my riding. Although I wasn't elected, my campaign helped to get out our ideas about saving what's left of this planet.

Then came another real turning point, when I decided to start up Sudden Death Records again as a serious label. This breathed new life into me and into D.O.A. Our first release was *Festival of Atheists*. We got in a lot of shit with religious groups for that title. Kuba joined D.O.A. as our live bassist, and later, the Great Baldini took over on the drums. I ran for city council again in '99, and again I was not elected. I also put out a solo acoustic album called *Beat Trash* and started playing acoustically at protests and on picket lines. During this period, we did lots of Canadian dates, five European tours, and three big US tours.

BLACK SPOT TOUR

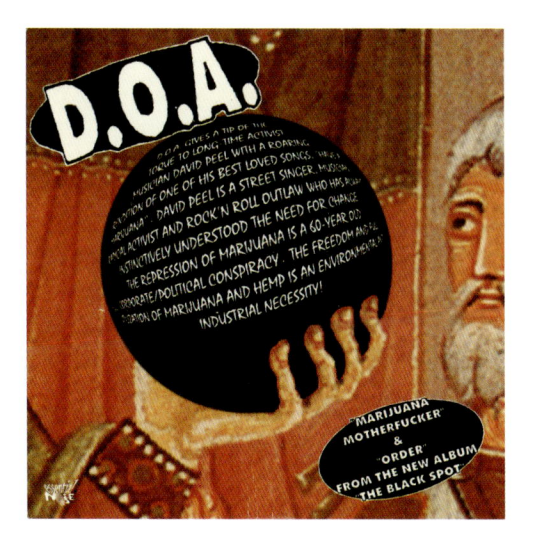

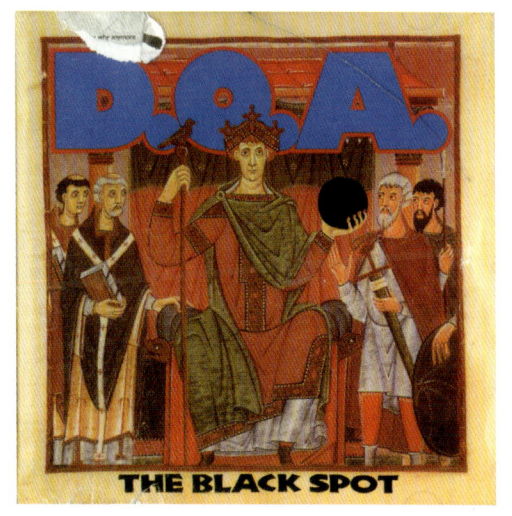

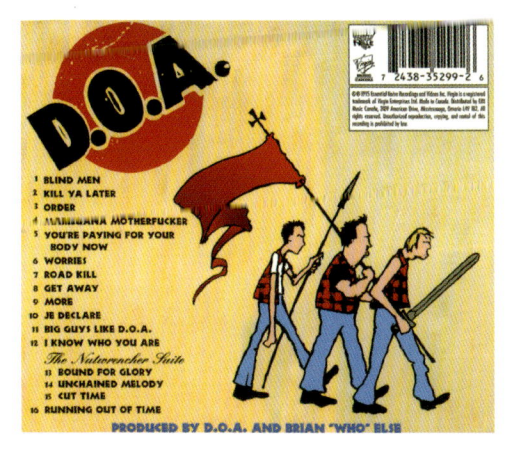

In the fall of '94 before Ken Jensen passed away, we had been working on demos for a new studio album. After Ken's funeral in Victoria, John Wright volunteered to fill in on drums for the upcoming disc the Black Spot. We recorded the bed tracks at Mushroom Studio and finished it up at Green House Studios, with John, Ford, Wimpy, Brian "Who" Else, and myself co-producing. It was released in the fall of 1995.

Once the album was out, we did a cross-Canada tour with our new drummer, Brien O'Brien. The poster, above left, is from our stop in Toronto at Lee's Palace, inspired by Wimpy's song "Big Guys Like D.O.A."

WORRIES
KILL YA LATER
ORDER

```
        D.O.A. TOUR SCHEDULE
        as of Nov. 6th, 1995

   * Nov.  3 - Republik - Calgary
   * Nov.  4 - The Power Plant - Edmonton
   * Nov.  6 - Student Union - Regina
   * Nov.  8 - Townehouse - Sudbury
   * Nov.  9 - Barrymore's - Ottawa
   * Nov. 10 - Foufoune Electrique - Montreal
   * Nov. 11 - Almonte Community Hall - Almonte
   * Nov. 13 - L'Importateur - Quebec City
   * Nov. 15 - The Capri Club - Sydney
   * Nov. 17 - Pyramid Club - Fredericton
   * Nov. 16 - Madhatter's - St. John, N.B.
   * Nov. 18 - Birdland - Halifax
   * Nov. 19 - Venue TBA - Bathurst, N.B.
   * Nov. 21 - Market Hall - Peterborough
   * Nov. 22 - The X Club - Hamilton
   * Nov. 23 - The Volcano - Kitchener
   * Nov. 24 - Lee's Palace - Toronto
   * Nov. 25 - The Hideaway - St. Catherines
   * Nov. 26 - The Embassy - London
   * Nov. 28 - Crocks'n Rolls - Thunder Bay
   * Nov. 29 - The Pyramid - Winnipeg
   * Dec.  2 - The Garage - Nelson, B.C.

Attention: Doug Caldwell
cc: Geoff, Nancy and all concerned parties!
Please note latest additions!
```

I'M RUF
BIG GU
FUCK YOU
ALREADY DEAD
I KNOW WND
OVERTIME

219

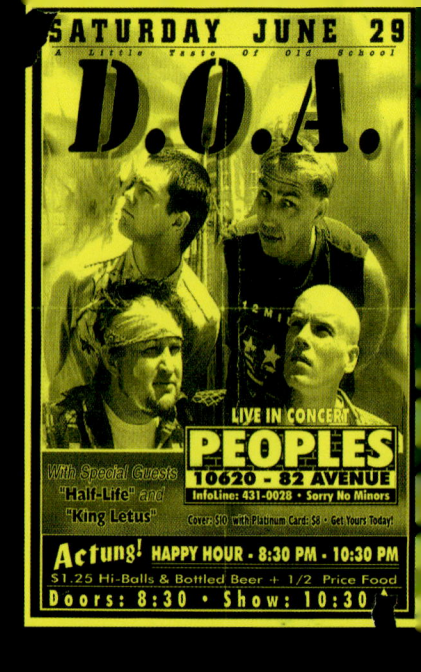

We headed off in late August for a European tour. The first stop was Poznan, Poland. When we arrived at the open air festival (we headlined the first night), our roadie Bob Dog discovered that some of the would-be attendees were stashing various crude weapons, such as machetes and clubs, underneath the stage. Bob alerted me and we moved the weapons to where these goons could not find them. As the show proceeded, we discovered that two of the bands each had a skinhead following from the separate towns they came from. So when the music started, all hell broke loose, as the gangs fought to the last dislocated knuckle. We told the promoter: No security, no D.O.A. show. Thirty minutes later, in marched a ton of burly guys in matching almost fascistic black jackets; that was our security. But by the time we played, the skinheads were worn out and they left, dragging their knuckles all the way to the train station.

On tour back in the US, we played in Baltimore, Maryland, not far from Lexington Market. After the show it was my turn to sleep in Reid Fleming and be the van guard so our shit didn't get ripped off. I was about to crash out when these gangbangers noticed me in the van, which was parked in a lot just behind the hotel. They started giving me grief, suggesting I come on out. I put the key in the ignition so I could run the fuckers down if push came to shove. Out of nowhere this old, streetwise homeless guy came up, saw what was happening, and chased them off. He said, "I'll wash your windows for ya, man." I gave him ten bucks. At the Lexington Market that day, Ford had purchased some raw oysters and called us wimps for not partaking. The next day we drove Ford to John Hopkins' Hospital Emergency for food poisoning. Ford barely recovered, but he got up and managed to play the show.

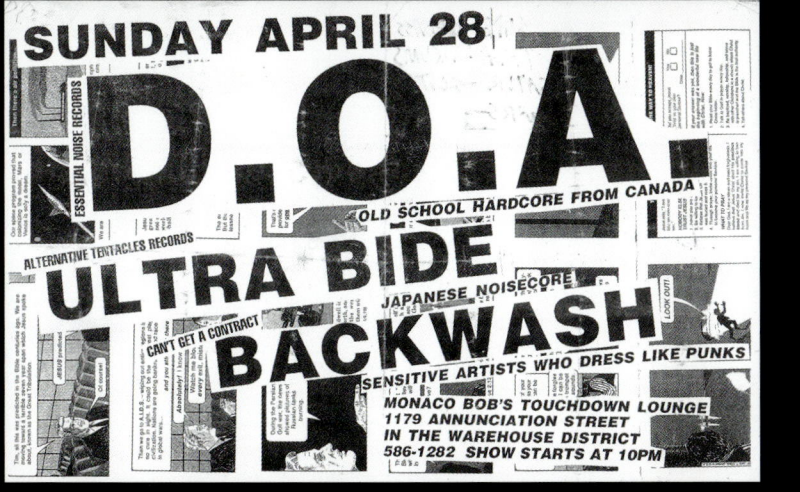

We had just finished a three-week tour from California to Texas with NMN. Then we started for another three weeks touring the eastern half of the USA with the ultra cool Ultra Bide from Japan. Our show in New Orleans was at the absurdly named Monaco Bob's Touchdown Lounge. Ford decided to test the strength of the local alcoholic drink "the Hurricane." I told him more than two would be disaster, but Ford decided four or five along with a dozen beer would do the trick. Let's just say D.O.A. played a nouveau jazz set that night.

Back in Rome at Europe's greatest squat, Forte Prenestino, about 3,000 fans and troublemakers attended. This was the third time we had played at the Forte. It is, in some ways, one of the most amazing places I've ever been to. It's a squat featuring living space, a recording studio, and an outdoor venue large enough to hold over 3,000 people. The Forte was originally built for the defence of Rome in the 1800s, then the Germans used it as their headquarters during World War II. It's great to think something that had housed war criminals could now be used for the people, by the people.

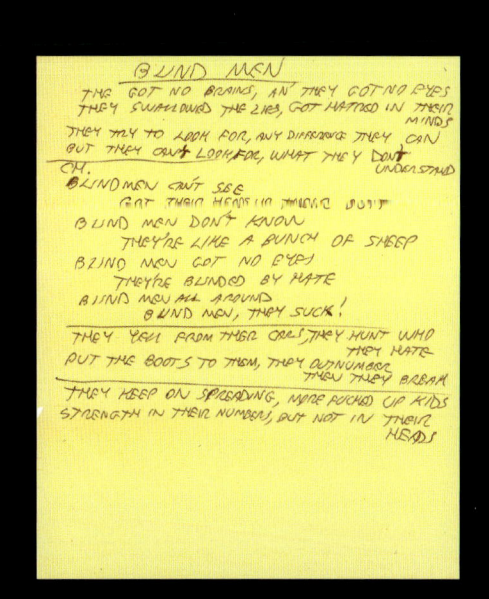

[X] VOTE GREEN PARTY

JOE KEITHLEY
(IN BURNABY WILLINGDON)

[X] JOE KEITHLEY:

"I am running for the Greens because the other parties just don't seem to get it...we need to conserve & preserve what is left of the planet,"

Joe is a life long Burnaby resident. He is married and has two children.

Joe is lead singer for the internationally renowned alternate music group D.O.A. D.O.A. has supported environmental and progressive causes for over ten years. Joe is active in the struggle to save Discovery Park.

JOEY — Beware of False Prophets!

1. Dump The Bosses
2. There's a man goin' around takin' names
3. You won't stand alone
4. The Yuppie has to die

(same tracks on both sides)

BEWARE OF FALSE PROPHETS!

My name is Joe Keithley
-friends call me Joey!

I was one of the first punk rock singers with my band **D.O.A.**
D.O.A. is about SOCIAL ACTIVISM - our slogan is "TALK MINUS ACTION EQUALS ZERO"
- and we have played hundreds of benefits for activist causes over the last 17 years. But punk rock has become a fashion statement now, and I ain't the most fashionable guy in the world!
To me punk rock has always been about doing my own thing, about not taking bullshit and about thinking for yourself.

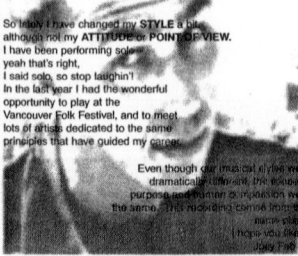

So lately I have changed my STYLE a bit, although not my ATTITUDE or POINT OF VIEW. I have been performing solo, yeah that's right, I said solo, so stop laughin'!
In the last year I had the wonderful opportunity to play at the Vancouver Folk Festival, and to meet lots of artists dedicated to the same principles that have guided my career.

Even though our musical styles were dramatically different, the sense of purpose and burning conviction were the same. This recording comes from that same place.
I hope you like it.
Joey Feb 97

All songs © Joe Keithley (p) 1997 Prisoner Publishing
Track 1 words John Brillo arrangement Joe Keithley
Track 2 words Leadbelly arrangement Joe Keithley
1&2 arrangement © arrangement Joe Keithley
(p) 1997 Prisoner Publishing
thanks to FDI

Recorded at Goldrush Studios by Si Garber January 1997
Management : Laurie Mercer
P.O. Box 27070 Collingwood P.O.
Vancouver, B.C. V5R 6A8 Canada
Phone 604.438.2285 fax 604.438.2287
email laurie@conspinpy.com
Joey's got a website at http://www.conspiracy.com/joey
and you can email joey@conspiracy.com

Acoustic four-song demo cassette.

a nite of rant'n'roll

JOEY KEITHLEY
EUGENE RIPPER
FORD PIER
thursday May 22

BEWARE OF FALSE PROPHETS!

THE BRICKYARD
315 Carrall Street ph 685-3922
Doors 9:00pm tix $5 at the door.

DON'T MISS
eugene ripper's fast folk underground
featuring
JOE KEITHLEY
JIM CUMMINS
FIRE ANT
Plus a possible appearance by "the madman in love" ABDALA BUCARAM
MONDAY MARCH 24
THE RAILWAY CLUB

A local forest in my hometown was on the verge of getting cut down to make room for a high-tech industrial park. I got involved in the effort to save the forest, and was asked to run for the Green Party in Burnaby in the next provincial election, which I did.

In early '97, I started working on acoustic songs with producer Cy Garber. Laurie Mercer and I worked hard at promoting my "anarcoustic" and spoken word side over the next couple of years.

D.O.A. was in Surrey playing a fundraiser for a food bank. We were getting back in full swing; Wycliffe was the temporary bassist. Drummer Brien O'Brien and I were recording demos for a new album, for which I filled in on bass.

We were invited to play our first gig in Prince George, BC, at the town's annual party, Prince George Days. At the venue there were a slew of death metal/cookie monster bands playing as support, so we hung out in the van and kept our beers on the down low, to avoid getting busted by the Mounties. It proved to be a pointless exercise, as the 400 kids that showed up were getting completely wasted and smashing their bottles everywhere in and out of the venue. Finally the dreary dirge ended inside, and it was time for D.O.A. We had played about two songs when the Mounties showed up and cut the power to the stage. They sent a messenger to tell me I had to announce that the gig was being cancelled. I said I would do it. They turned the power back on and we started playing "The Enemy." We got about halfway through, and the cops cut stage power again. They sent up another message about announcing that the show was over, figuring I had misunderstood it the first time, so I said sure. The power came on, and we charged headlong into "the Prisoner." Well, that lasted about thirty seconds. Not wanting to tempt fate, we snuck out of town that night as the cops were busy busting and cuffing everybody who came near them. The next day the local newspaper headline read: "Heavy Metal Band D.O.A. Causes Riot!"

Kuba and Joe give a free demonstration of Canadian hockey know-how to an unfortunate sap.

HAMMER HORROR
D.O.A.
Clockwork
Medusa
Blatant Decay
Ludicrous

Saturday August 23rd 1997

doors at 7:30   tickets $10

Aug 23

...ce of Death
...nt Day
...mortals join hands
...ons in a
...d measure that
...cho the steps
...nd Eve

In January, 1998, I restarted Sudden Death Records as a serious label. Our first release was *Festival of Athiests*. I played the bass, guitars, and sang lead vocals on the album; Brien O'Brien played the drums and did a lot of the artwork. Sudden Death also released *The Lost Tapes*, a collection of hard-to-find and previously unreleased D.O.A. tracks. An album from a young band called d.b.s. was the third release for SDR.

Kuba became our new permanent bass player and we set forth on the *Festival of Athiests* tour. When we first released the album, we sent out an email to 10,000 members of various right-wing Christian groups, telling them about the joys of atheism. We got bombarded by hate messages through email and telephone. One lost soul even emailed us the entire Bible. Later that year, when we played way up north in the Yukon, a religious group held a protest in front of the arena. A protest against D.O.A.! Now the shoe was on the other foot.

SUDDEN DEATH RECORDS

JOEY "SHITHEAD" KEITHLEY SLASHES YOU WITH HIS NEW LABEL: SUDDEN DEATH RECORDS

20 YEARS OF BUCKING THE SYSTEM

FESTIVAL OF ATHEISTS
Featuring "DEATH TO THE MULTINATIONALS," "IF THERE'S GOD," "YOU WON'T STAND ALONE" and "WORLD FALLS APART." New 13-track studio album. Explore the eyeopening world of atheism through the music and even further with this extensive CD-ROM. The most wildly divergent D.O.A. album since *War On 45*. (On CD-ROM and LP. Cassette available in April.)

THE LOST TAPES
Featuring "NO GOD NO WAR", "KILL KILL THIS IS POP," and "THE MUTANT." 16 previously unreleased tracks — by the original D.O.A. guys: Joe Shithead, Chuck Biscuits, Randy Rampage, Dave Gregg, Dimwit + Wimpy. 1976-1984; 6 tracks never before released and 10 more alternate versions of some old D.O.A. faves. (On CD and LP. Cassette available in April.)

A BRAND NEW GENERATION OF TROUBLEMAKERS

I IS FOR INSIGNIFICANT
Featuring "HOMOPHOBIA IS A CRIME AND YOU'RE A CRIMINAL," "DAVID O IS A NAZI," "SUNDAY" and "SO POPPY IT'LL MAKE YOU PUKE, PART ONE & TWO." The third album by North Vancouver's teenage punks. This incredible band have been blasting it out for 5 years and touring North America when they're not in high school. (On CD)

DISTRIBUTED BY FAB IN CANADA.
LICENSED & DISTRIBUTED TO PLASTICHEAD FOR U.K. AND EUROPE (EXCEPT GERMANY, AUSTRIA & SWITZERLAND) & TO EMPTY/E.F.A. FOR GERMANY, AUSTRIA & SWITZERLAND)
SUDDEN DEATH RECORDS: MOSCROP PO BOX #43001, BURNABY, BC CANADA V5G 3H0 / email: sudden@concentric.net / website: w.suddendeath.com / Orders by phone (604) 439-9046 / USA promotion: Bob Cutler, email corn@idic.net, phone (913) 842-0161 / Canadian promotion: Melanie Kaye, email caution@sprint.ca, phone (416) 504-5070
PLASTICHEAD: phone +44-1491-825-029, email plastichead@compuserve.com / EMPTY: phone +49-911-790-5338, fax +49-911-790-5543

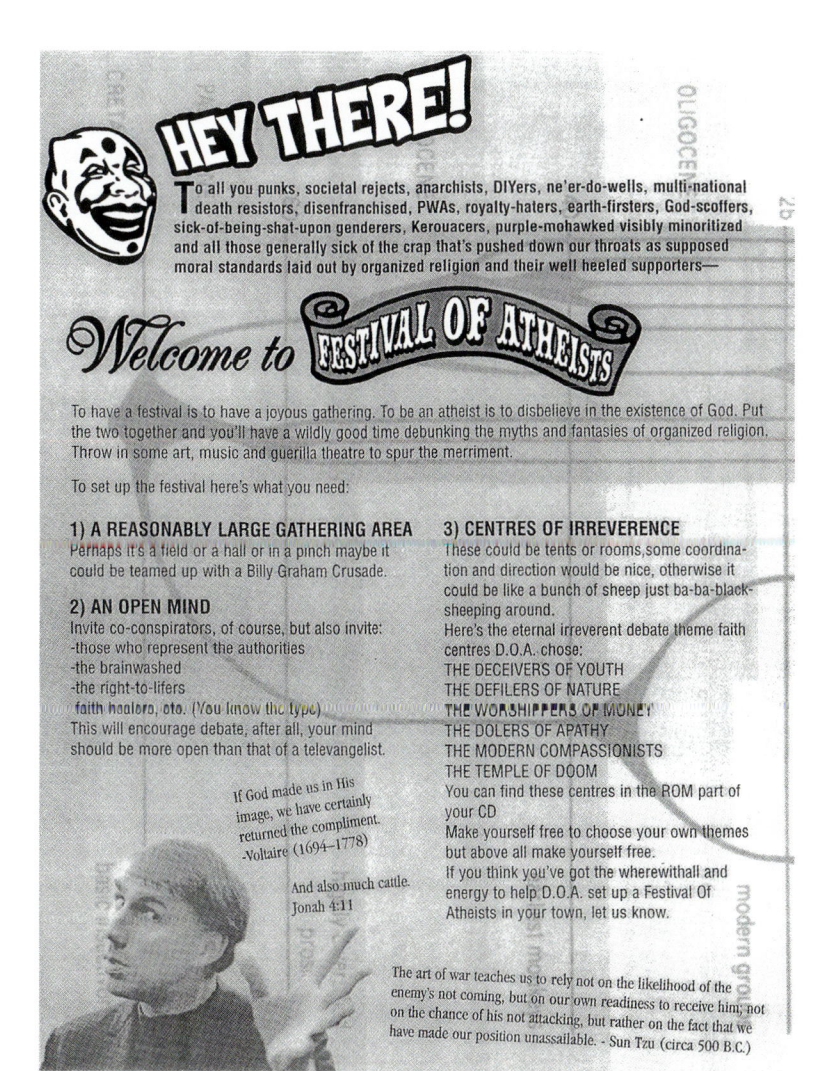

HEY THERE!

To all you punks, societal rejects, anarchists, DIYers, ne'er-do-wells, multi-national death resistors, disenfranchised, PWAs, royalty-haters, earth-firsters, God-scoffers, sick-of-being-shat-upon genderers, Kerouacers, purple-mohawked visibly minoritized and all those generally sick of the crap that's pushed down our throats as supposed moral standards laid out by organized religion and their well heeled supporters—

Welcome to FESTIVAL OF ATHEISTS

To have a festival is to have a joyous gathering. To be an atheist is to disbelieve in the existence of God. Put the two together and you'll have a wildly good time debunking the myths and fantasies of organized religion. Throw in some art, music and guerilla theatre to spur the merriment.

To set up the festival here's what you need:

1) A REASONABLY LARGE GATHERING AREA
Perhaps it's a field or a hall or in a pinch maybe it could be teamed up with a Billy Graham Crusade.

2) AN OPEN MIND
Invite co-conspirators, of course, but also invite:
- those who represent the authorities
- the brainwashed
- the right-to-lifers
- faith healers, etc. (You know the type)
This will encourage debate, after all, your mind should be more open than that of a televangelist.

3) CENTRES OF IRREVERENCE
These could be tents or rooms, some coordination and direction would be nice, otherwise it could be like a bunch of sheep just ba-ba-black-sheeping around.
Here's the eternal irreverent debate theme faith centres D.O.A. chose:
THE DECEIVERS OF YOUTH
THE DEFILERS OF NATURE
THE WORSHIPPERS OF MONEY
THE DOLERS OF APATHY
THE MODERN COMPASSIONISTS
THE TEMPLE OF DOOM
You can find these centres in the ROM part of your CD
Make yourself free to choose your own themes but above all make yourself free.
If you think you've got the wherewithall and energy to help D.O.A. set up a Festival Of Atheists in your town, let us know.

If God made us in His image, we have certainly returned the compliment.
-Voltaire (1694–1778)

And also much cattle.
Jonah 4:11

The art of war teaches us to rely not on the likelihood of the enemy's not coming, but on our own readiness to receive him; not on the chance of his not attacking, but rather on the fact that we have made our position unassailable. - Sun Tzu (circa 500 B.C.)

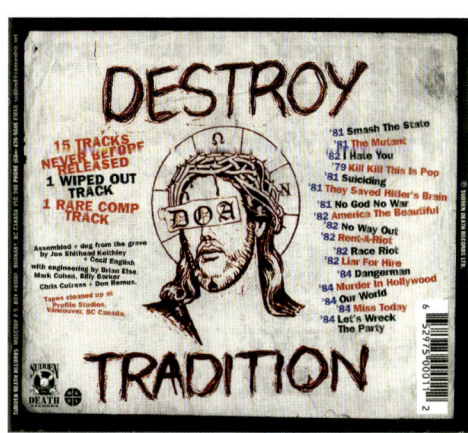

DESTROY TRADITION
15 TRACKS NEVER BEFORE RELEASED
1 WIPED OUT TRACK
1 RARE COMP TRACK

Assembled + dug from the grave by Joe Shithead Keithley + Cecil English
with engineering by Brian Else, Mark Cuban, Billy Barker, Chris Cuiteras + Don Remus.
Tapes cleaned up at Profile Studios, Vancouver, BC Canada.

'81 Smash The State
'84 The Mutant
'82 I Hate You
'79 Kill Kill This Is Pop
'81 Suiciding
'81 They Saved Hitler's Brain
'81 No God No War
'82 America The Beautiful
'82 No Way Out
'82 Rent-A-Riot
'82 Race Riot
'82 Liar For Hire
'84 Dangerman
'84 Murder In Hollywood
'84 Our World
'84 Miss Today
'84 Let's Wreck The Party

You Won't Stand Alone

Time to make a stand, Time to have a say
Don't buckle under, Get in the way
'Cause there's many ears to listen, And many hands to help
Time to wake them up, And give the liars hell

Ch: When you face the storm, You won't stand alone
We'll all fight back, With every stone
Not just for yourself, We do it for all
Reach out for our help, You won't stand alone

Bridge   They climb the corporate ladder
They take the kickback
They'd sell out their mother
They can go to hell

2   They'll line you up to listen, In front of the TV
And make you fell lucky, 'Cause you've something to eat
And you'll pee in a jar, Just to keep your job
Unless you're downsized, Like another useless cog

The world falls apart ah ah
falls apart

There's a mean streak in the air
There's a heartlessness that's being taught
You read + hear about it
And a safety net that's being dropped
There's an old man got in a wheel chair
There's a single mom with 2 starving kids
There's an abused girl who ran away
And dying people who got too rough
And they have all hit the skids
Our world falls apart
In Vancouver / In Toronto / In Montreal
Ain't no compassion / Ain't no compassion
On the eastside   Just pawns in the game
Our world falls apart
On the eastside

The world falls apart

You can sleep in a dumpster
And eat from a garbage can
There used to be jobs
Now there's a food bank man

                                                                Nothing
I never met anyone who wants to be a victim
I never met anyone who wanted to be kicked
I never met anyone
But I sure know a lot of scapegoats
There's it a phoney war that nobody wins
You can't throw a bandaid at poverty's kin
It's a phoney war that nobody wins
                        That nobody wins
There's a bureaucrat who's tryin to save his ass
There's a politician that wants to edit those towers
There's a TV that needs to   and dying people who're

The 20th Anniversary Show was a whole lot of fun. We organized it so we could go through the various line-ups in chronological order, with each line-up playing four to five songs from that era. At the very end, we got everybody on stage, with a multitude of amps and vocal mikes. We had three drummers—Brien O'Brien, John Wright, and Zippy Pinhead—beating out a fearsome tattoo. Well done, everybody! Fabulous!

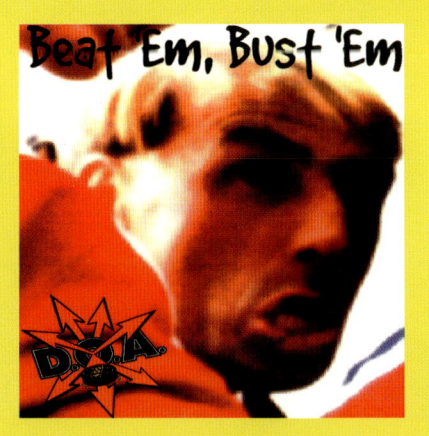

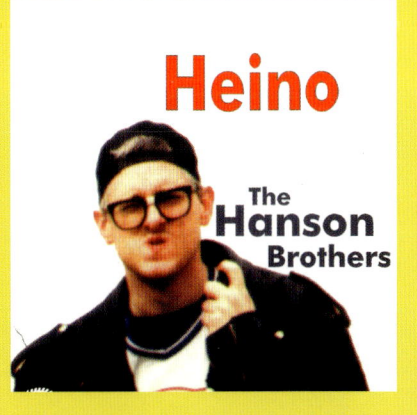

FESTIVAL OF ATHEISTS TOUR

Di. 3. Sept.
Einlaß: 20⁰⁰ Start: 21⁰⁰

D.O.A.

Vorverkauf:
Rave Up, Why Not, Flex (Tel. 533 75 25)

FLEX
1, Donaukanal, U-Station Schottenring

MERCOLEDI' 25 MARZO
HARDCORE MASTERS
per la prima volta a Genova
DAL CANADA
dalle ore 22.00

D.O.A.
+ D.B.S.

Centro Sociale Occupato Autogestito
EMILIANO ZAPATA
via Sampierdarena 36 - ex Magazzini del sale - Genova

We booked a spring European tour that went from Berlin to Poland to Prague in the Czech Republic. After the show in Poznan, Poland, we left for Prague; part way there, one of the d.b.s. guys (support band for the tour) realized he left his passport back at the apartment. We had to turn around, and that shithook back into the Poznan traffic jam cost us about two hours. When we finally got on the highway to Prague, it was jammed up worse than a Los Angeles freeway on a Friday night. The road systems in the east were not built to handle the influx of cars and trucks after the collapse of communism. We were going nowhere fast and were worried we might miss the show. Our sound man Bob Cutler said, "Hey, why don't you try that road over there?"

It was a five-foot-wide dirt road running into the forest. I thought, "Well, you only live once! And this is probably it." It got us past the traffic jam and onto the correct road, but we got into Prague really, really late. Ziggy, our Polish merch guy, said he knew a little Czech, so we got him to ride shotgun so he could ask the locals for directions and read the map at the same time. We started circling the same part of Prague in a seemingly endless loop. Finally I yelled, "Were going to miss the fucking show! Let me see that fucking map!" I understood no Czech, but I had us there in five minutes. As we pulled up to the Roxy Club, the promoter had just cancelled the show and was starting to hand out refunds. I told the promoter that we could be loaded and have the support band d.b.s. on stage in ten minutes! And we did it: d.b.s. got up there and rocked, and so did D.O.A.

The next day we had to get to the show in Vienna, which meant entering Austria and, consequently, entering the EU. We had two yellow Mercedes rental vans. I was driving the lead one with our band and all the musical equipment. The lead singer of d.b.s. was driving the second van with his band mates and all the merch. The Austrian border guard asked if we had anything to declare. I said no, and Jesse said the same, but the guard pulled us in for inspection. We had a whole bunch of cassettes and vinyl from Poland, outside the EU. To make a long story short, the border fucker fined us $7,000 and took so long doing the paperwork that we missed the show in Vienna. All in all, that day cost us about $10,000 … Fuck.

Another day we were driving toward Calle, France, to catch the ferry for the UK portion of the tour. Dooza, who was at the wheel, suddenly said, "Shit, we have no oil pressure!" We pulled over; the engine was hooped.

I walked up the highway against a gale-force wind and got a tow truck. We eventually hooked up with d.b.s. and stuck them with the broken van, then they nearly got busted by the *gendarmes*, because D.O.A. had not paid the bill. Eventually, we all hurried off to the ferry and got to Birmingham super late. The promoter "claimed" he had refunded all the tickets and wouldn't pay us. We said "Fuck that!" and played anyways for the people who were still there.

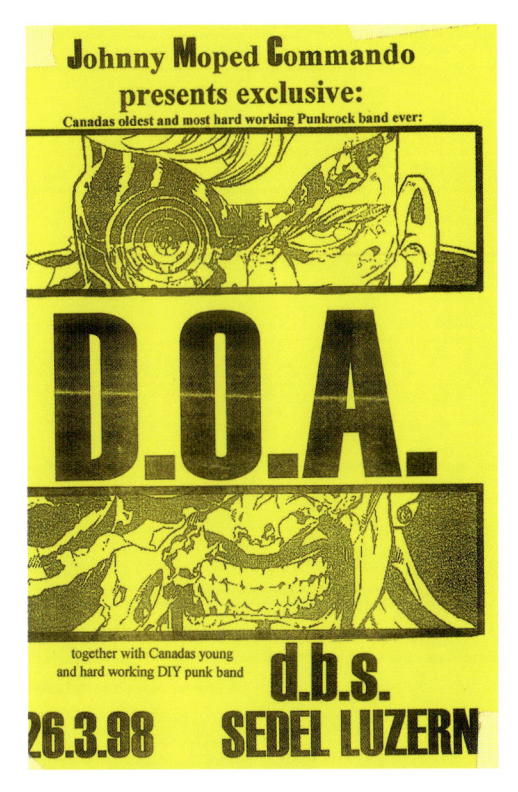

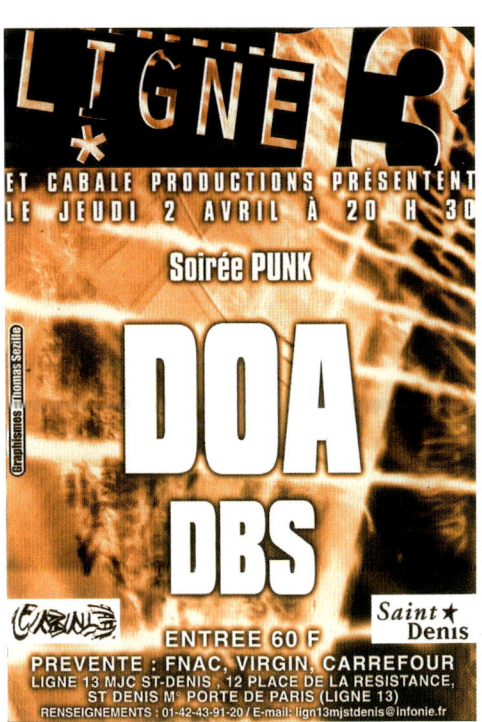

21 and over

FRIDAY

Unity Skateboards Presents Another All Ages Benefit - Food Bank
Vancouver's Best! Punk Rock Legends **DOA** Superstars **DBS** new CD Release but wait there's more **Tommy Middlefinger** plus local exotic dancers **Kore Society**

Four bands $10 plus 2 cans of food Bring food no excuses
Doors 7:30 Show 8pm
APRIL 24th Roberts Creek Hall
tickets @ Unity Skateboards call: 885-5535 we're (Across from McDeaths)

Concert Café
SUNDAY JUNE 7
20th Anniversary World Tour
D.O.A.
ALL AGES • DOORS 6:30 • SHOW 7:00
Zeke • Pontos River • The Derks
Concert Café • 1116 Main, Green Bay
Info 435-0880
TICKETS $8 ADVANCE $10 DAY OF SHOW
TICKET OUTLETS: SURFIN' BIRD GREEN BAY
EXCLUSIVE COMPANY GREEN BAY & APPLETON
DR. FREUD'S MANITOWOC APPLETON IMPORTS OSHKOSH
RADIO KAOS STEVENS POINT MUSIC REPLAY OSHKOSH
ORDER BY PHONE (920) 435-0880
A POWERBOMB PRODUCTION

2B1 Presents at the Maritime Hall
D.O.A
WITH **ZEKE • BIMBO TOOLSHED • DORK**
SUNDAY MAY 10
DOORS OPEN AT **7 PM**
FOR TICKETS AND INFO CALL:
(415) 974-0634
$10 ADVANCE • $12 AT SHOW
450 HARRISON STREET SAN FRANCISCO
FLIER BY CHRIS X 707.778.3882

D.O.A
Fresh from the clutches of corporate meddlings
These Legendary Paladins of Heresy
ANARCHY INTERNATIONAL in conjunction with SHAMELESS PROMOTIONS
The Great Khan Job
Festival of Atheists
PLUS **ZEKE**
TUESDAY • MAY 12th $8.00 adv $10.00 door
PALOOKAVILLE
16 & OVER WELCOME **(408) 454-0600** 9:00 PM SHOWTIME
1133 PACIFIC AVENUE • DOWNTOWN SANTA CRUZ PHONE • ENTER FROM LINCOLN AVE.

featuring **C.J. RAMONE**...ONES
The BREAKROOM

TICKETMASTER • 206.628.0888
SHOW INFOLINE • 206.346.0225

Pure Water • VANS • Odwalla
SINGLES GOING STEADY

MAY 8

$8 at the doo

20th Anniversary Tour!

D.O.A.
ZEKE
with HELLVIS

Thursday June 4th

Euclid Tavern
11629 Euclid Ave. Cleveland (216)229-7788

DIMANCHE 11 OCTOBRE

D.O.A.

DOG EAT DOGMA

PIGMENT VEHICLE

L'Arlequin
8$

1070 rue St-Jean, Québec
Tel/info/fax (418) 694-1422
http://www.arlequin.qc.ca

In the spring of 1998, we headed out on a thirty-day tour of America with the ever-excellent and frantic Zeke as support. The tour went pretty smoothly, but one day we were kicking the soccer ball around to stay in shape and Brien tweaked his back. We didn't think too much of it till the home stretch of the tour. Brien had fucked up his sciatic nerve; he could neither sit nor stand without pain and he certainly could not drum anymore. So in Green Bay, Wisconsin I had Zeke's drummer Donny Paycheck on standby to fill in and halfway through the show he did. We flew Brien back to Vancouver and Donny filled in for five shows as we headed back west. But when Zeke split off eastwards again, we had no drummer and three shows left. I called ahead to Salt Lake City, Missoula, and Spokane and asked the promoters to get us the best punk drummer in town. Then we showed up at sound check and ran over the entire set with the drummer; it actually turned out to be three special shows, but I felt like PT Barnum— the show must go on! That injury finished off Brien O'Brien for touring. In the fall, we did a cross-Canada tour, and Kuba's buddy Ted Simm (SNFU) filled in on drums; he did a great job. We took newly signed Sudden Death label mates Dog Eat Dogma and Pigment Vehicle along as support for the tour.

To start 1999, we had a tour to California booked in January, but Brien O'Brien called two days before the tour to say, "Hi, my back is out again." It was suggested that I get Jan Rodgerson of Dog Eat Dogma to fill in (later he was given the Great Baldini nickname by Rampage). Baldini was a real powerhouse; he drummed for D.O.A. for the next seven years. After a big show in Poland, D.O.A.'s twentieth anniversary and the powerful Dezerter's fifteenth anniversary, these three guys came backstage wearing T-shirts that spelled out D.O.A., one letter per guy. We posed for a photo, and surprised them with a Canadian beer assault.

Later that year, other members of the Burnaby Greens and I started a civic party, C.E.R. (Community Environment Responsibility). We ran four candidates in the city election. Again none of us were elected, but we pushed our Earth-first agenda further into public consciousness.

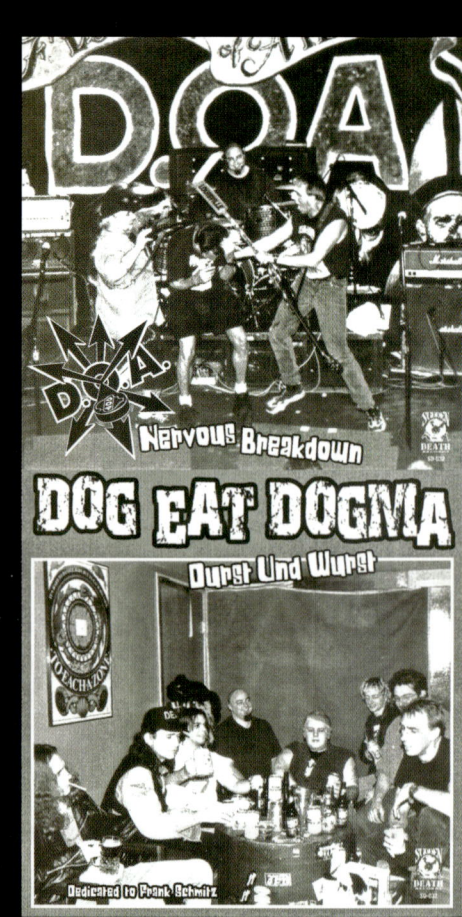

JOEY "SHITHEAD" KEITHLEY PRESENTS
20 YEARS OF BUCKING THE SYSTEM

PUNK ROCK GARAGE SALE

WEST COAST PUNK ROCK/HC
BLACK FLAG, DEAD KENNEDYS
SUBHUMANS, CIRCLE JERKS

D.O.A.

VINYL
POSTERS
CD'S
MEMORABILIA
SATURDAY
MARCH 6
1PM-6PM
RAILWAY CLUB
(BACK ROOM)
579 DUNSMUIR
VANCOUVER, BC

SUDDEN DEATH RECORDS MOSCROP PO BOX #43001, BURNABY, BC CANADA V5G 3H0
email: suddend@concentric.net / website: www.suddendeath.com / phone: (604) 439-9046 / fax (604) 439-9097

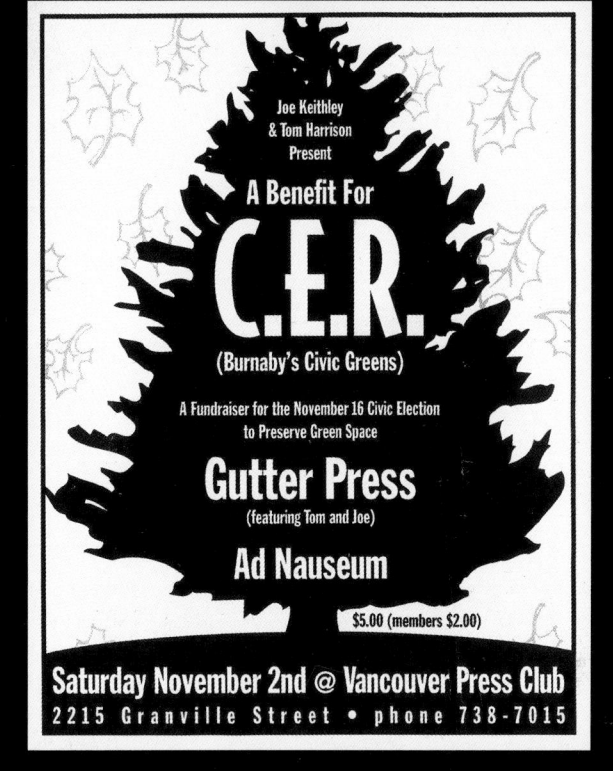

Joe Keithley & Tom Harrison Present

A Benefit For

C.E.R.
(Burnaby's Civic Greens)

A Fundraiser for the November 16 Civic Election to Preserve Green Space

Gutter Press
(featuring Tom and Joe)

Ad Nauseum

$5.00 (members $2.00)

Saturday November 2nd @ Vancouver Press Club
2215 Granville Street • phone 738-7015

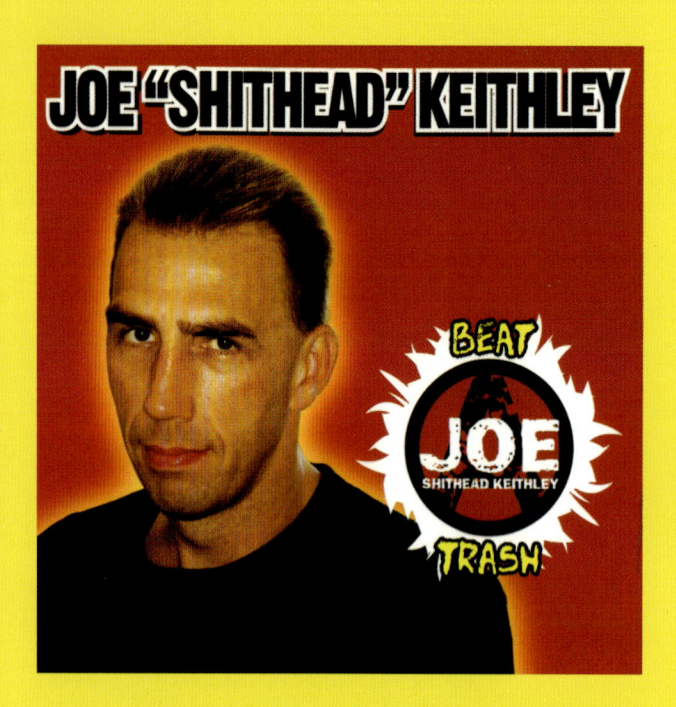

In 1999, Sudden Death released my first solo album. Cecil English and I had started working on it in the fall of 1998. After finishing the last guitar track, I was driving home from the studio when a car ran a stop sign at about forty miles an hour. I nailed that car with my van's front end and then spun around and nailed him again with the back of the van. When I came to a stop, I was facing the opposite direction from where I had started, the horn was jammed on, and the airbag was deployed. About thirty neighbourhood people ran out and figured we were all dead. I was lucky I had just broken my left hand, but hey, no problem, I had finished all the guitar tracks! The album was a mostly acoustic tribute to a couple of heroes of mine, Woody Guthrie and Leadbelly.

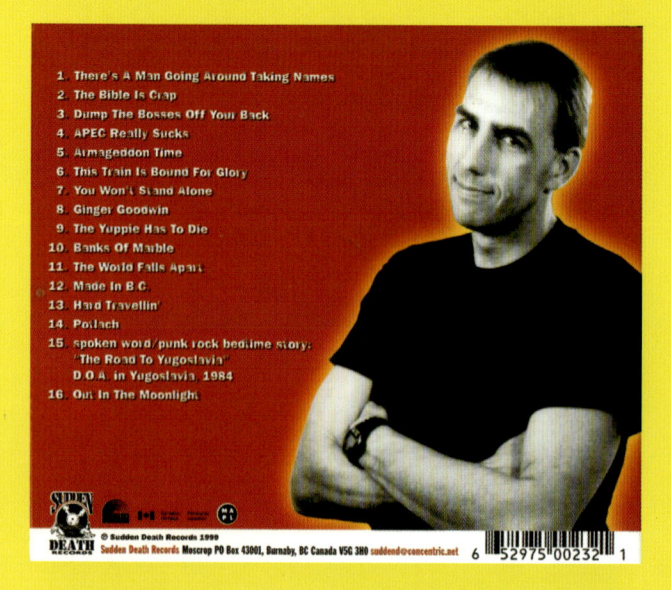

THE YUPPIE HAS TO DIE

① Here's a story sad and low about a yuppie that I know
He never stopped to look in the mirror
He tried to buy a broken dream, he would be in control
But the dream had a large appetite
He clawed here and gouged there, up the ladder he went
But every rung was slicker than the last
His conscience deserted him and his friends did too
Is it blood or money in his veins?

CH. He was a yuppie to the end, he was terrorized
He only had one truth, that was consume or die
And all of his money, his lies and his nerve
Couldn't stop his victims from screaming out th[e]
The yuppie has to die

② He never had enough, because he got too greed[y]
He never learned to put any back
He stocked up and stock piled, he thought he w[as]
But now he's the one that's getting stalked
And his friends that he used, that got him where
Have not forgotten where he is
And all the pieces of his life are inside his lapto[p]
Even all the pieces that want out

BRIDGE Now we know by this point, that he's going to [die]
It's just a matter of how and when, I sure as hel[l]
'Cause the wages of sin, they are death
So I'm going to tell you, how we put him to rest

Punks took his laptop, I got his I Phone
We emptied his bank account, YOU KNOW WHAT HAPPENED NEXT?
He just shriveled up and died

We did a month-long summer tour of the US with thirteen other punk bands, called Social Chaos. It was a wild and woolly tour to be sure, marked by some big crowds and then some that were not so big, which left the promoters scrambling to pay the bands. Along the way, guns were pulled, cops waded in, and the beer was crap. D.O.A. made it a regular plan to scour the venues for beer—after all, if they were gonna serve us hard-working bands Miller and Bud light, we were damn well gonna take anything good that was lying around. So after about a week the other bands would beat a path to Reid Fleming (D.O.A.'s tour van), knowing we had a big supply. The most ridiculous show of the tour was when we were plunked down into the middle of the Milwaukee Metal Fest. The bands had about thirty minutes per set. Murphy's Law was on before us and played for waaaaay too long, and of course, they had also covered the entire stage with beer (as any self-respecting punk band would). When we got up there, Kuba slipped on the beer and he and his bass amp went crashing down. It took about ten minutes to get it working again. In the meantime, Baldini and I played a ten-minute version of "Folsom Prison Blues," just stalling for time. By the time the three of us were ready to go, we only had ten minutes left. We played three songs, then the stage manager cut the power in the middle of "The Prisoner." Baldini and Kuba got into a pushing/yelling match with the stage manager (who was acting like a real dickhead), and they got kicked out of the venue.

Below, D.O.A. with one of New York City's finest.

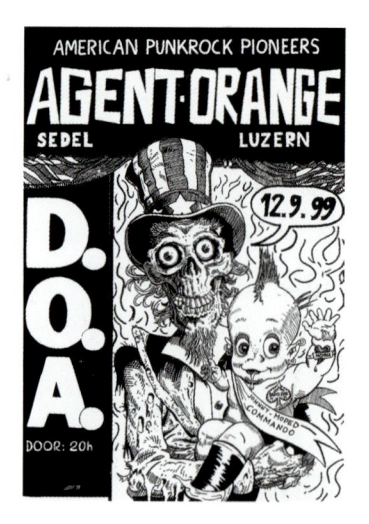

"A little shack outside La Grange."

Joe, Baldini, and Kuba doing their Ogie Oglethorpe imitations in front of good ol' Reid Fleming.

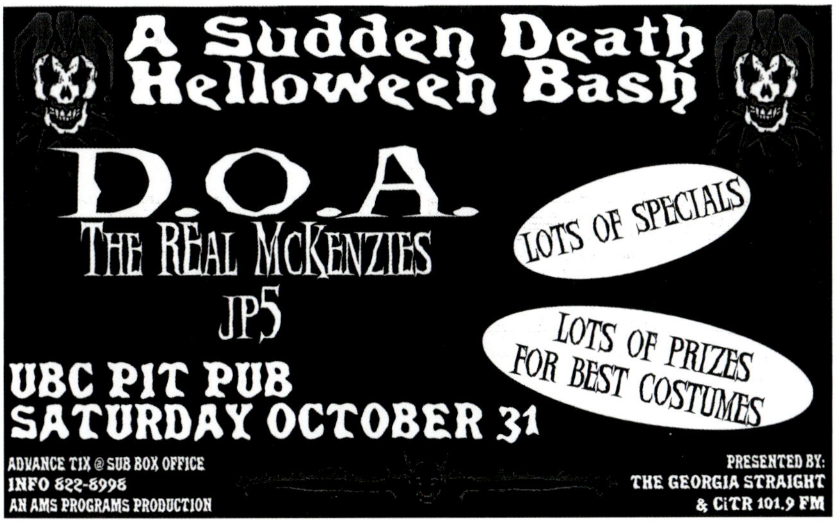

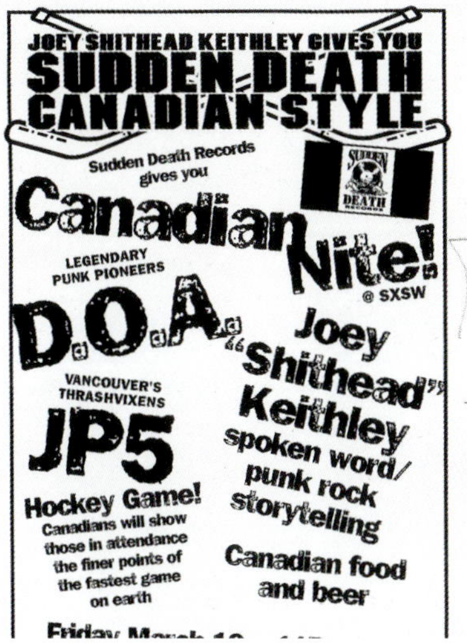

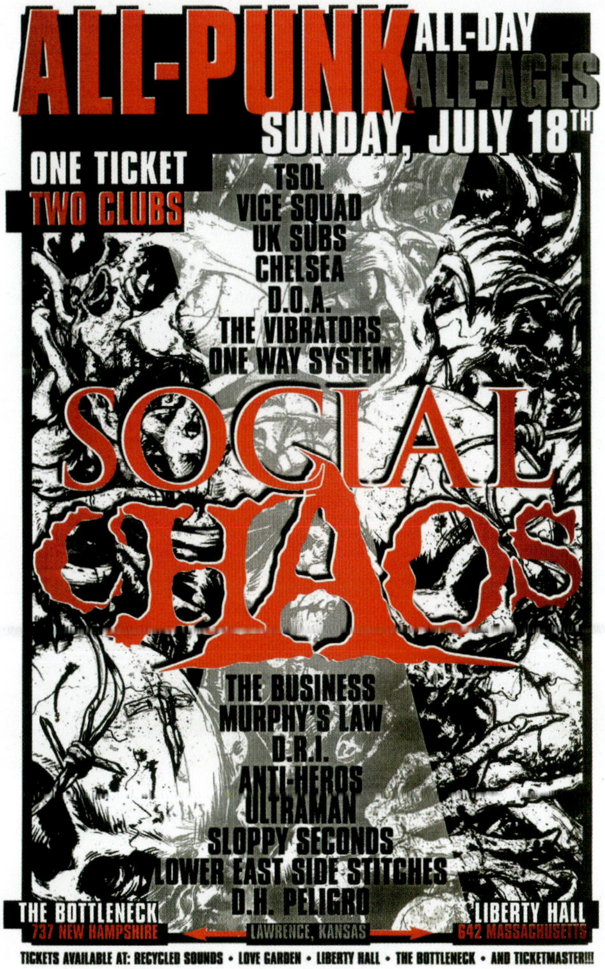

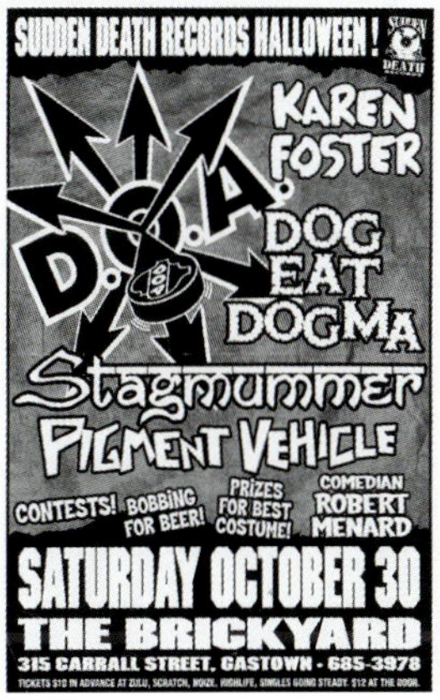

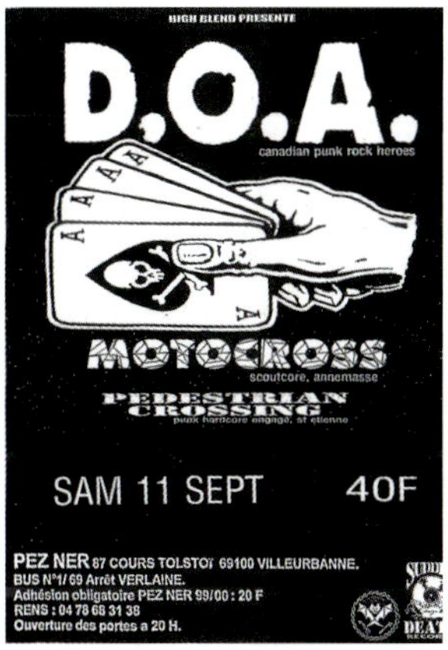

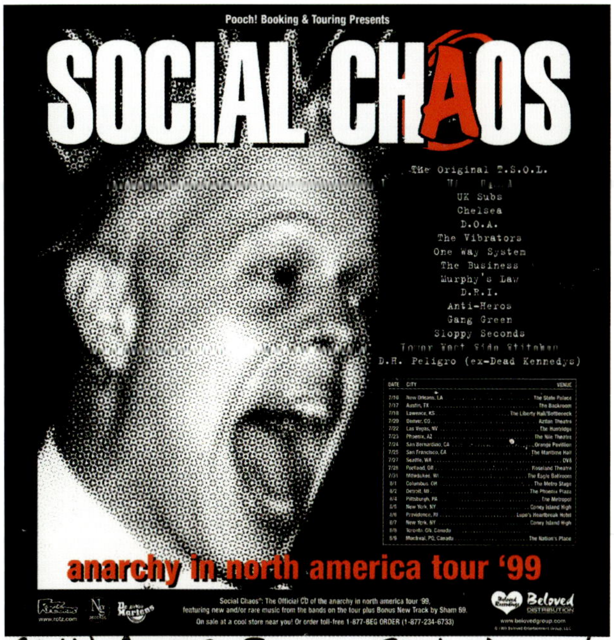

SUN AUG. 8 Tix Here!

NOW @ BIG BOP

csoa Forte @ Prenestino

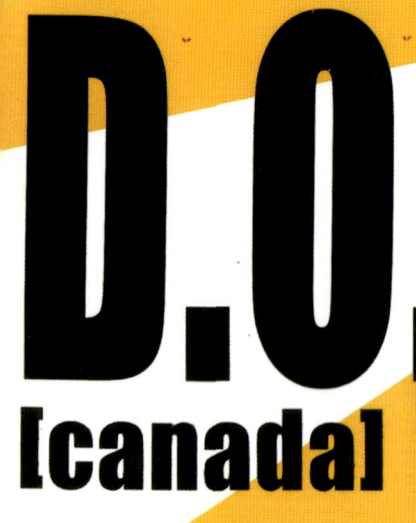

D.O.A [canada]

DEEP REDUCTION
[ex radio birdman-australia]

FLU!

D.O.A. LIVE — Alternative Wednesday, Mittwoch, 17. Mai 2000, 21:00, Fr. 12.–/15.– — GASWERK!

SO. 7. MAI 2000
...KANADA WIE ES SINGT UND LACHT...
D.O.A. & DAYGLO ABORTIONS
CLUB VAUDEVILLE, VON-BEHRING-STRASSE, LINDAU
20.–DM/140.–SCHILLING/17.–FR

special delivery from:
Sudden Death Records
Moscrop PO Box # 43001
Burnaby, BC
V5G 3H0 Canada
suddend@concentric.net
www.suddendeath.com

D.O.A. SPECIAL STICKERS SET EUROPEAN TOUR 2000

in concerto

In 2000, D.O.A. went to Europe again, where we played a great event in Berlin called Holidays in the Sun with Stiff Little Fingers, Angelic Upstarts, and the always great UK Subs. We played a show in Lindau in the south of Germany where the Dayglo Abortions were the support act. While they played, their singer Jimbo dumped all the Dayglo's beer onto the crowd. We could hear the other band members angrily denouncing Jimbo for wasting the beer. They hatched a plan to grab ours, but we had taken our entire rider and stashed it by our drum kit. When they found there was no D.O.A. beer to grab, we heard the sound of fists hitting Jimbo …

Later that year, I got involved with this great jazz group called the Hard Rubber Orchestra. They organized an extravagant show at St. Andrew's-Wesley United Church in Vancouver where I sang demented versions of Elvis Presley songs—pretty cool shit for sure. At the end of the year, I thought that D.O.A. needed to spice things up, so I got Randy Rampage playing bass again. Back to the future.

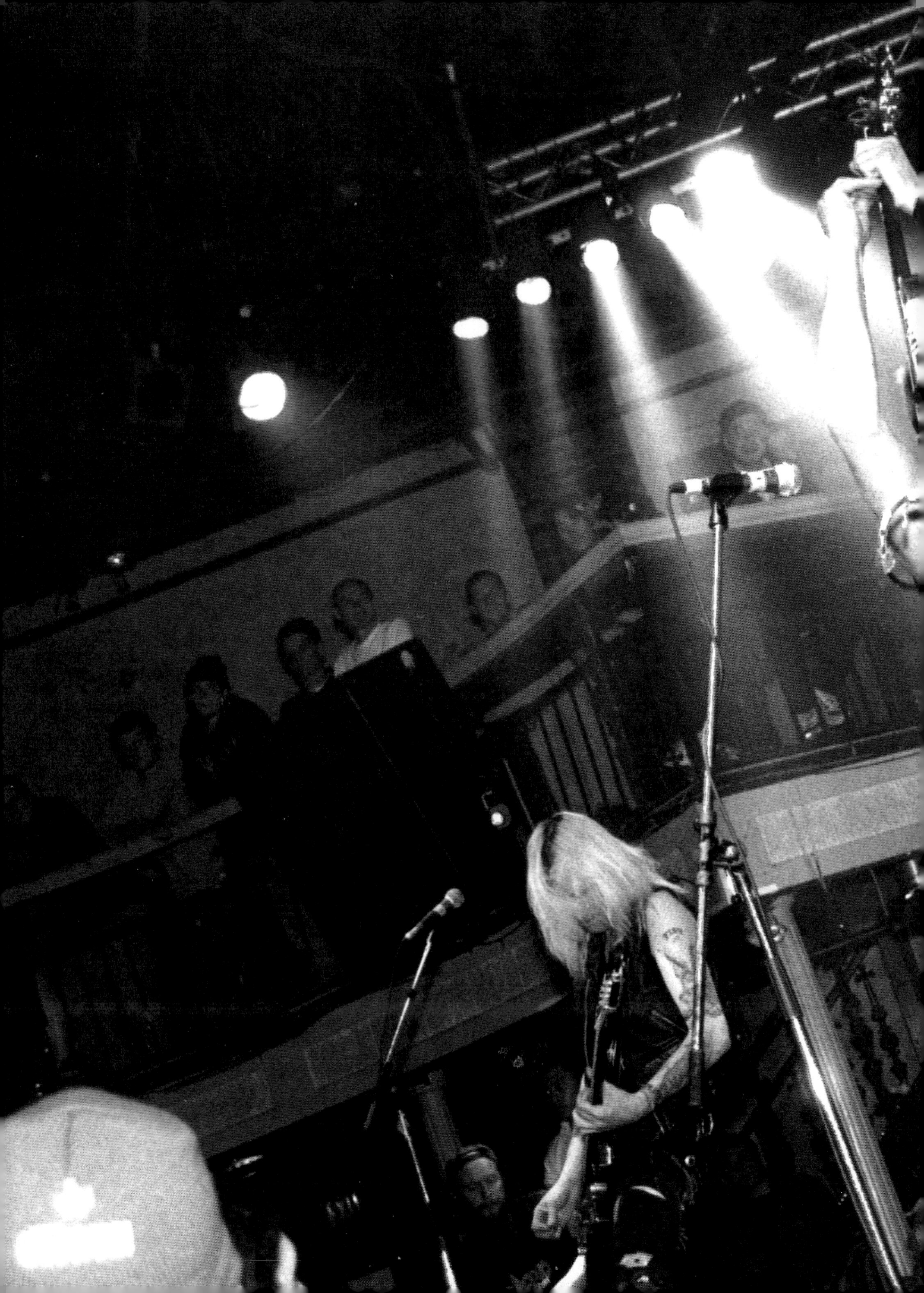

Chapter 9

2001–2004

WIN THE BATTLE

2001, I got hired as a fulltime talk-show host on MyCityRadio.com, which was live-streamed radio on the 'net. We called it the *Joe Show*. I got to gab with politicians, artists, scenemakers—anyone I wanted to talk with. Randy, Baldini, and I started recording the *Win the Battle* album, released in 2002. In 2001, I ran for the Green Party again in the provincial election, getting fifteen percent of the vote, the second-highest by a Green candidate that year. We also went to Japan for the first time; that was a trip.

By the start of 2002, Kuba was back on bass. Baldini, Kuba, and I toured across Canada and ventured over to Europe again. In 2003, Dirty Dan Sedan took over on bass, and we recorded D.O.A.'s eleventh studio album, *Live Free or Die*. We played a lot of anti-globalization benefits and anti-war concerts at this time, too. Some things never change.

Joe with Billy Hopeless.

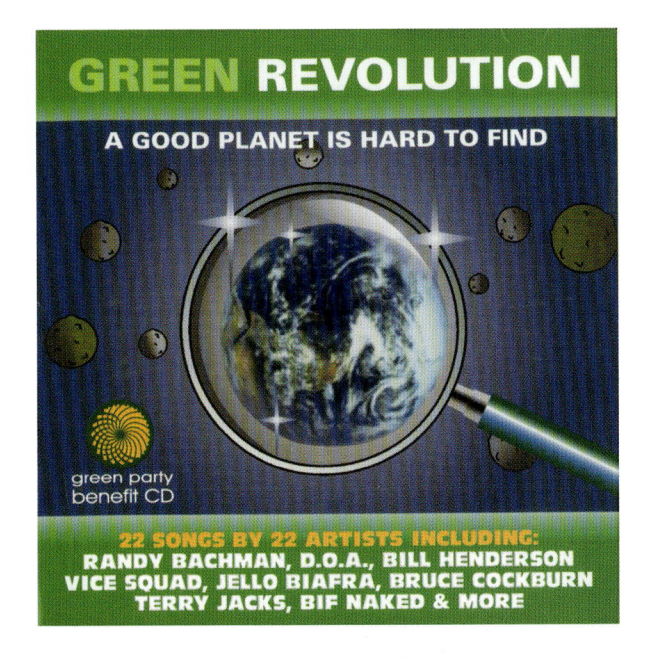

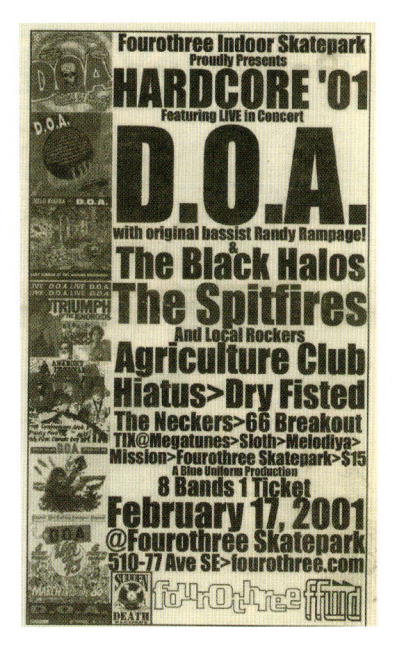

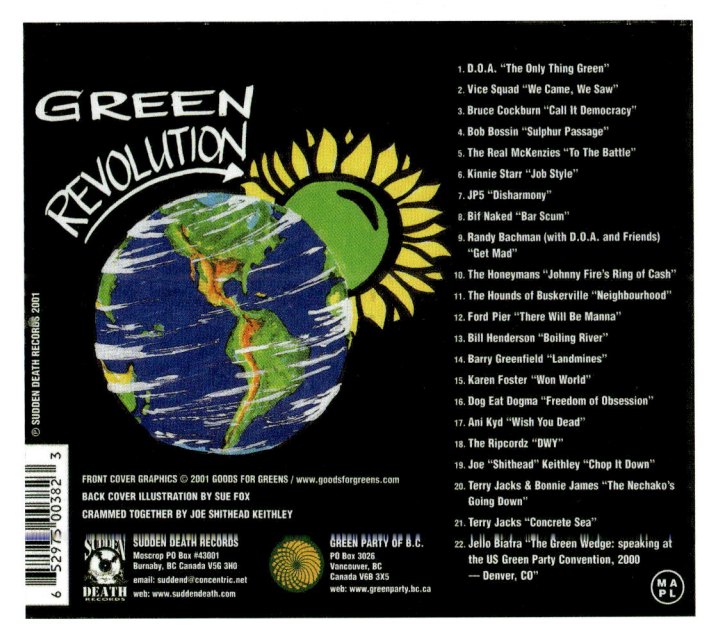

In 2001, Sudden Death released a benefit compilation album for the Green Party. I did a solo set at the benefit show. It was very cool to see all of these bands working together to kick some ass for the Earth.

D.O.A.'s first show with Rampage, Baldini, and me was a Skate-board Festival in Calgary with the Black Halos. It was a barnstormer. After the gig, Billy Hopeless (above right) tried to get the secret of rock 'n' roll out of us with a bottle of Jack; a good tactic, as Billy knows rock.

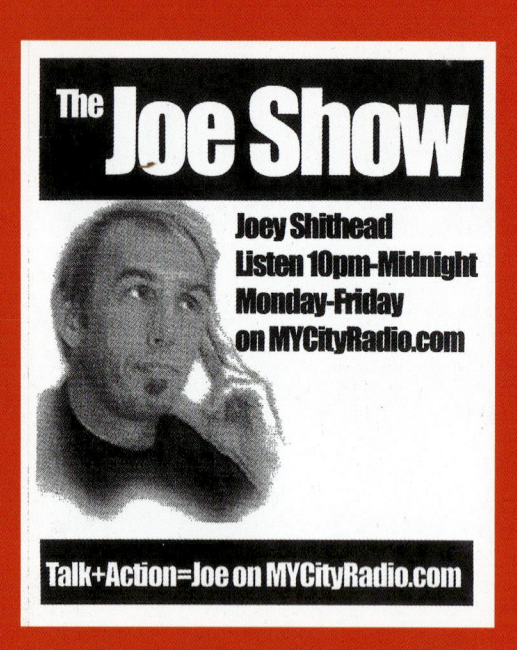

The Joe Show

Joey Shithead
Listen 10pm-Midnight
Monday-Friday
on MYCityRadio.com

Talk+Action=Joe on MYCityRadio.com

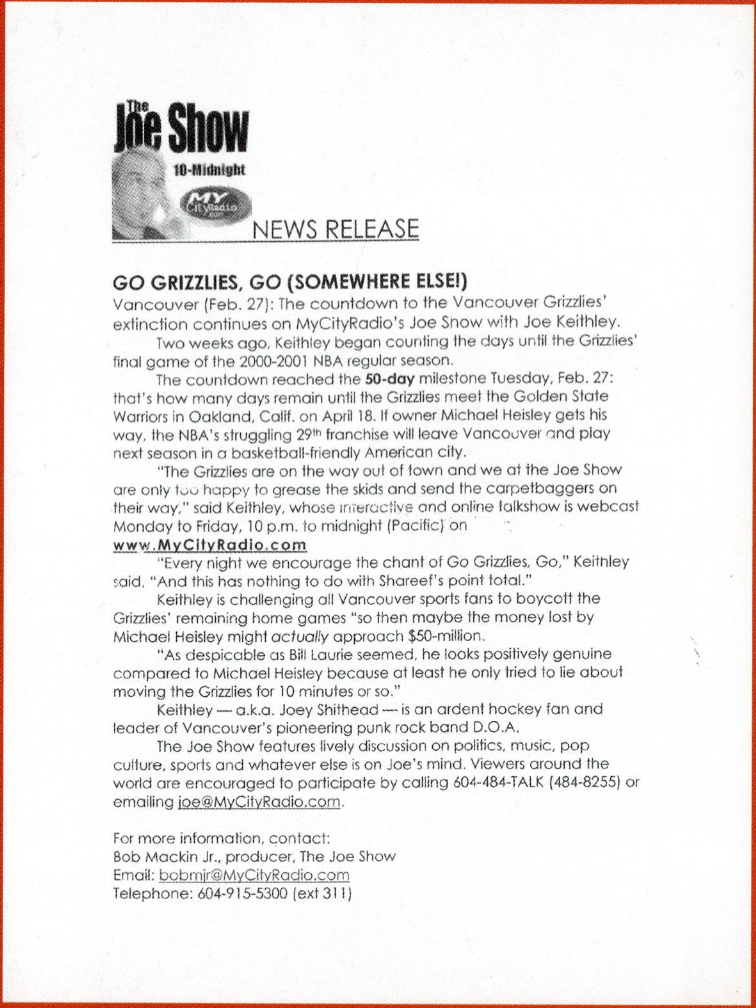

The Joe Show
10-Midnight
MyCityRadio

NEWS RELEASE

GO GRIZZLIES, GO (SOMEWHERE ELSE!)

Vancouver (Feb. 27): The countdown to the Vancouver Grizzlies' extinction continues on MyCityRadio's Joe Show with Joe Keithley.

Two weeks ago, Keithley began counting the days until the Grizzlies' final game of the 2000-2001 NBA regular season.

The countdown reached the **50-day** milestone Tuesday, Feb. 27: that's how many days remain until the Grizzlies meet the Golden State Warriors in Oakland, Calif. on April 18. If owner Michael Heisley gets his way, the NBA's struggling 29th franchise will leave Vancouver and play next season in a basketball-friendly American city.

"The Grizzlies are on the way out of town and we at the Joe Show are only too happy to grease the skids and send the carpetbaggers on their way," said Keithley, whose interactive and online talkshow is webcast Monday to Friday, 10 p.m. to midnight (Pacific) on **www.MyCityRadio.com**

"Every night we encourage the chant of Go Grizzlies, Go," Keithley said, "And this has nothing to do with Shareef's point total."

Keithley is challenging all Vancouver sports fans to boycott the Grizzlies' remaining home games "so then maybe the money lost by Michael Heisley might *actually* approach $50-million.

"As despicable as Bill Laurie seemed, he looks positively genuine compared to Michael Heisley because at least he only tried to lie about moving the Grizzlies for 10 minutes or so."

Keithley — a.k.a. Joey Shithead — is an ardent hockey fan and leader of Vancouver's pioneering punk rock band D.O.A.

The Joe Show features lively discussion on politics, music, pop culture, sports and whatever else is on Joe's mind. Viewers around the world are encouraged to participate by calling 604-484-TALK (484-8255) or emailing joe@MyCityRadio.com.

For more information, contact:
Bob Mackin Jr., producer, The Joe Show
Email: bobmjr@MyCityRadio.com
Telephone: 604-915-5300 (ext 311)

2000
THE GEORGIA straight
Vancouver's News & Entertainment Weekly

READERS' CHOICE MUSIC AWARDS

Favourite Local Male
Joe Keithley

The *Joe Show* was pretty cool, We had a great street-level location in downtown Vancouver. We would tape segments on the street and had plenty of guests that ranged from politicians to actors to artists. The show was going really well; I felt it was funny and political. Well, it was going well till the company went bankrupt. My broadcasting career had ended just as quickly as it had started!

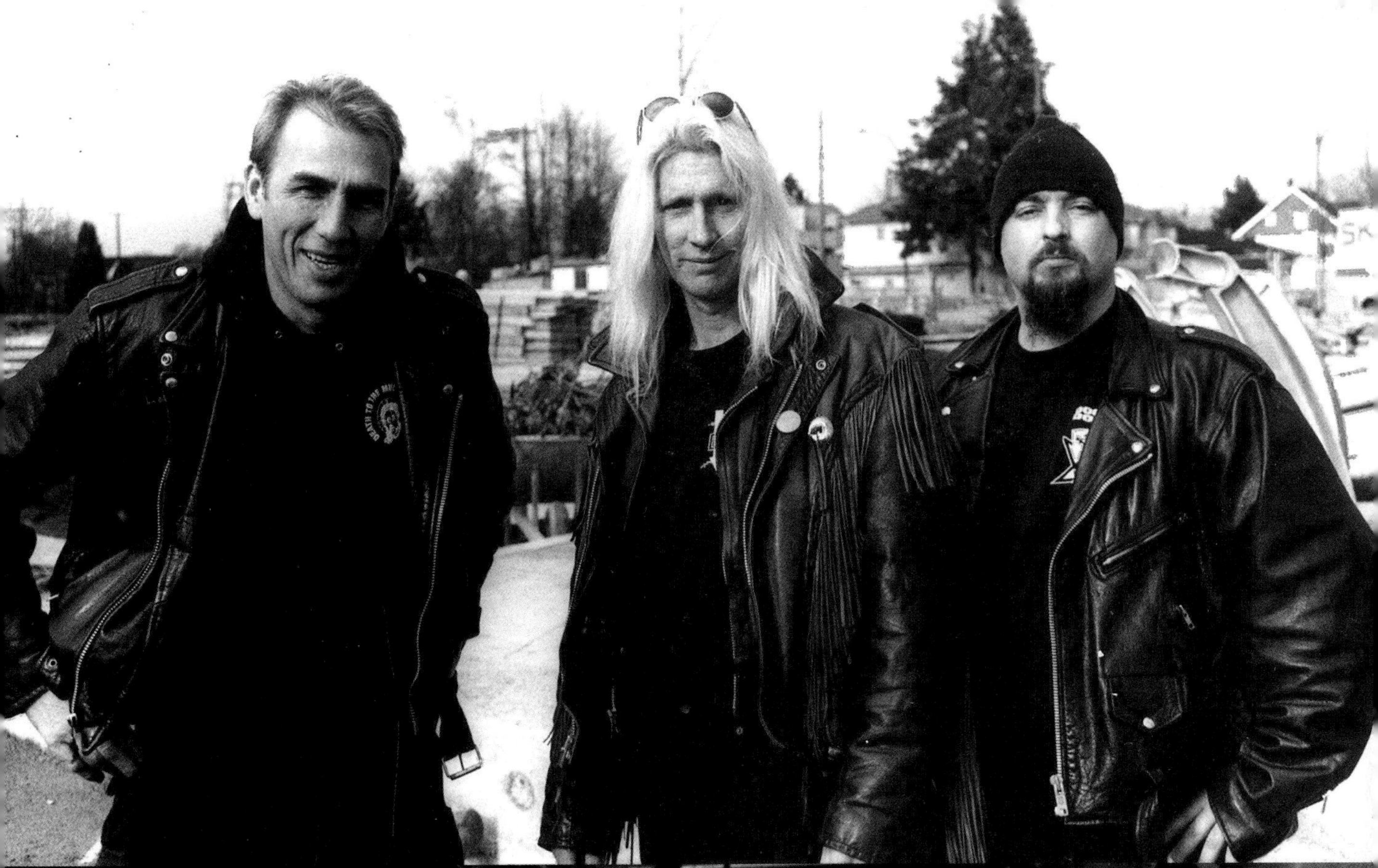

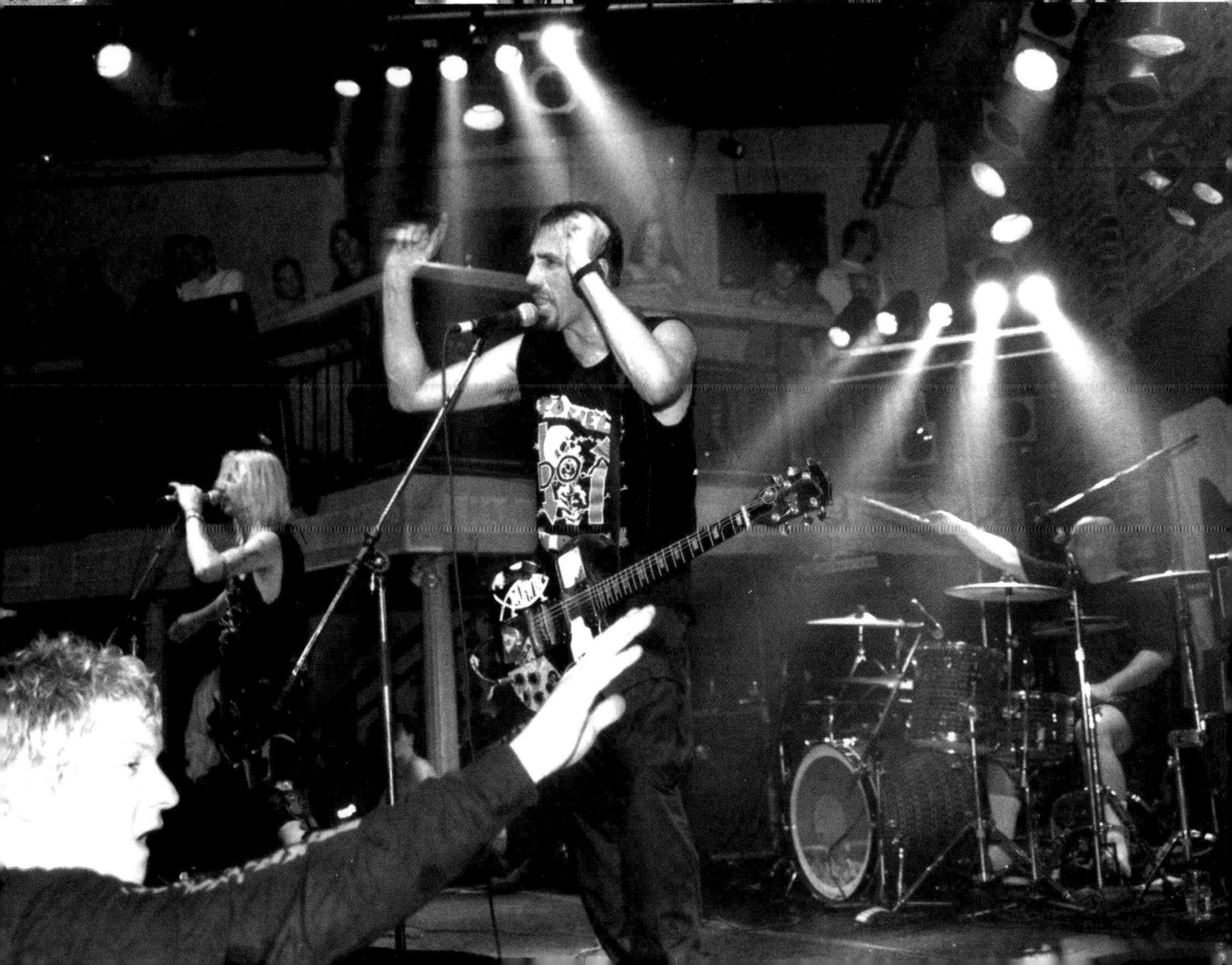

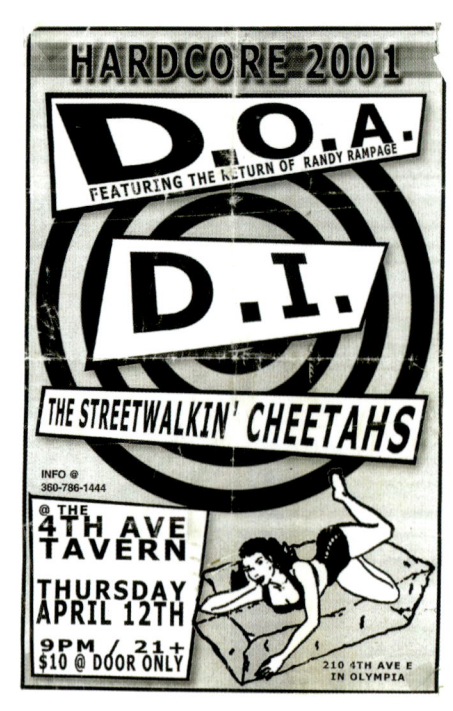

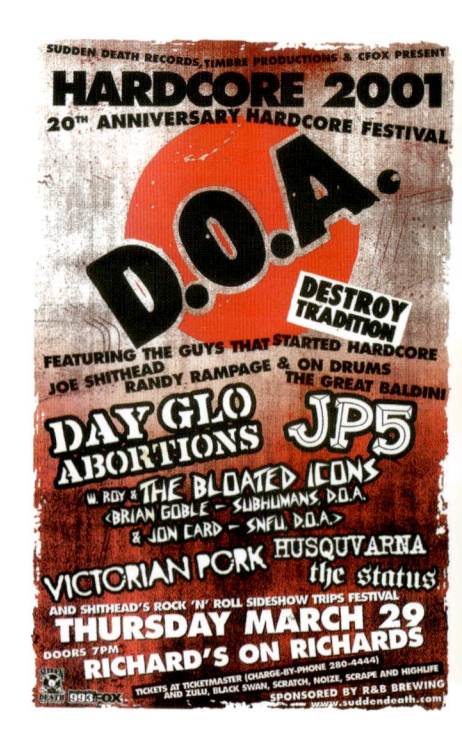

The twentieth anniversary of *Hardcore 81*: Hardcore 2001 and the start of a Northwest tour with our old pals D.I.

The mini-tour stopped in Seattle for two shows. Our muffler was fucked up, so Baldini patched it with an old coffee can and some bass strings. That Baldini is a talented mofo, for sure.

When I decided to run for MLA (Member of the Legislative Assembly), I never thought I could get elected, but I believed I could make people think. It's a funny thing running for elected office; it always seems like too much compromise is involved. But I knew I could operate in my usual maverick fashion. The press would ask me what kind of record I had to stand on. I'd say "I've got lots of good records to stand on." In the end I quit the Green Party and stopped running for office, because people will always vote for shitheads, but not necessarily Joe Shithead.

GREEN PARTY

Campaign to Elect
Joe Keithley
MLA Burnaby-Willingdon

Strong

Representation in

Burnaby-Willingdon

Britsh Columbia's

Green Party

Good Government

If elected your M.L.A. in Burnaby-Willingdon, I would stand up for your interest first and foremost. Throughout my career I have learned how to overcome many obstacles that have been thrown in my way, by circumstances, and less than open minded people.

The N.D.P. have become bankrupt of good ideas and in some cases, morally bankrupt as well.

Gordon Campbell and the Liberals have borrowed their economic plaform from Ronald Reagan. Their trickle down theory of big tax cuts for huge companies and multi-millionaires won't help you and I (just check where their campaign contributions are coming from).

I believe in people first and the power that we, the people have. That power must be exercised.

"We in B.C. need a new direction, political will and leadership. One that puts YOU THE PEOPLE first!!. The Green Party can provide that. Our leader Adrienne Carr has made a career out of standing up for the people's interest. I believe that I too, can do that for you, and would be honoured to serve as your M.L.A.",

Joe Keithley

Domenica 17 giugno

D.O.
+ Special guest

FUCKING GOOD CONCERTS
presents

D.O.A.
+ special guests

am
Donnerstag, 14.06.01
im
Limelight/Stuttgart
Einlaß: 20.30 Uhr

VVK: 16,- DM (+ Geb.)
AK: 20,- DM (incl. 7 % MwSt.)

Keine Haftung für Sach- und Körperschäden. Zurücknahme der Karte nur bei Absage des Konzerts. Das Mitbringen von Dosen, Glasbehältern sowie Waffen ist verboten! Keine Erlaubnis für Ton-, Film- und Videoaufnahmen. Das Fotografieren ist ausdrücklich erlaubt. Dem Club und dem Veranstalter obliegt das Hausrecht (betr. Nazis, Randalierer u. Gesocks). Kein Sitzplatzanspruch . . . ist ja wohl klar!!!

№ 151

STOP G8

D.O.A.: EUROPE 2001

The flight over to Germany was a smooth one. Lufthansa now ranks as my favorite airline, if only because they get you drunk. Tons of free booze, red and white wine and cognac! We had a minor setback when Randy (Rampage) Bob, the sound guy and myself went for a bite to eat at the Frankfurt airport, not realizing we had to go through security again on the way back to the gate. We ended up missing our connecting flight to Hamburg. It worked out because there was another flight leaving every hour, but I learned a valuable lesson for a roadie; If you fuck up and get lost you better have one of the band guys with you or you are getting left behind

June 13, Schweinfurt, Germany

Schweinfurt, translated, literally means "fort swine," I believe, so it was appropriate that the venue was located right across the street from the police station. Just a little hall that felt like any small North American town, especially considering the opening bands were from New Jersey and Delaware. Jan, the drummer got really sick, which I suspect had something to do with drinking an entire bottle of vodka with Randy Rampage. He had a big barf-o-rama in the parking lot. I ate something that I was allergic to and had to induce vomiting as well.

I puked about a dozen times. An interesting start to the trip. That night, I began my tour of duty sleeping in the van.

June 14, Milan, Italy

We didn't get more than an hour outside of Schweinfurt before the van started shaking and making strange sounds. All of a sudden smoke started to pour out of the back and we had to pull over to the side of the Autobahn and push it to the nearest gas station. Turns out we had blown a rod and cracked a head gasket. We called the insurance company and they sent some guy to come and confirm the fact that our vehicle was totalled. This took two hours. He took one look at the liquid spewing out of the tail pipe and said; "Kaput." Yeah, that was what we thought. So then we had to wait for a tow truck to take us to Werzburg.

When we got to the nearest car rental place they told us that they would have had a van except it was a holiday weekend and all they had was their own Mitsubishi mini van, a five-seater for six of us. We ditched half the gear and brought a pair of socks a pair of pants and a t-shirt each and roared like hell down the Autobahn. The entire time, Ziggy the Polish merch guy Randy and I took turns sitting on the console and having Joe "accidentally," stroke their leg every time he geared down.

When we finally got to the Radio Blackout Festival, that evening's venue, and they said "Hey, you're on in ten minutes." After a few minor equipment failures, everything was going fine until the kids at the front of the stage knocked down the security barrier and started fighting with the festival security. This seemed a little silly since the barrier was positioned in a way that they could easily have walked around it but hey, what do I know.

They were eventually able to settle the dispute in a non-violent fashion and the show went off without a hitch.

That night I got to stay in a hotel room (albeit next to Bob's legendary snoring) and had a decent breakfast, before taking one picture, of a side-street and bidding farewell to Milan.

June 15, Torino, Italy

Got a nice bottle of Chianti at one of the gas stops for the equivalent of maybe five bucks. Not bad at all. The venue was an empty factory with dirt on the floor about an inch deep but it still had an outdoor bar. There were all kinds of crusty kids with their dogs, smoking opium. I got a little drunk at dinner and woke up to someone shaking the van. You've not lived fully until you've had the experience of being awakened from a dead sleep (in a car no less) by Joey Shithead screaming and shaking you. I have experienced this a lot.

After a few Red Bulls I was alert enough to tune the guitars and everything went off as planned.

June 16, Vicenza, Italy

Had my first bidet experience at a coffee shop across the street from the squat.

At some point the lights went out in the tiny bathroom and I had to finish the unpleasant task in the dark.

The venue was an abandoned factory. Dirty, dusty and tons of crusty punks with dogs boozing it up and having a good time.

The monitors at the front of the stage kept getting knocked over and I had to shuffle around on my knees and prop them back up. The crowd was very enthusiastic. At some point a kid grabbed one of the water bottles on the stage, slammed back about half of it and then exploded projectile vomit all over the stage, which I thought was just spilled water and wiped up with a towel. Afterward Rampage said "Wow, I can't believe you wiped up that guys puke." I had no idea what he was talking about. It was also at this show that a guy, pointing at me, asked Randy "Is that the guy from Kids In The Hall?" From then on, every night when Joe introduced the band and crew, he'd say "This is Rusty the roadie. He's got a television show in Canada called The Kids In The Hall," and I would stand up and take a bow.

June 17, Roma, Italy

I'll tell you one thing, Italians really dig their soccer. The day we got into Rome, they won the Italian soccer championship for the first time in something like twenty years. They started honking their horns when we got there and they hadn't stopped when we packed the gear up at night. People were driving in zig-zag patterns (even more than drivers in Rome usually do) with huge flags hanging out the side of their cars yelling "Campione! Campione!"

The show itself was at the biggest, coolest squat in Europe, the Forte Prenestino. The Fort used to be an old army base in World War II. It looks like a castle and has a huge outdoor stage.

I'm not sure if it was too much Grappa or not enough back-lighting on the stage but at one point during the show I looked over at where Rampage had been standing, and he wasn't there anymore. He had kept walking where the stage ended, done a little pirouette and fallen ass backward into the crowd. Everyone headed for higher ground and left him to land flat on his back. He kept playing anyhow. So I helped hoist him back

---

Above is Rusty the roadie's diary.

We started the tour in Schweinfurt, Germany. The next show was in Milan, about 600 miles (1,000 km) away and through the Alps, so we got going early. I was doing 100 mph (160 kph) on the autobahn when this horrendous bang came out of our engine. I looked at the driver's side mirror and there was James Bond-like smoke coming out of our tailpipe. I got the van off the road and we pushed it into a gas station. After two hours the AAA (ADAC) guy showed up and said the engine was "Kaput." I said we knew that two fucking hours ago! Now we needed a rental van, but because it was some sort of ridiculous religious holiday, the touring vans were all rented, so all we could get was a fucking mini-van! We had to cram six guys, half the gear, and a box of merch inside the van. Since we had taken out the last row of seats, there were only five seats for the six of us. It meant two guys had to split the front seat. I decided at this point that I would drive the whole way for all six Italian shows. But whenever I went to shift gears, I would hit whoever was sitting in the middle of the front seat (which was generally Rusty, the skinny roadie) in the left leg with the stick shift. We barely made the Milan show, which was a big outdoor Radio Blackout Benefit. We hustled onto the stage in fifteen minutes and the lighting guy turned up the stage smoke to the fucking max! As we were playing, I could see neither Randy or Baldini. By about the third song, the anarchist punks started a brawl with the security guys across the barricade. They didn't want a barricade at all; a people's band like D.O.A. had to be right close to the people. A couple of days later we were at Forte Prenestino, the squat in Rome. As we were playing, the bass suddenly stopped. I looked around and I couldn't see Rampage. He had gone for a jump and plunged off the six-foot-high stage, landing right on his tail bone. Jan and I filled with another impromptu version of "Folsom Prison Blues" till Randy came to and got back on stage.

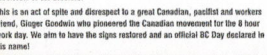

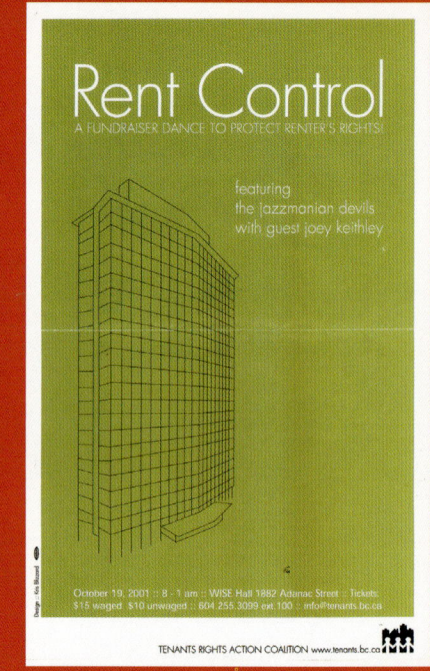

My acoustic duo, the Rabble Rousers, played a rent-control benefit in Vancouver (above right).

We got asked to play a benefit concert (above left) by the Vancouver Island Labour Council to preserve the legacy of a revered BC labour activist, Ginger Goodwin. In 1915, he led the first strike in Canada for an eight-hour work day. After Ginger and fellow workers won that right, he was assassinated by a government agent.

At the Vancouver Folk Festival (right), I was jamming with Peggy Seeger and Dick Gaughan.

While busy recording our new album with Cecil English at Profile Studios, we did a song about 9/11, "All Across the USA" with the talented Bif Naked on board as guest vocalist. That song became part of the *Just Play It Over and Over Again* EP. Rot n' Hell did the artwork; he also did the Sudden Death logo.

ALL ACROSS THE U.S.A.
WITH BIF NAKED
LA GRANGE
DEAD MEN TELL NO TALES
JUST SAY NO TO THE WTO
MEXICAN HOLIDAY
AND OVER AGAIN

#SDR-0047
SUDDEN DEATH RECORDS
MOSCROP PO BOX #43001, BURNABY, BC CANADA V5G 3H0
email: info@suddendeath.com / web: www.suddendeath.com

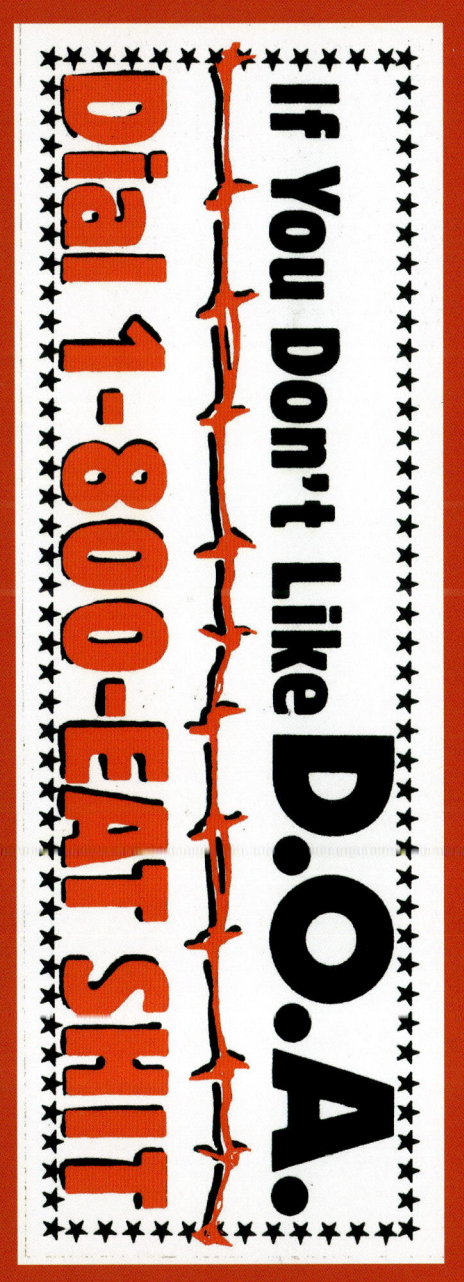

If You Don't Like D.O.A. Dial 1-800-EAT SHIT

What an extraordinary experience the Japanese tour was. The first show up north in Sendai was nothing to write home about, but it got better as we went. There were four to five support bands a night (mostly the bands that had recorded the D.O.A. tribute album). The other bands would play about twenty minutes each, then we played for about an hour, and the show would be over by nine-thirty p.m. Then the whole gang would head out to a restaurant for dinner, sake, and beer. The food was over-the-top good, and each night our tour hosts Toshio and Hitoshi would make sure it was quite different than the previous one. After dinner, the four of us (Ernie from Removal came along) would end up either at Toshio's warehouse, where the bed would be a flattened cardboard box on a linoleum floor, or at Hitoshi's (he lived in an old video store inside a covered mall, it was very surreal) where the bed would also be a flattened cardboard box on a linoleum floor. One morning we got up at about seven a.m. and took five different packed subways to get to Tokyo's airport. Then we flew to Miyazaki, one of Japan's southernmost cities. When we arrived, there were about thirty kids there to greet us, holding up D.O.A. signs and screaming and waving. Miyazaki rocked. One night we played in Noborito, a suburb of Tokyo; the road was so congested that it took us three hours to get there even though it was only about fifteen miles from where we started. After the show, Toshio said there was no rush to get out of there because the traffic was too heavy. We left the club at one a.m., and it took us two hours to drive back through that insane traffic. At the Narita airport we said sayonara to Hitoshi and Toshio. I didn't think Randy was keeping it together, so not long after we got back to Canada, I told him he was out as our bassist.

We Still Keep Running on With D.O.A. was recorded just in time for the tour of the D.O.A. tribute album. Six Japanese bands recorded two D.O.A. songs each. D.O.A. pitched in with two songs as well. What a great compilation!

JAPANESE TOUR

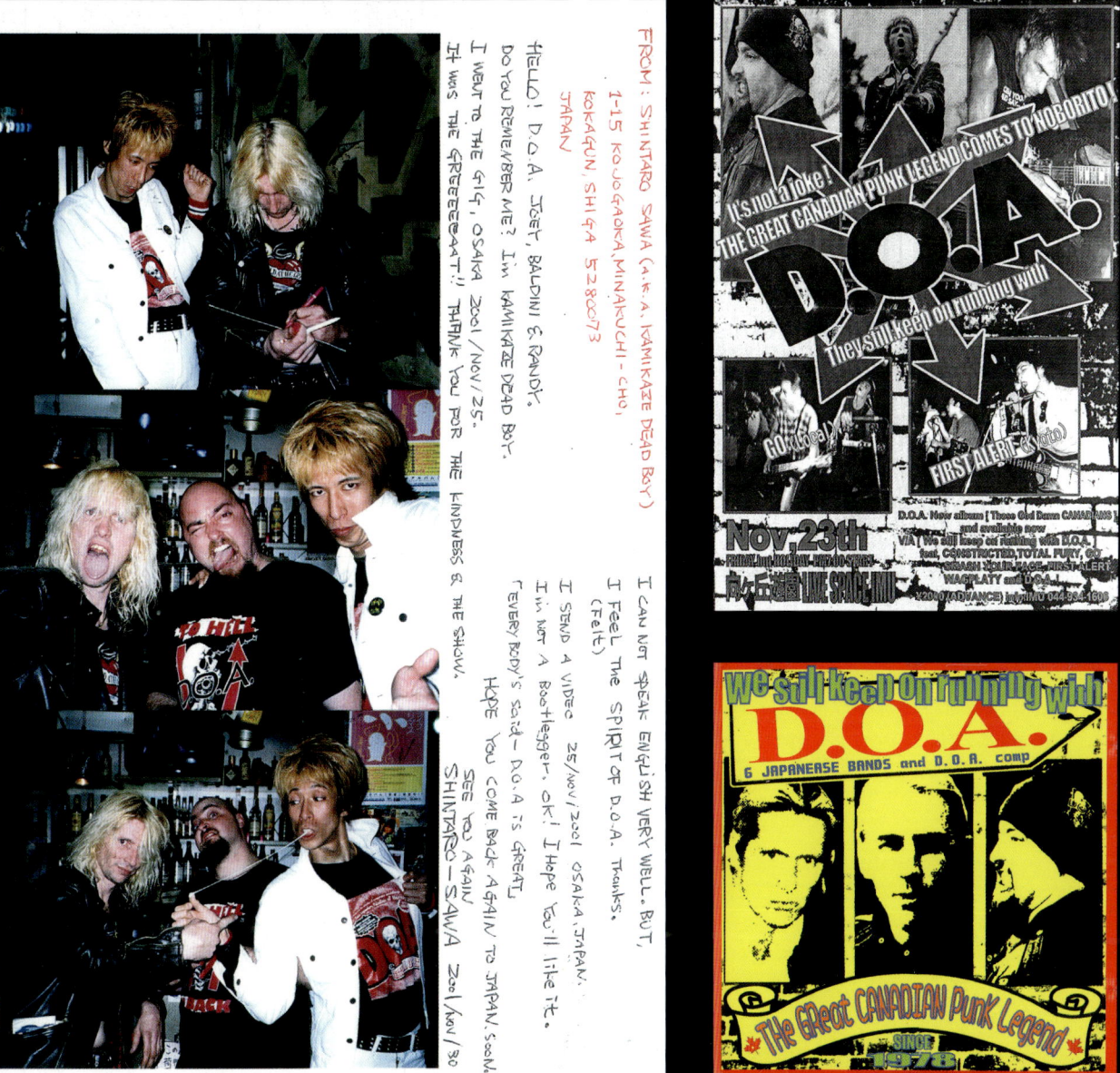

FROM: SHINTARO SAWA (a.k.a. KAMIKAZE DEAD BOY)
1-15 KOJOGAOKA, MINAKUCHI-CHO,
KOKA GUN, SHIGA 5280073
JAPAN

HELLO! D.O.A, JOEY, BALDINI & RANDY.
DO YOU REMEMBER ME? I'M KAMIKAZE DEAD BOY.
I WENT TO THE GIG, OSAKA 2001/NOV/25.
IT WAS THE GREEEEEAAT!!! THANK YOU FOR THE KINDNESS & THE SHOW.

I CAN NOT SPEAK ENGLISH VERY WELL. BUT,
I FEEL THE SPIRIT OF D.O.A. THANKS.
(Felt)
I SEND A VIDEO 25/NOV/2001 OSAKA JAPAN.
I'M NOT A BOOTLEGGER, OK! I HOPE YOU'LL LIKE IT.
EVERYBODY'S SAID — D.O.A IS GREAT.
HOPE YOU COME BACK AGAIN TO JAPAN, SOON.
SEE YOU AGAIN!
SHINTARO-SAWA 2001/NOV/30

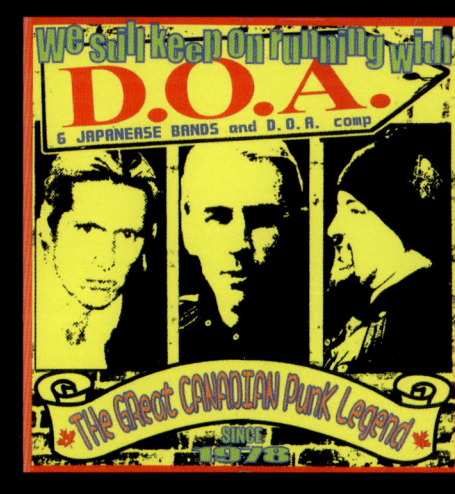

255

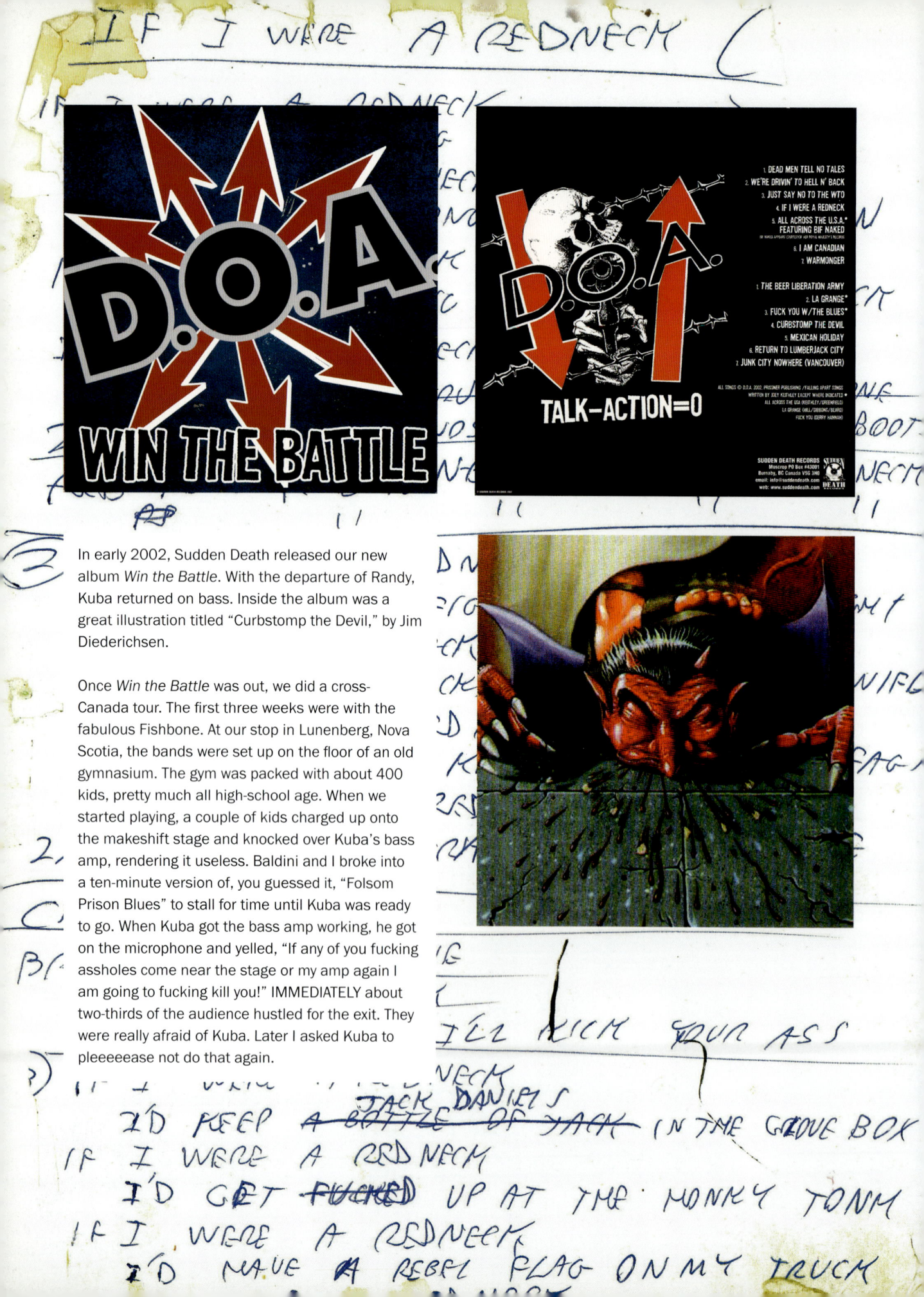

In early 2002, Sudden Death released our new album *Win the Battle*. With the departure of Randy, Kuba returned on bass. Inside the album was a great illustration titled "Curbstomp the Devil," by Jim Diederichsen.

Once *Win the Battle* was out, we did a cross-Canada tour. The first three weeks were with the fabulous Fishbone. At our stop in Lunenberg, Nova Scotia, the bands were set up on the floor of an old gymnasium. The gym was packed with about 400 kids, pretty much all high-school age. When we started playing, a couple of kids charged up onto the makeshift stage and knocked over Kuba's bass amp, rendering it useless. Baldini and I broke into a ten-minute version of, you guessed it, "Folsom Prison Blues" to stall for time until Kuba was ready to go. When Kuba got the bass amp working, he got on the microphone and yelled, "If any of you fucking assholes come near the stage or my amp again I am going to fucking kill you!" IMMEDIATELY about two-thirds of the audience hustled for the exit. They were really afraid of Kuba. Later I asked Kuba to pleeeeease not do that again.

JUST SAY NO TO THE WTO

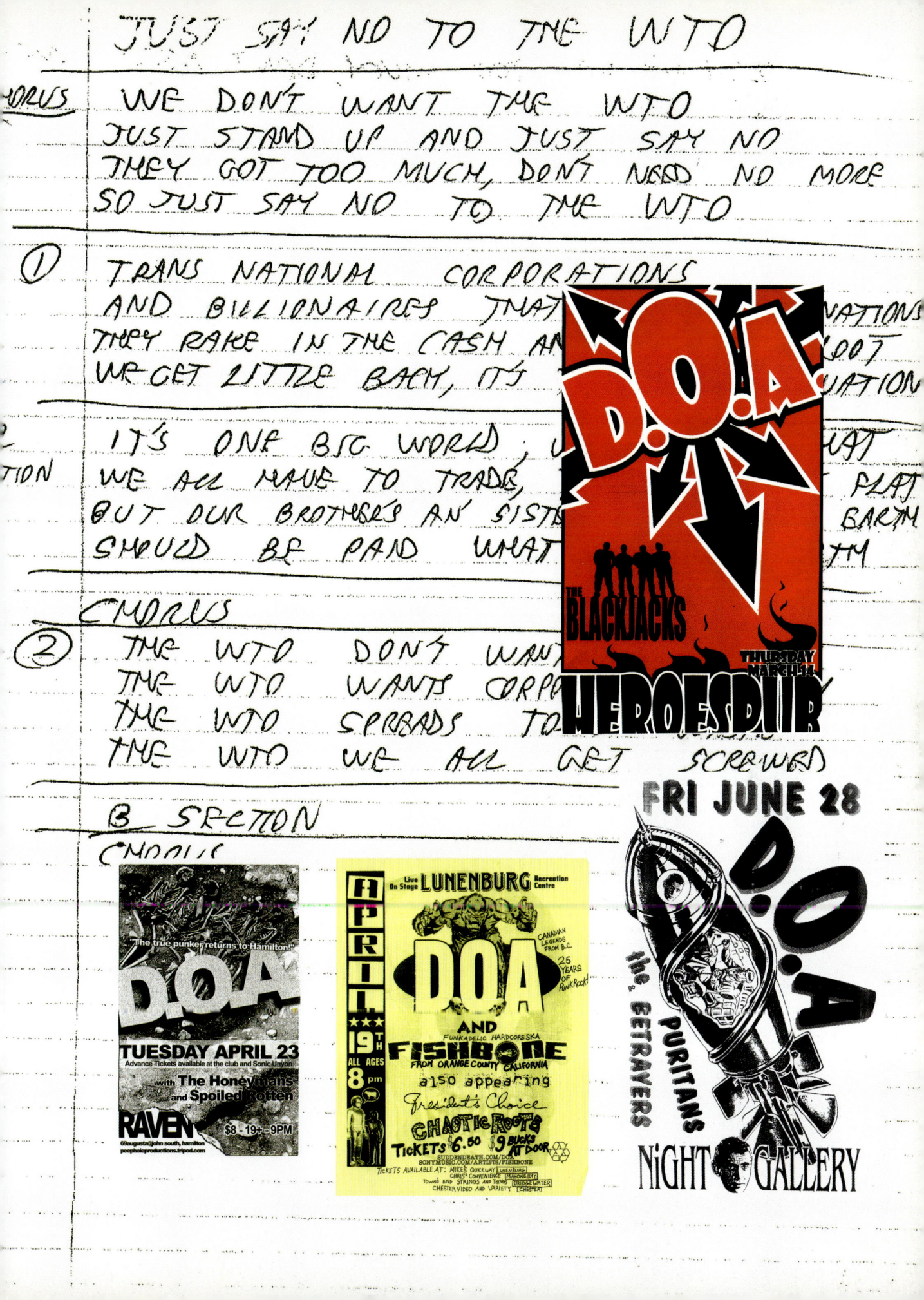

CHORUS
WE DON'T WANT THE WTO
JUST STAND UP AND JUST SAY NO
THEY GOT TOO MUCH, DON'T NEED NO MORE
SO JUST SAY NO TO THE WTO

① TRANS NATIONAL CORPORATIONS
AND BILLIONAIRES THAT ... NATIONS
THEY RAKE IN THE CASH AN... LOOT
WE GET LITTLE BACK, IT'S ...UATION

IT'S ONE BIG WORLD, ...AT
WE ALL HAVE TO TRADE, ... PLAY
BUT OUR BROTHERS AN' SIST... BARM
SHOULD BE PAID WHAT ... ...M

CHORUS

② THE WTO DON'T WAN...
THE WTO WANTS CORP...
THE WTO SPREADS TO...
THE WTO WE ALL GET SCREWED

B SECTION

CHORUS

HERE WE STAND!
Peace Arch Park May 18th, 2002

12:30	**Traditional Greeting**
1:00	**John Juliani and Agrippa The Poet** — Recreating the roles of Harvey Murphy and Paul Robeson at the original 1952 concert
1:20	**The Jewish Folk Choir** from Vancouver
1:40	**D.O.A.** — Vancouver's punk rock activists perform Chee Lai - a Robeson favorite
2:10	**Madeleine Parent** — Keynote Speaker and labour hero, imprisoned under Quebec's notorious "padlock law"
2:30	**Bronwyn, Sara & Tanya** — Grassroots hip-hop from Vancouver
2:35	**The Seattle Labor Chorus**
2:50	**Alden Bryant** — WW II veteran accompanied by Harold Brown on the same piano used in the 1952 concert
3pm	**Ronnie Gilbert** — Activist & member of the legendary Weavers (blacklisted, like Robeson, during McCarthyism)
3:20	**The Total Experience Gospel Choir** from Seattle
3:50	**Danny Glover** — US actor and political activist, with the words of Paul Robeson
4:10	**Solidarity Notes Labour Choir** from Vancouver
4:30	**Jim Sinclair** — President of the BC Federation of Labour
4:45	**Here We Stand Mass Choir** — An adhoc conglomerate of the choirs from throughout the day

ALSO ON SITE:
- An opportunity to hear stories of the lives & struggles told by olders in social action at the olders' stage
- A workshop for activist stage bands from both sides of the border
- Onsite activities such as displays, stilt walkers, information tables and more
- Free face-painting, a children's art corner and a Peace banner created on site by children
- History, in the form of memorabilia from the original concert and visual and recorded information
- An area for groups from both sides of the border committed to social justice, to share their information and ideas

Your emcees for the afternoon are John Juliani and Vancouver activist Jackie Larkin.
US organizer Diane Sosne will also speak. NOTE: The line-up and times are subject to change

---

At the Peace Arch Canada–US border crossing a celebration was held to commemorate the fiftieth anniversary of Paul Robson's concert there in 1952. Robeson was a communist during the McCarthy era and the US government took away his passport. So labour unions in BC and Washington State helped to organize Robeson's performance at the Peace Arch, where 40,000 people heard his magnificent voice. I was honoured when the organizers asked me to sing Robeson's most famous song, "Old Man River," which I sang a capella. Then the rest of D.O.A. joined me on stage for a set.

Above right, D.O.A.'s set list from the Paul Robeson concert with activist-actor Danny Glover's autograph.

We had never been to Sicily before—man, was it hot. We swam in the Mediterranean one day, it was fucking unreal. We played the Delirium Festival in Palermo and everything went well. For the next show, we had to travel through the heat of Sicily, and it was about 107°F (42°C). Our Irish roadie, Jason, was driving when out of the blue he pulled the van over and started puking on the side of the highway. As we worked our way north while playing shows, everybody in the entourage got the Sicilian bug too. We had to stop the van at almost every gas station as it was coming out both ends, so to speak. I guess our lightweight northern digestive systems could not handle what was in the water. I drove most of the way through Italy, not having been bothered by it too much, till we finally got to Switzerland. The boys dropped me off at the hotel as I could barely walk, and they did the sound check without me. After a couple of hours, I woke up in a sweat and staggered down to the club. I almost got killed by a car when I attempted to cross a nearly deserted street. One day, after we had all been sick for a week, Baldini exclaimed, "Man, I can't stop pissing out my asshole!" Ziggy, the merch guy, said, "You have diarrhea?" Baldini replied, "Where the fuck have you been for the last week? Everybody's got the Sicilian bug!" Then Ziggy gave Baldini these little brown pills he had brought from Poland, which killed the bug almost immediately! Thanks, Ziggy!

259

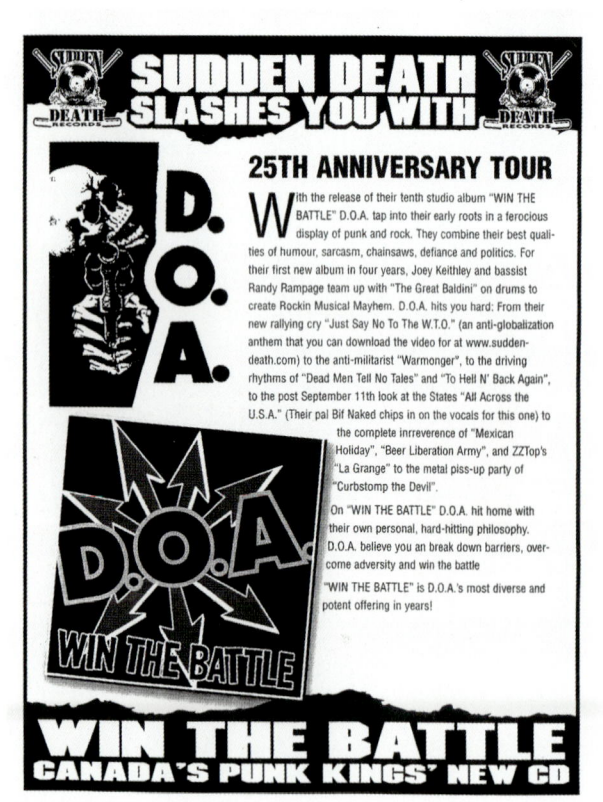

On December 21, 2002, newly elected Mayor of Vancouver Larry Campbell's (now Senator Campbell) first official act was the declaration of D.O.A. Day in Vancouver. I was playing an acoustic show at the Railway Club when city councillor Jim Green came down and read out the declaration in the middle of the show. He was taking a bit long (in a fun way) reading aloud all the various "whereas D.O.A. did this blah blah blah ..." So I grabbed it from him, sped up the reading, and carried on with the show. Thanks very much, Vancouver!

Office of the Mayor
CITY OF VANCOUVER
BRITISH COLUMBIA

Proclamation

"CELEBRATION OF 25TH ANNIVERSARY OF DOA"

WHEREAS	The punk rock band DOA celebrates its 25th Anniversary this month;
AND WHEREAS	DOA was formed in the midst of the punk/new wave explosion in 1978;
AND WHEREAS	DOA burst out of Vancouver's underground to become one of the most influential bands on the punk circuit;
AND WHEREAS	DOA have gained world-wide renown through annual tours of Europe, retaining a stronghold in Germany, Italy and the UK;
AND WHEREAS	DOA's exceptional longevity as a band in a milieu known for the early demise of musical groups is to be highly commended;
AND WHEREAS	The City of Vancouver recognizes the Band's contribution to the vibrant punk-rock scene in Canada:
NOW, THEREFORE,	I, Larry Campbell, Mayor of the City of Vancouver, DO HEREBY PROCLAIM Saturday, December 21st, 2002 as

"CELEBRATION OF 25TH ANNIVERSARY OF DOA"

in the City of Vancouver.

Larry W. Campbell,
MAYOR

$15 IN ADVANCE
MORE AT THE DOOR
ALL AGES

TIC
DOC WIL

WITH SPECIAL GUEST
GRIM HYMN & THE HORR

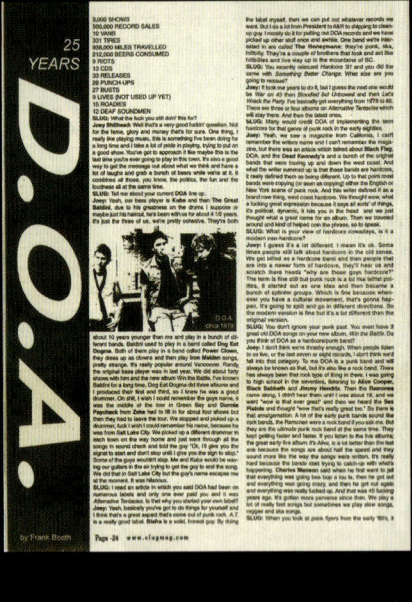

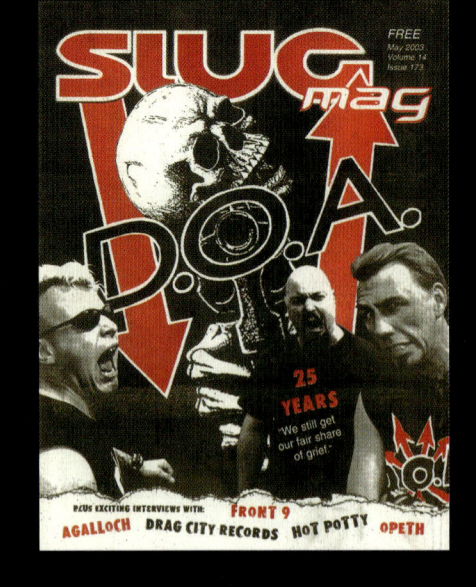

The cover of *Slug Mag*—the cool side of Salt Lake City—and a Belarussian mag in the Cyrillic language.

Right after a show in Long Beach, California, we left for our next gig in Las Vegas, just so we could get an early start on losing our dough in Sin City. About three a.m. we were way east of L.A., just getting deep into the desert in San Berdu (San Bernadino County). We were partying as we raced along, when all of a sudden the Five-O was flashing their lights behind us. A solo cop came near the van and then darted back to his cruiser. Next thing we knew there were six cop cars, lights a blazin' in the desert night. They pulled out their guns and cuffed all six of us, then threw us in the back of the cars. It turned out that the cop that first pulled us over looked at our British Columbia licence plate and figured that we had a mobile meth lab fresh up from Central America. Yeah, right! When they finally cut us loose, the only African American cop of the six asked us what our band's name was. When I told him D.O.A. he said, "I know you guys, can I get your autograph?" The white cops shot him a dirty look.

It took me about eight months to finish *I, Shithead*. Sometimes I cried when I typed, but mostly I laughed. I wanted this book to feel like you were riding in the old D.O.A. van Reid Fleming, rolling down the I-5 having a beer with the boys and me, listening to these stories. Thanks to Brian Lam and Arsenal Pulp Press for getting the ball rolling! To go along with *I, Shithead*, Sudden Death released a twentieth-anniversary best of D.O.A.

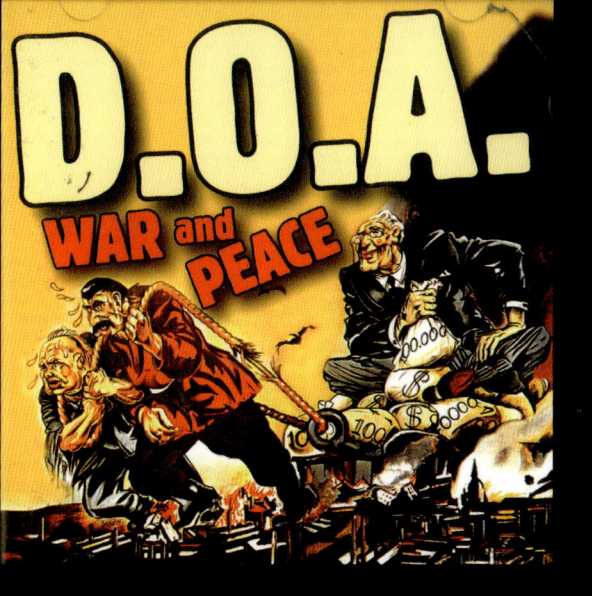

War and Peace, the twenty-fifth-anniversary release.

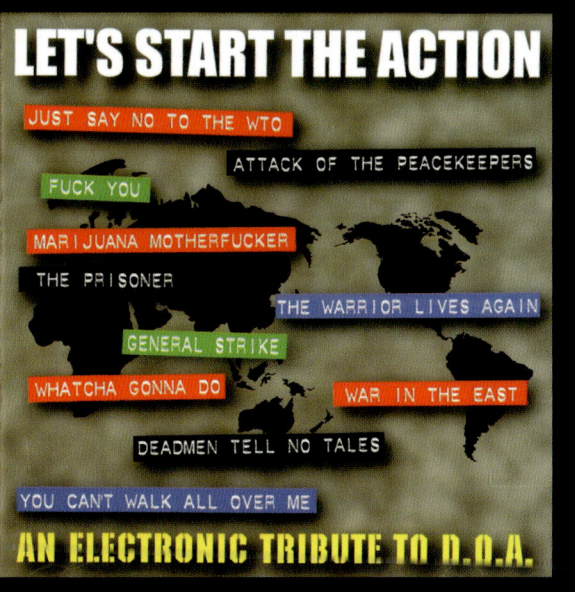

I got approached by the crazy cool Alexy of Ambassador 21 to do an electronic tribute to D.O.A. He was from Minsk, Belarus. I thought wow, what a weird fucking combo, this has got to be worth doing, it's so from left field. Twenty artists from all over world twisting D.O.A.—perfect.

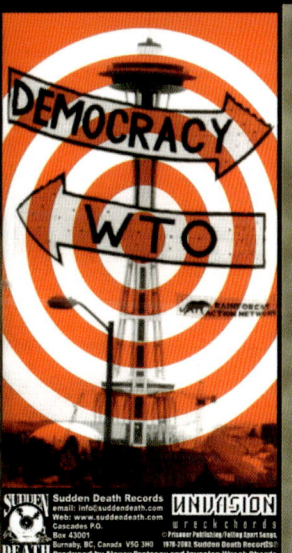

We were on tour in Ontario and this poster (bottom left) showed up. It's Jack Klugman in his role as "Quincy." *Quincy, M.E.* was a predictable '80s TV show and in one of its "best" episodes Quincy came to the conclusion that "Punk rock killed that person!" D.O.A. lived through that, when we partied with Keith Morris (Circle Jerks) and two people were killed in some sort of Satanic ritual/revenge killing in the apartment below us. The LAPD burst into our party with their guns drawn. The next morning the LA coroner's van was out front, and we looked around for Quincy. Wimpy wrote a song about that night called "Murder in Hollywood." That episode was the bookend for the '80s TV show *CHiPS*, which featured California highway motorcycle cops busting a punk rock band. TV paranoia to the max! They missed the whole point of punk. When you think about it, most people miss the point of punk.

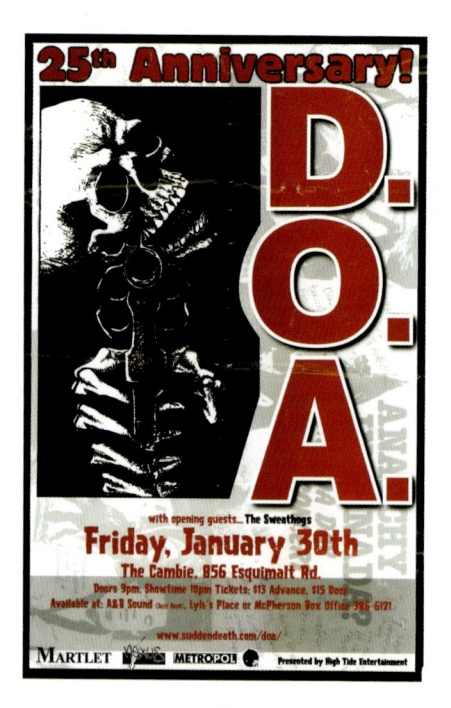

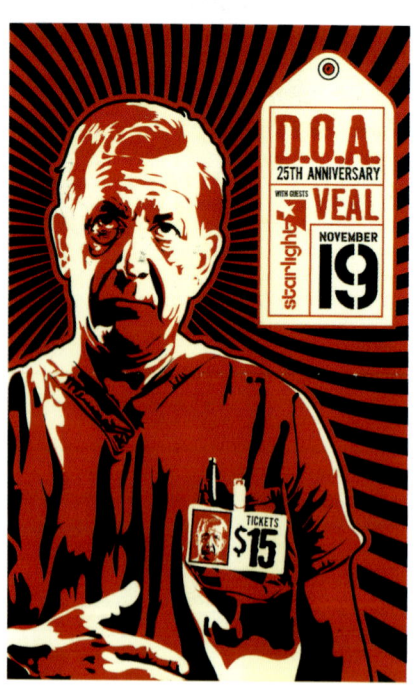

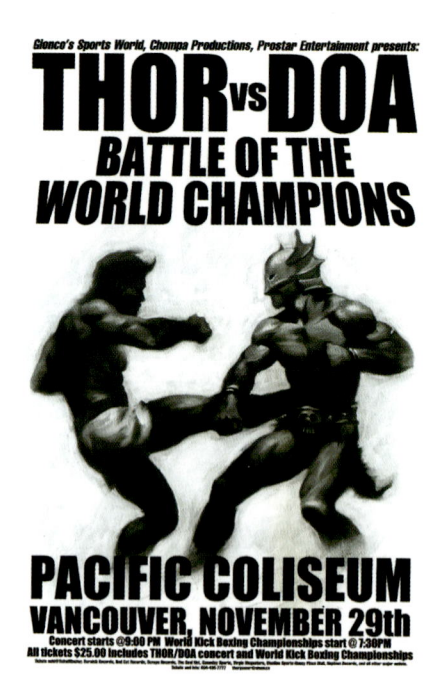

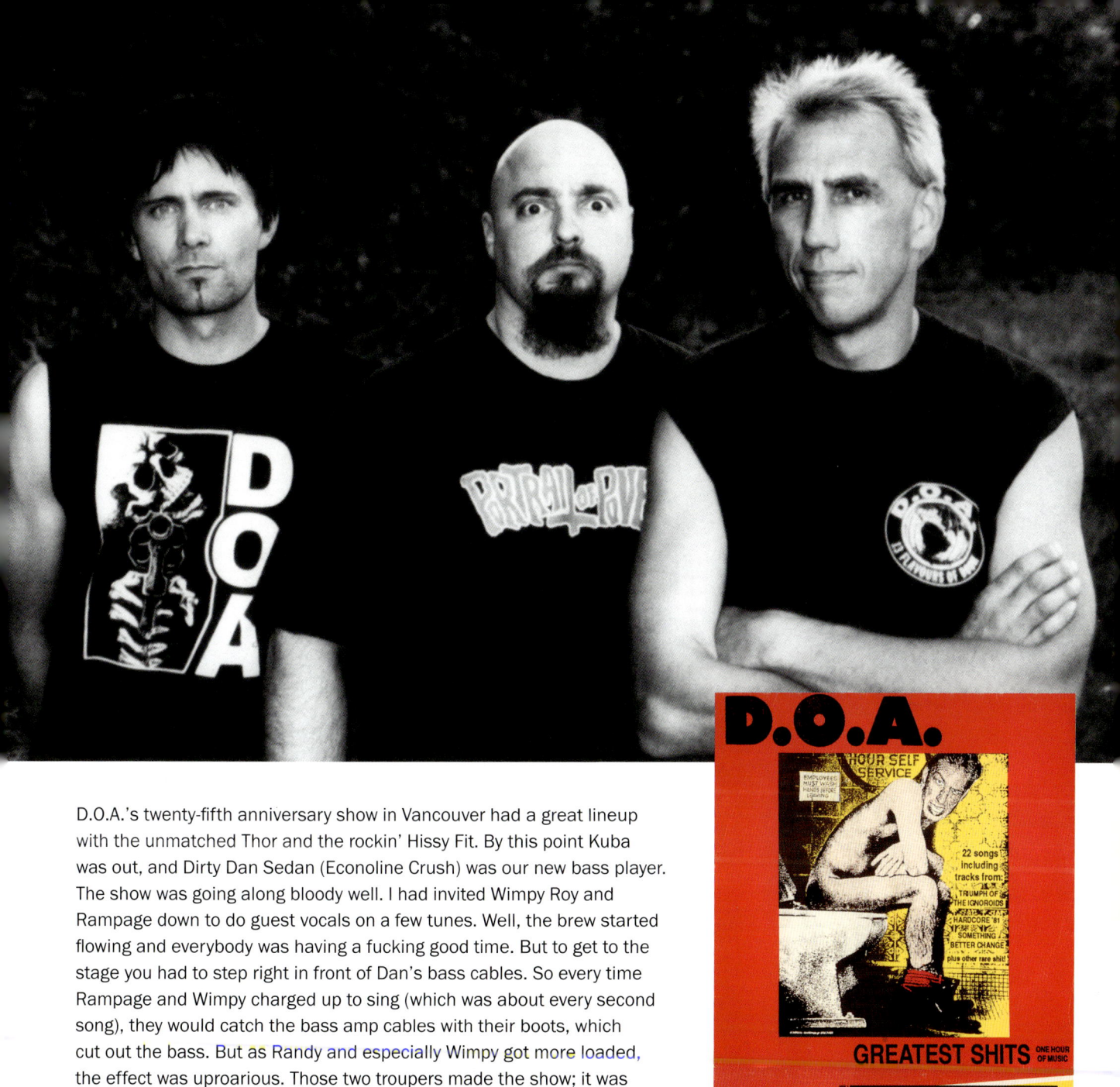

D.O.A.'s twenty-fifth anniversary show in Vancouver had a great lineup with the unmatched Thor and the rockin' Hissy Fit. By this point Kuba was out, and Dirty Dan Sedan (Econoline Crush) was our new bass player. The show was going along bloody well. I had invited Wimpy Roy and Rampage down to do guest vocals on a few tunes. Well, the brew started flowing and everybody was having a fucking good time. But to get to the stage you had to step right in front of Dan's bass cables. So every time Rampage and Wimpy charged up to sing (which was about every second song), they would catch the bass amp cables with their boots, which cut out the bass. But as Randy and especially Wimpy got more loaded, the effect was uproarious. Those two troupers made the show; it was something special.

I had become friends with Thor and he asked us if D.O.A. would play at the Pacific Coliseum at a kick-boxing event. In the centre of the arena they had a ring set up for the kick-boxers, and at the other end was a ring for D.O.A. and Thor. The floor filled up with about 5,000 people, half of them biker types. We played about four D.O.A. songs before the main event. Then Thor joined us on stage and we played four Thor songs. The whole thing was a riot, as our amps and drums were almost falling over as Thor stomped around the stage.

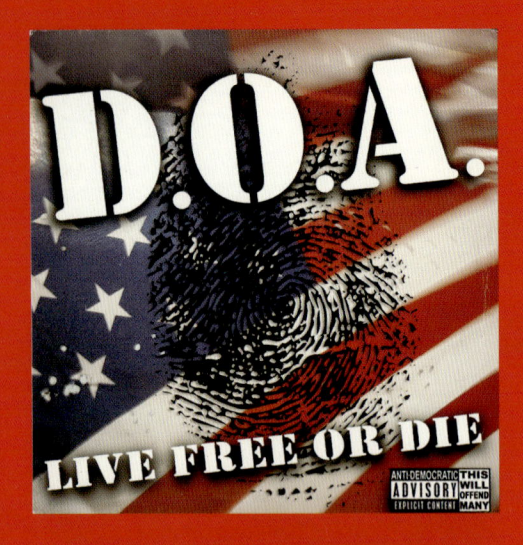

The decision to put the US flag with a big thumbprint on the cover of our *Live Free or Die* album was inspired by the new over-the-top Homeland Security approach to people's rights, a total disregard for democracy. The little advisory on the bottom right corner is also a spoof, but it looks so similar to the original that it fooled a lot of people.

We flew out to Toronto for Canadian Music week, and played a few shows. I hosted the awards show and D.O.A. got this shiny plaque (top centre).

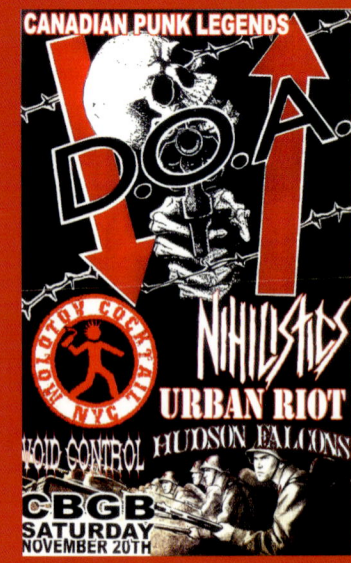

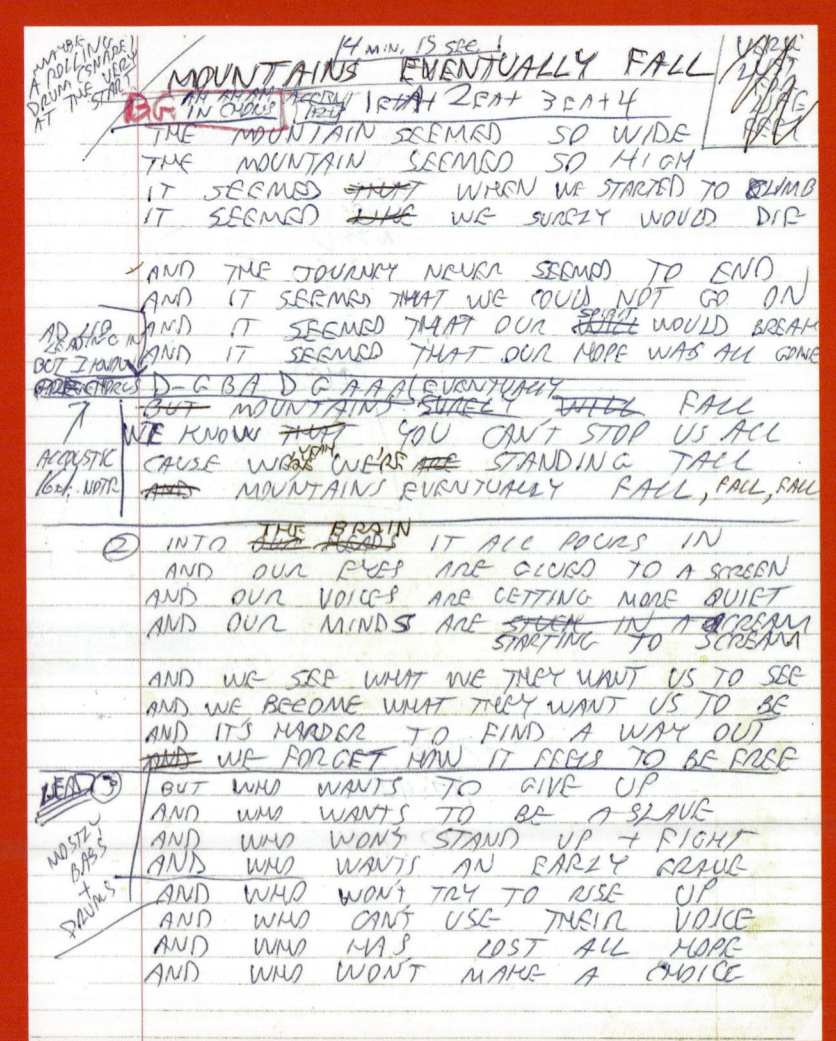

INTRO   BRIGANDS AND PIRATES

WE LOOKED FOR ADVENTURE ACROSS THE OPEN SE[A]

...ER WALK THE PLANK
        AN' FACE A WATERY GRA[VE]
THAN LOSE MY COURSE IN LIFE AN' LIVE LIKE A SL[AVE]
CH. BRIGANDS + PIRATES, THAT'S WHAT WE WERE BRAN[D]
    GOT NO REGRETS, YOU REAP WHAT YOU SO[W]
    WHEN THEY CATCH, THEY'LL CLAP US IN IRON[S]
    AND THE NOOSE WILL SEND US TO A
            GRAVE DOWN BELO[W]

FEEL SKA — I MAKE THIS WORLD
GUITAR ~~WORLD~~ KEEPS SPINNIN' ROUND

2,#,4
↓① THE OLD WORLD KEEPS SPINNIN' ROUND N' ROUND
     AN' IT'S TROUBLE TRIES TO HOLD ME DOWN
2,#,4 BUT I'M NOT A SLAVE, SO DON'T GET IN MY W
2,#,4 CAUSE THIS OLD WORLD, WON'T HOLD ME DOWN

PICKUP TIME / CHORUS
     BUT I DON'T GIVE A DAMN, THIS WORLD IS MIN
     I'LL RISE ABOVE THE RAGIN' TIDE
     LIKE AN EAGLE SOARIN' IN THE SKY
     CAUSE THIS OLD WORLD 3x ~~I MAKE THIS W~~ ~~THIS OLD WOR~~
     THIS OLD WORLD, I MAKE IT MINE
     ~~YEAH I MAKE IT, MAKE IT MINE~~

"D" 1 BAR STOP AT ② / 5 BEATS TOTAL

     I LIFT THE WEIGHT, I BREAK THE WAL
     I JETTISON THE PETTY AND SMALL
     I AIN'T GOT YOUR ANSWERS, NO I DON'
     BUT I DO MY BEST, TO TRY N' STAND TAL

(CHORUS)
   INSTRUMENTAL
③ THOUGH I MAY FALTER, THOUGH I MAY STUM
   THOUGH I MAY WEAVE, THOUGH I MAY FAL
   I WILL STAND UP TO IT, I'LL BEAT THE ODD
   CAUSE ~~I'M~~ GONNA GET THERE, EVEN IF I HAVE TO CR
                                    EVEN

(CHORUS)
   INSTRUMENTAL
④ THE WORLD LIVES ON THROUGH IT'S YOUTH
   THE CREATE AND FOLLOW THROUGH
   THEY STOMP THE STANDARDS, THEY RIP RIGHT THR
   THEY CUT THE CRAP, TAKE WHAT THEY CAN US

(CHORUS)

FULL ON
2x TRIPLETS w/ ① + ② OVER TOP IMPROV.
REPRISE 3x D-E / D-E / D-D w/ RETARD.

This was a great event. We were the warm-up act for activist Noam Chomsky on Sunset Beach near downtown Vancouver. A couple of days before, we whipped up a version of "Masters of War" and played that, of course. I have never heard such a large crowd (20,000) be so quiet as when Noam spoke. He was so soft-spoken that people were leaning in to hear his words—and what he has to say makes a lot of sense in this mixed-up world.

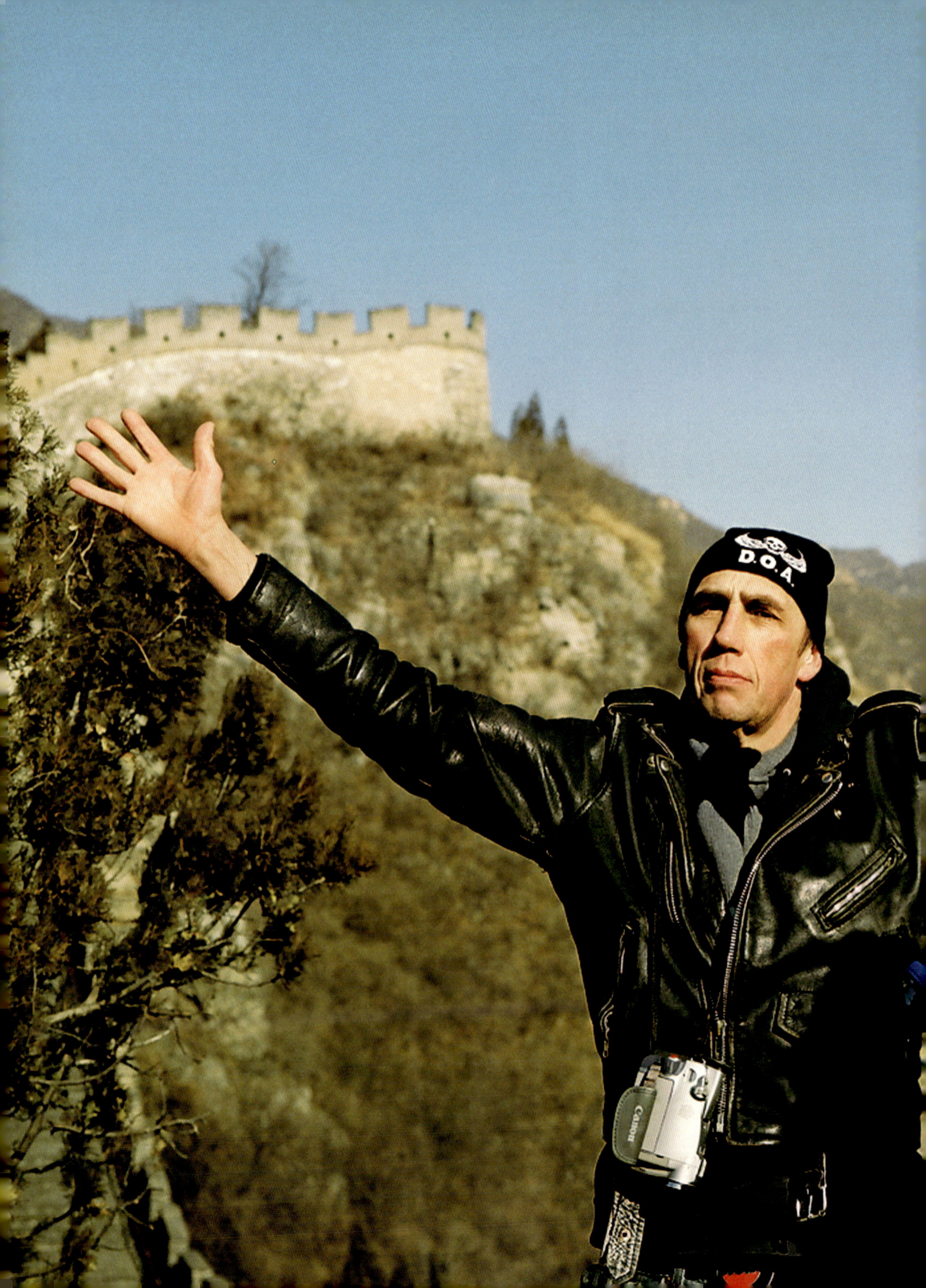
D.O.A.
Canon

Chapter 10

2005-NOW

POLICE BRUTALITY
LIAR FOR HIRE
HOCKEY SONG
D.O.A.
WAR
FUCK YOU
FUCKED UP HARPER
DISCO SUCKS
LA GRANGE
I HATE U
2+2
FOLSOM PRISON
MARIJUANA → SURFIN' BIRD
WOKE UP SCREAMING
SLUMLORD
CAPTAIN KIRK

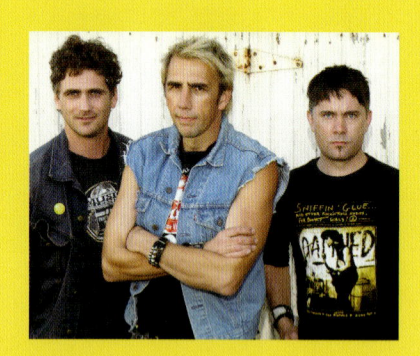

TALK–ACTION *STILL* = 0

Near the start of '05, I helped organize the re-release of 1979's *Vancouver Complication* compilation album and associated benefit show. At that show, Randy did a guest spot on bass with D.O.A. and we blew the doors off of the WISE Hall in East Vancouver, so Randy was back in as bassist. Early in 2007, I put together a cool DVD called *Smash the State,* which contains really raw early footage of D.O.A. That year, I also recorded a second solo album called *Band of Rebels*, an electric album with a ton of cool musicians helping out. D.O.A. also toured Australia for the second time in '07. Thanks, Nigel (RIP).

But it sure felt like the band needed a spark, and that came first in the form of a talented new drummer, Floor Tom Jones, and next when Bob Rock agreed to produce a new album for us. Randy, Floor Tom, and I worked on demos through the winter, and in February 2008, we recorded the bed tracks at the Warehouse Studios in Vancouver. With the help of co-producer Jamey Koch, Bob made it sound huge, which is what he's famous for. We called the album *Northern Avenger*; it's one of my favorites. By the time the album came out in September, Dirty Dan Sedan was on bass again, and that was cool—he's one of the best.

In January 2009, we broke some new ground when we became the first political punk band to tour China. It was amazing. In the spring, we went back to Europe for the first time in seven years. The tour was strong and we had some big-ass shows in Italy. In the summer, we went back to Germany for a week of festival concerts. Hey, we were going strong again, like a freight train rolling down the track; just don't get in our way! Sudden Death also released a twenty-six track retrospective DVD called *The Men of Action*. Well, that's who we are.

We decided to record another album in the winter of 2010 that Chon (from Profile Studios) and I produced. I thought it was fitting to call it

Talk–Action = 0. We finished the mix in April and slammed it out in time for a European tour that started in Zurich on May Day. A riot ensued: D.O.A. and the crowd got surrounded by a thousand cops. That summer, Floor Tom, Dan, and I played a bunch of crazy shows from Chicago to NYC, and these gigs were good 'n' hot. In the summer of 2010, Floor Tom Jones left D.O.A. and was replaced by the exciting whiz kid on drums Jesse Pinner. Dan, Jesse, and I did a massive Canadian tour that fall.

In December 2010, the *Vancouver Sun* newspaper finished an online poll that looked at British Columbia's most influential people of all time. Initially, I was supposed to be included in the list and then thanks to D.O.A. fans' online efforts, I came out number one in the poll. It don't mean much, but it was funny to beat out celebs, musicians, and historical figures.

Over the past couple of years, I've found the time to write all new music for a theatrical adaptation of the cult classic *Hard Core Logo* by Michael Turner. The playwright, Michael Scholar Jr., and I trained the actors/musicians, and *Hard Core Logo Live* made its theatrical debut in the fall of 2010. As of this writing, it's enjoyed successful runs in Edmonton and Vancouver.

It's a funny thing: As I travel around the world, I meet a lot of well-wishers who say, "Here's to another thirty years of D.O.A.!" I'm not sure it will go on quite that long, but come and visit me in 2040 or so, and you'll probably find me at some joint in Vancouver playing my old Gibson SG. I might even take requests.

But just remember this, my friends:

    WE CAN AND TOGETHER WE WILL
    CHANGE THIS WORLD INTO A BETTER PLACE
    TALK–ACTION = 0

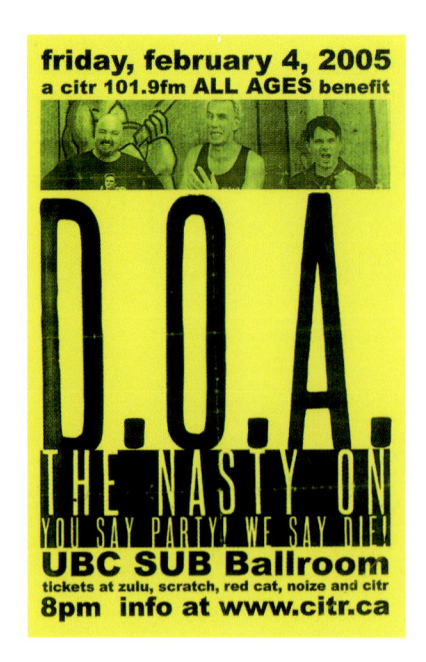

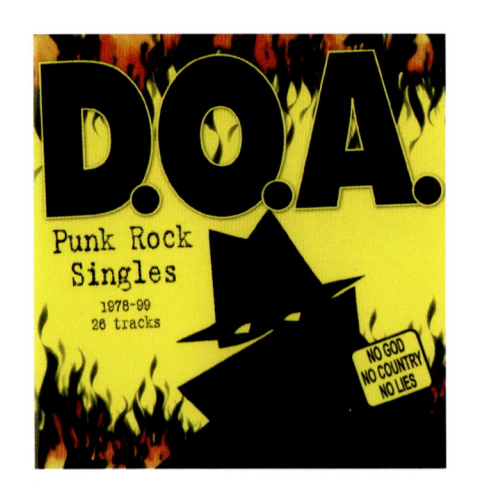

At a show at UBC (above, centre), we got about four songs into the set and the fire alarm went off. They cleared the ballroom, and after a few minutes they let the crowd back in. We played another three songs and the alarm went off again. Okay, one more time, everybody out! This happened four times; some fucker kept pulling the alarm. They finally just cancelled the gig.

After some amicable conversations, Sudden Death got permission from everybody involved to re-release the 1979 *Vancouver Complication* compilation. With a lot of help from Grant McDonagh, Steve Macklam, Phil Smith, Gerry Barad, and more, we had this great album ready to go again, after being out of print for twenty-five years. The real key was to make the re-release a fundraiser for the Vancouver Food Bank. To commemorate this milestone, we organized a show at the WISE Hall. I was the MC for the evening. Just before they came on stage for their set, I would ask the bands when was the last time they played? The Dishrags and the Shades both said twenty-six years ago. I was blown away! At the end, D.O.A. got up to play. Dan came up and played five songs, then Randy Rampage came up and joined us for another six or seven tunes; it rocked. Shortly thereafter, Dan was out and Randy was playing bass for D.O.A. for the third time. To date, the album has raised $6,500 for the food bank.

Sudden Death re-released the *War on 45* EP on CD with eleven additional tracks. We had an Xmas party on the third annual D.O.A. Day.

Sudden Death also put out all of D.O.A.'s 7-inch singles and EPs on *Punk Rock Singles*.

275

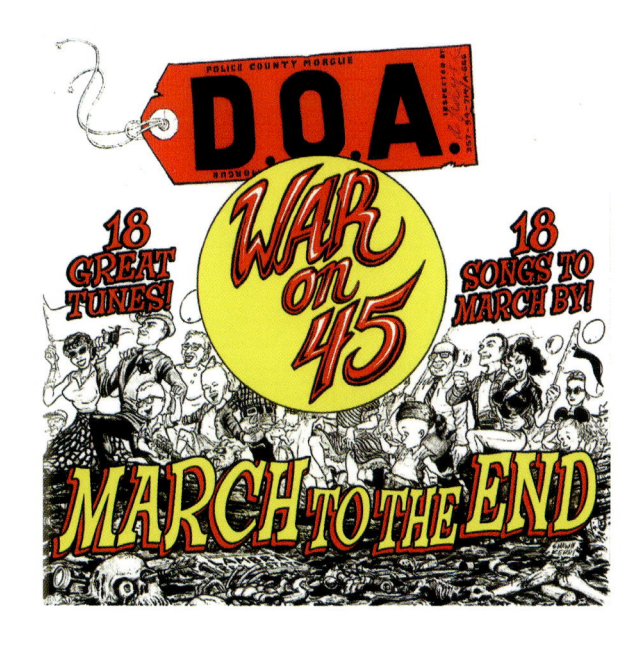

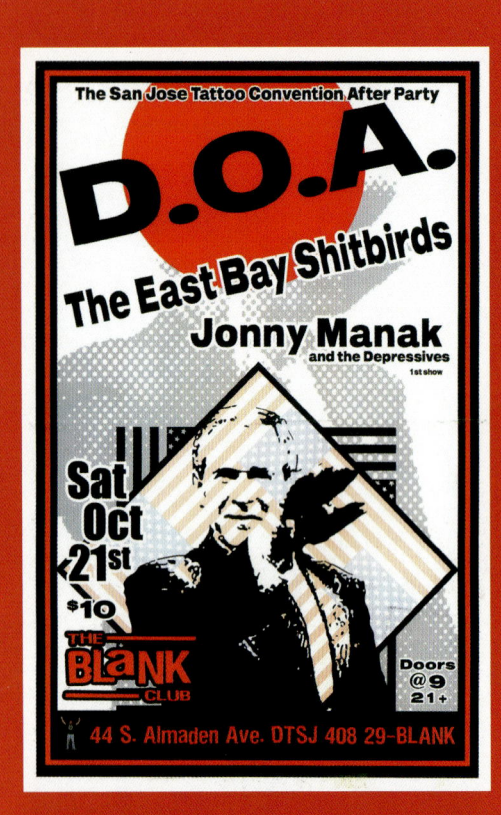

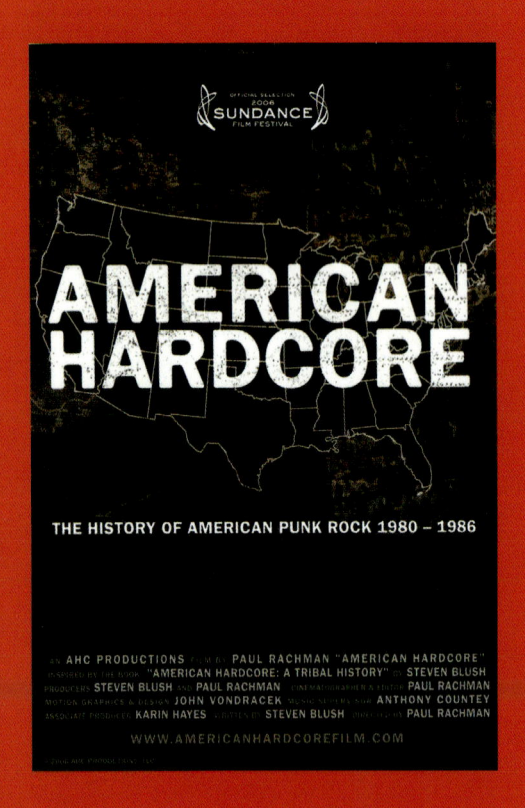

In San Jose, we wrapped up the tattoo convention. We got free tickets to see the San Jose Sharks and the Minnesota Wild play hockey. What a bloody game! Rampage passed out, so he didn't go, and I ended up having to sell his $100 ticket for $15. Baldini was in the shitter the entire game (he and I had been having a contest to see who could consume the most Mexican food each day; apparently I was the winner). The guys who got the tickets for us missed the entire game as they sat in the arena bar, and I spent the game explaining to our roadie, Tim the hippie, hockey rules! Fuck! The show was great. Jack Rabid was there, and he loved it.

American Hardcore was somewhat incomplete and not quite accurate, but it was entertaining, informative, and ultimately important documentary. The filmmakers, Steven Blush and Paul Rachman, arranged for us to play the film's premiere at the Sundance Film Festival in Park City, Utah, along with the Circle Jerks. It was really a riot, free food, free drinks wherever you went, and even all the celebrity swag that you hear about at these types of soirées. We were not on the A or B list, that's for sure, but the C list was okay, as was the show, once I got Randy to lay off the Grey Goose a bit. The Circle Jerks were fucking great, and Zander was an unholy character. Later on, we played the Canadian premiere of the film at the Toronto International Film Festival, but they sure didn't know how to party like Park City.

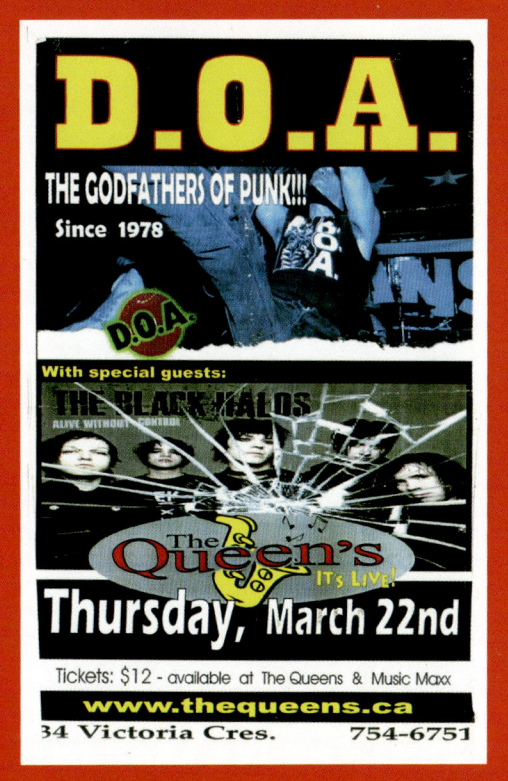

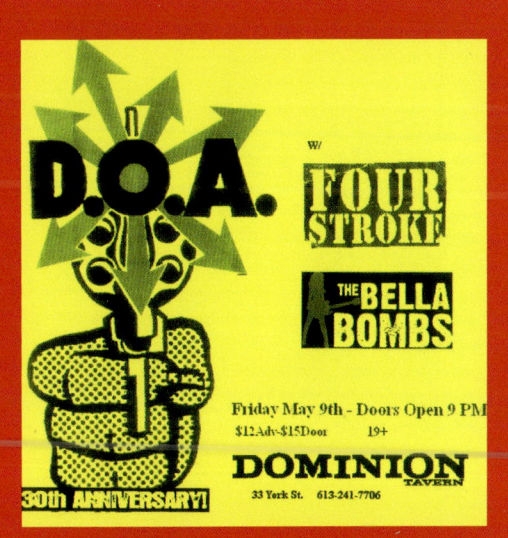

D.O.A. and the Black Halos burned down the Hub City (above). Billy Hopeless was a madman at large, as usual.

We were on tour in Ontario again and played one of the capital's oldest and finest dives, the Dominion Tavern. You needed a Japanese subway attendent to shoehorn them in that night. On the way back, we stopped at Niagara Falls (probably my tenth time there—I love it!) on the Canadian side. In the tourist/sucker pavilion they have a booth where you can look like you're going over the fucking falls in a barrel. It usually costs about twenty bucks, but when we got there the booth's attendant was absent, so I said, "Hey, here's a fucking freebie!" I gave the digi-cam to our roadie Handy Andy, and we piled into the barrel in unauthorized fashion. Out of the blue (and I don't mean in the coked-out Dennis Hopper way), the middle-aged attendant came out of the ladies' john screaming bloody murder! Oh shit, she was tough; she made me buck up the twenty bones, and the rest is history, as you can see.

277

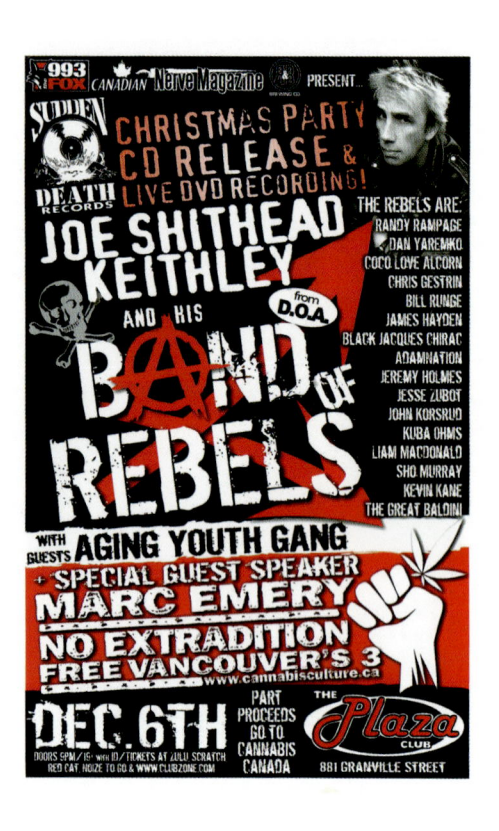

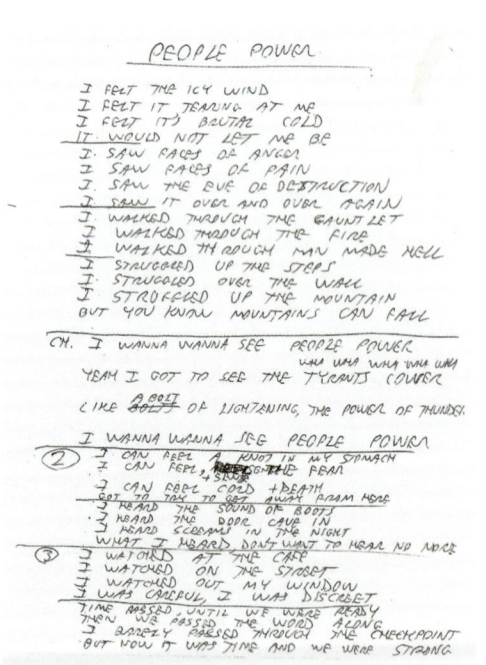

We went up to Whitehorse in Canada's far north and played two shows. It was beautiful, but I was surprised at the level of poverty up there. These would be the last shows we played with the Great Baldini. Too bad, he's a good guy. Maybe he was unhappy that we got paid with an autographed Bobby Orr hockey jersey! Nice touch on the poster with the cop car on fire.

I wanted to stretch out a bit musically, so I put together the Band of Rebels: a gang of desperados that should not be fucked with. In between appearances on stage and screen, the gang and I are usually holed up near BC's Anarchist Mountain, living on rations of poutine and R&B brew and clandestinely visiting Unity Skates in Osoyoos. Fuck the new fascists; we will survive.

Well, Baldini was out of the band, and Floor Tom Jones took over beating the tubs. His first show was this gig at the Plaza Club; it was cool, a breath of fresh air that D.O.A. needs from time to time. Some people may say I'm hard to get along with, but how tough can I be? Even Attila the Hun had his detractors. The *Smash the State* DVD faithfully covers D.O.A.'s early days, with footage from our sixth show and other early shows in the San Francisco Bay Area.

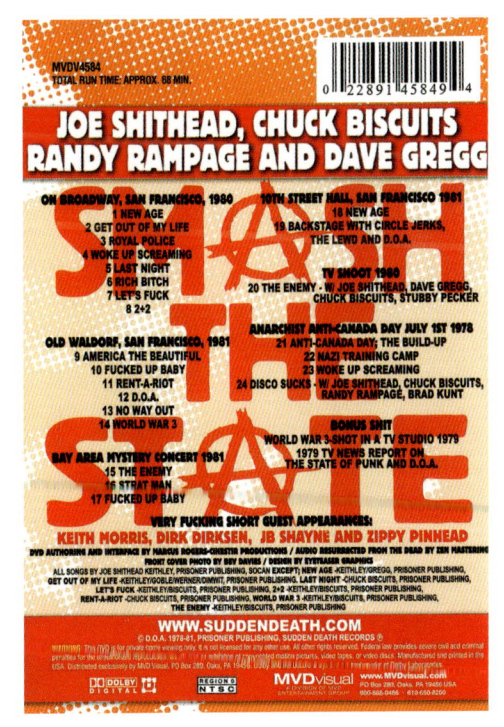

MONDAY MAY 12th!!!

ALL AGES

SUDDEN DEATH RECORDS AND LUCKYBAR PRESENTS DOADGAAWT!!!

D.O.A.
30th ANNIVERSARY SHOW!!!
with **DAYGLO ABORTIONS** and AWT

Friday April 18 - Doors at 10pm
$15 advance tix at Lucky, Lyle's, and Old Nick's

Lucky bar
METROPOL

WITH
TAURINE
AFTER THE INVASION
DAM

This was a great fucking show that ripped up sleepy Victoria, BC. Floor Tom Jones, Rampage, and I were on working on songs for a new album, and played a couple of them at this show.

POLICE BRUTALITY

Police, police, police brutality
That's, that's, that's reality
Police, police, police brutality
Police, police, police brutality
Lose your life, fascist reality
Police, police, police brutality

Got their tasers, got their guns
Got you and me, on the run
They're a law — unto themselves
Do as they please, put you on the ~~curb~~
Protect & serve, that's their motto
But they don't do, what they ought to
The cops always protect their own
But when they cover up, the mistrust grows

Your neighbor down the street, is a little crazy
Nothin' too bad, just a little off
The cops bust in, they take a stance
They gun him down, never had a chance
Some local kids, pull some minor shit
The cops react, an' have a fit
The people are mad, seen this before
They fight back, it's like a war

③ A summer night, too much heat
~~The~~ Tension is high, on the street
~~In a show of force~~
The bulls pull up, in a show of force
Start to push people around, got no remorse
But when push comes to shove, it's bound to blow
It's almost a riot, that's ready to go
Cause we can only, only take so much
Before we call, before we call their bluff

HUMAN BOMB

Gonna tell you once, ain't gonna say it twice
Ain't no second chance, you'll end up on ice
I'm like dynamite and the match is lit
Watch your step, 'cause you just might slip
The safety's not on and the hammer is cocked
Ain't got time, for your fascist talk

① I'm a human bomb and I'm ready gonna explode
So they better run for cover, they're gonna pay for what they've stole
They pushed ~~us~~ too far, with their corporate rules
They're planting the seeds, for riots on every Avenue
For riots on every Avenue

Ch. Get a blast of freedom from a human bomb
Gonna blow it apart, gonna have some fun
Don't need their lies, don't need their guns
But they better watch out, 'cause I'm a human bomb

② I'm like a public avenger, I try to even the score
When I get through with you, you won't be comin' back for more
I'm a deadly charge, packed with TNT
And I'm on the street, gonna blow a hole in your scheme
Gonna blow a hole in your scheme

③ So I hope your listening, an' your eyes are wide open
'Cause you think I'm bluffing, listen up, you're dead wrong
'Cause I'm a human bomb an' I'm ready to explode
I'm gonna get some justice, gonna gonna gonna, let it blow

Ch. That poor poor boy, he ain't got much chance
That poor poor boy, his momma abuse the substance
That poor poor boy, got nothin' to eat
That poor poor boy, he lives by his wits out on the street

D Yeah he grew up on that old Hastings Street
Where things are crap an' there's nowhere to run and hide
His family's a mess, but he try the best that he can
He try to survive an' bury the misery deep inside

Ch. That poor poor boy, he got no home
That poor poor boy, his daddy left home the day he was born
That poor poor boy, yeah he grab a gun
That poor poor boy, now the Five-0 got him on the run

② Got some sketchy friends an' they got a sketchy plans
They steal some dope from a local eastside gang
Now the trouble's comin' back like a boomerang
"Cause it's the jail house doors or the gun it bang

③ Now he's runnin' hard an' he ain't got much chance
They check the waterfront, they searchin' Chinatown
He's runnin' down Kingsway, he'll be lucky to make Main St.
He knows they're right behind him an' they're lookin' to bring him down

DEVIL'S SPEEDWAY

① You're drivin' down for a street race, yeah you think you're fuckin' cool
You think you'd kick anybody's ass, But your about to get schooled
You pull up beside a Cadillac, the Cadillac's red and so's the driver
He looks at you with a deadly smile, an' his eyes burn you like a dagger

Ch. The Devil's Speedway — He'll race you through a ring of fire
The Devils' Speedway — Welcome to your funeral pyre
The Devil's Speedway — His machine's the wickedest
The Devil's Speedway — You'll burn in hell, like all the rest

② You think they're fast at Talladega, You think it's tough at The Brickyard
You won't catch this cat at Monte Carlo, he's got more balls than Dale Earnhardt
Better keep your nerve, 'cause this is the shit, he plays bumper cars when he wants to pass
When it's your time, you start to crap, an' you can feel the Devil bite your ass

③ Well here's a fact that will burn yer balls, just when you thought you'd passed the test
But you're just another fuck up, you mess with him, die like the rest

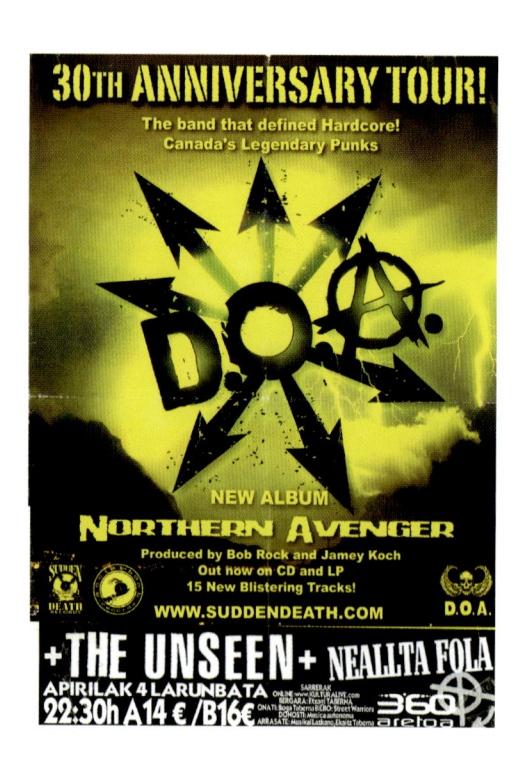

In February 2008 we did the bed tracks for the new album at the Warehouse Studio in Vancouver with Bob Rock and Jamey Koch producing. We would finish a take and I would say to Bob, "How was that?" He'd reply, "When are you going to start trying?" And I'd shoot back, "When are you going to start producing?" Lots of laughs on that one.

I told Bob that the name of the album was going to be *Northern Avenger*. He looked at me and then at my old Gibson SG and said, "No, *that's* Northern Avenger! Eric Clapton's got Blackie, Joe Shithead's got Northern Avenger!"

The album came out in the fall of 2008. We would never play those songs with Randy again, as it was time for the Rampage to go. Dirty Dan stepped back in as bassist.

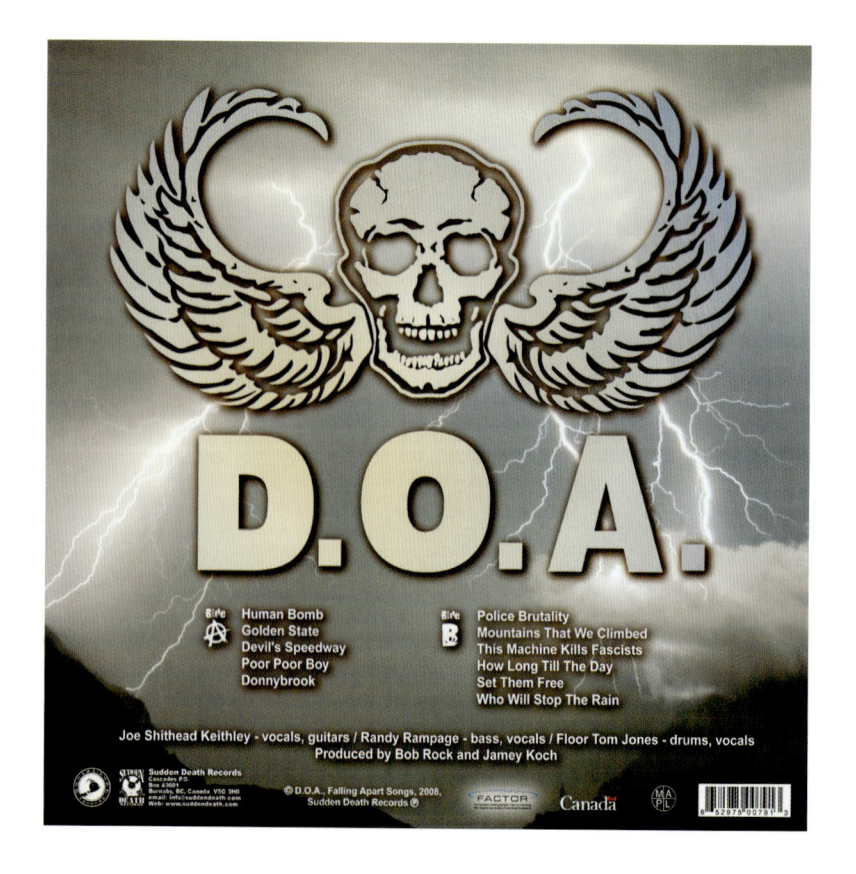

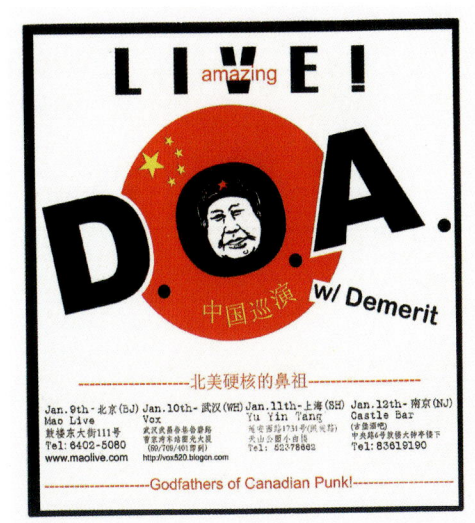

Bob Rock with Joe.

We had a new album, a new lineup, so why not tour a new country? How about the world's most populous: China? We were the first political punk band to go there. The trip did not get off to a smooth start. Dan and I flew in together, but Floor Tom Jones came by way of Tokyo. We were supposed to meet him at the Shanghai airport. We waited and waited, but he didn't show up. His plane sat on the tarmac for hours, but eventually he found us, almost by accident. China was one place where we found a tour manager indispensable. We had Abe Deyo, an American who speaks fluent Mandarin. We did two shows in Beijing, one in Shanghai, and one in Wuhan, spread out over eight days. I had never heard of Wuhan, but its population is six million! It was an endless sprawl of depressing, massive apartment blocks with hundreds of seemingly abandoned chemical drums scattered anywhere and everywhere. Travel in China was hectic; we moved about in planes, trains, and taxis. We almost got killed several times in cabs and ripped off as well. Crossing the street was tough, as regard for pedestrians there is the lowest I have ever seen. The shows were really good as were most of the support bands, one of the best being Demerit. When we saw the kids at the shows, it was like going back in a time warp to 1983. From the massive crowds of people everywhere to the poorest of the poor scratching out a living, to impressive sites like Mao's Tomb, the Drum Tower, central Shanghai, and the Forbidden City, it was an unforgettable experience. But my favourite part was the ride back from the Great Wall. We had hired a car and driver (whom we nicknamed Bob). He kept insisting that we were all friends from way back so we had a cover story if the police got us, 'cause he had no licence to drive tourists. Then he couldn't find Beijing (merely a city of twelve million). Abe had fallen asleep, so the driver kept trying to tell us stuff in Mandarin. Finally realizing we didn't understand a word, he started singing. Then he'd stop and look at me, and I would sing something in English. We traded songs back and forth, it was way cool. Music is the language that unites any culture, in any time.

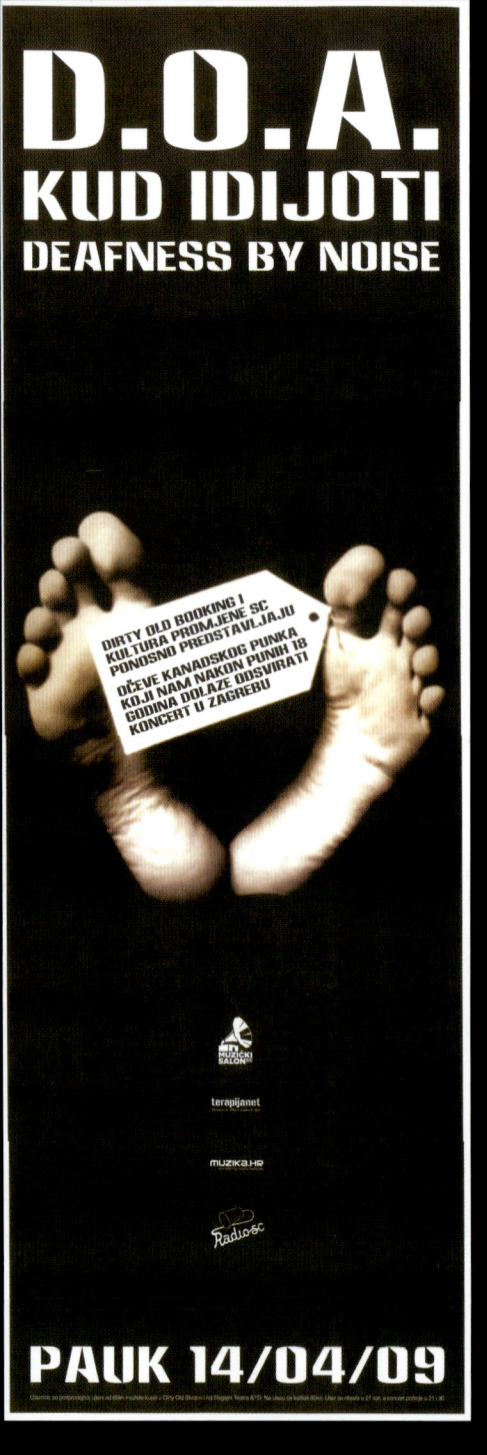

We went to Europe twice in 2009. Two shows in Spain, including this wild show in Euskadi, where we finished playing at four a.m. We moved onto Italy for eight shows, where we played "That's Amore" every night in the encore. The Italian punks would hear "Amore"'s first few bars, then link arms and all sing along.

We hit Zagreb for the first time in seventeen years. It was great to play with the great Kud Idijoti again. We continued on through France. Later in the summer, we flew back to Europe and played the waaaay too bizarre Force Attack Festival near Germany, the biggest punk festival on the continent. Our tour managers Andreas Gohlke and Till Von Hofmann (RIP) got supremely harassed by the cops as we entered the festival, where we came across a supreme clusterfuck of dirty punks, puke, and piss. We headlined the Saturday night, our set was over the top. Shortly after the tour our buddy Till passed away. It was pretty messed up; too many times I've had friends in their prime go. But at least we got a week to hang with him before he went.

MOUNTAINS THAT WE CLIMBED

① There's some things that you ought to know
I'm talkin' old school my friend
I'm talkin' hardcore
Yeah, the cops tried to put us to the end
Yeah we got some old guitars
An' made the scene as hard as we could
Society, ~~first~~ hated us
It was obvious, where we stood

CHORUS
Mountains that we climbed
We didn't care the cost
Rivers so wide, battles won + lost
We waved our own flag
Didn't give a damn
Man my heart bled
~~But what,~~ what — what the hell man

② 'Cause we made our own rules
People thought ~~that~~ we were strange
In every place that we ~~stopped~~
~~They treated us like the~~ black plague
You might think that we wasted our time
You might wonder why we tried
We felt like we found a new frontier
~~We screamed a~~ revolutionary cry

CHORUS

BRIDGE
Along some rocky roads, some died that way
Some went to the joint, they'll get out one day
Over valleys + plains, beat n' busted by cops
Over rivers + mountains, nazis that we fought
From New York to Florida, it was chaotic + hard
From Vancouver to Texas, searched by border guards
From Warsaw to London, we played every dive
Still I don't know how, we made it back alive

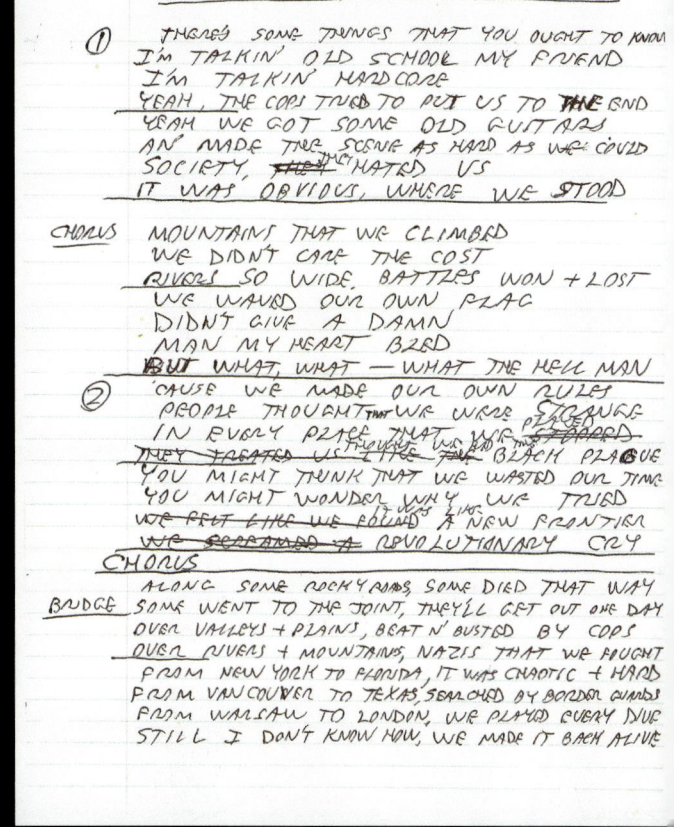

SET THEM FREE

① You organize the death squad
You do the ethnic cleansing
~~You brutalize the village~~
You're turning boys into soldiers
Abusing the innocent
You deal in human bondage

CH — But we're gonna set, set the people free
— Yeah no time to stall
~~We got to set, set the people free~~
— Eventually, the fascists must fall
— Break them out, of this penitentiary
Got to break, break these chains
— We got to set, set the people free

② You got your AK-47
You got ~~big~~ sidur landmines
You got your secret police
There's Islamo ~~fascists~~
An christian fanatics
They're god's destruction

③ We know what you've done
We'll find where you've run to
We're gonna track you down
You're gonna have to pay
For your mortal sins
You won't outlive your reknown

FRIDAY SEPT 8TH
DOA

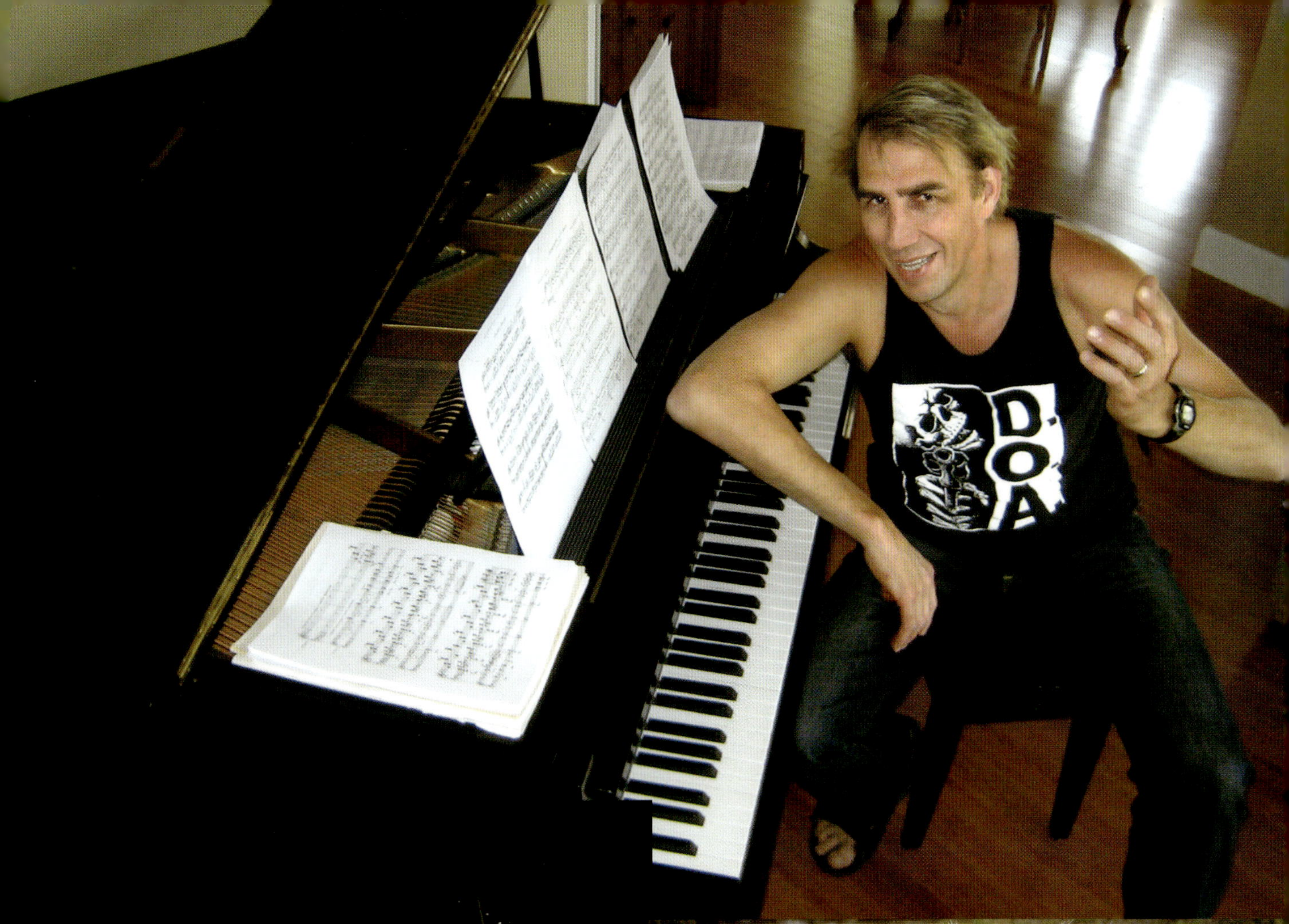
D.O.A
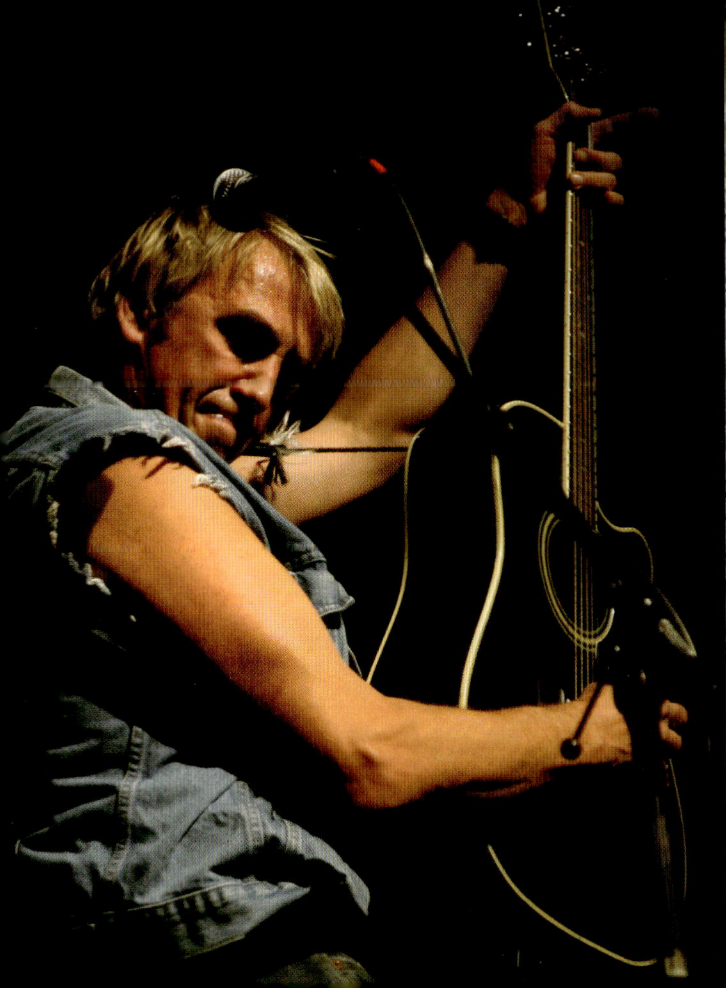
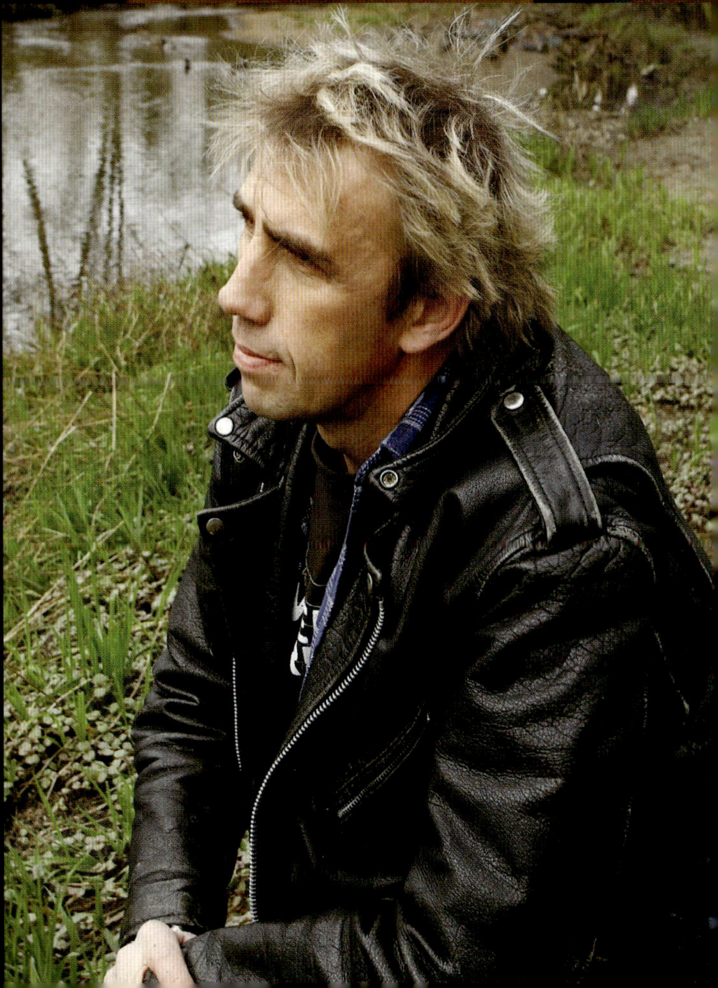

I guess you could say that D.O.A. invented hockey rock with the release of the "Taking Care of Business" video in 1987 (with apologies to Phil Esposito and Marcel Dionne). Once again, it was time to take on the opposition with a series of elbows, hipchecks, and a bit of slew footing. Better keep your head up on the blueline!

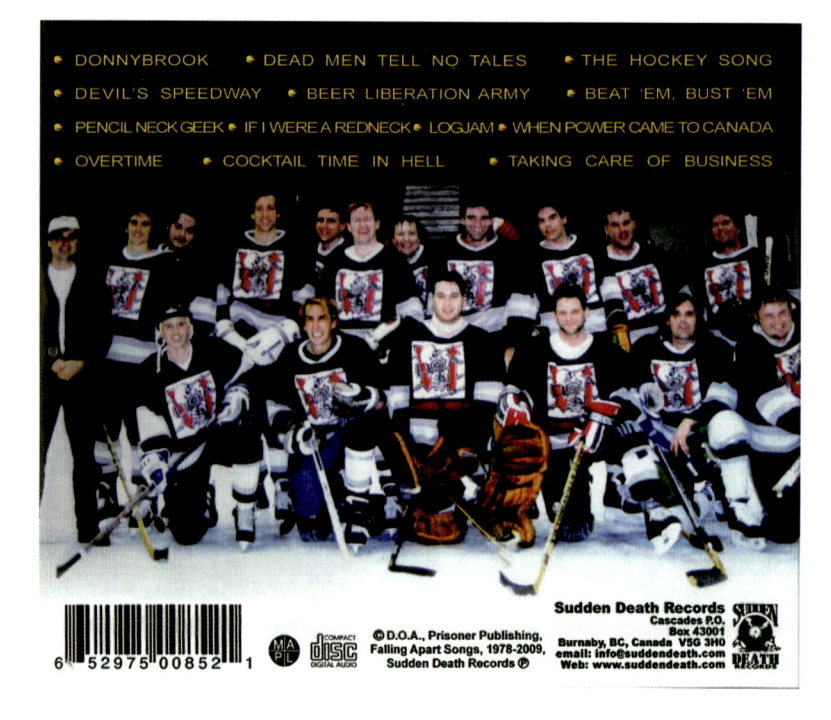

D.O.A.'s all-hockey compilation.

Golden State

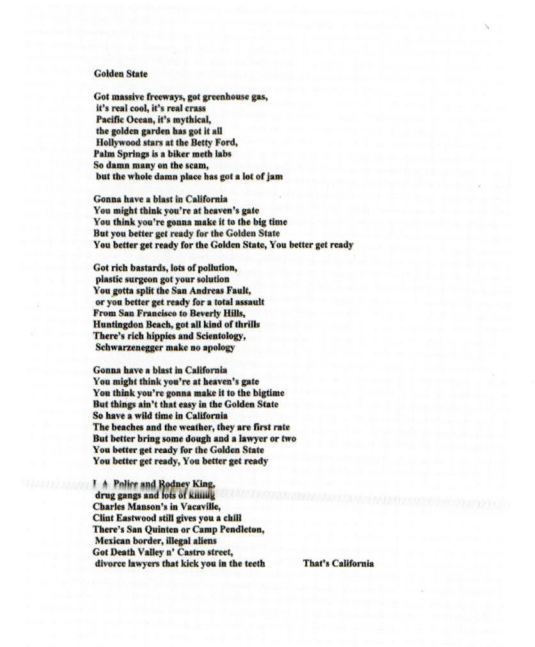

Got massive freeways, got greenhouse gas,
   it's real cool, it's real crass
Pacific Ocean, it's mythical,
   the golden garden has got it all
Hollywood stars at the Betty Ford,
Palm Springs is a biker meth labs
So damn many on the scam,
   but the whole damn place has got a lot of jam

Gonna have a blast in California
You might think you're at heaven's gate
You think you're gonna make it to the big time
But you better get ready for the Golden State
You better get ready for the Golden State, You better get ready

Got rich bastards, lots of pollution,
   plastic surgeon got your solution
You gotta split the San Andreas Fault,
   or you better get ready for a total assault
From San Francisco to Beverly Hills,
Huntingdon Beach, got all kind of thrills
There's rich hippies and Scientology,
Schwarzenegger make no apology

Gonna have a blast in California
You might think you're at heaven's gate
You think you're gonna make it to the bigtime
But things ain't that easy in the Golden State
So have a wild time in California
The beaches and the weather, they are first rate
But better bring some dough and a lawyer or two
You better get ready for the Golden State
You better get ready, You better get ready

! ♠ Police and Rodney King,
   drug gangs and lots of killing
Charles Manson's in Vacaville,
Clint Eastwood still gives you a chill
There's San Quinten or Camp Pendleton,
Mexican border, illegal aliens
Got Death Valley n' Castro street,
   divorce lawyers that kick you in the teeth   That's California

In August, 2009, we played the Warped tour old-school stage for four dates in California with bands like UK Subs, the Addicts, CH3, and Fishbone.

BACK FROM THE GRE

D.O.A.

Sudden Death Records Presents...

THE OWE-LIMPIC$ CAN GO TO HELL

D.O.A.

with **THE JOLTS** & **Fear Of Tomorrow**

Special guest speaker Professor Chris Shaw
author of Five Ring Circus, Myths and Realities of The Olympic Games

SAT FEB 20th — **RICKSHAW**

254 e Hastings . Vancouver . BC . Canada
Tix: ZULU, RED CAT, SCRATCH, densixx.com
doors at 8 PM ~ www.suddendeath.com

Sudden Death Records • Live It

APPEARING WITH:
MILLIONS O
DEFECT DE
PUKE N RA
9PM SAT. FEB

WHITE NORTH

FRIDAY JANUARY 29TH
D.O.A
AND THE FROSTBACKS

10PM - $15 IN ADVANCE
$20 AT THE DOOR
TIX AVAILABLE AT LYLES PLACE,
AND DITCH RECORDS

LIGHTHOUSE BREWING COMPANY

Lucky bar
517 YATES ST

That's Why I Am An Atheist (Joe Keithley, Prisoner Publishing, SOCAN, 2010)

It makes no sense, when you preach for god
Superstitions, to control the down trod
I read the bible, I've seen its plan
It told me a fable, about the creation of wo(man)
About the creation of wo(man)

Ch.
That's why I am an atheist
I'm not one of god's fascists
Don't need your mumbo jumbo
To know that I exist
That's why, I am an atheist

Extremists kill, extremists fight
The way they act, they'll never see the light
You see the priest, abuse some boys
Steal their youth, treat 'em like human toys
Like human toys

The fanatic tells, tells his flock
To spread the hatred, stone 'em with rocks
It's something to believe, thou shall not kill
And peace is king and live by your free will
Live by your free will

DEAD COPS
ECT
LY

8TH SE 8TH & MAIN ST.

PLAN B

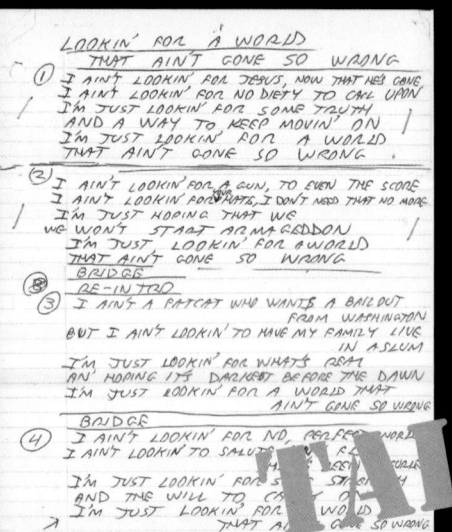

In 2010, Dirty Dan, Floor Tom Jones, Chon, and I had just recorded the new album *Talk – Action = 0* when we headed over to Europe again. Pretty well the first show was a May Day protest show in Zurich. The protestors were trying to make a point with their money-oriented city council that the city belonged to everybody, so they set up an outdoor show in a small park and flew in those noted troublemakers D.O.A. to play. We knew there was the potential for some shit to go down. We got to the park about the time the 2,000-strong May Day parade came marching into the park. We enlivened the radicals with songs like "The Enemy" and "General Strike." It all seemed easy enough. After we finished we noticed hat a lot of cops had shown up. The punks jeered at them, and soon the park was surrounded by 1,000 cops (a conservative estimate), four trucks equipped with water cannons, and a half dozen Toyota jeeps equipped to smash through barricades. They were in full riot gear and every third one brandished a gun with rubber bullets. When the cops finally entered the park, they did so in stages by advancing 150 feet (50 meters) at a time. Anybody who tried to run through their gauntlet was quickly surrounded to prevent cameras and phones from filming the takedown, however brutal. We hung around as long as we could, and when they got too close we made a beeline for the hall that was in the park. That day, the cops arrested 400 people in Zurich and got to practice their militaristic operation.

On June 17, we started an Eastern US tour in Philadelphia, and we ended it in Cleveland at a joint called Now That's Class—how apropos for D.O.A. In between we hit most of the major cities out that way. The most unforgettable show was Skatopia in hillbilly country Ohio: skaters, punks, dust, and dirt. Another was Punk Island in NYC. We had driven overnight from Boston and took a ferry to Governor's Island in the New York harbour. The show had seventeen stages (actually grassy areas) with six to seven bands playing on each stage. It was out of control, with about 7,000 kids in attendance. While waiting for our set, we got into the "General's House," a historic mansion where Ronald Reagan, Mikhail Gorbachev, and George H. Bush signed an agreement to end the cold war. It was cool to shave at the wet bar where they mixed drinks for those political giants. Sadly, this would be the last tour we would do with Floor Tom Jones.

TALK-ACTION=0 TOUR

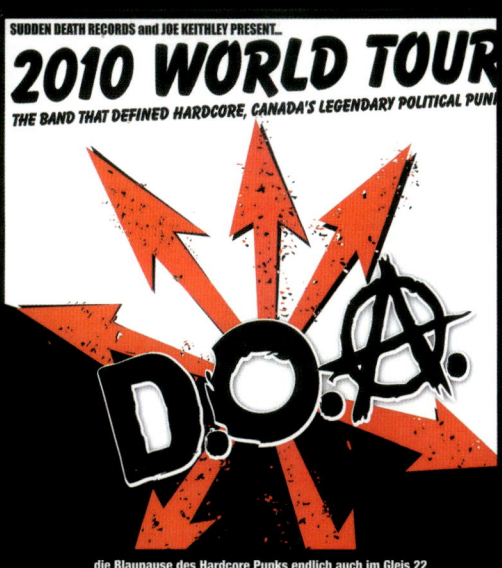

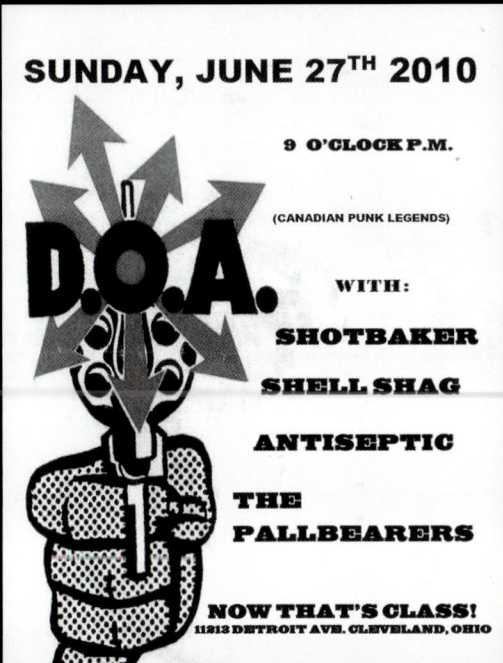

We found a new drummer, Jesse Pinner (Raised By Apes). The *Talk – Action = 0* album release party was Jesse's first gig in Vancouver with D.O.A., which was part of our cross-Canada tour.

I LIVE IN A CAR

CH. I WANNA GO HOME, BUT I CAN'T
'CAUSE NOW I LIVE IN A CAR
I USED TO HAVE A LIFE, I HAD A C[AR]
BUT NOW I'M BLEEDING AND SCARRED
I PARK BY THE WALMART, ~~ALMOST~~ EVERY NIG[HT]
~~TRY TO~~ KEEP MY EYES, WIDE OPEN FOR COP[S]

BUT ~~MY~~ GAS IS LOW, ~~AND~~
'CAUSE NOW ~~NOW WOW~~ AND I AIN'T GOT NO MO[NEY]
'CAUSE NOW I LIVE IN A CAR
  I LIVE IN A C[AR]

I WONDER IF YOU CAN SEE
WHAT THIS WORLD'S DONE TO ME
IT STRIPPED ME BARE
AND TOOK EVERYTHING
NOW THERE'S NOTHING LEFT
NOT A DAMN THING
~~THEY~~ TOOK MY JOB
MY WIFE AND MY KIDS
THE BANK FORECLOSED
I THINK I FLIPPED MY LID
NOW A WELFARE LINE
IS ALL THAT'S LEFT
YEAH I THINK I'M DYING
FROM THIS CORPORATE THEFT

② EVERY NITE, I GET IN LINE
I LINE UP, AT THE FOOD BANK
I SEE ALL MY NEW FRIENDS
THE OLD GUYS, HOOKERS AN' TWEAKERS ON CRA[NK]

BY DAY I PUSH A SHOPPING CART
I COMB THE ALLEYS, LOOKIN' FOR CANS
PEOPLE LAUGH, AN' COPS HARASS
I THINK I'VE HAD ABOUT ALL I CAN STAN[D]

Floor Tom Jones and the Wednesday Night Heros.

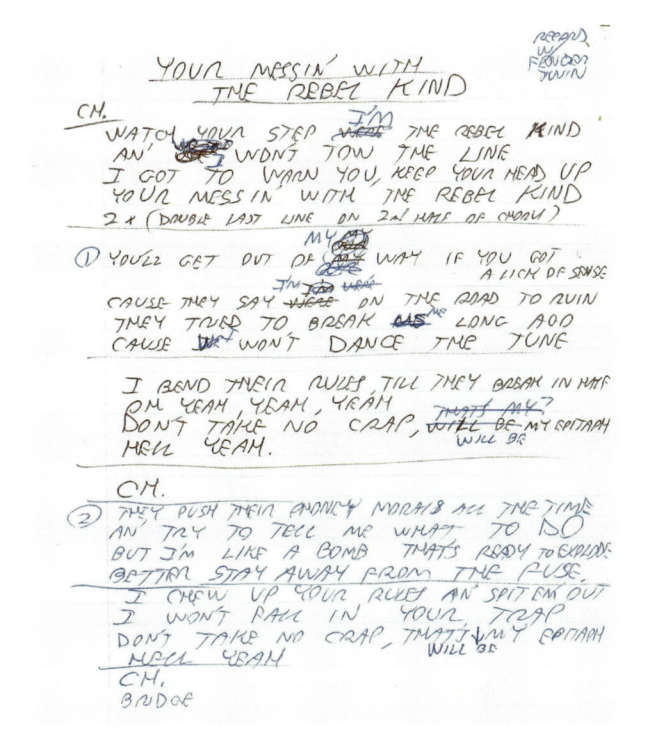

In the fall of 2010, I went to Edmonton to help prep the cast for the theatrical version of *Hard Core Logo Live*. The playwright, Michael Scholar Jr., finally convinced me to write new music for the play. After doing so, I became the musical director and helped select the cast. The play had its premiere in Edmonton in November 2010.

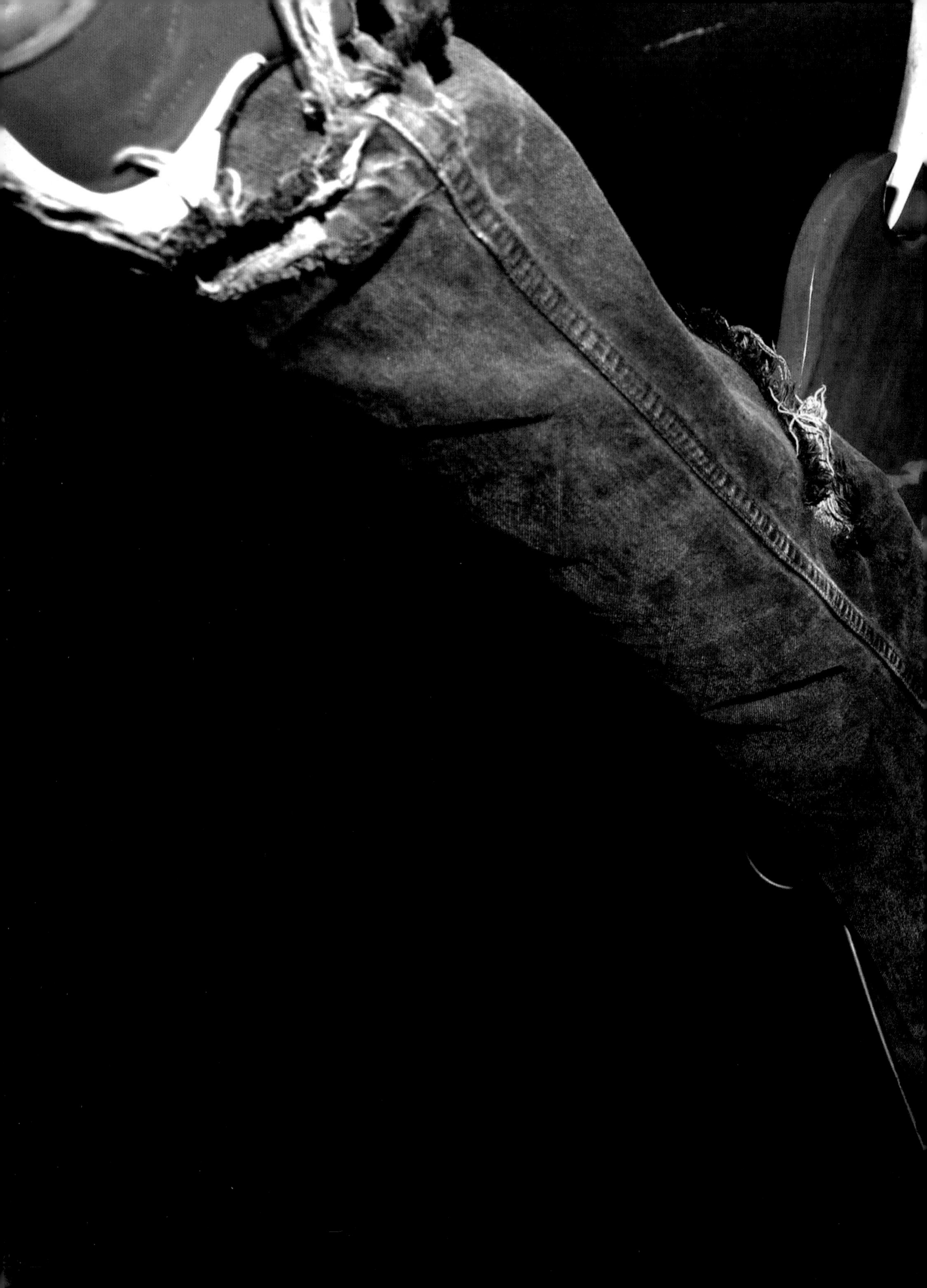

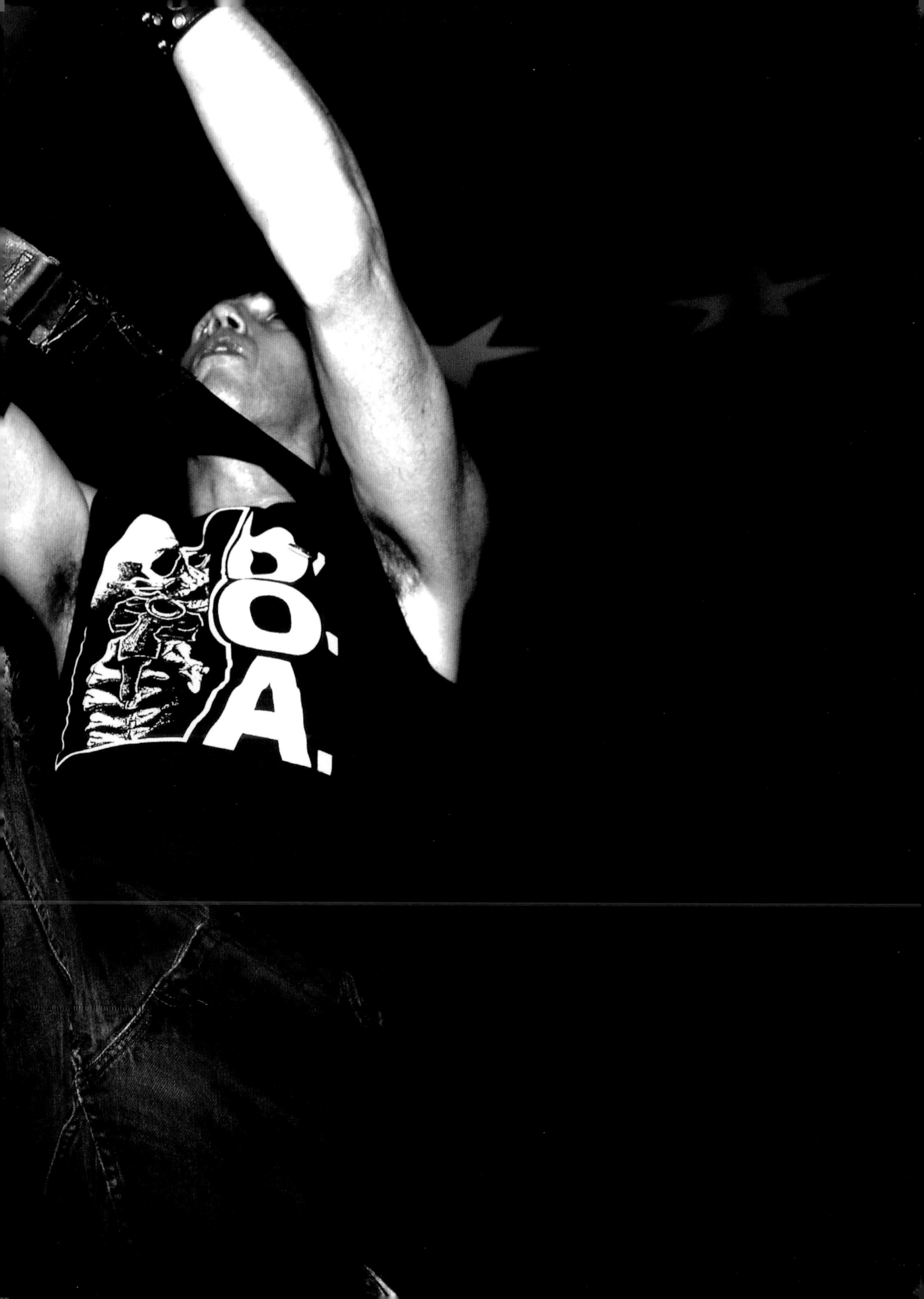
O.
A.

D.O.A. FAMILY TREE

#15 GREGG ↓ SHITHEAD ↓ WIMPY ↓ JON CARD ← SNFU / PERSONALITY CRISIS
JUNE 86 / N.Y.C.

#16 ← MOVED TO N.Y.C. "CHRIS" HUMPER PROHOM GUITAR ↓ SHITHEAD ↓ WIMPY ✗ CARD NOV. 88
DAY GLO ABORTIONS → TIL DEC. 13, 1990 THEN WE SPLIT UP

#17 ↓ SHITHEAD ↓ WIMPY ↓ KEN JENSEN ← WE REFORMED SEPT. 1992
RED TIDE

1994 SIMON WILDE DIES FROM A BRAIN TUMOR R.I.P.
1994 DIMWIT O.D.'s R.I.P.

#18 FORD PIER ↓ SHITHEAD ↓ WIMPY ↓ JENSEN SEPT. 94
JUNIOR GONE WILD → ROOTS ROUNDUP

JAN. 1995 KEN JENSEN DIES IN A HOUSE FIRE R.I.P.
SUMMER 1995 D.O.A. RECORDS THE BLACK SPOT WITH JOHN WRIGHT OF NO MEANS NO

#19 FORD PIER ↓ SHITHEAD ↓ WIMPY ↓ BRIEN O'BRIEN DRUMS ← CURIOUS GEORGE
EVIL TWANG ← ADIOS WIMPY NOV. 1996 SEPT. 1995
ADIOS FORD PIER SHOW BUSINESS GIANTS - SOLO

SUMMER + FALL 1997 JOEY + BRIEN RECORD FESTIVAL OF ATHEISTS

#20 SHITHEAD WYCLIFFE BASS ← BEACH MUTANTS O'BRIEN OCT. 1997

#21 TED SHITHEAD → KUBA BASS OUT! DRUMS TED SIM ← SNFU O'BRIEN ↓ JAN. 98 RETIRED

#22 ↓ SHITHEAD ↓ KUBA JAN. 1999 THE GREAT BALDINI ← DOG EAT DOGMA RETIRED

#23 ↓ SHITHEAD OUT HE'S BACK! RAMPAGE BALDINI SEPT. 2000

#24 ↓ SHITHEAD ← OUT KUBA ← BACK AGAIN BALDINI JAN. 2002

#25 ↓ SHITHEAD DAN YAREMKO → BASS BALDINI JULY 2003
BIF NAKED / CHOKING CRUSH

#26 SHITHEAD RANDY RAMPAGE BALDINI OUT MARCH 2005

#27 SHITHEAD RANDY RAMPAGE FLOOR TOM JONES DRUMS ← VON ZIPPERS AUG. 2007

#28 ↓ SHITHEAD OUT DIRTY DAN SEDAN YAREMKO BASS FLOOR TOM JONES OUT AUGUST 2008

#29 ↓ SHITHEAD DIRTY DAN JESSE PINNER ← RAISED BY APES AUGUST 2010

DISCOGRAPHY

YEAR	ALBUM	FORMAT	LABEL
1978	Disco Sucks	4 song 7-inch EP	Sudden Death Records
1978	Prisoner/13	7-inch single	Quintessence Records
1979	World War 3/Whatcha Gonna Do?	7-inch single	Sudden Death Records
1980	Something Better Change	album	Friends Records
1980	Triumph Of the Ignoroids [live]	4 song 12-inch EP	Friends Records
1981	Hardcore 81	album	Friends Records
1981	Positively D.O.A.	5 song 7-inch EP	Alternative Tentacles Records
1982	War On 45	8 song 12-inch EP	Faulty Products (US) / Alternative Tentacles Records (UK)
1982	Right To Be Wild (Burn it Down/Fuck You) [benefit]	7-inch single	Sudden Death Records
1983	General Strike [benefit]	7-inch single	Sudden Death Records
1983	Bloodied But Unbowed [compilation] [tracks are different on US and UK versions]	album	Alternative Tentacles Records
1985	Let's Wreck the Party [US and UK covers are different]	album	Alternative Tentacles Records
1985	Don't Turn Yer Back On Desperate Times	4 song 12-inch EP	Alternative Tentacles Records
1986	Expo Hurts Everyone [benefit with three other artists]	4 song 7-inch EP	Sudden Death Records
1987	True (North) Strong and Free	album	Rock Hotel/Profile Records
1989	Last Scream Of the Missing Neighbors with Jello Biafra	album	Alternative Tentacles Records
1989	Where Evil Grows	cassette single	Enigma Canada
1990	Murder	album	Restless Records
1990	Talk Minus Action Equals Zero [live]	album	Restless Records
1991	Greatest Shits [compilation]	album	QQYRQ Records
1992	Dawning Of A New Error [compilation]	album	Alternative Tentacles Records
1993	13 Flavours Of Doom	album	Alternative Tentacles Records

1993	The Only Thing Green [benefit]	7-inch single	Alternative Tentacles Records
1994	Loggerheads	album	Alternative Tentacles Records
1994	It's Not Unusual, But It Sure Is Ugly	single, CD/EP	Alternative Tentacles Records
1996	The Black Spot	album	Essential Noise
1996	D.O.A. split with Show Business Giants	5 song 10-inch EP	Essential Noise
1996	Marijauna Motherfucker [benefit] split with Colorifics	7-inch single	Canabis Canada Records
1997	D.O.A. split with Hanson Brothers	7-inch single	Empty Records
1998	Festival of Atheists	album	Sudden Death Records
1998	The Lost Tapes	album	Sudden Death Records
1998	D.O.A. split with d.b.s.	4 song 7-inch single	Empty Records
1999	Beat Trash [Joey Keithley solo]	album	Sudden Death Records
2000	Nervous Breakdown split with Dog Eat Dogma	7-inch single	Sudden Death Records
2001	Just Play It Over and Over Again	5 song 7-inch CD/EP	Sudden Death Records
2001	The End, live 1990 with Jello Biafra	DVD	Sudden Death Records
2002	Win the Battle	album	Rhino Records
2003	War and Peace [compilation]	album	Sudden Death Records
2003	Greatest Shits [tracks different than CD version]	DVD/VHS	Sudden Death Records
2004	Live Free or Die	album	Sudden Death Records
2005	War on 45 [compilation]	albun	Sudden Death Records
2007	Punk Rock Singles [compilation]	album	Sudden Death Records
2007	Smash the State	DVD	MVD / Sudden Death Records
2007	Band of Rebels [Joe Keithley solo]	album	Sudden Death Records
2008	Northern Avenger	album	Sudden Death Records
2008	Human Bomb / Crossfire	7-inch single	Sudden Death Records
2009	Kings of Punk, Hockey and Beer [compilation]	album	Sudden Death Records
2009	Men of Action	DVD	MVD / Sudden Death Records
2010	Talk – Action = 0	album	Sudden Death Records

TRIBUTE ALBUMS

Year	Title	Label
2001	We Still Keep On Running with D.O.A. 6 bands covering D.O.A. songs	Base Records (Japan)
2003	Let's Start the Action international electronic tribute to D.O.A.	Sudden Death Records

CREDITS

CHAPTER ONE
Page 13 photos by Gerry Hanna; page 14 poster by Bob Montgomery; page 21 photo by Al Steadman; page 27 photo by Don Denton; page 32 photo by Ross Burnett; pages 21, 28, 36 photos by Bev Davies.

CHAPTER TWO
Page 48 photo by Edward C. Colver; page 49 photos by Dean Kelly; page 52 poster by Raymond Pettibone; pages 40-41, 43, 46, 60, 63 photos by Bev Davies.

CHAPTER THREE
Page 64-65, 69, 83 photos by Bev Davies; page 83 (top) photo by Steve Shedroff.

CHAPTER FOUR
Pages 89, 98 photos by Edward C. Colver; pages 89, 90, 92 posters by Raymond Pettibone; page 93 photos by Peter Kers; page 99 photo by Steve Shedoff; page 104 (top) photo by Brian McLeod; page 104 (bottom) photo by Peter Kers; pages 105, 119 photos by Bev Davies.

CHAPTER FIVE
Page 124 photo by Connie Kuhns; page 125 (right) photo by Susan Springer; pages 127, 132 photos by David Lee; page 128 photo by Bev Davies; page 133 (top) photo by Laurence Acland; page 133 (bottom) photo by Iain C. Ross; page 144 photo by Peter Horwood; page 147 photo by Viliam; page 150 (top) photo by Naomi Petersen; pages 150 (bottom), 152-153 photos by Karen Lee Plessner; page 156 photo by Eileen Polk.

CHAPTER SIX
Page 158-159 photo by Naomi Petersen; page 165 (top) photo by Sylvia E. Thome; pages 165 (bottom), 177 (top right) photos by B. Gautier; pages 160, 172, 174 (top right), 176, photos by Dvorana Šcuc-a; page 174 (left column) by Kent Moore.

CHAPTER SEVEN
Page 178-179 photo by Alex Waterhouse Hayward; page 187 photo by Bev Davies; page 197, 202 (top) photos by Manfred Rahs; page 202 (bottom) photo by Dominik Schunk; page 220 photo by Paul Clarke.

CHAPTER EIGHT
Pages 214-215, 230, 241 photos by Ed Goralnick; page 219 photo by Jan Berman; page 224 by Ronnie Hall; page 235 photo by James Loewen; page 240 photo by James Richard.

CHAPTER NINE
Pages 242-243, 247 (bottom), 248 photos by Ed Gornalick, pages 247 (top), 261 photos by Bev Davies; 255 photos by Kamikaze Dead Boy; page 259 photo by James Richard; page 265 photo by Laura Keithley; page 269 photo by Jeff Keithley.

CHAPTER TEN
Pages 270-271 photo by Abran Deyo; pages 272, 287 (bottom right) photos by Kevin Statham; page 276 photo by Don Denton; page 280 photo by Kevin Lamb; page 283 photo by John Mackie; page 287 (bottom left) photo by Bev Davies; page 287 (top) photo by Malcolm Parry; page 295 (right) photo by Diane Foy; page 296-297 photo by Michael Loccisano.

D.O.A. logo on front cover by Eyeteaser.

Artwork by Gisele Grignet, Randy Iwata, Dave Lester, Ken Lester, Bob Mercer, and Bob Montgomery.

TALK-ACTION=0
Copyright © 2011 by Joe Keithley

All rights reserved. No part of this book may be reproduced or used in any form by any means—graphic, electronic, or mechanical—without the prior written permission of the publisher, except by a reviewer, who may use brief excerpts in a review, or in the case of photocopying in Canada, a licence from Access Copyright.

ARSENAL PULP PRESS
Suite 101, 211 East Georgia St.
Vancouver, BC
Canada V6A 1Z6
arsenalpulp.com • suddendeath.com

Efforts have been made to locate copyright holders of source material wherever possible. The publisher welcomes hearing from any copyright holders of material used in this book who have not been contacted.

The publisher gratefully acknowledges the support of the Canada Council for the Arts and the British Columbia Arts Council for its publishing program, and the Government of Canada through the Canada Book Fund and the Government of British Columbia through the Book Publishing Tax Credit Program for its publishing activities.

Book design by Shyla Seller

Printed and bound in Hong Kong

Library and Archives Canada Cataloguing in Publication

Keithley, Joe, 1956-

    Talk, action = 0 : an illustrated history of D.O.A. / Joe Keithley.

Includes discography.

Issued also in an electronic format.

ISBN 978-1-55152-396-5 (pbk.)

    1. D.O.A. (Musical group). 2. Punk rock musicians--Canada--Biography.